HISTORICAL ATLAS
of the
BRITISH ISLES

HISTORICAL ATLAS
of the
BRITISH ISLES

by

DR IAN BARNES

First published in Great Britain in 2011 by
Pen & Sword Books Limited
47 Church Street, Barnsley, South Yorkshire, S70 2AS

ISBN 978-1-84884-499-5

A CIP catalogue record for this book is
available from the British Library

Printed and bound in China by Printworks Int.Ltd

Pen & Sword Books Limited incorporates the Imprints of
Pen & Sword Aviation, Pen & Sword Maritime, Pen & Sword Military,
Wharncliffe Local History, Pen & Sword Select,
Pen & Sword Military Classics and Leo Copper

For a complete list of Pen & Sword titles please contact
PEN & SWORD BOOKS LIMITED
47 Church Street, Barnsley, South Yorkshire, S70 2AS, England
E-mail: enquiriers@pen-and-sword.co.uk
Website: www.pen-and-sword.co.uk

Contents

Map List

Introduction

This book is an historical atlas of all the British Isles and the key themes in the cultural and political development, and relationships between their component peoples and states. The British Isles are a mere geographical expression comprising different regions and peoples who evolved over time incorporating new arrivals into the islands or being absorbed by new migrants and their cultures. Various historical processes shaped and organised socio-political entities, eventually becoming Wales, Scotland, Ireland and England as a result of invasions, civil wars, religious change, and imperial enterprise.

An important aspect of the islands' history is a constant review of the past with changing interpretations of events and societies interpreted by archaeology and analytical technology. Evidently, society was not static, with mobile populations moving across the land-bridge when the British Isles were part of the European continent and then using the sea as a major means of communication for trade or conquests.

History was rewritten in 2010 when evidence of early humanoids was discovered on Happisburgh Beach, Norfolk. This part of Britain was occupied between 800,000 and 970,000 years ago, pushing back the date for the first humanoid settlement in northern Europe by at least 100,000 years. The stone tools found pre-dated the Neanderthals by 700,000 years. Another discovery occurred at the Starr Carr site near Scarborough, Yorkshire. Previously known for the remains of a domesticated dog, a wooden paddle and an antler head-dress, the site showed that the inhabitants hunted and killed stags rather than hinds or fawns, showing some basic skills at deer-herd management. During 2010 witnessed the uncovering of Britain's earliest surviving house dating from at least 8,500 BC, pre-dating Ancient Egypt's earliest human settlements. A large wooden platform next to the former Lake Pickering is currently being excavated which provides possibly the earliest evidence of carpentry in Europe.

The strong links with Europe are demonstrated by the remains of the Amesbury Archer buried near Stonehenge. This Bronze Age man's (2300 BC) dental enamel was subjected to oxygen isotope analysis and his origins placed him in an alpine region of Central Europe. An early Iron Age site at Culduthel, Inverness, showed a mix of cultures with stone arrow heads, bronze objects, amber and an arrow arm guard similar to new bow styles being imported from Europe. This was a period of a networked society with travel and trade as normal patterns of life. Likewise, the seabed off Salcombe, South Devon, has offered evidence of trade after divers found the cargo of a shipwreck. Nearly 300 items were found from this 3,000-year-old wreck. Tin ingots were part of this cargo, evidence of British produced tin bound for European metalworking centres. A gold bracelet and an 18-inch long European-style bronze leaf sword were part of the haul.

All this recently-found evidence points to a rich and complex island heritage which is subject to constant re-interpretation. The Celtic Bronze and Iron Age cultures which overlay and absorbed pre-Celtic peoples were ultimately attacked themselves and, in part, colonized by Rome. Four centuries of Roman rule integrated the province of Britannia into a vast empire via roads, commerce, administration and urbanization, although the peoples of parts of Scotland and all of Ireland were never subjugated.

The withdrawal of Rome, and its professional army, from Britain allowed Germanic peoples to cross from northern Europe in large numbers. The newcomers reduced the Celtic language area to Wales and Cornwell while their Old English or Anglo-Saxon became linguistically dominant, as did Germanic systems of law, which were customary, rather than involving universality as in the Roman imperial and legal system. Christianity was re-introduced into northern Britain by Irish missionaries while Roman priests converted the south. The Anglo-Saxons established the county system allowing uniformity in local government, making Anglo-Saxon England one of the best administered kingdoms in Europe, as well as a great source of efficient tax collection, as William the Conqueror appreciated after the Norman invasion in 1066. The shire system also allowed a successful defence against Viking incursions. William I helped establish an Empire reaching from England to Europe. The Anglo-Norman polity reduced Wales, briefly subjected Scotland until Robert Bruce bloodied an English army at Bannockburn in 1314. The invasion and seizure of Ireland opened up a source of violence and hostility undiminished in certain quarters today.

An important innovation in England, as a means of financing war against the Welsh, Scots and French, was the summoning by the King of England of representatives of land owners, towns burghers, and lords temporal and spiritual who would discuss and agree taxes. This Parliament was initially a tool of monarchy which claimed it represented the English. Likewise, the Scots had notions of their distinctive customs and speech while the Welsh rebelled in a 14-year campaign under Owain Glyndŵr ushering in a strand of Welsh identity.

The introduction of the Protestant Reformation in England, beginning under Henry VIII, created the Church of England, a catalyst in further developing national consciousness, this being strengthened by Queen Mary's cruelty and the fear of Roman Catholicism and Spanish enmity. The conflict with the old faith deepened the wounds in Ireland and impacted upon the Scots Reformation.

The Unification of the Crowns of England and Scotland under James, I of England and VI of Scotland, spawned two phenomena: firstly, authoritarian and intransigent monarchy conflicted with Parliament in a savage Civil War; and, secondly, James presided over the beginning of the first global English Empire. The struggle with Parliament under Charles I saw England suffer a revolution in the form of the republican government of the Cromwellian Commonwealth, the only time

England-Scotland pursued such an aberration.

The search for Empire saw Lowland Scots planted in Ulster and colonies established in the Americas, Bermuda and the Caribbean. This dominion was linked to Britain's increasing importance as a commercial hub with London and Glasgow as prime trading ports. The Empire expanded to Africa and, most importantly, India. The end of the first Empire under the impact of the American Revolution was followed by the growth of the second throughout the world, this endeavour being aided by all the British Isles' peoples, settlers creating new nations in Canada, Australia and New Zealand. The aftermath of surviving two World Wars saw a weakened Britain unable to sustain control over its vast Empire. The Dominions became independent states and colonies and territories in Africa, Asia and the Caribbean gained, or were given, their sovereignty and became members of the Commonwealth of Nations.

One final element in the islands' history has been constitutional change. In the nineteenth and twentieth centuries the electoral franchise was constantly widened until all 21-year-olds possessed a vote, this age restriction being reduced to 18 in 1970. The hereditary peers in the House of Lords have been reduced in number but not eliminated. After a violent struggle, Ireland, or the large part of it, became an independent state in 1922. Wales, Scotland and Northern Ireland have been granted their own devolved assemblies, each with a different system of proportional representation, a process continuing with elections for the Mayor of London and Members of the European Parliament. Finally, the separation of powers has been enhanced by the new Supreme Court which commenced operations in October 2009.

Recently, the British Isles has taken in migrants turning island communities into multicultural and multi-ethnic entities. The future will tell whether this socio-economic project is successful as full integration has yet to take place. Unresolved religious issues, extreme right-wing politics, severe economic crises and fear of terrorism hinder the growth of true harmony.

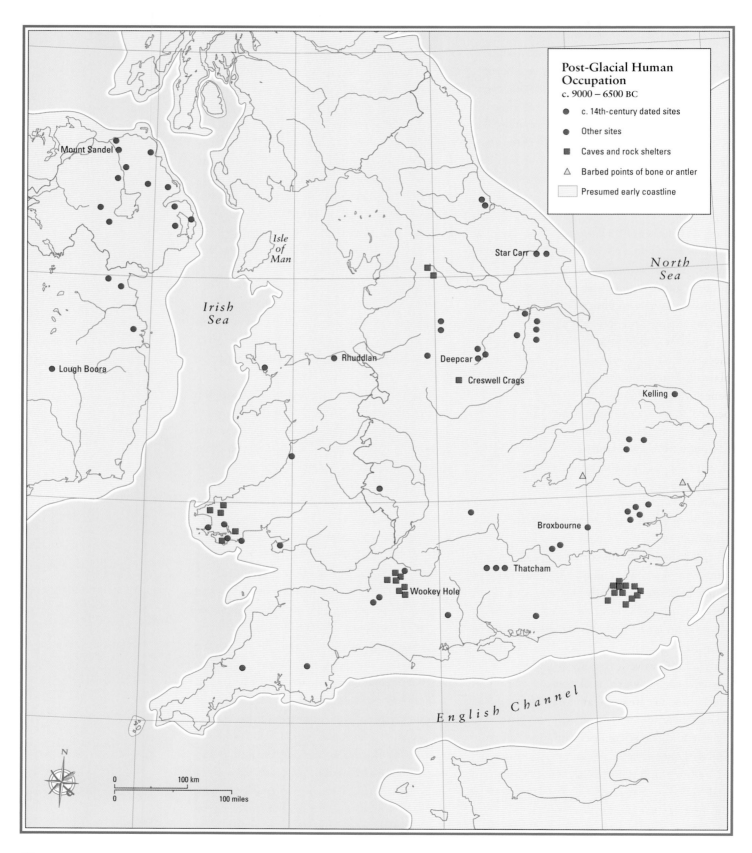

Post-Glacial Human
Occupation
c. 9000 – 6500 BC

● c. 14th-century dated sites

● Other sites

■ Caves and rock shelters

△ Barbed points of bone or antler

☐ Presumed early coastline

Mount Sandel

Isle
of
Man

Irish
Sea

North
Sea

Star Carr

Lough Boora

Rhuddlan

Deepcar

Creswell Crags

Kelling

Broxbourne

Thatcham

Wookey Hole

English Channel

N

0   100 km

0   100 miles

Early Peoples

What was to become the British Isles was a landmass attached to Europe by land-bridges which provided access for the first peoples to walk across, what is now the North Sea, to Britain, the Isle of Man, and Ireland as they are known today. These *Homo erectus* probably developed from earlier hominids but would be recognisable as human creatures capable of flaking stones to produce chopping tools. Evidence suggests that *Homo erectus* lived both in caves and on lake and river banks. Bands of these peoples became expert hunters, gatherers and fishers, having reached Europe some two million years ago, gradually moving northwards into the 'British Isles'.

Between 700,000 years ago to 11,000 BC, these first human groups traversed the sunken plain of the North Sea during the Ice Ages and penetrated the 'Isles'. During this early human occupation, *Erectus* moved north and south according to the pressure of the ice sheets, having first arrived during a warm period. During the last glacial period, modern man, *Homo sapiens sapiens*, appeared with a collection of tools including: carefully flaked long blades and artefacts made from antler, bone and ivory producing diverse awls, needles, harpoons, spears ornaments and whistles. Hunting was a major task and bones found in caves, especially at Badger Hole, in Lancashire, and Wookey Hole, in Somerset, include those of hyena, lion, otter, fox, brown bear, horse, giant Irish deer and reindeer. Caves in Creswell Crags, Derbyshire, witnessed early art works with a horse rib depicting a human, wearing an animal mask and using a bow.

After 10,000 BC, temperatures began to rise and early heath lands were gradually populated by birch and pine forests with large mammals following the retreating ice sheets leaving this new environment to become habitats for a variety of smaller animals. Rather than moving between summer and winter camps, people became less nomadic and extended their diet from mainly meat to include more plant foods. Evidence of camping sites has been provided by piles of flints, noticeably along the North and South Downs and the Weald. Starr Carr in Yorkshire is another site, and coastal Wales was a likely home. The first evidence of humans in Ireland is a concentration of sites in the Bann Valley of northern Ireland but no sites of this early period have been found in Scotland.

Humans now began to alter their environment by creating grazing areas within forests by felling trees. Hazels were encouraged to grow, ensuring a possible storable food supply. Deer would be easier to hunt now and evidence suggests that stags were culled. Also, dogs were being domesticated. People had now adapted their surroundings and were less likely to be at the mercy of nature and the elements. Bands of people spread further and excavations at Mount Sandel in the Irish Bann Valley have uncovered egg-shaped huts with enclosed fire-pits and hearths with outside hearths and flint-working areas. Bone remnants show the consumption of fish, young wild boar and birds, while hazel nuts and parts of an edible white water-lily were also eaten.

Shortly after 6,000 BC, temperatures had risen so much that melt waters from the ice sheets caused the sea-level to rise to such an extent that all land bridges between Ireland and Britain and Britain and the Continent were broken, leaving the British Isles in much the same shape as they are now. The islands' population increased and human habitation spread throughout the islands, as shown by the number of sites discovered. The disappearance of the land bridges did not cut off the islands from Europe. Boat building took place as shown by the 4.5-metre long dug-out canoe found in the River Tay at Friarton, Perth.

Post-Glacial Human Occupation

Around 10,000 BC, following a global temperature rise, people re-occupied what would become the British Isles, walking across the 'land bridge' from settlements to the east and south.

Skara Brae, Orkney

The well-preserved prehistoric village of Skara Brae was discovered in Orkney in 1850 after a powerful storm washed away a sand dune exposing this 5,300-year-old set of stone houses. Located on the Bay of Skaill on the west coast of Mainland, Orkney, this Neolithic community has won UNESCO World Heritage Site status. However, Skara Brae is just one of a series of similar villages found and excavated over the years. Other important examples of Neolithic houses and farms are: Links of Noltland on Westray; Knap of Howar on Papa Westray; Rinyo on Rousay; and, Barnhouse Settlement, adjacent to the Standing Stones O'Stenness on Mainland.

The Skara Brae dwellings were not sunk into the ground, instead being built into middens of domestic waste, thereby providing a layer of insulation against Orkney's ferocious winter climate. The lack of trees on Orkney caused the inhabitants of the village to construct their houses with local stone. Each house is virtually identical, suggesting a standardization of a successful design to be repeated over time, much like the more contemporary Orcadian croft houses existing today. Each house possessed a large square room, with a central hearth and a stone 'dresser' facing the door entrance, the latter being closable by a stone slab, held in place by a bar that slid in bar-holes cut into the stone door jambs. A bed was placed each side of the hearth, at some times free-standing, at others, recessed into the wall. The rooms also included cupboards, seats and storage boxes, and a drainage system providing a primitive toilet in each house. Stone seats or boxes were placed to the left of most entrances ensuring that a person entering the room would be directed to the right-hand side, often referred to as the male side. The alley ways connecting the houses are still roofed with their original stone slabs but the roofs of the houses no longer exist. Likely, the roofs were constructed from whale bone with drift wood rafters and covered with skins, turf, thatched

seaweed, or straw. Seaweed remained a roofing material in Orkney until recently.

One of the houses in the Skara Brae complex is interesting because it can only be locked from outside suggesting that the building was used as a ritual building for rites of passage or for excluding transgressors from the community or for these and other reasons. Another house had neither beds nor a dresser, instead having a partitioned recess. Archaeologists found the floor littered with pieces of chert and other stones, suggesting that the house was a work room. The house style is that different though it is similar to later Bronze Age Houses in Shetland so it might have been a later addition. The idea that the Skara Brae house design was static is incorrect as the houses were remodelled over the years so a new design could be readily incorporated.

The inhabitants of Skara Brae, variously estimated to have been from fifty to one hundred people, probably wore skins and furs since no evidence has been found of weaving. Bones found in the midden are made up of cattle and sheep, while wheat and barley comprised the community's cereal crops. Together with farm produce, fishing and limpet collecting provided dietary supplements. Stone boxes in the house formed from thin slabs with joints sealed with clay were probably waterproof containers to keep freshly-caught fish or to store limpets. Deer and boar were hunted for meat and skins while seals would be eaten as well as any whale which inadvertently beached itself, as still occurs. Birds eggs and birds were probably also eaten just as in recent Orcadian history.

A great variety of artefacts have been found at Skara Brae, some mysterious. Ten inch long ivory, walrus or whale, pins are similar to those located in an Irish Boyne Valley passage graves, suggesting either a cultural link or possibly parallel development. Other finds were constructed from animal, fish, bird, whale bone, whale and walrus ivory, and killer whale teeth. These artefacts included awls, knives, beads,

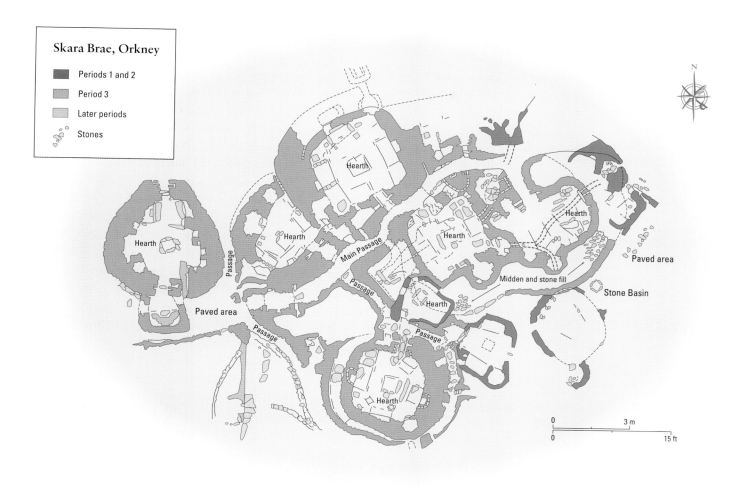

Skara Brae, Orkney

- ■ Periods 1 and 2
- ■ Period 3
- □ Later periods
- ⬚ Stones

Hearth

Hearth

Hearth

Main Passage

Passage

Passage

Paved area

Passage

Hearth

Hearth

Passage

Hearth

Hearth

Midden and stone fill

Paved area

Stone Basin

N

0   3 m

0   15 ft

adzes, shovels and small bowls, while other knives were made from flakes of sandstone cobbles. Decorations have included cross-hatchings and chevrons carved into lintels and bed post; some signs are redolent of runes or ogham but this is mere happenstance.

The most curious discovery was a number of carved stone balls, like the ivory pins, which again have been linked to the Boyne Valley in Ireland. The balls are spiked all over and might possibly be sun symbols or a ritual object. The Skara Brae people lived busy and creative lives and also appeared to be aware of celestial movements. The hearths, like those at Barnhouse, share identical alignments despite the doors facing in opposite directions. They were aligned with four solar directions: midsummer sunrise and sunset; and, midwinter sunrise and sunset.

Evidently, Orkney is the sole location in the British Isles where these four directions are perpendicular to each other, forming a cross. Of interest, a Neolithic 'road' connects Skara Brae with The Ring of Brodgar, the Standing Stones O'Stenness and Maes Howe, a major tomb, with a south-west facing entrance allowing the dying sun on midwinter's day to shine down its passage into the tomb chamber.

Skara Brae was occupied from about 3,200 BC – 2,500 BC. Climatic change occurred at the latter date ushering in a colder and wetter weather. Such conditions could have caused the village to have been abandoned. Or, maybe a severe storm created a panic and flight, since important possessions were left behind including food and a stream of broken beads in a doorway and in the outside passageway.

Skara Brae

Located in the Bay of Skaill, Orkney, it is made up of a cluster of compact houses. It is Europe's most complete Neolithic village, older than Stonehenge or the Great Pyramids at Giza.

Stone Circles and Henges

Avebury Site Plan

- Standing stone
- Fallen stone
- Stone hole
- Estimated position of a stone hole

Avebury, in Wiltshire, consists of a massive henge and a ditch with an external embarkment. This is the largest stone circle in Britain and one of the largest in Europe.

Stone Circles and Henges
Henges may have been constructed for many reasons – religious, cultural, trading centres or a combination of any or all of these. Stone circles have the same assumptions with the added use of celestial observation, which may have had a bearing on crop planning. The concentration of these structures is in the north and west of the British Isles, with relatively few found in the south-east. The significance of this remains unknown.

The period between 2,500 BC and 1,500 BC witnessed an astonishing growth in the construction of stone circles and henges, which gradually displaced megalithic tombs over a period of some 1,000 years, with megalithic tombs still being built in the Scilly Isles, the Orkneys and southern Ireland at the end of this millennia. A henge is essentially a ring bank with a ditch inside rather than outside, thus showing that an henge was not a defensive earthwork. These monuments are some times associated with stone circles, which can be incorporated in this monumental architecture.

The central area of the henge might be anything from 20 metres in diameter upwards and could contain stone circles as ritual structures, timber circles or coves which were three or four standing stones placed near to each other to give the appearance of a box within the henge. Avebury henge in Wiltshire and Mount Pleasant henge in Dorset include coves in their monuments.

Various types of henge exist: the circular or oval bank would have one entrance; a bank would be pierced by two entrances directly opposite each other; and some henges would have four entrances with two pairs facing each other in diametrically equally situated sitings. The late Neolithic or early Bronze Age people who built the henges are often associated with certain styles of pottery such as Grooved Ware, Impressed Ware and Beakers. The growth of henges and stone circles suggests that ancestor worship, associated with megalithic tombs when anyone could become a revered ancestor according to their role in a tribe, was changing. Building a megalithic tomb would take time but a monumental henge, perhaps with an associated stone circle, would take skilful organisation to build and the use of many months, or even years, of dedicated labour.

Logic indicates that important chiefs, controlling large areas, were alone in possessing the power and authority to order henge and stone monuments which became the sacred and secular sites of large chiefdoms, although some henges are associated with burials. Henges of this variety are found in north-west Britain, Ireland and Dartmoor but not in southern England; eastern England is markedly different with few henges and no stone circles. Some archaeologists have argued that stone circles and henges have astronomical significance. Lunar and solar alignments might exist with chiefs possibly using sight lines to predict a calendar for festivals and rituals and associated agricultural tasks, such as planting and harvesting. Such knowledge would ensure a chief accrued even more authority ensuring that a chief's leadership in sacred rites would elevate him into the role of priest-chief.

Important henges occur throughout the British Isles. Avebury comprises four interconnected monuments. The henge structure at Avebury, with three stone circles, is connected to a smaller henge (the Sanctuary), via an avenue of paired stones, while the fourth monument is Silbury Hill, the largest artificial mound of prehistoric Europe. This 130-foot high structure covers five acres and comprises 248,000 cubic metres of chalk and clay. One estimate has calculated that 500 men would have required 15 years to build and shape it. One interpretation is that a pan-southern British effort was needed to build the hill, and only possible at the behest of a very powerful priestly elite. The Ring of Brodgar in Orkney has a 380-metre ditch cut through bedrock and contains 27 out of an original 60 (estimated) stone megalith placed in a true circle. The Ring comprised part of a large Orcadian ritual complex including the Ring o'Stenness and, probably, the Ring o'Bookan. Nearby is the Comet

Stone Circles and Henges

- ■ Henge site
- ○ Stone Circle site
- ■ Henge and Stone Circle site

0   100 km
0   100 miles

Shetland Isles

Orkney Isles

A T L A N T I C
O C E A N

Recumbent
Circles

N o r t h   S e a

Balfarg

Beaghmore

Long Meg

Irish Sea

Druids
Circle

Llandegai

Monknewtown

Avebury

Marden

Stonehenge

Durrington
Walls

Mount
Pleasant

English Channel

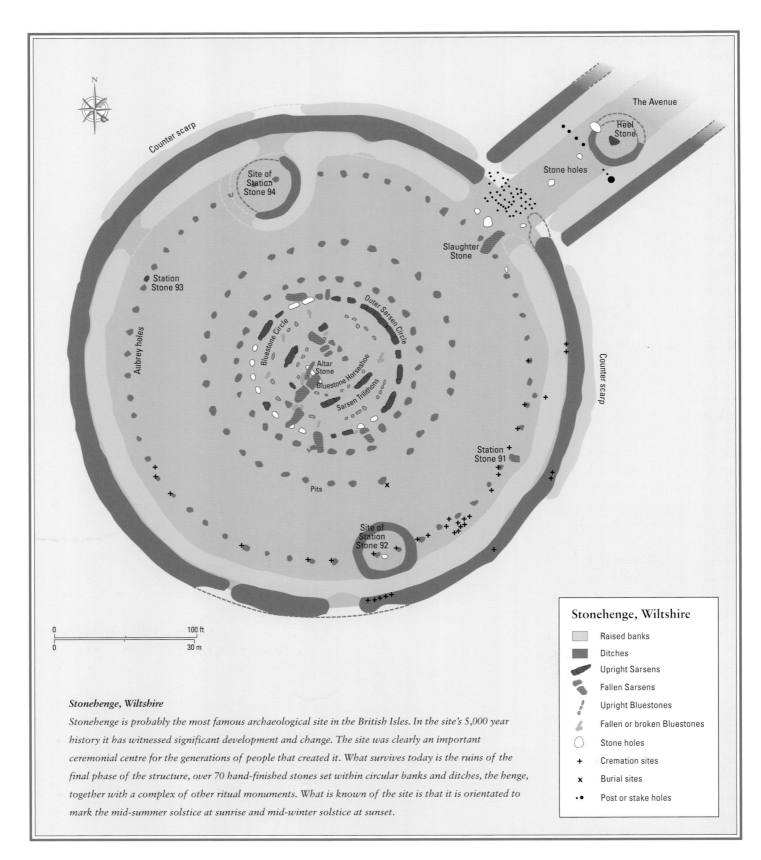

N

Counter scarp

The Avenue

Heel
Stone

Site of
Station
Stone 94

Stone holes

Slaughter
Stone

Station
Stone 93

Outer Sarsen Circle

Bluestone Circle

Aubrey holes

Altar
Stone

Bluestone Horseshoe

Sarsen Trilithons

Counter scarp

Station
Stone 91

Pits

Site of
Station
Stone 92

0   100 ft
0   30 m

Stonehenge, Wiltshire

Stonehenge is probably the most famous archaeological site in the British Isles. In the site's 5,000 year history it has witnessed significant development and change. The site was clearly an important ceremonial centre for the generations of people that created it. What survives today is the ruins of the final phase of the structure, over 70 hand-finished stones set within circular banks and ditches, the henge, together with a complex of other ritual monuments. What is known of the site is that it is orientated to mark the mid-summer solstice at sunrise and mid-winter solstice at sunset.

Stonehenge, Wiltshire

	Raised banks
	Ditches
	Upright Sarsens
	Fallen Sarsens
	Upright Bluestones
	Fallen or broken Bluestones
	Stone holes
+	Cremation sites
x	Burial sites
••	Post or stake holes

Stone, part of a stone cluster linking Brodgar to Stenness. Another interesting henge system is that at Thornborough Henges, Yorkshire, where three henges are aligned together. Wales has a relative paucity of henges and the few stone circles are in Gwynedd, south-west Dyfed, and on Mynydd Epynt in central Wales. In Ireland, there are no known definite henges but stone circles congregate in Cork and Kerry, with a few stray examples elsewhere. A final noteworthy minor henge is the Seahenge, Holme-next-the-Sea, Norfolk, comprising 55 split oak trunks in a nearly circular enclosure. Originally constructed during the early Bronze Age in saltmarsh lands, the area was inundated by the sea leaving the posts to be preserved in peat. Dendrochronolgy has shown that the felling of the oak trees took place in 2049 BC with between 16 and 26 different trees being used. Palynological evidence points to the timber being from local woods with 51 different axes being used to work the timber.

Stonehenge, the most famous henge with accompanying standing stones, remains an enigma. Possibly the most important sacred, or perhaps secular, site in the British Isles, its huge proportions represent a vast human effort employed into its construction. Situated in what was to become a sacred landscape full of prehistoric monuments, the bank and ditch were dug around 3,000 BC. Stones were set up in a rectangle with a long axis aligned on the northerly setting of the midwinter moon while the short axis pointed at midsummer sunrise. Near 2,100 BC, the henge was modified with a widened entrance and a ditched avenue laid out in a straight line for 530 metres. The centre of the henge was witness to the erection of a double circle of blue stones, possibly from the Preseli Mountains of south-west Wales, which suggests shipping up the Severn River followed by a lengthy portage on rollers to Salisbury Plain. Finally, 70 blocks of sarsen sandstone, each weighing 26 tons, was moved from the Malborough Downs to Salisbury Plain. Upright stones were linked via stone lintels, locked into place by mortice and tenon joints and carved out of stone. Further modification took place with horseshoe and double circles, finishing in 1,500 BC.

A further point to be made about Stonehenge is the environment of burial mounds covering the period of the henge construction. Evidence found in the excavation of mounds suggests a wealthy culture or, at least, elite wealth. A man buried under nearby Bush Barrow had a decorated gold lozenge on his chest and was accompanied by three bronze daggers. Additionally, there was a stone mace and a baton decorated with gold. One dagger handle was inlaid with thousands of tiny gold pins. Such wealth indicates the presence of powerful chieftains who were undoubtedly connected with the rituals of the area. Other surrounding graves demonstrate links with Europe, with materials from Cyprus and exchanges of products with Brittany confirming long distance trade routes and influences at the time.

The archaeology of Stonehenge continues to develop as modern technologies find new structures in the environs. Some recent fieldwork by Professor Gaffney and team from the University of Birmingham and the Ludwig Boltzmann Institute for Archaeological Prospection and Virtual Archaeology in Vienna are pioneering the use of very sophisticated survey equipment and computer software. A geophysics plot has found a circle of some 24 postholes within two arcs of some ten pits. The totality is enclosed within a bank containing the normal henge ditch. The find was previously thought to be a ploughed up burial mound or barrow from the Bronze Age. Artist drawings of the site have been published in the British press and the *British Archaeology* magazine. This survey is part of a major survey of the Stonehenge landscape and there are hopes that further finds might provide more information for debates and differing interpretations of Stonehenge's past functions, although these will probably never really be fully understood.

First Farmers

The transition from the Neolithic (Late Stone Age) to the Bronze Age was characterised by technological and agricultural revolutions. Farming as a means of food production began in the Near East between approximately 11,000 BC and 9,000 BC, before spreading through the Balkans, then radiating east and west, reaching the British Isles between 5,000 BC and 4,500 BC. New migrants brought the farming concept across the Channel or 'British' natives went to Europe and imported new ideas, grains and livestock, or there was a mixture of both methods. Whatever the case, farming spread through the Mesolithic into the Neolithic era, taking some 2,000 years to percolate throughout the islands.

The gradual change from managed hunting to agriculture saw the introduction of early cattle, sheep and goats from Europe. The animals themselves were probably important in clearing undergrowth and dense forest, thereby changing the landscape of lowland Britain and facilitating cereal production. A more sedentary lifestyle developed with people dwelling in round houses and evidence exists of field systems.

Technological development continued, witnessing the development of pottery in various forms, together with the appearance of metalworking, after small furnaces were fashioned and used with bellows to achieve high temperatures. Copper was the easiest metal to mine and noticeable production centres were at: Great Orme, Llandudno, Wales; Alderley Edge, Cheshire, England; and Mount Gabriel, West Cork, Ireland. Historians have calculated that the Mount Gabriel mine extracted 32,570.15 tonnes of rock, gangue and ore. Useable copper ore comprised 162.85 tonnes, resulting in a finished smelt of 146.56 tonnes. The making of bronze followed, this metal comprising 90 per cent copper and 10 per cent tin, the latter being mainly mined in Cornwall. Bronze and copper were used for spearheads, axes, knives, daggers and arrowheads. Gold was also mined and used in the decorative arts, mainly jewellery.

The increased use of bronze technology generated an increase in commercial travel as formerly Neolithic self-sufficient settlements needed to trade with copper and tin bearing regions. Along trade routes travelled ideas and art designs resulting in greater cultural uniformity.

As population densities increased, different regions became populated with groups of distantly related families, the precursors of tribes. These larger groups began constructing ceremonial sites and hill forts, such as Windmill Hill, near Avebury, which could be used for rituals, the exchange of goods, the storage of grain, and defence. Other major constructions were tombs and elongated earthen mounds known as long barrows. The types of barrows varied by region: for example, long barrows were prevalent in southern England, round cairns and barrows in Scotland, and passage graves in Ireland, amongst others. This Megalithic Age saw elite burials in stone lined chambers inside the mounds where the dead would be accompanied to the afterlife with grave goods. Amongst grave goods were often found specifically designed pottery beakers giving rise to the name, Beaker People. Possibly the most spectacular passage grave was at Newgrange in Ireland where an entrance stone was carved with *triskeli*, a motif familiar in the current Manx flag.

Around 600 BC, waves of Celts reached the British Isles infiltrating and mixing with the local populations. Celtic language and culture became dominant and spread throughout the islands. That the Celts reached the British Isles is testament to the quality of contemporary ship construction. Boats have been found at Ferriby in the Humber constructed from planks sewn together, some being 40 feet long. In 2009, Bronze Age artefacts were found off Salcombe in Devon. The 285 finds, including tin and copper ingots, suggest a coastal, if not a cross-Channel, trade. A shipwreck in Langdon Bay, Kent, carried a cargo of scrap metal and bronze implements; the objects were of Continental origin, again pointing to maritime trade.

Spread of Agriculture
Farming became established in the Near East around 11,000 BC. It spread into south-east Europe and by c. 5,000 BC had reached the British Isles.

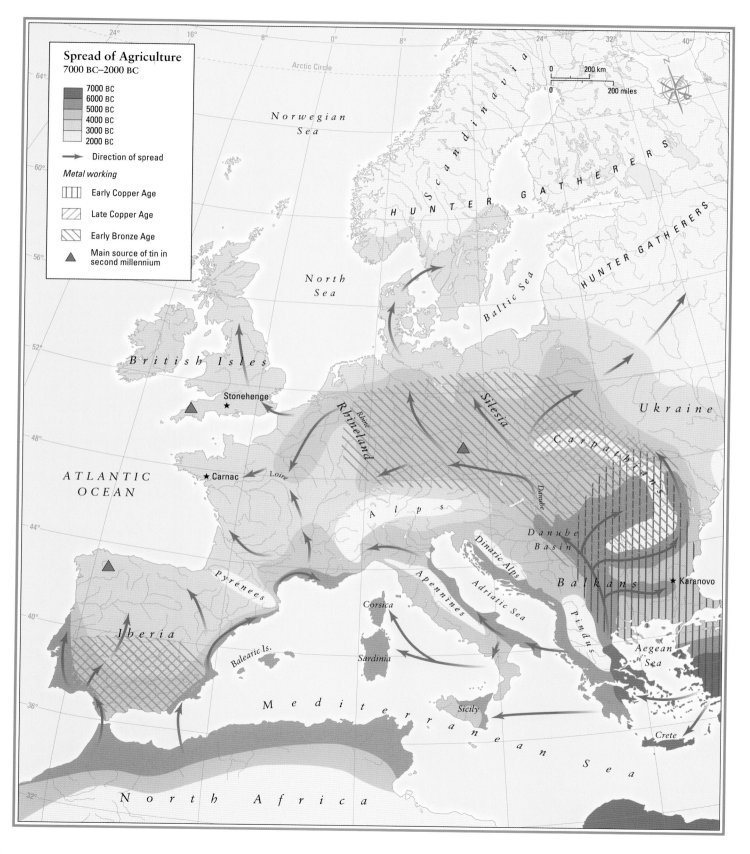

Spread of Agriculture
7000 BC–2000 BC

7000 BC
6000 BC
5000 BC
4000 BC
3000 BC
2000 BC

→ Direction of spread

Metal working

||| Early Copper Age

/// Late Copper Age

▨ Early Bronze Age

▲ Main source of tin in second millennium

Epoch of the Celts

Celtic culture is first associated with a burial ground at Salzkammergut in Austria. This Celtic Hallstatt period (750–450 BC) spread its Iron Age technology and civilisation throughout the Balkans, central Europe, France, Spain and probably entered Britain, according to archaeological evidence around 400–500 BC. These Celts used their iron tools to fell forests and clear land for agriculture and their weapons were used in raids on neighbours or amongst themselves. Hallstadt society was organised into tribes which were subdivided into families, with loyalty being given to a chieftain, wise in peace and skilled in warfare. Society comprised chiefs, warriors, druids, craftsmen, farmers, servants and slaves. Aristocratic women were given parity with men, as discovered in the burial finds at Vix, France, displaying a princess or druidess with vast accumulations of wealth. Female power and authority is sustained by the life and actions of Boudicca, Queen of the Iceni.

The next period of Celtic culture, La Tène, was named after a Celtic archaeological site on Lake Neuchâtel in Switzerland, and existed from approximately 450 BC to its collapse when Julius Caesar conquered Gaul in 58 BC. This period witnessed many Celts leaving their central European homeland to cross the Alps and settle in the fertile, alluvial river valleys of northern Italy, fighting and destroying many Etruscan cities in the process. In 38 BC, the Celts sacked Rome and raided south to Sicily but were eventually defeated and forced back to the Alpine foothills. Celtic control of Europe continued with a consolidation in central Europe and incursions into the Carpathians and Balkans. Some tribes, under Brennus, invaded Bulgaria, Thrace and Macedon, and looted the Greek temple of the god Apollo at Delphi before being defeated by the Greeks and driven back. Some of these defeated Celtic tribes established a fortress on the site of the future Belgrade, while others crossed the Dardanelles

into Anatolia and settled in the region of Galatia. Smaller Celtic groups established footholds on the northern Black Sea coast at Tyra, Olbia and Chersonesus, even reaching the Sea of Azov in Russia. Meanwhile, other groups percolated into France, the British Isles and some crossed the Pyrénées into Spain to form Cetiberian communities, such as that around Numantia or to 'Celtify' existing peoples.

While the continental Celts were eventually squeezed between the rising powers of the Roman Republic to the south and the German tribes to the east, the La Tène culture flourished in the British Isles where this new wave of Celts intermingled with existing populations, developing peculiarly British forms of Celtic art work, many of which can be seen in the British Museum, London. Examples include the Desborough Mirror and the Battersea Shield. These Celts developed two insular dialects: Brythonic, which was spoken across lowland Britain and the mountains of the west, and eventually exported to Brittany by British migrants where it superseded Gaulish; and Goidelic, spoken in Ireland and eventually carried to Scotland and the Isle of Man. The other language spoken in Scotland was Pictish, variously described as an Indo-European language of a Celtic-type related to the Brythonic of southern Britain. Another way of dividing British Celts is by linguistic nomenclature: P-Celtic and Q-Celtic. An early 'q' sound was replaced by a 'p' sound. Thus, the word for son in Brythonic Welsh is 'map' whereas in Goidelic Irish or Scots it is 'mac.'

The Celtic and Celtic-acculturated peoples of the British Isles were divided into a number of tribes, many possessing connections with similarly named tribes on mainland Europe. Julius Caesar's writings pointed out that continental Celts had recently settled in Britain. The Belgae and the Atrbates of central southern Britain and the Yorkshire Parisi had links with tribes in

Epoch of the Celts
By the late 19th century, archaeologists had defined the La Tène with its proceeding Hallstadt cultures with their distinctive styles and burial rites as 'Celtic' assuming a close link between ethnicity, language, artistic and ritual styles. Archaeologists based their originals to the area of northern France to south-western Germany, a homeland from which they spread reaching the British Isles around 400–500 BC.

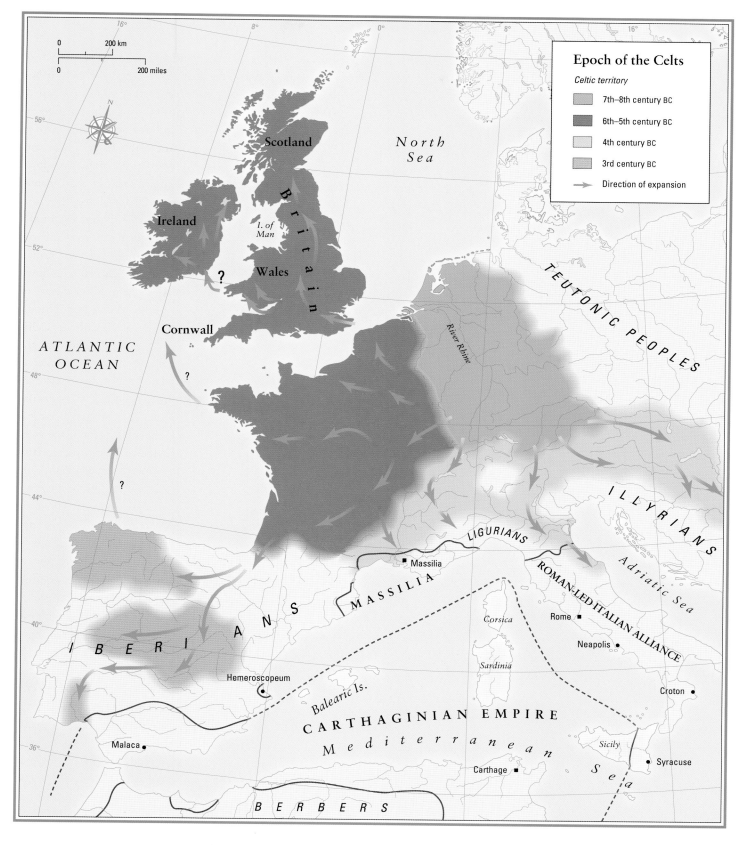

Epoch of the Celts

Celtic territory

- 7th–8th century BC
- 6th–5th century BC
- 4th century BC
- 3rd century BC
- Direction of expansion

16° 8° 0° 8° 16°

56°

Scotland

North Sea

Ireland

B r i t a i n

I. of Man

Wales

52°

?

ATLANTIC OCEAN

Cornwall

?

River Rhine

TEUTONIC PEOPLES

48°

?

44°

?

ILLYRIANS

LIGURIANS

Adriatic Sea

MASSILIA

■ Massilia

ROMAN-LED ITALIAN ALLIANCE

I B E R I A N S

Corsica

Rome ■

40°

Neapolis ●

Hemeroscopeum ⊙

Sardinia

Balearic Is.

Croton ●

CARTHAGINIAN EMPIRE

M e d i t e r r a n e a n   S e a

36°

Malaca ●

Sicily

Syracuse ●

Carthage ■

B E R B E R S

Orkney Islands

North
Sea

Pre-Roman British Isles

- ● *Oppidum*
- ▨ Major area of hillforts
- ▧ Minor area of hillforts

CORNAVII

CARINI

SMERTAE

Outer
Hebrides

LUGI

TAEXALI

CARNONACTAE

DECANTAE

CERONES

CALEDONII

VACOMAGI

EPIDII

VENICONES

DAMNONII

SELGOVAE

Traprain Law

VOTADINI

Eildon Hill

CORIONOTOTAE

NOVANTAE

ROBOGDII

VENNICNII

CRUITHIN

Stanwick

GAHRANIOVICES

ERDIN

DANNI

Isle of
Man

BRIGANTES

NAGNATE

VOLUNTII

Barwick in Elmet

PARISI

EBDANI

Irish
Sea

SETANTII

BLANII

AUTEINI

Isle of
Anglesey

CAUCI

DECEANGLI

CONCANI

DOMNAINN

GANGANI

CORITANI

MENAPII

ORDOVICES

CORNOVII

ICENI

GAGANI

USDIAE

LUCENI

CORIONDI

CATUVELLAUNI

VELABRI

BRIGANTES

Wheathampstead

IVEMI

VODIAE

DEMETAE

Salmonsbury

Grim's Ditch

TRINOVANTES

Colchester

UTEMI

Bagendon

St Albans

SILURES

DOBUNNI

ATREBATES

Dyke Hills

Oldbury

Canterbu

BELGAE

Silchester

CANTIACI

Winchester

REGNI

ATLANTIC
OCEAN

DUMNONII

DUROTRIGES

Hengistbury

Chichester/Selsey

English Channel

0		100 km
0		100 miles

northern Gaul. Historians have claimed that the Belgae sailed to Britain between the late second and early first centuries BC, maybe under pressure from encroaching German tribes, possibly the migrating Cimbri and Teutones, and also the pressure from the newly created Roman province of Gallia Transalpina in France. Yet, some archaeological evidence suggests the Belgae moved into southern Britain simultaneously with occupying the region of modern Belgium. Parisi graves in the Yorkshire Wolds have distinct similarities with those of the Champagne Parisi. These comprise elaborate chariot burials, such as those at Garton Slack and Wetwang Slack, with at least another twelve such burials.

The Celtic peoples, the majority being farmers, inhabited a variety of dwellings, the most common being a round house occupied by an extended family. A museum example of the Ballacagan Round House and its construction can be found in Manx museums in Douglas and Peel. Two interesting reconstructions are those of the Great Roundhouse at Butser Ancient Farm, Hampshire, which shows that British dwellings differed from continental rectangular versions. Another example, containing far less detail, is that at Rydale Folk Museum, Hutton-le-Hole, Yorkshire.

In Scotland and in the northern and Western Isles, Celts began building *broch*s. Constructed from local stone, being 12 to 25 metres in diameter at the base, the *broch*s were at least 15 metres high. Built without using mortar, they had an inner and outer wall, tapering towards the top, fastened together by long stones. Between the two walls were staircases which led to interior gallery rooms. The *broch* was surrounded by a wall, the totality providing protection and accommodation. Over five hundred *broch*s were built, examples being found at Dun Carloway Lewis, and the Broch of Mousa, Shetland. In Ireland and sometimes Scotland, the Celts sometimes constructed *crannóg*s. These comprised a group of palisaded buildings on an artificial island or platform raised on stilts over water, connected to land by a bridge. A good reconstruction exists at Graggaunowen, County Clare, with a Scots example on Loch Tay, Perthshire.

Most British hillforts were built during the Bronze Age but the Celts redeveloped some of these constructing multi-vallate forts with cleverly constructed gateways capable of enfilade fire in killing grounds. Such a fort is Maiden Castle, revamped with stone revetments but was incapable of withstanding a Roman army which stormed the fort and destroyed its gateways. Other architectural developments were the introduction of *oppida*, city states, sometimes fortified, such as those at Colchester and St Albans that became centres of power, as did those at Silchester, Braughinng, Canterbury and Winchester. So powerful were these states that they minted their own coinage. Inscribed in Latin, coins have been attributed to Commius, King of the Atrebates, and Cunobelinos of the Catuvellauni.

Coinage is symptomatic of established trade patterns and commerce was important, even showing that Chinese silk had reached the Celtic world. In the seas surrounding the British Isles, the Celts built strong ships that traversed the Irish Sea and the English Channel. The self-sufficient Celts produced surpluses of grain, cattle and hunting dogs that could be sold, the proceeds purchasing tin, salt, iron, wine, copper and other goods. Traders from the Mediterranean bought Cornish tin. In return for trade in livestock, hides, gold and copper, produce from Greece, Carthage, Etruria, and Rome reached the islands. Kings in their *oppida* imported Roman silver and glass ware, Arretine pottery, and fish sauce (*garum*) from either southern Iberia or Brittany. Strabo, the Greek historian and geographer, claimed that Roman trade with Britain produced more revenue than if it had been a Roman province, a preferred option to the cost of conquering, holding, and administering the islands; ironically some British exports supplied the Roman army.

Pre-Roman Britain

The peoples of the British Isles had absorbed and adopted influences from the Continent as well as developing their own unique styles and cultures. There were regions where hillforts dominated the landscape. Other defended settlements emerged, mostly in the north, like brochs *and* duns. *Oppidum,* important trading centres, were founded, some of which survived into the Roman period as capitals of client kingdoms like Camulodunum (Colchester).*

The Stamp of Rome

Rome was hostile to the Celts ever since the Celtic leader Brennus, leader of the Gallic Senones, had sacked Rome in 387 BC. This was a culmination point of gradual Gallic (Celtic) tribal movements through the Alps to settle in northern Italy where they often allied with the remnants of Etruscan power. After the defeat of the Carthaginians in the Second Punic War (218–201 BC), the Romans sought retribution on those northern Italian Gauls who had supported Hannibal. The subsequent Gallic defeat saw Rome advance north of the River Rubicon creating the Roman province of Cisalpine Gaul.

After the Punic Wars, Rome allied itself to the large city state of Massilia (Marseille). When this ally was threatened by neighbouring Gallic tribes, a Roman army marched to its rescue. After a Roman victory they built Aquae Sextiae (Aix) which housed a Roman garrison. Roman campaigns against the Gallic Allobroges and Arverni saw the foundation of the first colony of Roman citizens at Narbo Martius (Narbonne) in Gaul, leading to southern Gaul being formed into the Roman province of Transalpine Gaul in 118 BC. Roman Spain was thereby linked by the Via Domitiana with Italy, and the trade routes of the Rhone Valley were controlled, as was the port of Massilia. Narbo was the base from which Julius Caesar set out to conquer the Gauls, approximately modern France and the Low Countries.

In 58 BC, Julius Caesar was awarded the governorship of Cisalpine Gaul, Transalpine Gaul, and Illyricum. Immediately, Caesar crushed the Germanic Helvetii who were migrating from their homeland. Caesar defeated them at Arar and Bibracte and drove them back into what is now Switzerland, only 110,000 remaining from the original migratory 368,000. During this chaos, the Germani Suebi had occupied Gallic territory, a situation remedied by Caesar when he defeated Arovistus' Suebi at the battle of the Vosges and forced the Germans back across the Rhine.

Caesar saw Gaul as a rich resource which he could conquer and loot to pay off his debts incurred in securing his posts and promoting his status in Rome. A series of alliances were arranged with some Gallic tribes while he moved against Belgic tribes such as the Nervi and Atrebates. Their surrender allowed Caesar to campaign against the Atlantic coastal tribes in 56 BC. Here, the Romans constructed a fleet to destroy the sea-going Venetii who controlled one of the major maritime routes to Britain. In 55 BC, the Romans mounted a reconnaissance force to Britain to prevent the Britons supplying aid to their Celtic cousins in Europe. Harsh weather destroyed much of the Roman fleet and Caesar withdrew to Gaul.

In 54 BC, Caesar returned to Britain with some 25,000 men. His major opponents were the Catuvellauni commanded by CassivEllaunus who waged guerrilla warfare against the Romans as he lured them further inland. The eventual British capitulation led to nothing. However, Caesar made alliances with various British tribes, especially the Trinovantes, and in c. 15 BC, Caesar Augustus recognised Tincommius of the Atrebates and Tasciovanus of the Catuvellauni as client kings, a status kept until Claudius invaded Britain in 43 BC.

Meanwhile, Caesar had to crush rebellions of the Nervi, Eburones, Treveri and Menapii, eventually leaving these tribes under the direction of his ally, Commius of the Atrebates. The Eburones had suffered greatly during this campaign, having their houses burnt and their cattle and crops seized, leaving much of the population to die of starvation. Next, Caesar faced a pan-Gallic alliance against Rome led by Vercingetorix, leader of the Arverni of central Gaul. The eventual Gallic defeat at the Siege of Alesia in 52 BC saw the Gallic leader surrender and eventually strangled at Caesar's triumph in Rome. Julius Caesar made so much money he could liquidate his debts and eventually march on Rome itself in a bid for supreme power. A permanent Roman road to Btitain now lay open.

Caesar's Conquest of Gaul
The Roman campaigns in Gaul, led by Julius Caesar, saw the Roman Empire established on the Oceanus Britannicus (English Channel) and, in 54 and 55 BC, the Romans, for politically and military reasons, mounted a reconnaissance in force during which new economic opportunities were revealed.

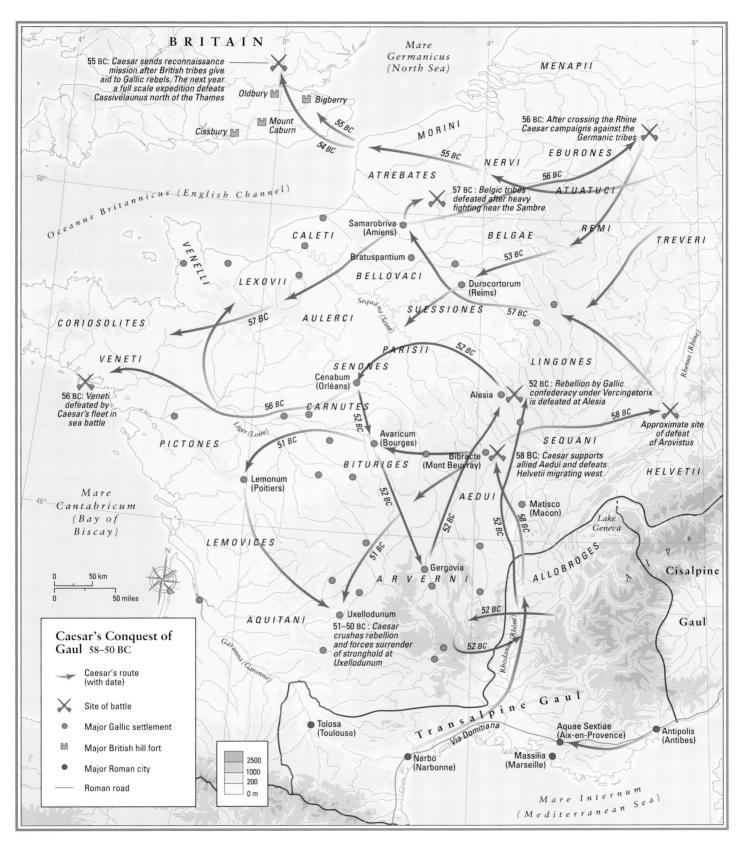

BRITAIN

55 BC: *Caesar sends reconnaissance mission after British tribes give aid to Gallic rebels. The next year a full scale expedition defeats Cassivelaunus north of the Thames*

Oldbury

Bigberry

Cissbury

Mount Caburn

55 BC

54 BC

Mare Germanicus (North Sea)

MENAPII

56 BC: *After crossing the Rhine Caesar campaigns against the Germanic tribes*

MORINI

EBURONES

ATREBATES

NERVI

ATUATUCI

55 BC

56 BC

57 BC: *Belgic tribes defeated after heavy fighting near the Sambre*

REMI

TREVERI

Oceanus Britannicus (English Channel)

CALETI

Samarobriva (Amiens)

BELGAE

VENELLI

LEXOVII

Bratuspantium

BELLOVACI

53 BC

Durocortorum (Reims)

Sequana (Seine)

SUESSIONES

57 BC

Rhenus (Rhine)

CORIOSOLITES

AULERCI

57 BC

PARISII

52 BC

LINGONES

VENETI

SENONES

Cenabum (Orléans)

52 BC: *Rebellion by Gallic confederacy under Vercingetorix is defeated at Alesia*

56 BC: *Veneti defeated by Caesar's fleet in sea battle*

56 BC

CARNUTES

Alesia

58 BC

Approximate site of defeat of Arovistus

Liger (Loire)

51 BC

52 BC

Avaricum (Bourges)

SEQUANI

PICTONES

BITURIGES

Bibracte (Mont Beuvray)

58 BC: *Caesar supports allied Aedui and defeats Helvetii migrating west*

HELVETII

Mare Cantabricum (Bay of Biscay)

Lemonum (Poitiers)

52 BC

AEDUI

Matisco (Macon)

Lake Geneva

LEMOVICES

52 BC

52 BC

52 BC

58 BC

Gergovia

ARVERNI

ALLOBROGES

Cisalpine

A L P S

N

0   50 km

0   50 miles

52 BC

Gaul

AQUITANI

Uxellodunum

51–50 BC: *Caesar crushes rebellion and forces surrender of stronghold at Uxellodunum*

52 BC

Rhodanus (Rhone)

Garumna (Garonne)

Caesar's Conquest of Gaul 58–50 BC

→ Caesar's route (with date)

✕ Site of battle

● Major Gallic settlement

⌂ Major British hill fort

● Major Roman city

— Roman road

2500
1000
200
0 m

T r a n s a l p i n e   G a u l

Via Domitiana

Aquae Sextiae (Aix-en-Provence)

Antipolis (Antibes)

Tolosa (Toulouse)

Narbo (Narbonne)

Massilia (Marseille)

Mare Internum (Mediterranean Sea)

Invasion AD 43–83

The Roman invasion of Britain in AD 43, under Aulus Plautius, comprised some 40–50,000 men including four legions: (Legio II Augusta, Legio XX Valeria, Legio XIV Gemina and Legio IX Hispana), the remainder being lightly armed cavalry and allied infantry, raised in places like Gaul, Thrace, and Germania. The timing of the invasion was motivated by the death of King Cunobelinus of the Catuvellauni, whose lands fell into the rule of his two Roman-hating sons, Caratacus and Togodumnus. The Atrebates living south of the Thames were pressured by the new leaders, whose tribe had previously seized Trinovatan lands and the Atrebatan King, Verica, was expelled from his territories and fled to Rome; this led the Catuvellauni to demand his extradition.

Emperor Claudius was insistent upon supporting Verica's treaty rights as a client king. The Romans landed at Richborough and soon confronted the locals when attempting to force the Medway. The Britons eventually retreated after a two-day battle and the Romans crossed the Thames after waiting for Claudius to catch up. Meanwhile, Togodumnus had fallen in battle and Caratacus had escaped to the west. Camulodunum was occupied and eleven British kings surrendered to the Emperor, who only stayed sixteen days, merely to gain the glory of meeting the vanquished.

The rest of Britain needed subduing. Legio XX made a base at Colchester while Legio IX and Legio XIV moved into the north and west Midlands. To the south-west Legio II campaigned against the Durotriges in Dorset. Vespasian subdued the Isle of Wight and some twenty hill forts, including Maiden Castle. Supplies could now be moved into Britain via Noviomagnus (Chichester). Roman occupation required the building of forts at key points, garrisoned by auxiliaries. Many forts were located near major concentrations of British populations, such as Verulamium (St. Albans) and Gosbecks, near Colchester. Legionary forts were also established as at Colchester to contain the Legio XX but the other legions were divided into smaller units being emplaced in forts in quieter areas such as Longthorpe, near Peterborough. The Rivers Trent and Severn became a border region or frontier zone, along the Fosse Way, with deep defences running from Lincolnshire to Devon. This delineated the new province acquired for Rome by Aulus Plautius.

Elsewhere, Caratacus fought a guerrilla war for nine years and the Romans felt compelled to advance to the Severn, building new legionary fortresses at Viroconium (Wroxeter) and Glevum (Gloucester). The Roman campaign against the Silures and Ordovices in Wales impinged upon the Brigantes, a powerful tribal confederacy in the north of Britain. The league was split between a major leader, Venutius, who wished to confront Rome, and his wife, Queen Cartimandua, who sought to reinforce her personal position within the tribe by seeking a détente with Rome. It was she who captured Caratacus and handed him over to the Romans in chains. Then, Cartimandua was forced to seek Roman aid against her ex-husband's revolt against Rome.

Later, successive Roman governors waged war against the Welsh tribes breaking off to defeat the Iceni Revolt after crushing the druids on Mona (Anglesey). Venutius was defeated, c. AD 70, leaving the Brigantes and neighbouring Parisi to be Romanised. The Welsh tribes were subdued with a new legionary base built at Caerleon, and important gold mines at Dolaucothi were developed. In AD 78, Agricola was appointed governor and finally subdued any possibility of further revolt in north Wales, Mona and Brigantia. He then marched against the Selgovae in southern Scotland and established Roman control over their lands and throughout Scottish Lowlands in north-eastern Scotland. Forts were built in the Lowlands, Caledonians defeated at the Battle of Mons Graupius in AD 83 and a Roman fleet sailed around the coast of Scotland in AD 84.

Roman Conquest of Britain
Between AD 43 and 83 Roman campaigns continued, conquering large parts of the British Isles. Trade contacts were developed with Hibernia (Ireland) and a kind of edgy peace was maintained with the Caledonian tribes in the north.

Orkney Islands

Roman Conquest of Britain
AD 43–83

→ First Roman landing AD 43

▨ Roman advance AD 43–47

▨ Roman advance AD 47–59

▨ Roman advance AD 61–74

▨ Roman advance AD 78–84

⌂ Major Roman fort

⌂ Marching camps for Agricola's campaigns AD 78–83

✕ Major battles with dates

▨ Major areas of native resistance

- - → Route of Roman fleet AD 84

ICENI Tribe names

CORNOVII

CAERENII

SMERTAE

TAEXALI

Thornshill
Cawdor
Bellie
Auchinhove
Ythan Wells
Dumo

CARNONACAE

Outer
Hebrides

CALEDONIAN
FEDERATION

DECANTAE

CREONES

VACOMAGI

Mons Graupius?
AD 83

CALEDONES

Strathcathro
Finavon
Cardean
Inchtuthil
Carpow
Bonnytown

VERTURIONES

Dalginross
Menteith
Ardoch
Dunblane
Camelon

EPIDII

DAMNONI

VOTADINI

Castledykes

Newstead

Beattock

SELGOVAE

NOVANTAE

Dalswinton
Corbridge
Luguvalium
(Carlisle)
Nether
Denton

Mare Germanicus
(North Sea)

CARVETII

B R I G A N T E S

PARISI

Eboracum
(York)

Ribchester

Mare Hibernicus
(Irish Sea)

SETANTII

IRELAND

Anglesey
AD 60

Newton-
on-Trent

Lindum Colonia
(Lincoln)

DECEANGLI

Deva
(Chester)

CORITANI

GANGANI

Wroxeter
(Viroconium)

ORDOVICES

CORNOVII

Letocetum
(Wall)

Ratae
Corieltauvorum
(Leicester)

Longthorpe

ICENI

TRINOVANTES

DEMETAE

Clyro

DOBUNNI

CATUVELLAUNI

Camulodunum
(Colchester)

SILURES

Usk

Glevum
(Gloucester)

Verulamium
(St Albans)

Isca Augusta
(Caerleon)

Durocornovium
(Swindon)

Londinium
(London)

Rutupiae
(Richborough)

BELGAE

ATREBATES

CANTIACI

South Cadbury
AD 44?

Hod Hill
AD 44?

REGNI

Noviomagnus
(Chichester)

Boulogne

North Tawton

ATLANTIC
OCEAN

Isca
Dumnoniorum
(Exeter)

Maiden Castle
AD 44?

Fishbourne

DUROTRIGES

DUMNONII

Nanstallon

AD 43

Oceanus Britannicus (English Channel)

G A U L

0   100 km

0   100 miles

Revolt of the Iceni

The west, roughly modern Wales, remained an area of resistance to Roman rule, especially since Anglesey was the home of the Druids. Roman energies were directed towards its conquest in AD 60 and victory celebrations were marred by news of Boudicca's revolt in the south-east of Britain.

In what is now East Anglia, there existed the client-state of the Iceni ruled by Prasutagas, whose lands would default to Rome on his death. His wife, Boudicca, contested this inheritance when Roman officials arrived to claim lands and property while financiers called in their loans. Boudicca was flogged and her daughters gang-raped, irrespective of their age. The Iceni exploded in rebellion and were soon joined by the Trinovantes who deeply resented the existence of Roman colonists at Camulodonum (Colchester). Locals had been mistreated by Roman colonisers and hated paying for the new Temple to Claudius. Roman settlements were attacked as the Britons moved towards Colchester where they butchered 3,000 and besieged a small party who locked themselves in the Temple of Claudius. This was torched and razed to the ground.

The XI Hispania legion sent a relief force of 2,000 men who were slaughtered in an ambush, possibly near Wormingford, north of Colchester. With no protection, London was destroyed with the killing of thousands of Romans. Boudicca's march on Verulamium (St. Albans) led to the destruction of that municipality but the inhabitants had already fled. The Roman governor, Suetonius Paulinus, force-marched from Anglesey to London but then retreated leaving the city, a major commercial centre, to its fate while he found a site to both resist the Britons and be near lines of communication with Isca Dumnuniorum (Exeter) where the II Augusta legion was stationed and summoned as reinforcements.

The Romans and Britons met in battle in the Midlands along Watling Street, possibly at Mancetter in Warwickshire. The Romans found a position with a secure wood to their rear with a defile to the front which would make it difficult for Boudicca to deploy her superior numbers. The Romans numbered some 10,000 men, mainly legionaries but supported by several thousand auxiliaries to the front and on the flanks as cavalry. The Romans, unable to cover the British front, were divided into three divisions but were prepared to defend themselves at all points whether attacked by infantry or by chariots. The Britons drifted into the battle zone in no great order, bolstered by courage and bravado to the extent of bringing their wagon park to the rear where non-combatants could watch the spectacle.

The British approached the Roman lines in an undisciplined mass, lacking any organization or officers, only to be met with a hail of javelins followed by a charge into the British ranks with close quarter fighting. This benefited the Romans with their short thrusting gladius sword against the long slashing British swords. The battle lasted most of a day, with chariot charges scattering Roman ranks until the drivers were shot down by archers. The melée was an intense formless swirl of fighters but the Romans maintained their discipline and formations, which more than matched the crazed Celtic attacks. The legionaries' steady advance pressed Boudicca's warriors back against the wagon park where many were cut down; be they men, women, children or animals.

Roman losses reached the hundreds but the Britons lost at least 8,000 with the dispersal of the rest. Boudicca committed suicide following the pattern of many defeated Celts. Emperor Nero was so horrified at the revolt that he even considered evacuating Britain. Paulinus next devastated the lands of the defeated tribes, disarming them, while fortresses and towns were strengthened. His measures were so harsh that he was replaced by the more conciliatory Petronius Turpilianus. Southern Britain now became peaceful as Romanization in administration and trade developed.

Boudiccan Revolts

High-handed Roman policies outraged the Iceni, who attacked Romans in a killing frenzy. Boudicca wished to annihilate all Romans and Britons who had been seduced by the invaders. No prisoners were taken and no mercy shown to woman or child. Tacitus claims Boudicca slaughtered 70,000 people in Colchester, St Albans and London. Her achievements are celebrated by a monument on the Thames Embankment, which made her into an iconic freedom fighter.

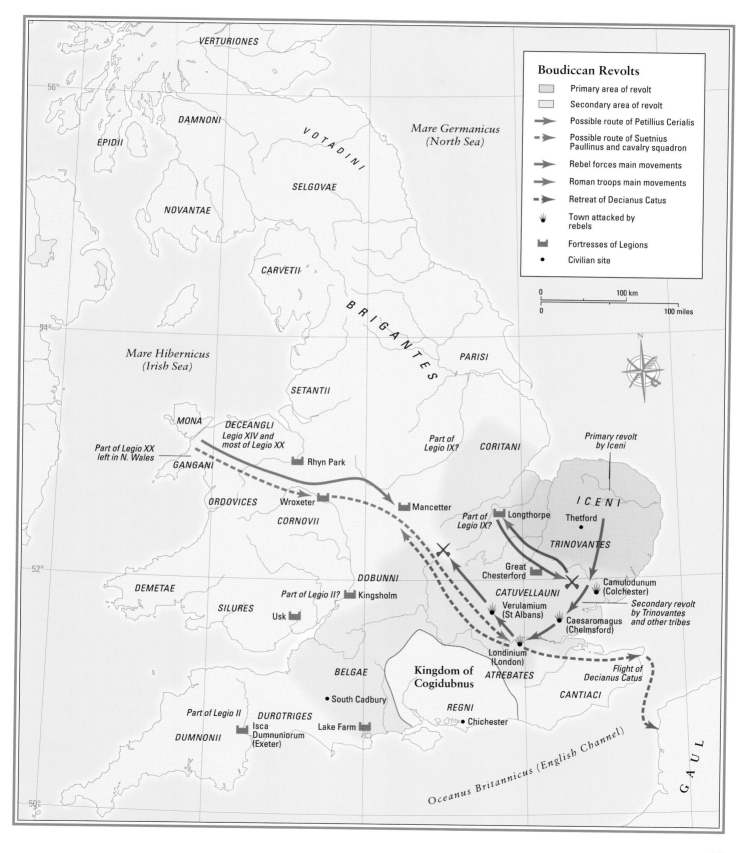

Boudiccan Revolts

Primary area of revolt

Secondary area of revolt

Possible route of Petillius Cerialis

Possible route of Suetnius Paullinus and cavalry squadron

Rebel forces main movements

Roman troops main movements

Retreat of Decianus Catus

Town attacked by rebels

Fortresses of Legions

Civilian site

0   100 km
0   100 miles

VERTURIONES

DAMNONI

EPIDII

VOTADINI

Mare Germanicus (North Sea)

SELGOVAE

NOVANTAE

CARVETII

B R I G A N T E S

Mare Hibernicus (Irish Sea)

SETANTII

PARISI

MONA

DECEANGLI
Legio XIV and most of Legio XX

Part of Legio XX left in N. Wales

GANGANI

Rhyn Park

Part of Legio IX?

CORITANI

Primary revolt by Iceni

ORDOVICES

Wroxeter

CORNOVII

Mancetter

Part of Legio IX?

Longthorpe

Thetford

I C E N I

TRINOVANTES

DEMETAE

DOBUNNI

Part of Legio II?

Kingsholm

Great Chesterford

Camulodunum (Colchester)

CATUVELLAUNI

Secondary revolt by Trinovantes and other tribes

SILURES

Usk

Verulamium (St Albans)

Caesaromagus (Chelmsford)

Londinium (London)

BELGAE

Kingdom of Cogidubnus

ATREBATES

Flight of Decianus Catus

South Cadbury

REGNI

CANTIACI

Part of Legio II

DUROTRIGES

Isca Dumnuniorum (Exeter)

Lake Farm

Chichester

DUMNONII

Oceanus Britannicus (English Channel)

G A U L

Londinium – Provincial Capital

Before the Romans invaded Britain in AD 43, there was no significant settlement where the future Londinium would be built. When Aulus Plautius pursued Caratacus northwards, he built a temporary bridge allowing his men to cross the River Thames. This bridge has been excavated and found to be very near the modern London Bridge. Some historians argue that Plautius awaited the arrival of the Emperor Claudius on the site of Londinium but archaeological evidence suggests otherwise. Interestingly, at the line of Watling Street, an early Roman road extends from the invasion base at Richborough in Kent to the Thames but bypasses the Londinium site, instead leading to a possible crossing at Westminster. The native road north of the Thames leads directly north to a British oppidum, later Verulamium. Eventually, Roman roads leading to London cut across Watling Street and extended to the later Roman London Bridge.

One historical theory argues that Londinium was never a military base but was founded around AD 50 as a well-planned civil trading settlement of Roman merchants. This port became important as a supply centre to supply the army and new Roman towns. Growing importance and its sack by Boudicca in AD 60 led to it superseding Camulodunum (Colchester) as the administrative capital of the Roman province of Britain. Hence, originally, Londinium was a deep-water port, a necessity for merchants engaged in commerce in this new province. Additionally, Londinium possessed a Roman bridge at the lowest crossing-point on the river. Thus, the city became an important communications centre with a network of roads fanning out across the country to important settlements like Dover, Chichester, Silchester, Chester, York and Norwich.

The importance of the Londinium entrepôt is evidenced by the goods found in archaeological excavations. The traders were not native Britons but businessmen from the Roman world trading with Gaul, Germania and the Mediterranean thereby linking Londinium into a sophisticated international trading network. Italy supplied fine glass tableware, decorated pottery lamps, and even re-coloured pottery tableware made near Vesuvius and containing volcanic ash. Central and southern Gaul supplied more colourful tableware, especially red-glossed Samian ware, in addition to southern Gaul's wine. Southern

Londinium

The first settlement lay north of the River Thames and to the east of the Walbrook Stream. The settlement spread slowly westward and was constructed mostly of timber. However, after the Boudiccan Revolt of AD 60, the town was rebuilt using stone for the major buildings and defensive works. It grew like other towns of Roman Britain, housing communities of craftsmen and merchants. By the fourth century the city had become important enough to be granted the title of 'Augusta' and was the headquarters of the 'vicarius', the Emperor's representative, of the four Roman provinces that made up Roman Britain.

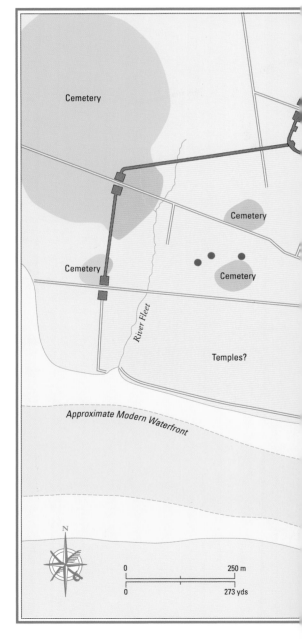

Spain's Seville traded globular amphorae, probably containing olive oil, while Rhodes in the Greek islands supplied wine and Syria provided well-designed glassware.

When London was rebuilt after AD 60, it accumulated all the architectural attributes of a typical Roman city with: a Temple of Mithras, baths (Huggin Hill), a *forum* and *basilica* (town hall), an amphitheatre, and a governor's palace. Remembering Boudicca's revolt, a stone wall was constructed around Londinium, roughly coterminous with the modern city. The wall was 3 kilometres long and 2.7 metres thick at its base and stood over 6 metres high, taking within its environs the Cripplegate Fort in northwest Londinium. Detachments from various legions served in the fort: auxiliary Tungrians, Legio II Augusta, Legio VI Victrix and Classis Britannica, the Roman fleet providing support for military operations in the provinces.

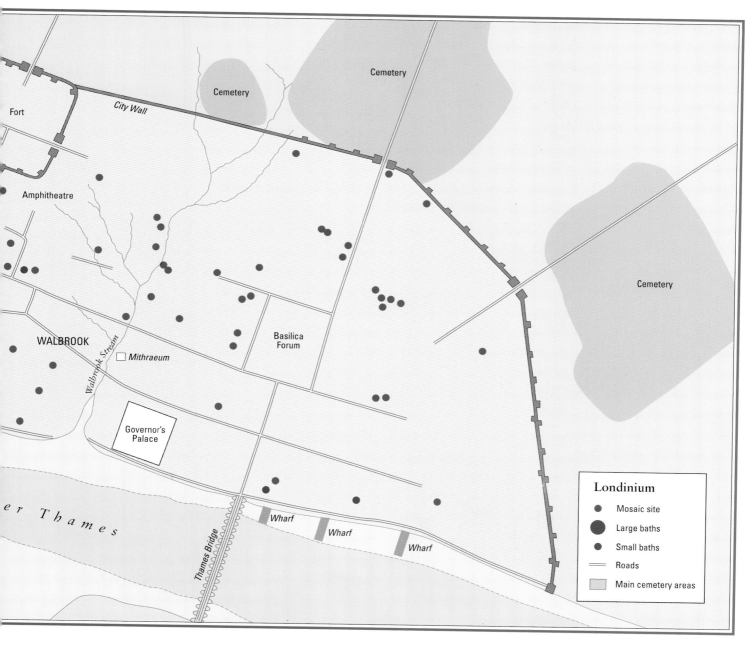

31

Roman Occupation and Rule

Roman Provincial Development
● Provincial capitals
○ Diocesan capitals

Claudian

Later First and Second Centuries

Roman Britain ranked as a consular province, to be ruled by a senator who had held the consulship. As governor, he was the Emperor's deputy for military and civil affairs. Not only had the governor to defend the borders but, even on campaign, civil affairs had to be handled. His brief was to oversee the civil communities, to build and maintain roads, and make the imperial postal system run efficiently. Additionally, he was responsible for military recruitment and ran a legal court of appeal, handling important issues of capital punishment or sentencing people to the mines, a recipe for a tortuous death. As more towns were founded, the governor acted as a virtual circuit judge. In case a governor might misbehave, a procurator was also appointed to be in charge of financial affairs while monitoring the governor's actions.

The system of local government existing in Gaul was transposed to Britain. The Celtic tribes were organised into *civitates*, each *civitas* having a capital town. The names of many *civitates* are known from archaeological inscriptions naming a *civitas* with a tribal suffix, such as Ratae Coritanorum (Leicester) and Corinium Dobunnorum (Cirencester). *Civitas* capitals were normally built on the site of an old Roman fort, which turned into a capital. This was serviced by a developing community. Town planning was probably the norm evidenced by the grid-street patterns. Verulamium, the capital of the Catuvellauni, became an autonomous borough (*municipium*), an institution having certain legal rights including the granting of Roman citizenship to the hundred-man council, or *ordo*. In these tribal areas, towns ranked as a *vicus* if they possessed some degree of self-government. The rural areas were divided into units known as *pagi*, whose meaning and function are uncertain.

The Romans also introduced communities of Roman veterans (*coloniae*) into Britain. These towns of self-governing citizens were partially designed to show the Celtic tribes the virtues of Roman civilisation. The three such communities in Britain were founded at Colchester, Lincoln and Gloucester (and later York) with *municipium* being developed too. Each *colonia* was surrounded by its own territory.

In the *civitas* towns, founded by imperial charter and run according to a simplified constitution of republican Rome, the ruling organ was the *ordo* comprising up to a hundred members, the *decuriones*. Heading the council were either two or three pairs of presiding officers. The two chief magistrates were the *duoviri iuridicundo* running the law courts while one would act as the chairman of the *ordo*. Next in the pecking order were the *aediles*, who handled the street-cleaning, waste disposal, aqueducts, water distribution and sometimes the supply of entertainment such as the theatre in Petuaria of the Parisi, now Brough-on-Humber. Occasionally, a third pair of officials was the *quaestores* who were responsible for financial affairs for the chief magistrates. To finish, a final group of officials were the *severi Augustales*, six priests, whose task was to hold ceremonies linked to the imperial cult.

The Roman towns developed a vibrant urban life with houses of timber, then stone, being built in the squares created by a grid-street system. Public buildings were constructed like the town *basilica* where the *ordo* met. The towns were eventually linked by more than 11,900 kilometres of roads, which facilitated commerce and the regionalisation of certain product manufactures.

In the reign of Emperor Septimus Severus (AD 193–211), Britain was divided into Upper and Lower Britain. Later, Domitian (AD 286–305) divided Lower Britain into Britannia Secunda and Flavia Caesariensis in the north, and split Upper Britain in the south into Britannia Prima, with a capital at Cirencester and Maxima Caesariensis administered from London. Each of these four provinces had its own governor responsible to the Emperor's representative, the *vicarius,* who had his base in London.

Just as local government followed the Gallic system, so did the Romanisation of other aspects of life and culture. The *civitates* and *municipia* of Britain were substantial but not in comparison with their Mediterranean origins, quality, and architectural proportions. Instead, the system of villas was much more important, especially in the civilian settlement areas south of the Fosse Way, the road linking Exeter (Isca) to Lincoln (Lindum). North of this line, the military was more in evidence, certainly as Hadrian's Wall was approached.

The towns occupied key points where trade routes crossed and served as market places to exchange surplus products such as Cotswold wool, Devon pottery, or jet from the Whitby area. Additionally, markets brought in goods from Europe such as Samian-ware pottery, Falernian wine, olives and olive oil. A coin-based economy led to service businesses in municipal areas such as bakeries, shoe-making, mosaic setting and interior painters. The Roman taxation system enhanced productivity and generated financial stability, a prerequisite for economic activity. Towns housed temples, *basilicae* and the *forum,* together with temples and public baths with the complete range of rooms from the *frigidarium* to the *caldarium*. Many towns possessed an amphitheatre like that at Chester or theatres, and some towns still have the remains of the enclosing walls.

Most people in Britain lived in the countryside inhabiting the traditional circular wattle and daub houses used traditionally by Iron Age Britons. Others lived in villas and these prosperous farms were home to Romans, wealthy Romano-Britons, and to Celtic servants and labourers. Some villas were sumptuous with beautiful mosaics such as the Orpheus mosaic at the Roman villa at Littlecote Manor near Hungerford. Some villas have now been identified as hostelries, sometimes associated with neighbouring temples like that of Nodens at Lydney Park in Gloucestershire.

Villas tended to be farms laid out in various patterns following a rectangular style. Important examples can be visited at Littlecote, Brading and Newport in the Isle of White. Villas included outbuildings such as barns for animals, storage, and servants' quarters. Ownership of villas varied with some farm-owners present but those comprising parts of larger estates would be managed by bailiffs. Vectis, the Isle of Wight, owns eight identifiable villas representing all the types found amongst the 700 villas found in Britain. These are found at Brading, Newport, Combley (Arreton), Carisbrooke, Clatterford, possibly Bowcombe, Rock (Brighstone) and Gurnard.

Vectis became a well populated Romano-Celtic society, peaking in prosperity between AD 250–300. The villas practised mixed farming, using crop rotation with green manure as well as animal. Cereal crops such as wheat and barley were grown on the downs and corn was exported. Meadows were used to raise cattle while chicken, geese, goats and oxen were common. The downs were also used for sheep grazing and for small enclosed fields, which can be seen via aerial photographs. The northern part of the island was thick with forest and was used for foraging pigs and hunting deer, boar and birds. The sea provided a rich harvest as it still does. The prosperity of the island partially relied on the easy access to markets, with the Solent providing multiple routes to the mainland. Ptolemy dubbed the Solent network as the Magnus Portus and anchorages have been found at Yarmouth and Wootton Creek.

The Romans wished to develop British resources such as the lead and silver mines, with occasional gold workings in Wales. Cornish tin was useful for making bronze but was often alloyed with lead to make pewter. The Sussex and Kentish Weald were home to iron smelting as was the Forest of Dean. Trade was extensive and London became a major city exporting corn, wool, textiles and jet, the latter even reaching the Rhineland.

Third Century

Early Fourth Century

Caledonia

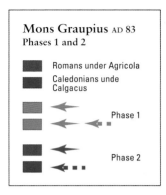
After Agricola's victory at Mons Graupius, the Romans apparently constructed a frontier along the Gask Ridge, a series of 'glen-blocker' forts, and consolidated a Forth–Clyde defensive line, the future site of the Antonine Wall. This occupation of Lowland Scotland was apparently brief; the second century witnessed the forts of southern Scotland being destroyed or burnt with a new frontier being built along the Stanegate (c. 105), a road built by Agricola from Carlisle to Corbridge.

A new line was built, Hadrian's Wall, running from Bowness on the Solway Firth to Wallsend on the River Tyne. A later fortification, the Antonine Wall, was established from the Firth of Clyde to the Firth of Forth in AD 142.

The Gask Ridge stands some 70 metres above sea level and is situated between the Highland massif and the rich lands of Fife, comprising part of a corridor northwards towards the coastal strip of fertile agricultural land that reaches to the Moray Firth. The Gask frontier includes a line of forts, fortlets and watch-towers along a military road and might be the earliest Roman *limes* ever built. Beginning at Glenbank, north of Dunblane, it extends to Bertha near Perth on the Tay. The fortifications were so close together that they were part of a frontier scheme rather than a signalling system. The Gask lines were abandoned, possibly because of troubles on the Danube in AD 85, which led to the withdrawal of the Legio II Adiutrix and auxiliary units from Britain. Possibly, Britain was regarded as so peripheral that the loss of some border lands was acceptable for the greater good of the Empire.

Emperor Hadrian visited Britain in AD 122, ordering a wall built just north of the Stanegate. Some 70 miles long, the stone-built wall was ten feet wide, extending from Newcastle to the River Irthing after which a turf wall was built to Bowness-on-Solway. The mile-castles were built from turf and timber on the turf wall and elsewhere of stone. Two small turrets were emplaced between each mile-castle. The front of the wall was protected by a large ditch except where the wall followed steep cliffs or an escarpment. The wall incorporated fifteen forts and was further protected to the south by a military zone and an earthwork, the Vallum, a ditch between two mounds. The Cumberland coast beyond the wall also had a chain of mile-castles and towers. The wall was intended as an obstacle to the Caledonian tribes and to keep the Brigantes in.

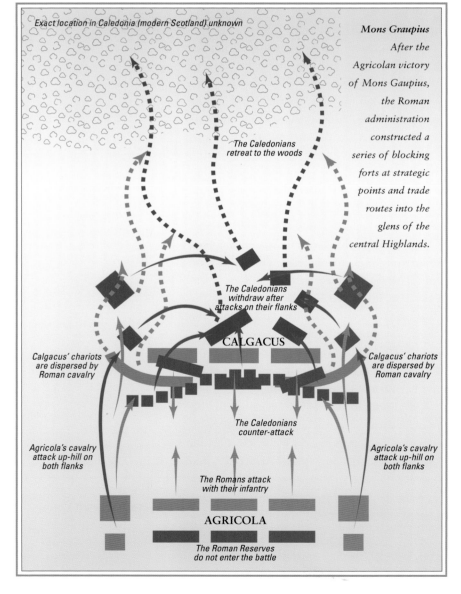

Exact location in Caledonia (modern Scotland) unknown

Mons Graupius

After the Agricolan victory of Mons Gaupius, the Roman administration constructed a series of blocking forts at strategic points and trade routes into the glens of the central Highlands.

The Caledonians retreat to the woods

The Caledonians withdraw after attacks on their flanks

CALGACUS

Calgacus' chariots are dispersed by Roman cavalry

Calgacus' chariots are dispersed by Roman cavalry

Agricola's cavalry attack up-hill on both flanks

The Caledonians counter-attack

Agricola's cavalry attack up-hill on both flanks

The Romans attack with their infantry

AGRICOLA

The Roman Reserves do not enter the battle

In AD 138, Emperor Antoninus Pius re-evaluated the frontier system, giving a new governor, Quintus Lollius Urbicus, the duty of re-occupying southern Scotland and erecting a new wall across the Forth–Clyde gap. The legions built the wall, which stretched 37 miles, with a turf rampart built on stone foundations. The wall, 13 feet high and 15 feet wide, was fronted by a wide level space, a berm and a ditch. Nineteen forts were incorporated, being about two miles apart. The Wall was abandoned around AD 158 and then re-occupied for a while before a final

retreat was made to Hadrian's Wall (c. AD 163) Emperor Septimus Severus campaigned in AD 208–09 and 210 respectively. Sections of the Antonine Wall were repaired while Severus won several victories over the Caledonii.

Seemingly, the Romans never intended to occupy the Highlands. However, Scotland was remote, not tied into a market economy and the costs of the wall impinged upon the imperial budget. The major threats to the Empire lay on the Danube and Rhine against the Germans, so a withdrawal to Hadrian's Wall made sense.

Hadrian's and Antonine Walls
Hadrian's Wall was the first established fortified frontier. In AD 146, the Antonine Wall was constructed. It remained the frontier until abandoned in AD 163, when the frontier moved back to the line of Hadrian's Wall.

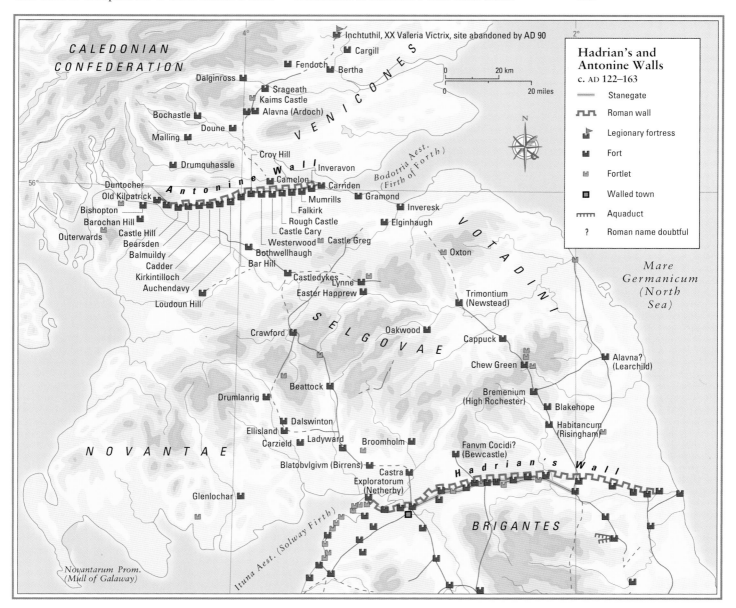

Britain's Trade with the Empire

Britain's Trade with the Empire AD 180

——	Trade routes	⌑	Forts
▣	Regional capitals	⊞	Naval bases
⊙	Cities	····	Continuous fortification line
○	Towns	·· ··	Fortification line
◼	Legionary bases	——	Roads
◻	Other bases		

The province of Britain, in the far north-west of the Roman Empire, linked the islands to a vast array of products, mostly from the western provinces. These included pottery, everyday necessities such as olive oil and fish sauce, and exotic products like silk from China. In return, Britain exported lead, tin, copper, gold, silver, cattle, wheat and slaves.

NAVARI

BASTARNAE

OSTOBOCI

ROXOLANI

Tissum
Gherla
apoca
Potaissa
pelum
Tibiscum
avia
Drobeta
Pontes
Sucidava
Romula
ratiaria
aissus
Oescus
MOESIA INF.
Nicopolis
Serdica
THRACIA
Stobi
Philippopolis
Nicopolis
ONIA
Hadrianopolis
ella
Thessalonica
ea
Cassandrea
Dium
Demetrias
Pharsalus
RUS
Delphi
Patrae
Corinthus
Elis
Argus
mpia
Magalopolis
Sparta
ACHAIA

Curaidava
Castra Traina
Pons Aluti
Durostorum
Tropaeum Traini
Arbittus
Marcianopolis
Odessus
Mesembria
Anchialus
Apollonia
Byzantium
Perinthus
Chalcedon
Trajanopolis
Lysimachia
Mare
Alexandria
Troas
Magnesia
Smyrna
Chalcia
Athens

Olbia
Ordessos
Tyras
Neapolis
Chersonesus
Panticapaem
Theodosia
Phanagoria
Agrippia
Hermonassa
Caesarea
Bata

Pontus Euxinus

SINDI
HENIOCHI
ZICHI
ABSAGI
COLCHIS
Dioscurria
Phasis
IBERI
Harmorica
ALBANIA

Sinope
Amastris
Tieum
Heraclea Pontica
Nicomedia
Nicea
Apamea
Prusa
Cyzicus
Parium
Illium
BITHYNIA ET PONTUS
Pompeiopolis
Amisus
Amasia
Zela
Gangra
Ancyra
Germa
Pessinus
GALATIA
Dorylaeum
PONTUS
Cotyoro
Cerasus
Nicopolis
Trapezus
CHALYBES
ARMENIA MINOR
Satala
Carana
Caenopolis
Artaxata
Artagira
Araxes
ARMENIA
SOPHENE
Tigranocerta
Amida
CORDUENE
ADIABENE
Gazaca
REGNUM PARTHORUM

MYSIA
Pergamum
ASIA
Sardes
Ephesus
LYDIA
Laodicea
CARIA
Miletus
Halicarnassus
Cnidus
Rhodus
Magnesia

Germa
Pessinus
Iconium
LYCAONIA
Cremna
Parlais
Lystra
Comama
Olbasa
Attalia
Aspendus
Selinus

Caesarea
Archelais
Tyana
CAPPADOCIA
Ariarathia
Melitene
Arsameia
OSROENE
Samosata
Edessa
Zeugma
Cyrrhus
Carrhae
Rhesaenae
Nisibis
Singara
Arbela
Arela

Tarsus
CILICIA
Pompeiopolis
Seleucia
Laodicea
Antiochia
Beroea
Sura
Apamea
COELE-SYRIA
Epiphania
SYRIA
Emesa
Palmyra
Circesium
Dura
MESOPOTAMIA
Tigris
ASSYRIA
Seleucia
Ctesiphon
Babylon
Euphrates
Nicephorium
Hatra
Dara

Cydonia
Cnossus
Crete
Gortyn

ERNUM

Cyprus
Paphus
Salamis
Aradus
Tripolis
Berytus
PHOENICIA
Tyrus
Ptolemais
Caesarea
JUDAEA
Neapolis
Hierosolyma
Gaza
Hebron
Masada
Raphia
Elusa
Oboda
NABATAEI
Aila
ARABIA
Heliopolis
Damascus
Bostra
Gerasa
AGRAEI

us
Apollonia
cus
Cyrene
Darnis
Semeros
Halivros
Antipyrgos
NAICA
CYRENE
MARMARICA
Paraetonium
Alexandria
Sais
Sebennytus
Pelusium
Memphis
Babylon
Fossatum
Arsinoe
AEGYPTUS

37

Rome's Retreat in the West

Western Europe was an agriculturally-rich land, with its interior connected to the seas by broad navigable rivers. Cities grew along these routes and became nodes of trade and communications. The region was well populated, as the Romans found, when they seized control from its Celtic or Gallic peoples. The Celtic tribes were farmers and their villages survived after conquest but were eventually incorporated into the great estates of a provincial Roman or Celtic-Roman aristocracy, depending upon how much inter-marriage existed. Celtic status changed as formerly free landholders became peasants without freedom and were coerced into paying rents and taxes to the Gallo-Roman elite. When barbarian Germanic tribes were invited into the Empire as military allies or *foederati* to defend the frontiers against other barbarians, the newcomers lived amidst the Celts, bringing new ideas, laws and a degree of military security against increasingly frequent raids.

The peoples outside the Empire's frontiers lived in settled agricultural villages and had traded with the Romans for years, with many surplus young men being recruited into the Roman army. Roman culture was absorbed and Christianity had won many converts. Despite the occasional border raids and counter-raids, the Germanic tribes were not hell bent on expansion but remained content with their artisans producing fine metalwork, iron tools and weapons. By the time of migrations into the Roman Empire, the enemies at the gates were fairly stable dynastically. When a king died, a tribal assembly would elect the best possible successor from his family which might not be the eldest son.

By the end of the fourth century, the Huns emerged from the steppe surging westwards while conquering one tribe after another. They subordinated the Ostrogoths who inhabited a kingdom east of the Dniester on the shores of the Black Sea but the Visigoths, who dwelt in an area from the Dniester to the Danube, escaped begging the Romans for sanctuary on the Roman side of the Danube . The Eastern Emperor Valens allowed them to settle in Moesia in AD 376 maybe because he was an Arian Christian like the Visigoths. More and more Germanic war bands and their families migrated into the Empire and often behaved like conquering kings, creating their own power centres, thereby reducing the amount of taxation going to Rome.

The Visigoths were so badly treated by corrupt Roman officials that they rebelled and savaged the Balkans. Valens took the field and lost the battle of Adrianople and his life, being succeeded by Theodosius I. When he died in AD 395, the Empire was split between East and West, each part being given to a son: Arcadius in the East and Honorius in the West. The Visigoths renounced their allegiance to Rome, invaded Greece and migrated to Italy. The Germanic Vandals invaded France in 406 and then Spain in 409. The Visigoths sacked Rome in 410 and traversed the Pyrénées into Spain where they fought the Vandals. The latter, led by Gaiseric, crossed to North Africa in 429, defeated the Romans and seized Carthage in 439, making it the capital of a Vandal kingdom. They had captured Rome's breadbasket and Vandal pirate fleets raided Sicily, Sardinia and Corsica. In AD 455, they entered Rome and sacked it for two weeks before moving to devastate Greece and Dalmatia, which forced the Emperor Zeno to recognize Gaiseric and conclude peace in 476.

Visigothic King Theodoric I, based in Spain and Provence, died fighting Attila the Hun at Châlons in 451 while allied to Rome. A successor, Euric, declared independence from Rome while using aspects of Roman governance and law. He absorbed the Suevi Kingdom in north Portugal in 469 but was defeated by the forces of Clovis I, King of the Franks, at Vouillé in 507, losing most of Provence but being left with Iberia.

Rome's Retreat in the West
The year of AD 410 saw the Roman Army abandon the province of Britain. Rome gradually lost control over its western territories over the following decades. Britain became increasingly vulnerable to external threats, which duly arrived in the form of Angles and Saxons from the east, and Picts and Scots from the north and west. It was these peoples who would shape Britain's post-Roman future.

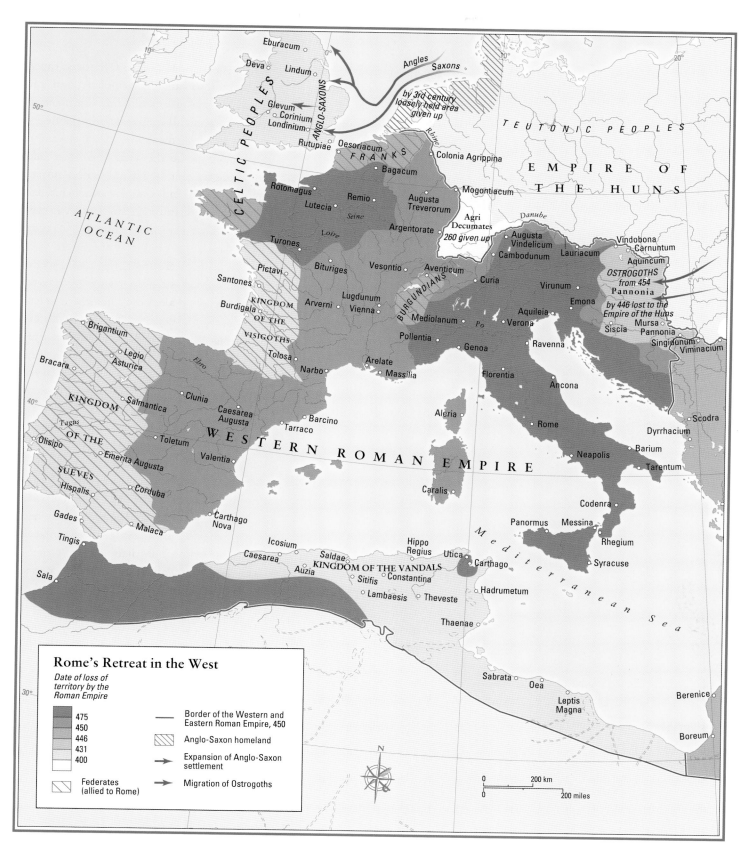

Rome's Retreat in the West

Date of loss of territory by the Roman Empire

475	
450	
446	
431	
400	

—— Border of the Western and Eastern Roman Empire, 450

Anglo-Saxon homeland

→ Expansion of Anglo-Saxon settlement

→ Migration of Ostrogoths

Federates (allied to Rome)

CELTIC PEOPLES

TEUTONIC PEOPLES

EMPIRE OF THE HUNS

FRANKS

BURGUNDIANS

OSTROGOTHS from 454 Pannonia

by 446 lost to the Empire of the Huns

Pannonia

KINGDOM OF THE VISIGOTHS

KINGDOM OF THE SUEVES

WESTERN ROMAN EMPIRE

KINGDOM OF THE VANDALS

ATLANTIC OCEAN

Mediterranean Sea

Angles

Saxons

by 3rd century loosely held area given up

Agri Decumates 260 given up

Eburacum
Deva
Lindum
Glevum
Corinium
Londinium
Rutupiae
Oesoriacum
Colonia Agrippina
Mogontiacum
Rotomagus
Bagacum
Remio
Lutecia
Augusta Treverorum
Argentorate
Turones
Vesontio
Aventicum
Augusta Vindelicum
Cambodunum
Lauriacum
Vindobona
Carnuntum
Aquincum
Biturges
Pictavi
Curia
Virunum
Emona
Santones
Lugdunum
Vienna
Mediolanum
Aquileia
Verona
Siscia
Mursa
Arverni
Burdigala
Po
Ravenna
Singidunum
Viminacium
Brigantium
Pollentia
Genoa
Legio
Asturica
Tolosa
Arelate
Massilia
Florentia
Ancona
Scodra
Bracara
Narbo
Clunia
Caesarea Augusta
Aleria
Rome
Dyrrhacium
Salmantica
Barcino
Tarraco
Barium
Toletum
Valentia
Neapolis
Tarentum
Olisipo
Emerita Augusta
Caralis
Hispalis
Corduba
Codenra
Panormus
Messina
Gades
Malaca
Carthago Nova
Rhegium
Tingis
Icosium
Hippo Regius
Utica
Syracuse
Caesarea
Saldae
Carthago
Sala
Auzia
Sitifis
Constantina
Lambaesis
Theveste
Hadrumetum
Thaenae
Sabrata
Oea
Leptis Magna
Berenice
Boreum

Rhine
Danube
Seine
Loire
Ebro
Tagus

N

0	200 km
0	200 miles

An Imperfect Empire

The third century saw the Roman Empire being subject to barbarian raids, financial instability owing to inflation, and governmental interference in the provinces. In AD 276, the Franks and Alemanni entered the Empire and devastated large numbers of Gaullish cities where urban areas were largely without walls. This was not the first time. Emperor Probus (276–82) drove the Franks and Alemanni from Gaul, the Burgundians and Vandals out of Raetia, and the Goths and Getae out of the Danubian provinces. In comparison, Roman Britain remained peaceful, with minor foreign raids and was still wealthy. Until the fourth century, Britain's defences were a barrier to barbarians.

Britain's defences were extensive, with Hadrian's Wall and Pennine forts warding off attacks from the north. Most urban centres possessed walls and the coasts were studded with forts to deter and counter incursions from Ireland. The south and east coasts along the 'Saxon Shore' were fortified to resist Saxon attacks from across the North Sea. This particular danger was faced in a co-ordinated fashion on both sides of the Channel with a headquarters at Boulogne.

Unfortunately, Britain faced domestic political problems that probably weakened its security position. In approximately AD 286, Carausius, commander of the British fleet, was accused of various crimes, including peculation, and Rome ordered his death. He reacted by seizing Britain and declaring himself Emperor. He invaded Gaul, capturing its northern parts, but was pushed out by Caesar Constantius who invaded Britain in 296, killing Allectus after the finance minister of Carausius had murdered his master and grabbed control of Britain himself.

AD 305 witnessed Constantius' return to refurbish some northern forts while 342–43 saw Emperor Constans arriving, it is thought, to build the fort at Pevensey. The projecting towers of the forts were designed as artillery platforms to extend the forts' defensive reach. In 367, the Picts, Scots and German Allacotti co-ordinated the Grand Alliance, an onslaught against Britain, which captured the Roman commander of the north and killed the Count of the Saxon Shore. The defensive system suffered severe desertions and bandits roamed Britain. Roman commander Count Theodosius was sent from Europe to keep the peace and rebuild shattered defences. However, archaeological evidence shows little urban damage at this time demonstrating the success of town walls.

In AD 383, Magnus Maximus, a Roman commander in Britain, declared himself Emperor, taking part of the army in Britain to Europe to expand his territory. In 398, Roman General Stilicho invaded Britain and restored legitimate imperial control. Troops in Britain again elected an Emperor, Marcus, in 406, who was deposed by Gratian. Constantine was exchanged for Gratian and the new Emperor crossed to Gaul taking the British garrison with him to confront a barbarian invasion from across the Rhine

In AD 410, Britain was now alone to face Saxon invasions. Emperor Honorius informed the British cities that they must carry out their own defence. The same year, Alaric the Visigoth seized Rome, a telling point that the Roman West was now the barbarian West. Honorius fled to Ravenna and was forced to promote his main military commander as co-Emperor Constantius III.

Regional Fragmentation

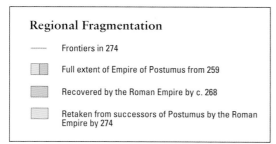

— Frontiers in 274

Full extent of Empire of Postumus from 259

Recovered by the Roman Empire by c. 268

Retaken from successors of Postumus by the Roman Empire by 274

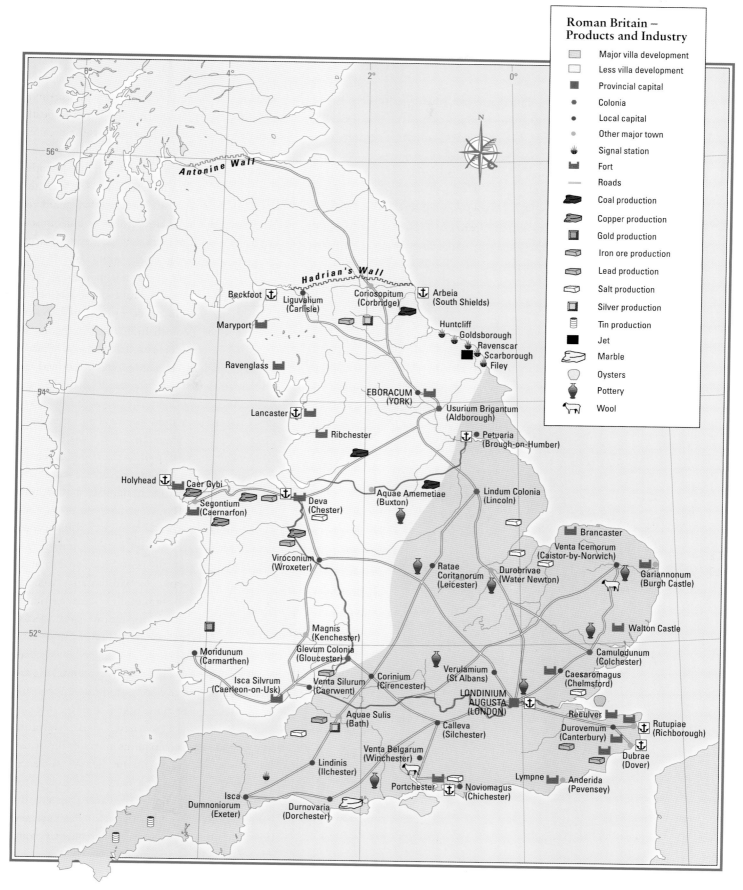

Roman Britain – Products and Industry

- Major villa development
- Less villa development
- Provincial capital
- Colonia
- Local capital
- Other major town
- Signal station
- Fort
- Roads
- Coal production
- Copper production
- Gold production
- Iron ore production
- Lead production
- Salt production
- Silver production
- Tin production
- Jet
- Marble
- Oysters
- Pottery
- Wool

Antonine Wall

Hadrian's Wall

Beckfoot
Liguvalium (Carlisle)
Coriosopitum (Corbridge)
Arbeia (South Shields)
Maryport
Huntcliff
Goldsborough
Ravenscar
Scarborough
Filey
Ravenglass
EBORACUM (YORK)
Lancaster
Usurium Brigantum (Aldborough)
Ribchester
Petuaria (Brough-on-Humber)
Holyhead
Caer Gybi
Deva (Chester)
Aquae Amemetiae (Buxton)
Lindum Colonia (Lincoln)
Segontium (Caernarfon)
Brancaster
Viroconium (Wroxeter)
Venta Icemorum (Caistor-by-Norwich)
Ratae Coritanorum (Leicester)
Durobrivae (Water Newton)
Gariannonum (Burgh Castle)
Magnis (Kenchester)
Walton Castle
Moridunum (Carmarthen)
Glevum Colonia (Gloucester)
Corinium (Cirencester)
Verulamium (St Albans)
Camulodunum (Colchester)
Caesaromagus (Chelmsford)
Isca Silvrum (Caerleon-on-Usk)
Venta Silurum (Caerwent)
LONDINIUM AUGUSTA (LONDON)
Aquae Sulis (Bath)
Calleva (Silchester)
Reculver
Durovemum (Canterbury)
Rutupiae (Richborough)
Lindinis (Ilchester)
Venta Belgarum (Winchester)
Dubrae (Dover)
Lympne
Anderida (Pevensey)
Isca Dumnoniorum (Exeter)
Durnovaria (Dorchester)
Portchester
Noviomagus (Chichester)

41

The Saxon Shore

Portchester Castle

— Roman walls
— Probable Roman walls
— Post-Roman buildings
— Probable post-Roman walls

The third century saw the Roman Empire establishing a chain of coastal forts on both sides of the English Channel for reasons which historians cannot agree. Known as the Saxon Shore, the forts in Britannia were commanded by the Count of the Saxon Shore who used the fleet, the *Classis Britannica*, to protect the coast from seaborne raiders. However, as pretenders to the Imperial Purple emerged in Britain, such as Carausius (AD 286–293), the fortifications could also defend the province against rival emperors from the Continent.

The very terminology of Saxon Shore is open to debate. Did the shore and its hinterland possess settled Saxons or was the shore fortified against Saxons? Also, do the names of the raiders – Angles, Saxons and Jutes – marry up to the variety of peoples reaching Britain's shores? A Roman source, the *Notitia Dignitatum*, stated that many German tribes were serving as *numeri* and *laeti* in the Roman army and veterans settled in Roman provinces. Those Germanic tribes arriving in Britain included Frisians and Franks. History suggests that Jutes, led by Hengist and Horsa, were first invited into this country by the Romano-British leader, Vortigern, and were given the Isle of Thanet as a recompense for mercenary service against other potential raiders. However, archaeological evidence exists demonstrating that settlements of merchant Angles and Saxons were already present in the coastal areas of Yorkshire and Lincolnshire, and also inland at Dunstable in Bedfordshire and Abingdon in Oxfordshire but no reason has been established to explain these places as commercial centres.

Whatever the interpretation of events, the Saxon Shore was closely linked with the southern Channel coastline military regions of the *dux Belgicae Secundae* and *dux tractus Amoricani et Nervicani*, intimating a unified defensive structure. On the other hand, the Saxon Shore forts were built at the estuaries of navigable rivers, implying that they were fortified logistic centres and transport points in the trading network between Britannia and Roman Gaul. Additionally, the ports were important as bases for the *Classis* (Fleet) in its campaign aiding Agricola (AD 81–85) in his Caledonian campaign, as described by Tacitus and in the Emperor Severus' (AD 208–210) operations against the Picts.

The historiographical interpretations are various and differ concerning centuries considered. What is certain is that Germanic settlers, most probably Romanized, lived in Britain prior to the Anglo-Saxon invasions and that the forts were used against 'feral' Saxons at a later date, with the finest fortification still existing at Portchester. The Venerable Bede attested this Saxon presence with: 'In 501, Port came to Britain with his two sons … and two ships, to the place called Portsmutha.'

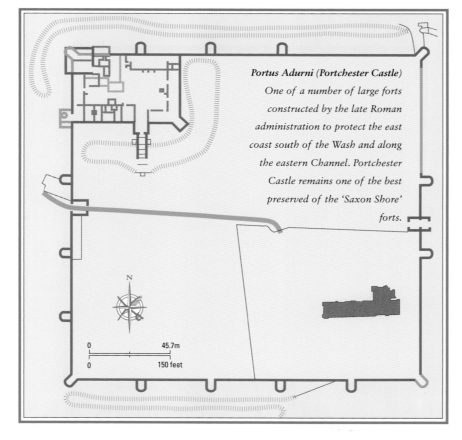

Portus Adurni (Portchester Castle)

One of a number of large forts constructed by the late Roman administration to protect the east coast south of the Wash and along the eastern Channel. Portchester Castle remains one of the best preserved of the 'Saxon Shore' forts.

N

0   45.7m
0   150 feet

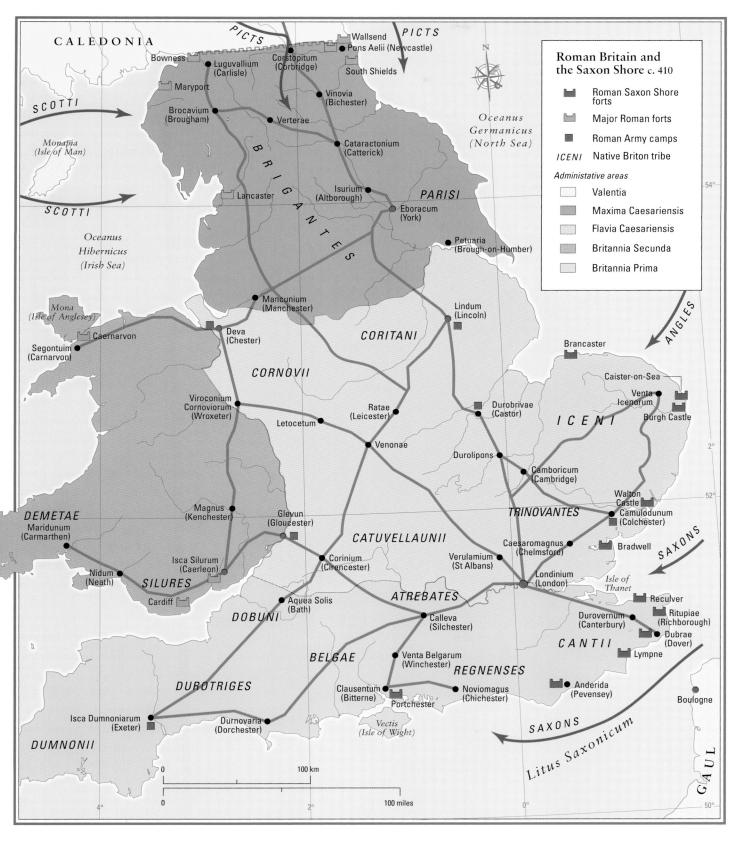

Roman Britain and the Saxon Shore c. 410

- Roman Saxon Shore forts
- Major Roman forts
- Roman Army camps
- *ICENI* Native Briton tribe

Administative areas
- Valentia
- Maxima Caesariensis
- Flavia Caesariensis
- Britannia Secunda
- Britannia Prima

CALEDONIA

PICTS

PICTS

SCOTTI

SCOTTI

Monapia (Isle of Man)

Oceanus Germanicus (North Sea)

Oceanus Hibernicus (Irish Sea)

Bowness
Luguvallium (Carlisle)
Corstopitum (Corbridge)
Wallsend
Pons Aelii (Newcastle)
South Shields
Maryport
Vinovia (Bichester)
Brocavium (Brougham)
Verterae
Cataractonium (Catterick)
Lancaster
Isurium (Altborough)
Eboracum (York)
PARISI
Petuaria (Brough-on-Humber)
BRIGANTES
Mancunium (Manchester)
Lindum (Lincoln)
CORITANI
Mona (Isle of Anglesey)
Caernarvon
Segontuim (Carnarvon)
Deva (Chester)
CORNOVII
Brancaster
Caister-on-Sea
Venta Icenorum
Burgh Castle
ICENI
Viroconium Cornoviorum (Wroxeter)
Ratae (Leicester)
Durobrivae (Castor)
Letocetum
Venonae
Durolipons
Camboricum (Cambridge)
DEMETAE
Maridunum (Carmarthen)
Magnus (Kenchester)
Glevun (Gloucester)
Walton Castle
Camulodunum (Colchester)
TRINOVANTES
Isca Silurum (Caerleon)
CATUVELLAUNII
Caesaromagnus (Chelmsford)
Bradwell
SILURES
Nidum (Neath)
Corinium (Cirencester)
Verulamium (St Albans)
Londinium (London)
Isle of Thanet
SAXONS
Cardiff
Aquea Solis (Bath)
Calleva (Silchester)
ATREBATES
Reculver
Durovernum (Canterbury)
Ritupiae (Richborough)
DOBUNI
BELGAE
Venta Belgarum (Winchester)
CANTII
Dubrae (Dover)
Lympne
REGNENSES
DUROTRIGES
Clausentum (Bitterne)
Portchester
Noviomagus (Chichester)
Anderida (Pevensey)
Boulogne
Isca Dumnoniarum (Exeter)
Durnovaria (Dorchester)
Vectis (Isle of Wight)
DUMNONII
SAXONS
Litus Saxonicum
GAUL

ANGLES

0   100 km

0   100 miles

Invasions – Briton c. AD 550

The desertion by Rome left Britain to disintegrate into a collection of petty kingdoms ruled by Romanized Celtic leaders. Ranging from the Picts of Scotland through to the Channel was a series of statelets which, from AD 410, mirrored Christian diocesan districts which were probably based upon ancient tribal land holdings. The Celtic successor states faced the Angle and Saxon onslaught, which became a torrent of settlers from the sixth century.

A range of sources from this period paints a vague picture of the political configuration of Britain. The West Country was divided into Dumnonia, based on modern Dorset, the home of the old Durotriges, while Kernow (Cornwall) was a separate kingdom. Wales fell apart into the four areas of Irish dominated Gwynedd, eventually to be taken over by migrating Votadini from Gododdin in the Scottish Lowlands. Powys occupied central Wales, the home of the Cornovii, Dyfed remained in Demetae hands, and Gwent belonged to the Silures. Matters were complicated when these areas sub-divided into Buellt, Ceredigion, Glywysing and Brycheiniog.

Elmet covered much of central northern England which kept the Angles of Deira in check for a while and was based upon the originally unruly Brigantes. Rheged occupied Cumbria with a capital at Liguvallium (Carlisle) and the Kingdom of Strathclyde in Galloway was ruled from Dumbarton, the kingdom being in conflict with the Dál Riada, migrants from Ulster. In Scotland, the Picts, for the moment, were the dominant force.

Sub-Roman Britain, the remainder of Britain in the south, became united under the High-King, Vortigern (c. 425–55). Sixth-century historian Gildas, in his *On the Ruin and Conquest of Britain* (*De excidio et conquestu Britanniae*), points out that Vortigern invited some Saxons to settle in Britain as mercenaries to replace the Roman forces and confront Jute invaders. Hengist was granted Kent as an ally but broke his contract and turned Kent into a Jutish kingdom, inherited by his son, Ærc. However, some Saxons, originally soldiers and auxiliaries of Rome, had retired in Britain. Archaeologists examining Anglo-Saxon cemeteries from Yorkshire to Kent suggest that these hired men settled with their families rather than arriving as raiders. These hired Saxons were placed to guard the estuaries of the Humber, Wash and Thames from coastal invasion and their defence in depth reached up the Thames Valley to Oxford. These mercenaries eventually became so strong that they rebelled.

Other Saxons invaded, with AD 480 witnessing the Saxon Ælle reaching Selsey Bill on the Sussex coast after which he pushed out the Celtic Britons from the New Forest. Some Saxons arrived at the coast near today's Southampton and established the West Saxon, Wessex, kingdom. Arguably, Cerdic was the Wessex leader who also captured the Isle of Wight, starting his campaigns with only three ships of warriors who landed at Southampton. Conflicts occurred with the Celts of Dumnonia and the south coastal areas of Sussex and Wessex were linked when the Saxon, Port, disembarked at Portsmouth.

Elsewhere, the Angles created Bernicia, Lindsey and Deira and some surged into East Anglia meaning the communities of north and south folk became Norfolk and Suffolk. Tradition claims that Bernicia established the fortifications at Bamburgh c. 547. Many Angles advanced into Elmet and founded Mercia leaving the remnant of Elmet at the other side of the Trent. The so-called middle Saxons founded Middlesex and eventually captured London. This Anglo-Saxon advance marched ever westwards, acquiring submissive British subjects while driving out other natives who retreated before them to leave Roman Britain in foreign hands while Scotland, Wales and Cornwall became the refuge of independent Celts. This historical period is home to the legends of Ambrosius and King Arthur who defeated the invaders at Mount Badon (c. 500) generating peace for several years.

The British Isles, c. 550
Small and aggressive Anglo-Saxon kingdoms appeared on the east coast of what would become England. They would advance westward at the expense of the Celtic-British kingdoms.

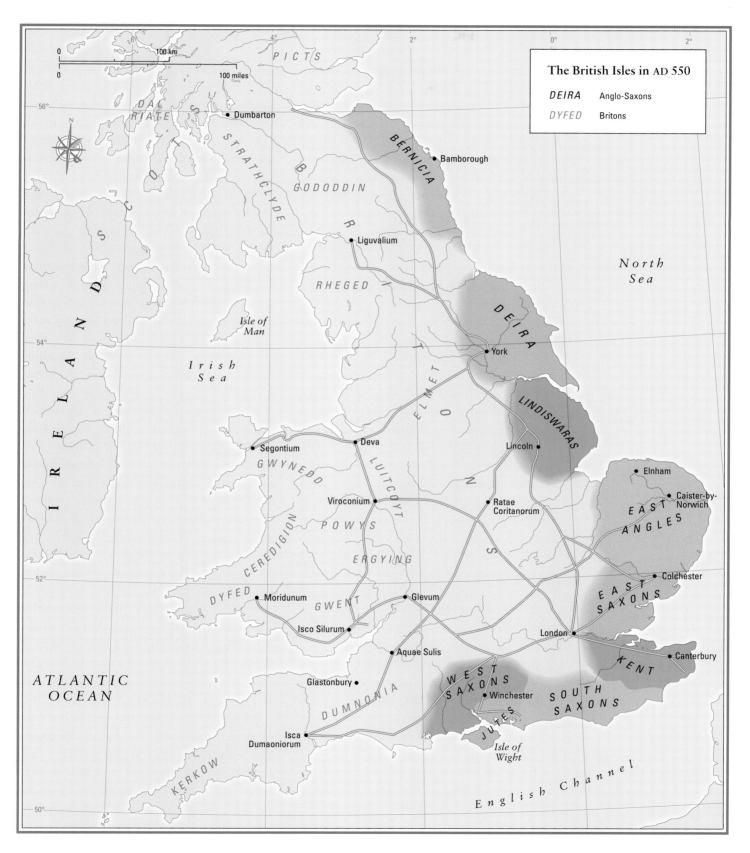

Anglo-Saxon Kingdoms c. 500–770

The history of Anglo-Saxon England is the subject of historical dispute. Did the Germanic invaders arrive en masse and drive the Romano-Celtic Britons into western territories or did small elite groups arrive and co-exist with the local population, while assuming the administration of the country? Co-existence seems to be the currently accepted interpretation while realising that considerable British–Saxon warfare took place. Also, internecine Germanic strife was common with Saxons allying with Britons against kinsfolk, as did Penda of Mercia in an alliance with Welsh Cadwallon of Gwynedd against Edwin of Northumbria in AD 633.

A heptarchy of states constantly jostled to attain some degree of hegemony in Anglo-Saxon lands. The main kingdoms of Wessex, East Anglia, Mercia and Northumbria which contained the sub-kingdoms of Deira and Bernicia, competed amongst themselves while seeking to dominate the minor kingdoms of Kent, Sussex and Essex. Even this delineation of power was a result of earlier political contests. Initially, in the last years of the sixth century, Æthelberht of Kent controlled lands up to the Humber but, after his death in 616, he was superseded by Rædwald of East Anglia. The latter's death allowed Northumbria to seek dominance resulting in long conflicts with Mercia. Even this Midlands kingdom's major enemy changed as the seventh and eighth centuries were spent fighting British Powys, resulting in Offa of Mercia building his 150-mile dyke which constituted the Welsh-English border.

English politics were generally characterised by the slow but permanent absorption of the smaller kingdoms into the larger. Bernicia digested Deira to create Northumbria in 651, while Mercia, between the kingships of Penda (d. 655) and Offa (d. 696), overran all the other kingdoms of the Midlands and the south-east, such as Hwicce, Surrey, Kent and Sussex at Mercia's greatest extent. Elsewhere, the kingdom of Wessex, established by Cerdic in Hampshire, acquired Devon, Dorset and

Somerset before eventually moving into the south-east to contest Mercia. A minor part of the Wessex expansion saw King Caedwalla invading Jutish Wightwara in 685/86, killing its King, Arvold, and eradicating Jute power. This strategic acquisition gave Wessex control of the entire Solent with its important ports and links with Europe.

Southern England became increasingly wealthy and developed powerful commercial interests, using trading centres like London, Southampton and Portsmouth in Wessex; Ipswich in East Anglia and York in Northumbria. Each port became an international marketplace evidenced by archaeological analysis. By the mid-seventh century, Canterbury was minting coins, originally gold but eventually becoming the silver sceattas, often called pennies, which helped develop a money economy since the coins have been discovered all over southern England.

An important development in Anglo-Saxon England was the spread of Christianity, with missionaries being sent from Ireland and Rome. Irish Christianity grew with St. Patrick being reputed with the mass conversion of the Irish, resulting in a rich development of monasteries and virtual religious villages. Northern seas became a highway for religion with St. Columba leaving Ireland to build a religious centre on Iona from where he converted the Picts. St. Aidan followed, establishing a monastery in the Lindisfarne Islands (635–651), near to the Northumbrian capital at Bamburgh, while St. Fursa preached in East Anglia. Thus, the Irish variant of Christianity percolated through Northumbria and down the eastern shires of England. English priests, trained by Irish monks, then introduced Christianity into Mercia.

In 597, further south, St. Augustine converted the Kingdom of Kent and founded the See of Canterbury. Priests of the Roman rites evangelised in Sussex, Wessex and Wight, especially under the auspices of St. Wilfred. Kingdoms were generally considered converted when a king entered the faith, with the bulk of the populations following.

Anglo-Saxon Kingdoms
Warfare between the Anglo-Saxon statelets and their Celtic neighbours was endemic but their armies were relatively small and poorly armed compared with the Romans. When the Gododdin of Din Eiydn (Edinburgh) attacked the Angles at Catraeth (c. 600), they numbered 300 fighters and were wiped out.

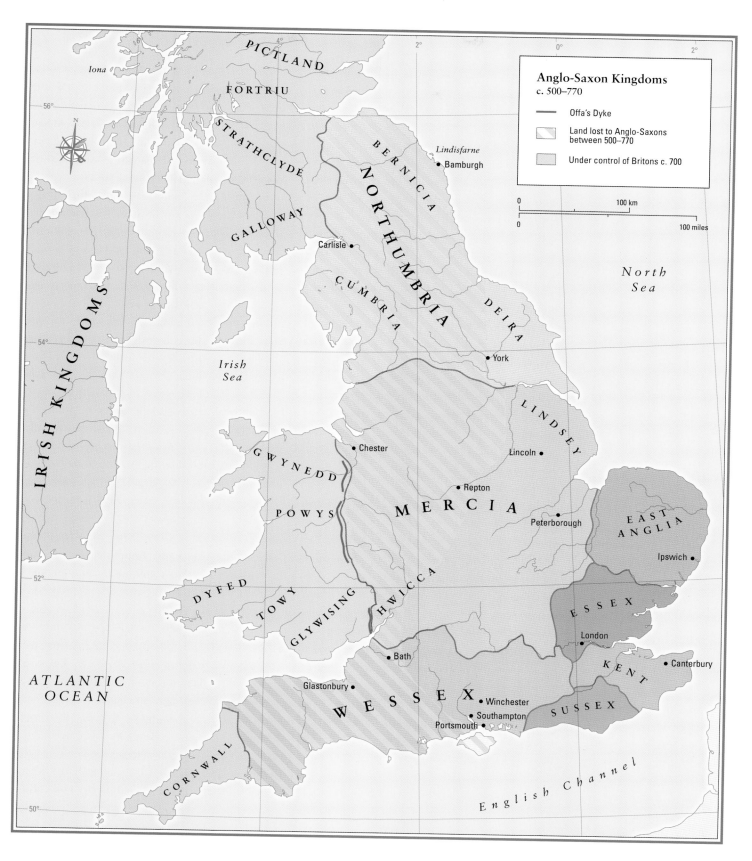

Anglo-Saxon Kingdoms
c. 500–770

— Offa's Dyke

Land lost to Anglo-Saxons between 500–770

Under control of Britons c. 700

0   100 km
0   100 miles

PICTLAND

Iona

FORTRIU

STRATHCLYDE

GALLOWAY

Carlisle

CUMBRIA

BERNICIA

NORTHUMBRIA

Lindisfarne
• Bamburgh

DEIRA

North
Sea

• York

IRISH KINGDOMS

Irish
Sea

GWYNEDD

• Chester

LINDSEY

Lincoln •

MERCIA

• Repton

Peterborough •

EAST
ANGLIA

Ipswich •

POWYS

DYFED

TOWY

GLYWISING

HWICCA

ESSEX

London •

KENT

• Canterbury

ATLANTIC
OCEAN

• Bath

Glastonbury •

WESSEX

• Winchester

• Southampton
Portsmouth •

SUSSEX

CORNWALL

English Channel

47

Viking Raiders

Throughout time, Scandinavia had exported its surplus population from a region which possessed limited arable land. In 113 BC, the Cimbri and Teutones, from Jutland, invaded the Roman Empire and the Goths, Burgundians and Vandals entered the Empire in the fifth century AD, claiming that they originated in the Scandinavian Peninsula. By the eighth century, the Vikings, or Northmen, were well known in European trading centres, reaching across the Baltic, to Ireland, England and Francia. They developed their own international trading centres at Ribe, Hedeby and Kaupang. Viking trade ensured that knowledge of foreign politics, geography and sea routes were understood wherever their long ships could reach.

Suddenly, in the eighth century, the Vikings expanded overseas driven by population pressure again, for trade, as an escape for those mavericks hostile to state centralisation in Norway and Denmark, or maybe for ideological reasons. The first violence at their hands in England occurred at Portland (c. 789) when three ships from Norwegian Hörthaland killed the local king's reeve and his men.

In 793, the monastery at Lindisfarne was sacked, with monks being slaughtered or taken for slaves though some treasures survived. Further attacks followed on nearby religious centres, while raids on Scotland, Ireland and Francia soon followed. A recent theory suggests that the Vikings began engaging in a pagan crusade as a response to events in Francia. In 771, Charlemagne gained power and began a campaign to convert heathen neighbours and destroy their beliefs, culture and political systems and turn them into Christians and subjects. The Saxons bore the brunt of this cultural and armed invasion. Charlemagne forcibly baptised 4,500 Saxon prisoners at Verden, toward the Danish borderlands and then killed them. The Vikings were understandably horrified, visualised a similar fate and decided to fight back. Attacking the Carolingian military was not an option but attacking soft-targets like monasteries, the encroaching symbols of an invasive counter-culture, was easy. Hence, the Viking raids on the West were fuelled by religious hatred, in defence of Thor and Woden. Loot, of course, was an extra benefit.

The English response to raids lay in blocking rivers with bridges, preventing riverine penetration, causing the Vikings to direct their major efforts against the Low Countries, Francia and Ireland. The early ninth century witnessed renewed attacks on Britain, seeing a seesaw of English and Viking victories and defeats. However, English successes still made England a thorny target compared with Europe, after the break-up of the Carolingian Empire, with defence devolving to local lords and the collapse of centralized control.

In 865, a large Danish army arrived in East Anglia commanded by Halfdan and Ivar the Boneless. The Danes were able to acquire horses and allowed to cross the kingdom to attack the collection of small English kingdoms using the tactics of mobility and speed. In 866, the Danes captured York, with the Northumbrians being defeated next. A large Danish-controlled Kingdom of York was founded in 876 by Halfdan. Elsewhere, 869 saw East Anglia conquered. Its King, Edmund, was killed. In 873, after several years campaigning, the Danes defeated Mercia, capturing its capital at Repton. Large areas of Mercia around Nottingham and Lincoln then became Danish Mercia.

The Danes finally turned their attentions to Wessex where the forces of King Ethelred and Prince Alfred defeated them at the Battle of Ashdown, which witnessed incredible slaughter on both sides. During 871 saw major warfare with Alfred, now King, losing at Wilton. Alfred took refuge in the Somerset Levels seeking to rebuild his fortunes at Athelney and engage in guerrilla warfare against the Danes. A crushing victory where 800 Danes were killed at Countisbury Hill in 878, was followed by a Danish defeat at Eddington, which led to the Danes agreeing to leave Wessex.

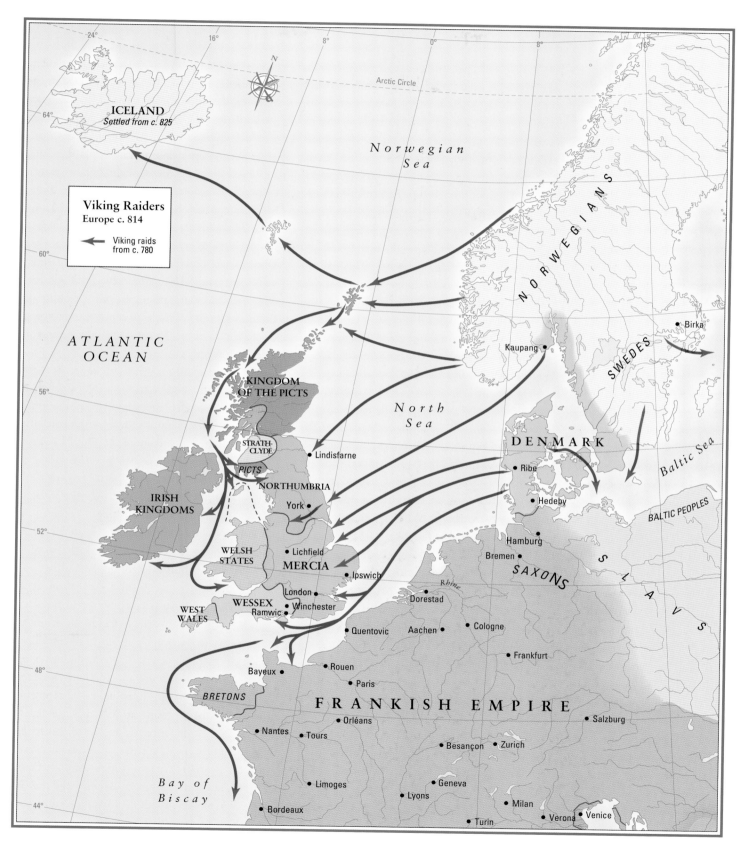

Viking Raiders
Europe c. 814

→ Viking raids
from c. 780

ICELAND
Settled from c. 825

*Norwegian
Sea*

Arctic Circle

N
O
R
W
E
G
I
A
N
S

• Birka

S
W
E
D
E
S

Kaupang •

ATLANTIC
OCEAN

*North
Sea*

DENMARK

Ribe •

Baltic Sea

BALTIC PEOPLES

KINGDOM
OF THE PICTS

STRATH-
CLYDE

PICTS

• Lindisfarne

Hedeby •

S
L
A
V
S

IRISH
KINGDOMS

NORTHUMBRIA

York •

Hamburg •

SAXONS

Bremen •

WELSH
STATES

• Lichfield

MERCIA

• Ipswich

Rhine

WEST
WALES

London •

WESSEX
Ramwic • Winchester

Dorestad •

Cologne •

Quentovic •

Aachen •

FRANKISH   EMPIRE

Frankfurt •

Bayeux •

• Rouen

• Paris

Salzburg •

BRETONS

• Orléans

• Nantes   • Tours

• Besançon   • Zurich

*Bay of
Biscay*

• Limoges

• Geneva

• Lyons

• Milan

• Bordeaux

• Turin

• Verona   Venice

Viking Settlements

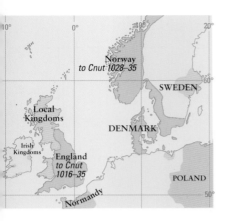

The Empire of Cnut the Great

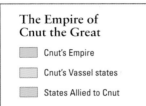

Cnut's Empire

Cnut's Vassel states

States Allied to Cnut

The Empire of Cnut the Great
King Cnut (Canute) became King of England in 1016, then King of Denmark in 1018. In 1028, he took over Norway assuming Kingship. He also controlled large areas of southern Sweden. Across what is now modern Scotland, local kings gave him their submission. In Ireland strong links were maintained even after Brian Boru's defeat of the Vikings at the Battle of Clonarf in 1014. After the battle the relationships were more of a commercial nature rather than conquest. His first wife was from the English nobility, He later married Emma of Normandy, forming family ties between England and Scandinavia, as well as the Dukedom of Normandy. Cnut died in 1035 and was buried in Winchester. He had created a stable and prosperous Empire.

The Norse and Danes turned the Irish Sea into a virtual Viking lake for nearly 400 years between 800 and 1170. Their military prowess and economic strength allowed them to take control of trade routes and create mini-states around the sea's littoral. Olof the White, from the Norwegian line of Vestfold kings, founded a dynasty which utilised Dublin as a base to control all Norse colonists on the Irish coast and those of the Hebrides and Galloway while conducting raids in Scotland and Ireland. Others conquered York and Northumbria so the Vikings encircled the Irish Sea by the tenth century when Norse migrants surged into north-west England and colonised the territory between the Wirral and Galloway. Large numbers of settlements in Cumbria and Westmoreland meant that a Viking land bridge spanned northern England from the Irish to the North Sea.

In Scotland, the early raids were eventually transformed into building settlements on the islands and along the Galloway coast to the Moray Firth. In Orkney and the Shetlands, the Celts were subordinated and absorbed and ninety-nine per cent of place names are of Norse origin. However, in the Hebrides and south-west, the subordinate Celts inter-married with the Norse to produce an ethnic fusion called, by the Irish, the Gall-Gaedhil or foreign Gaels. Celtic influence meant that Celtic Christianity spread amongst the Norse by 900. By the end of the century, the Vestfold Kings of Norway gained sovereignty over the Orkneys, creating an earldom there which rapidly assumed authority over the Norse areas of Scotland.

Elsewhere, York became a major commercial centre and still retains Viking street names today such as Goodhamgate and Swinegate; 'gate' comes from 'gade', meaning 'street'. The monk William of Malmesbury (c. 1080/94–1143) recorded that ships from Scandinavia, Ireland and Germania traded here. In the Irish Sea, Dublin was a fortified staging post providing protection and sanctuary to Viking merchants and raiders who sailed the Atlantic route which connected to Francia and the Mediterranean. The Norse only controlled the coastal margins of south-east Ireland rather than a large settled hinterland as in England around York. The Vikings of Dublin and York constantly sought to co-operate with each other but communications were difficult.

Viking influence grew in the Isle of Man as attested by the major Viking finds there. Burial mounds include that of longships at Knock y Doonee and Balladoole, plus other mounds at Cronk ny Arrey Lhaa, Jurby and Knock-y-Dowan. Additionally, Norse crosses can be found at Andreas, Braddan, Jurby, Maughold and Kirk Michael showing a spiritual change to Christianity and wealth in commissioning such objects. Likewise, crosses can be found at Gosforth in England.

Dublin began to re-orientate its trade as did Norse Wexford and Waterford. Ships sailed to Caen and Rouen in France and to Southampton, Wight and Sandwich. Commerce with Bristol was especially important, as were staging posts on the Welsh coast at Haroldston, Skomer and Flat Holm. Dublin changed in other ways as Christianity took hold, with King Olof Cuaran making pilgrimage to Iona in 980. Dublin possessed a Norse bishop and diocese and kept its Norse flavour and culture until the Anglo-Norman invasion in 1169.

Viking success in Ireland was short-lived. They made no great or lasting territorial conquests but probably weakened Irish kingdoms in their immediate vicinity. The Norse towns fought amongst themselves and Dublin Vikings were often intent on securing York (Jorvik) in England for themselves thereby not totally concentrating on their Irish interests. Only Irish disunity allowed the small, hemmed-in Norse communities to survive. Despite raids on monasteries, no major monastery ceased functioning. In fact, Christianity converted many Vikings and repeated inter-marriage created the Hiberno-Norse who spoke Gaelic rather than Norse.

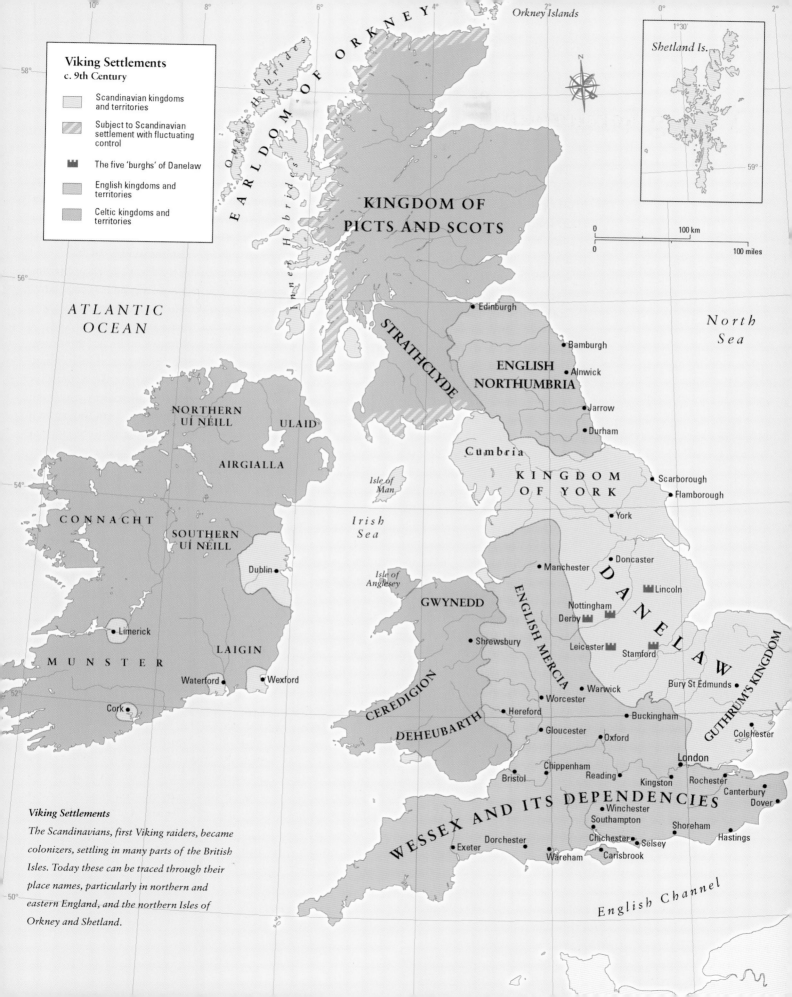

Viking Settlements
c. 9th Century

Scandinavian kingdoms and territories

Subject to Scandinavian settlement with fluctuating control

The five 'burghs' of Danelaw

English kingdoms and territories

Celtic kingdoms and territories

Orkney Islands

Shetland Is.

1°30'

59°

ORKNEY ISLANDS

E A R L D O M   O F   O R K N E Y

Outer Hebrides

Inner Hebrides

KINGDOM OF
PICTS AND SCOTS

ATLANTIC
OCEAN

• Edinburgh

STRATHCLYDE

*North
Sea*

• Bamburgh

ENGLISH
NORTHUMBRIA

• Alnwick

• Jarrow

• Durham

Cumbria

NORTHERN
UÍ NÉILL

ULAID

AIRGIALLA

*Isle of
Man*

KINGDOM
OF YORK

• Scarborough

• Flamborough

*Irish
Sea*

• York

C O N N A C H T

SOUTHERN
UÍ NÉILL

Dublin •

*Isle of
Anglesey*

GWYNEDD

• Manchester

• Doncaster

D A N E L A W

■ Lincoln

Nottingham ■

Derby ■

■ Leicester

■ Stamford

• Shrewsbury

• Limerick

L A I G I N

M U N S T E R

Waterford •

• Wexford

Cork •

CEREDIGION

DEHEUBARTH

ENGLISH MERCIA

• Warwick

• Worcester

• Hereford

• Gloucester

• Buckingham

• Oxford

Bury St Edmunds •

GUTHRUM'S KINGDOM

• Colchester

• London

• Chippenham

• Reading

• Kingston

• Rochester

• Bristol

• Canterbury

Dover •

WESSEX AND ITS DEPENDENCIES

• Winchester

• Southampton

• Shoreham

• Chichester

• Selsey

• Hastings

• Exeter

• Dorchester

• Wareham

• Carisbrook

English Channel

Viking Settlements

*The Scandinavians, first Viking raiders, became
colonizers, settling in many parts of the British
Isles. Today these can be traced through their
place names, particularly in northern and
eastern England, and the northern Isles of
Orkney and Shetland.*

0 100 km

0 100 miles

The Making of England

The Kingdom of England was born after Alfred's death in the tenth century. Succeeding kings ruled over lands constantly embroiled in warfare until the Danes had been brought to heel by an increasingly confident English army with monarchs, using the influence of the Catholic Church. The military conquest of the Vikings was merely the first stage of the unification process as the Wessex Kings of England needed to unify their disparate territories into a single political entity. This endeavour was not always a total success.

Alfred's son, Edward the Elder, continued the alliance with Mercia, aided by his sister, Æthelflæd, who succeeded to the Mercian throne on her husband's death in 911. This Lady of the Mercians co-operated in joint campaigns against Danish settlements in the Midlands and East Anglia. Using the burh system of fortified settlements, these key points were bases for an offensive that forced the Danes to withdraw or weaken their forces in costly frontal assaults against their walls. This offensive strategy served the brother and sister well, with Danish political independence being destroyed. As a result the Danish settled areas of most of the east Midlands were re-conquered, its settlers integrated into English society.

Edward was succeeded by his three sons: Athelstan (924–39), Edmund (939–46) and Eadred (946–55). Athelstan faced the problem of the Viking Kingdom of York. In 937, Olaf Guthfrithson, Gallo-Norse King of Dublin, sought to ensconce himself in York, which led to a bloody battle between his Dublin and York Vikings, Constantine II of the Scots and Owen I of Strathclyde on one hand, and Edward and his brother Edmund's Mercians and West Saxons at Brunanburh in 937 on the other. Seventeen more years followed before King Eadred pushed out Eric Bloodaxe from York. The seesaw of events changing territories between sides ended in 954 when Northumbria became a permanent, if reluctant, part of England, with rule even extending into Lothian.

Reconquest and Unification of England

King Edward the Elder of Wessex forcibly extended English control over Danish lands. His son, Athelstan, continued this process until his domains reached the border with the newly-emerging Scottish state. The Welsh Principalities to the west retained their independence during this violent process.

Masters of England, the Wessex monarchy, now needed to administer the various regions with their different customs. Different land tenure systems meant some former landowners were sacrificing some independence in return for a lord's protection, a form of early feudalism. Linguistic and dialect differences compounded problems, as did different currencies. Even land was divided variously with different names. The new English monarchs exercised the influence of only one coinage.

A degree of uniformity in administration was established with the Wessex system of shires being established in Mercia and then further north. The shires were sub-divided into hundreds except in the former northern Danelaw where wapentakes existed instead. The still existing shires or counties had their own administrators and courts established on a common model in the kingdom. The courts established in each hundred were to meet every four weeks to decide local legal matters, while the shire court met twice a year and borough courts thrice.

Meantime, the Church had divided England and Wales into dioceses and parishes where the local people had priests to conduct services. Ecclesiastical organizations had to be rebuilt in Danish areas, monasteries reformed, since some were ordered by secular priests, and general reforms introduced like those generated by the Cluniac movement, based upon the original Benedictine Rule. Accordingly, Edgar promoted three reformers to key positions: Dunstan to Canterbury; Æthelwold to Winchester; and Oswald to Worcester, and then York. Secular priests were ousted and worldliness and complacency attacked.

Unity, however, although growing, was subject to some setbacks. The nobility from north of the River Trent seldom attended court, while the far northern earls remained semi-independent. The lords of former Berenicia were left to defend England against the Scots. Ealdormen (governors) were appointed to bring Northumbria under effective royal control but with immense difficulty.

The Reconquest and
Unification of England
916–919

Wessex and allies 916

Conquered by Wessex 917

Conquered by Wessex 917–918

Under English control to 918

Under English control 916–919

——— Old Shire boundaries

• Towns or Mints

*Burghs –
Anglo-Saxon fortified towns*

Established before 916

Established after 916

SCOTIA

• Edinburgh
LOTHIAN

STRATHCLYDE

Galloway

CUMBERLAND

NORTHUMBERLAND

WESTMORLAND

St Cuthbert's
Land

*Isle of
Man*

Unshired lands
annexed
to Yorkshire

YORKSHIRE

Irish Sea

• York

Between Ribble
and Mersey

North Sea

Anglesey

LINCOLN

• Torksey
• Lincoln

CHESHIRE
• Chester

DERBY

NOTTINGHAM

GWYNEDD

Derby •
• Nottingham

STAFFORD
• Stafford

LEICESTER

Stamford •

NORFOLK

Shrewsbury •

Tamworth •

• Leicester

• Norwich

SHROPSHIRE

WARWICK

NORTHAMPTON

HUNTS

CAMBRIDGE

SUFFOLK

• Thetford

DEHEUBARTH

WORCESTER

Warwick •

Northampton •

Huntingdon •

• Bury St Edmunds

HEREFORD

Worcester •

BEDS

• Cambridge

Sudbury •

• Ipswich

• Hereford

Bedford •

ESSEX

• Colchester

GWENT

• Winchcombe

BUCKS

HERTFORD

• Buckingham

Aylesbury •

Hertford •

• Waldon

• Gloucester

OXFORD

London •

Horndon •

GLOUCESTER

Oxford •

Cricklade •

Wallingford •

• Southwark

• Rochester

MORGANNWYG

Malmesbury •

Reading •

• Canterbury

• Sandwich

Bristol •

WILTS

BERKS

SURREY

KENT

• Dover

Bath •

Great Bedwyn •

HANTS

• Guildford

SOMERSET

Warminster •

Salisbury •

• New Romney

Watchet •

Langport •

Cadbury •

Bruton •

• Wilton

• Winchester

SUSSEX

Taunton •

Ilchester •

Shaftesbury •

Southampton •

• Hastings

Crewkerne •

Milbourne
Port

DORSET

Bridport •

Chichester •

Steyning •

• Lewes

DEVON

Launceston •

• Lydford

• Exeter

Dorchester •

• Wareham

*Isle of
Wight*

English Channel

FRANCE

CORNWALL

Totnes •

0   100 km

0   100 miles

Scotland's Peoples

Scotland's Peoples

The Kingdom of Scotland slowly emerged when the Scots of Dál Riada had assimilated the Picts. By the eleventh century they had conquered the Britons of Strathclyde and won the Angles of Lothian. Scotland in its modern form had emerged.

Main Kin of the Scots of Dal Riada

It was the Scots of Dal Riada who, after their integration with the Picts, would give their name to the new kingdom of Scotland.

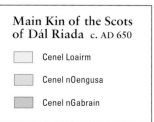

Main Kin of the Scots of Dál Riada c. AD 650

- Cenel Loairm
- Cenel nOengusa
- Cenel nGabrain

The Gaelic Irish colonizers from Dál Riada in Antrim were the driving force in unifying the different Celtic-speakers of Scotland. The earliest native inhabitants of Britain north of the Clyde-Forth diagonal line were the Picts, whom the Irish Scotti displaced in Argyll, Arran and Bute. The Scotti split into three separate tribes in these coastal regions. The most important were the Cenél Loairn dominating the southern entrance to the Great Glen and the Cenél Gabrain settled Kintyre, Cowal and the coastal access to the Clyde. The Cenál n Oengusa occupied Islay.

As well as warriors, the colonizers brought Christian missionaries with their families. The sixth century witnessed Brendan of Clonfert founding monasteries in the Firth of Lorne at Elechnave and Lismore and religious houses on the isles of Rum, Eigg and Tiree. Columba went to Hinba and Iona in approximately 563 and this new Scottish Church campaigned amongst the Picts, especially to Bude mac Maelchon, a King of the Picts and overlord of the northern isles. It is not known whether the Pictish King was already a Christian or was converted by Columba. Whatever the case, the Picts were eventually converted and gradually absorbed Scottish influences in art and sculpture.

The Picts used the matrilineal line in royal succession and, as Scots and other kings married elite Pictish women, even more avenues opened for further Dál Riada influence. Eventually, the Picts were absorbed by the Scots but this took a long time since the last years of the seventh century observed Brude mac Bile ruling the Picts from the Orkneys to the Firth of Forth.

Scotland, south of the Clyde–Forth diagonal, was home to the British kingdoms of Strathclyde and the Gododdin of Lothian, heirs of the Votadini. Southern Lothian came under attack from the Angles of Berenicia, being absorbed into Northumbria. The Angles were attempting to expand northwards under their leader Ecgfrith (671–85). Incursions into Pict territory north of the Forth was met by an angry Brude mac Bile at Nechtanesmere in 685. His ambush resulted in Ecgfrith's death and the slaughter of his forces. Despite being defeated, the Angles held Lothian until the ninth century, allowing their language to permeate the area. The Forth continued to be the border between Pict and the Angles.

The British Kingdom of Rheged in Galloway also succumbed to English pressure. Aedán mac Gabhrán, a Dál Riada King and Columba's friend, waged war against Aethelfrith of Bernicia, a blood feud owing to the death of Aedán's son at the hands of Anglo-Saxon raiders. A Dál Riadan's army was defeated at Degsastan in 603 and the Scots never made war against the Lothian Angles again, especially after Aethelfrith added Deira to Bernicia, creating a Northumbrian overlordship.

A balance of power was established between the Scots, Picts, British, and Angles by the eighth century until the Vikings arrived. By the mid-ninth century, Scandinavian colonists had occupied the Orkneys, Shetlands, Caithness, Sutherland and the west coast down to Islay. Dál Riada now lay open to Viking attacks and settlement. Intermarriage created a Gallo-Norse population, especially in Orkney and Caithness.

Under the leadership of Kenneth mac Alpine, the Scots of Cenél Gabrain moved away into the central Lowlands and dominated the southern Picts south of the Mounth from their new capital at Scone. The Cenél Loairn migrated up the Great Glen invading and acquiring the northern Pictish kingdom, which became the Kingdom or Mormaerdom of Moray. The mac Alpines expanded into Lothian, Strathclyde and Cumbria eventually pushing the Scottish border to the Tweed. While the Norse occupied the Hebrides and west coast islands down into Galloway, the Scots created a kingdom across central Scotland, while Moray was run by a separate dynasty.

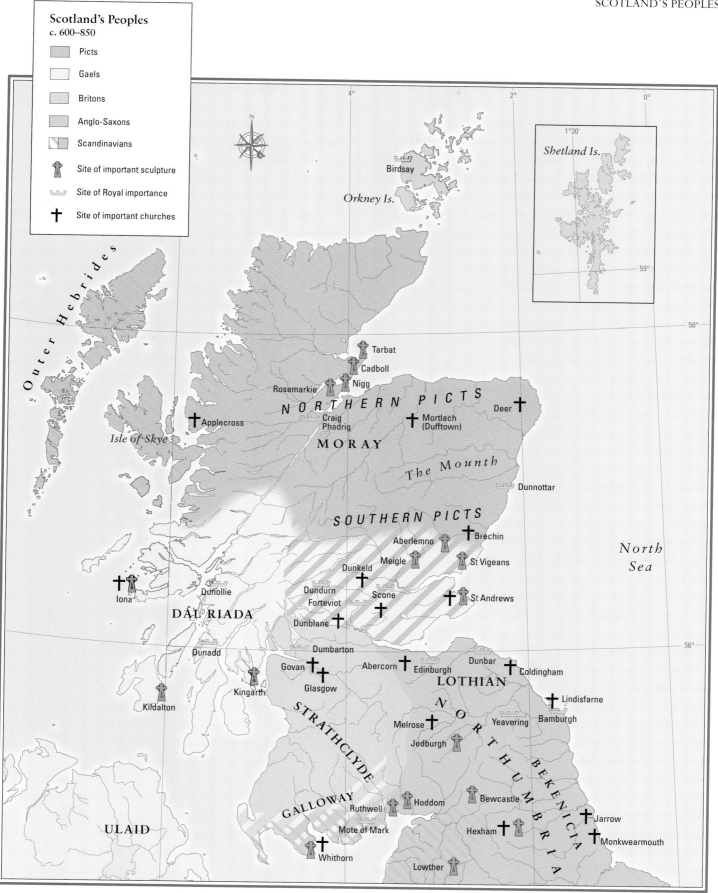

Scotland's Peoples
c. 600–850

- Picts
- Gaels
- Britons
- Anglo-Saxons
- Scandinavians
- Site of important sculpture
- Site of Royal importance
- Site of important churches

Shetland Is.

1°30'

59°

Birdsay

Orkney Is.

Outer Hebrides

58°

Tarbat
Cadboll
Nigg
Rosemarkie
Applecross
Craig Phadrig

NORTHERN PICTS

Deer
Mortlach (Dufftown)

MORAY

Isle of Skye

The Mounth

Dunnottar

SOUTHERN PICTS

Aberlemno
Brechin
Meigle
St Vigeans
Dunkeld
St Andrews
Dundurn
Forteviot
Scone
Dunollie
Iona
DÁL RIADA
Dunblane

North Sea

56°

Dunadd

Dumbarton
Govan
Glasgow
Kingarth
Kildalton

Abercorn
Edinburgh
Dunbar
Coldingham
LOTHIAN
Lindisfarne
Bamburgh
Melrose
Yeavering
Jedburgh
STRATHCLYDE
NORTHUMBRIA
BERNICIA

GALLOWAY
Ruthwell
Hoddom
Bewcastle
Mote of Mark
Hexham
Jarrow
Monkwearmouth

ULAID
Whithorn
Lowther

55

Ireland and Wales – 6th–8th Century

Ireland's Golden Age – Stronghold of Christianity

- ● Paruchia of Patrick (churches linked to Armagh)
- ● Paruchia of Colum Cille
- ● Other principal monasteries and churches
- ✝ High Crosses
- ▢ Illuminated Manuscripts

Ireland's Golden Age

By the sixth century, most of Ireland's churches were under the rule of a monastic hierarchy. Monasteries that were believed to have a common founder were grouped together in what was known as a 'paruchia'.

The arrival of Christianity in fifth century Ireland created monasteries and the growth of learning based on the use of Latin. This lead to written early histories, allowing later historians to piece together the changing political map of Ireland. By the seventh century, an alliance of dynasties ema-

nating from Connacht pushed north and east creating the Northern Uí Néill, Airgialla, and Southern Uí Néill respectively. The formerly powerful Ulaid were squeezed against the northeastern coast encouraging the Dál Riada to migrate to Scotland. Tara was seized from the Laigin and other tribes felt obliged to migrate: the Laigin to north Wales; the Déisi Muman to south Wales; and, the Uí Liatháin to Cornwall and Devon.

An important Irish development was the emergence of high status churches ruled by monasteries as opposed to individual missionaries, these monasteries being linked together according to their original founder. Hence, the paruchia, ecclesiastical jurisdiction, of St. Patrick and St. Columba (Colum Cille) became important. Interestingly, the early drive towards monasticism originated in the missionary work of St. Enda from Whithorn, St. Finnian from Llancarfan, and St. Máedóc from St. David's.

The monks developed the early Irish 'Golden Age'. The monasteries became centres of learning, collecting early Church writings and literature from across Ireland written in both Latin and Irish. The libraries saved literature and records from destructive Angles and Saxons in what became England and religious education generated a high level of scholarship and holy men. Irish missionaries then became active in Britain and Europe while St. Columbanus sailed to Gaul in 591. The increasingly wealthy monasteries were patrons of the arts resulting in the Ardagh and Derrnaflan chalices, stone High Crosses (High Cross of Moone, Kildare), the La Tène-style Moylough Belt Shrine, and the illuminated manuscripts known as *The*

Book of Durrow and *The Book of Kells.*

The years following the Roman exodus are poorly recorded in history. However, it seems that the Romano-Celtic Britons, led by a legendary leader, sometimes called Arthur, or by Ambrosius Aurelianus as recorded by Gildas, defeated the advancing Saxons at Mount Badon (c. 516). This victory was overturned c. 577 when the West Saxons were victorious at Dyrham, leading to the loss of Gloucester, Cirencester, and Bath, which pushed the Britons firmly westward towards what would become Wales. Now, a wedge was driven between the Britons of Wales and Cornwell which opened up the Severn valley to Saxon settlement.

Meanwhile, in Wales, Brythonic leaders were unable to continue Roman modes of governance and therefore established a number of small kingdoms in the hill and mountain country. Gwynedd, Powys, Dyfed and Seisylwg, Morgannwg and Gwent became the heirs of Romano-Britain, protecting their Celtic heritage resolutely fighting the Anglo-Saxon kingdoms of Mercia, Northumbria and Wessex. The constant warfare eventually fixed a border between Wales and England that roughly stands today.

Gwynedd was established by the legendary warrior, Cunedda, a Gododdin leader, who led the Votadini from north of the Tyne to north Wales. In the seventh century, Cornoviian Powys stopped further Mercian encroachments causing Aethelbald of Mercia to defend his recently acquired Brythoic territories by building a border earthwork, Wat's Dyke. The later Mercian King Offa developed Wat's into Offa's Dyke, which extends to around 185 miles.

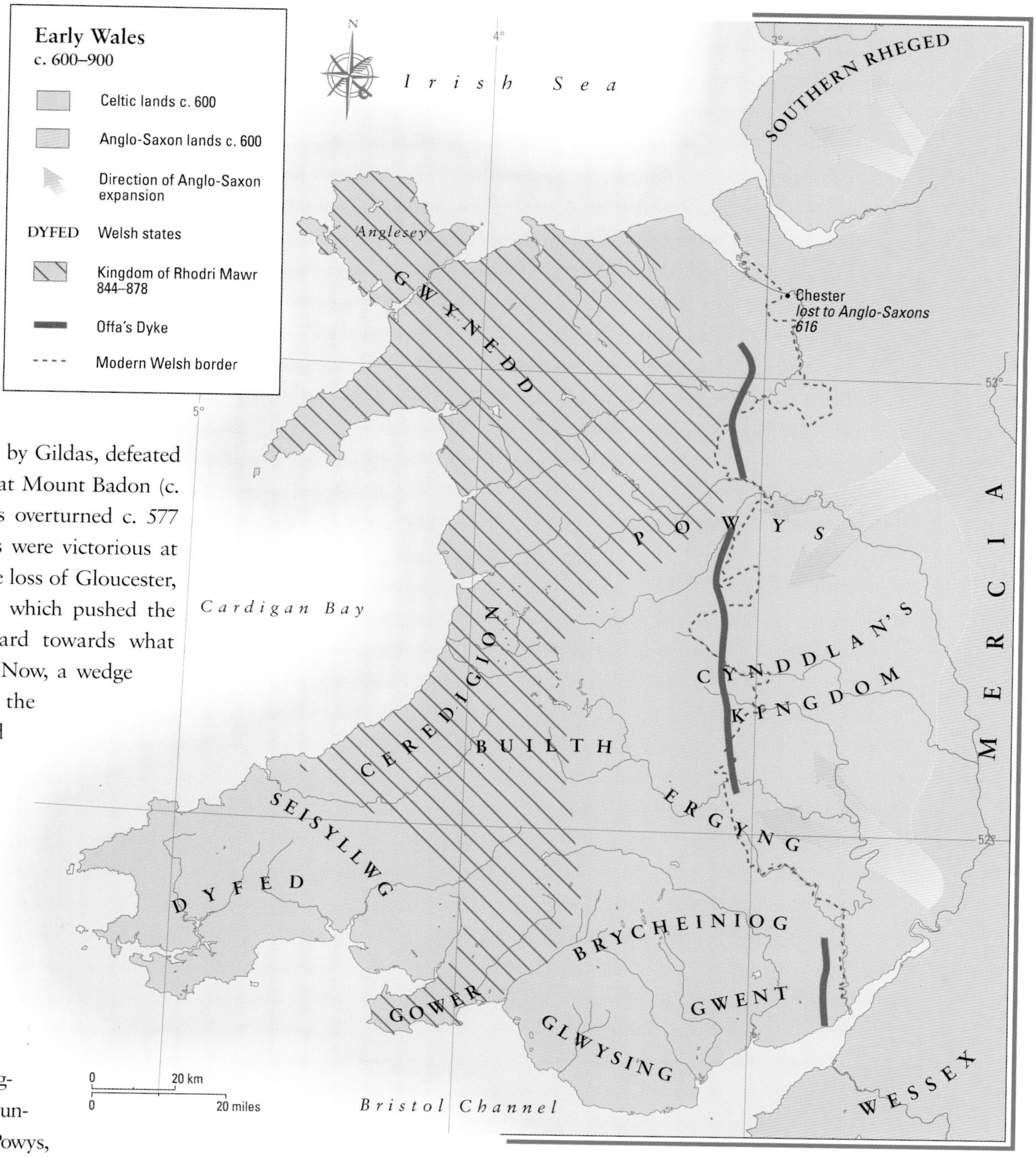

Early Wales
c. 600–900

Celtic lands c. 600

Anglo-Saxon lands c. 600

Direction of Anglo-Saxon expansion

DYFED — Welsh states

Kingdom of Rhodri Mawr 844–878

Offa's Dyke

Modern Welsh border

Irish Sea

Cardigan Bay

Bristol Channel

SOUTHERN RHEGED

Anglesey

GWYNEDD

Chester
lost to Anglo-Saxons
616

POWYS

CYNDDLAN'S KINGDOM

MERCIA

CEREDIGION

BUILTH

ERGYNG

SEISYLLWG

DYFED

BRYCHEINIOG

GOWER

GWENT

GLWYSING

WESSEX

0   20 km
0   20 miles

Early Wales

The region was divided up by warring princedoms, equally happy to fight each other as well as the encroaching Anglo-Saxons. Rhodri Mawr of Gwynedd was the first King to rule a large area of what was to become Wales.

England in 1066

King Edward the Confessor's death in January 1066 left England without an heir of the royal blood line. Duke William of Normandy claimed that Edward had promised him the Kingdom in 1051 and that Harold Godwinson, Earl of Wessex, had sworn to be William's vassal and help him acquire the English throne. Whatever the case, Edward gave Harold the kingship on his death bed. However, other claimants existed despite tenuous claims. The Scandinavian kings were certain to cause trouble as Harald Hardrada of Norway did in September 1066. Another problem facing Harold Godwinson was his brother, Tostig, exiled in 1065, who joined Hardrada, hoping to regain his Earldom of Northumbria.

William of Normandy was not slow to summon his lords and began collecting an army and building an invasion fleet. A skilled war leader, William acquired military experience: in battle against rebellious Norman magnates: in warfare against the Bretons; and in the seizure of Maine in 1063. To counter William, Harold stationed an army along the south coast with a fleet based off the Isle of Wight.

Harold maintained a watch on the English Channel until September when his army's food ran out, leaving him to disband his levies and return to London. William's luck was poor as a prevailing wind bottled him up in port during the summer. Meanwhile, a Norwegian army landed in Yorkshire and defeated the Yorkshire earls, Morcar and Edwin at Fulford Gate, leaving the Vikings in control of York where the men of the shire, many of Viking descent, agreed to help in the conquest of England. However, Harold surprised the Norwegians at their camp at Stamford Bridge, leaving Hardrada and Tostig dead and the Norwegians routed. While celebrating his victory, Harold learnt that William had landed at Pevensey on 28 September with his army of Normans, Flemings and Bretons.

Harold marched 190 miles to London and then onwards to face William in Sussex on 13 October, taking his position on the slope of Senlac Hill. The English axe-men fought dismounted behind a shield-wall. The Norman mounted knights, some 2,000 in number, charged repeatedly against the well-ordered shield-wall and were thrown back time and time again. Eventually, William feigned retreat, while retaining a strong force under his personal command. Less well-trained English forces ran forward but were attacked in the flank by William's cavalry. Only the disciplined infantry surrounding King Harold kept formation and fought to the death under a hail of arrows and cavalry attack. The English suffered 4,000 casualties, with survivors fleeing the field. The Normans suffered 2,500 dead and wounded.

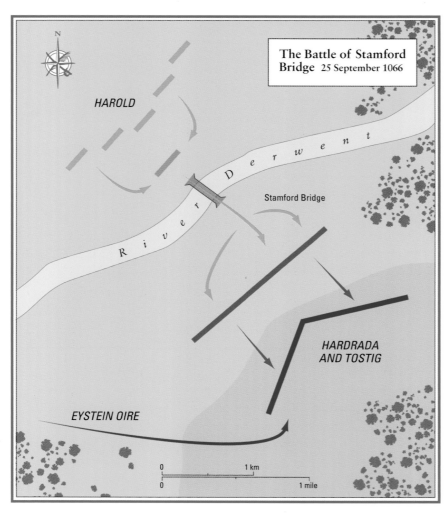

The Battle of Stamford Bridge 25 September 1066

HAROLD

River Derwent

Stamford Bridge

HARDRADA AND TOSTIG

EYSTEIN OIRE

0   1 km
0   1 mile

England in 1066

- Old Shire boundaries
- Shires under King Harold
- Ruled by Earl Gyrth
- Ruled by Earl Leofwine
- Ruled by Waltheof
- Ruled by Edwin
- Ruled by Morcar
- Disputed with Scotland
- Tostig, April–May 1066
- Harold, September 1066
- Harald Hardrada and Tostiq
- Battle site

King Harold ruled part of his new kingdom directly. The rest of the kingdom was governed by five trusted Earls. Harold's brother, Tostiq, exiled in 1065, remained intent on regaining his Earldom of Northumbria. He allied himself with Scotland and Norway, launching his campaign in April 1066. Unsuccessful he retreated north, joining Harald Hardrada and their combined forces returned in September.

EARLDOM OF ORKNEY

SCOTLAND

LOTHIAN
to Scotland

Galoway

NORTHUMBERLAND

CUMBERLAND
Disputed with Scotland

WESTMORLAND

North Sea

to Scotland
from Scotland

Isle of Man

Irish Sea

YORKSHIRE

Fulford Gate
20 September

York

Stamford Bridge
25 September

Between Ribble and Mersey

Anglesey

Linsey
May
Tostig defeated by Earl Edwin's forces

WELSH PRINCIPALITIES

CHESHIRE

DERBY

NOTTINGHAM

LINCOLN

STAFFORD

LEICESTER

SHROPSHIRE

WARWICK

NORTHAMPTON

HUNTS

CAMBRIDGE

NORFOLK

Tostiq raids East Anglia in May

WORCESTER

BEDS

SUFFOLK

HEREFORD

OXFORD

BUCKS

HERTFORD

ESSEX

GLOUCESTER

BERKS

LONDON

LONDON

WILTS

SURREY

KENT

Sandwich
Tostiq lands in May

SOMERSET

HANTS

SUSSEX

English fleet and army mobilised summer 1066.
Demobilised 8 September

DEVON

DORSET

Isle of Wight

English Channel

FRANCE

CORNWALL

0   100 km

0   100 miles

Norman Invasion

Conquest of England

Following the Battle of Hastings, Duke William seized Dover then marched on London. The city refused his demand to surrender, whereupon William began to devastate the surrounding countryside; London quickly surrendered. William's claim to the throne was acknowledged and he was crowned King on Christmas Day in 1066.

Learning of the Norman landing, Harold rushed south 190 miles to London, raised more troops and travelled a further 50 miles to Hastings, ready to fight the Normans, and all in 13 days. Apparently, Harold wished to surprise William but Norman scouts reported the English advance and 14 October witnessed the Anglo-Norman engagement at the ridge at what became known as Battle.

The English dismounted and formed a shield wall with their axe-men some 7,000 strong with the county levies. The Normans had larger forces with 6,000 infantry, including crossbowmen and archers, and some 2,000 knights. Battle began at 9 am and lasted all day, with repeated cavalry charges. Reports of the battle differ but many agree that a feigned retreat by the Normans caused the shield wall to

disintegrate as some soldiers rushed forward only to be scythed down by the returning cavalry. The English forces re-organized but Harold's brothers, Leofwine and Gyrth, were killed, Harold himself dying at dusk leaving his housecarls fighting to the death. The battle was close but William could view the slaughter of nearly all the Anglo-Scandinavian nobility as a precursor to their replacement with an entirely new layer of European aristocracy.

William needed to force an English surrender. Raids followed, with reinforcements landing at Chichester, capturing Winchester, the capital and treasury of old Wessex, then marching along the Thames to meet other Norman spearheads at Wallingford. Unable to force London Bridge, William burnt Southwark instead. Raids deep into Surrey and Hampshire and a vast raid

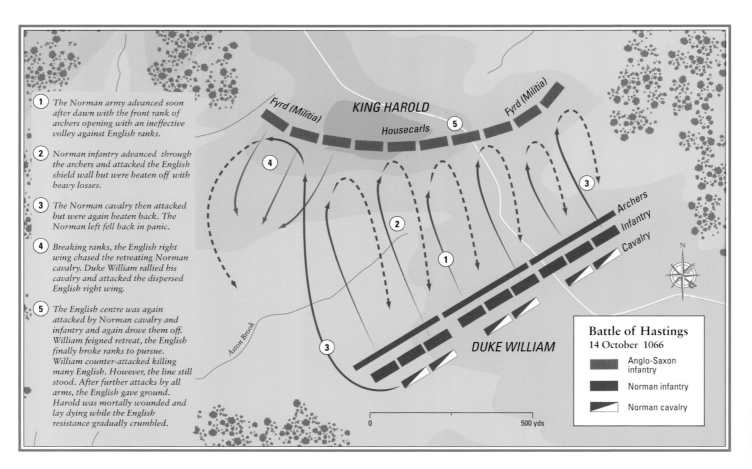

1. The Norman army advanced soon after dawn with the front rank of archers opening with an ineffective volley against English ranks.

2. Norman infantry advanced through the archers and attacked the English shield wall but were beaten off with heavy losses.

3. The Norman cavalry then attacked but were again beaten back. The Norman left fell back in panic.

4. Breaking ranks, the English right wing chased the retreating Norman cavalry. Duke William rallied his cavalry and attacked the dispersed English right wing.

5. The English centre was again attacked by Norman cavalry and infantry and again drove them off. William feigned retreat, the English finally broke ranks to pursue. William counter-attacked killing many English. However, the line still stood. After further attacks by all arms, the English gave ground. Harold was mortally wounded and lay dying while the English resistance gradually crumbled.

Fyrd (Militia)

KING HAROLD

Housecarls

Fyrd (Militia)

Archers
Infantry
Cavalry

DUKE WILLIAM

Aston Brook

N

Battle of Hastings
14 October 1066

Anglo-Saxon infantry

Norman infantry

Norman cavalry

0   500 yds

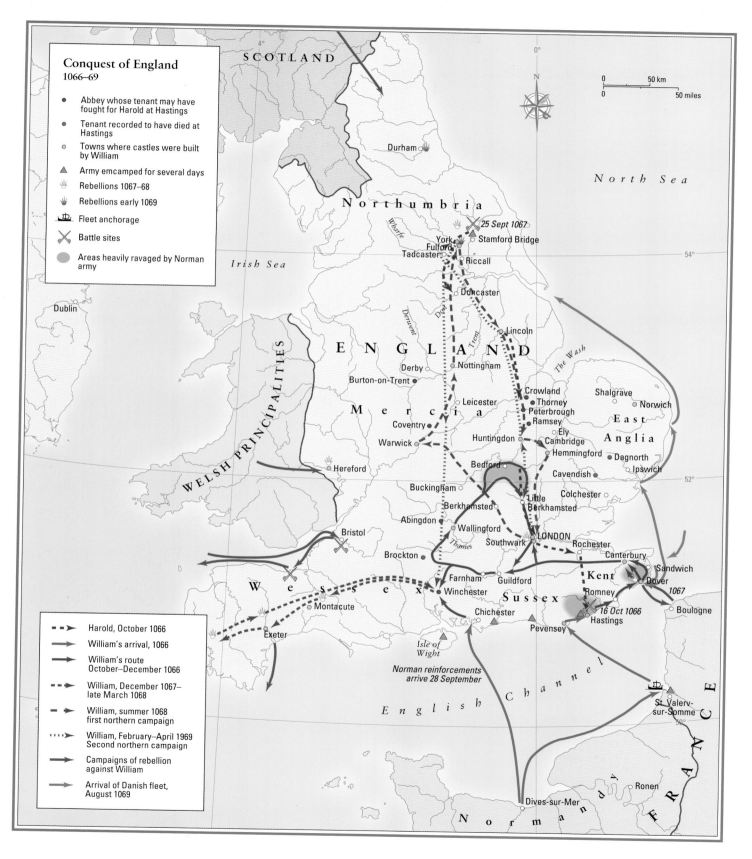

Conquest of England
1066–69

- ● Abbey whose tenant may have fought for Harold at Hastings
- ● Tenant recorded to have died at Hastings
- ◉ Towns where castles were built by William
- ▲ Army emcamped for several days
- ⚜ Rebellions 1067–68
- ⚜ Rebellions early 1069
- ⚓ Fleet anchorage
- ✕ Battle sites
- ⬤ Areas heavily ravaged by Norman army

SCOTLAND

North Sea

Durham

Northumbria

Irish Sea

25 Sept 1067
York ✕ Stamford Bridge
Fulford
Tadcaster Riccall

Doncaster

Dublin

ENGLAND

Lincoln

The Wash

Derby   Nottingham

Burton-on-Trent

Crowland   Shalgrave
Thorney   Norwich
Peterbrough   East
Leicester   Ramsey

Mercia

Coventry   Ely   Anglia
Huntingdon   Cambridge
Warwick   Hemmingford   Dagnorth
Cavendish   Ipswich

WELSH PRINCIPALITIES

Hereford   Bedford
Buckingham   Little   Colchester
Berkhamsted

Berkhamsted

Abingdon
Bristol   Wallingford   LONDON   Rochester
Brockton   Southwark   Canterbury   Sandwich

Thames   Kent   Dover
Farnham   Guildford   1067
Winchester   Romney
Sussex   Boulogne
Montacute   Chichester   16 Oct 1066
Exeter   Pevensey   Hastings

Isle of Wight

Norman reinforcements arrive 28 September

English Channel

St Valery-sur-Somme

FRANCE

Ronen

Dives-sur-Mer

Normandy

- ‑ ‑ ▶ Harold, October 1066
- ──▶ William's arrival, 1066
- ──▶ William's route October–December 1066
- ‑ ‑ ▶ William, December 1067– late March 1068
- ━ ━ ▶ William, summer 1068 first northern campaign
- ······▶ William, February–April 1969 Second northern campaign
- ──▶ Campaigns of rebellion against William
- ──▶ Arrival of Danish fleet, August 1069

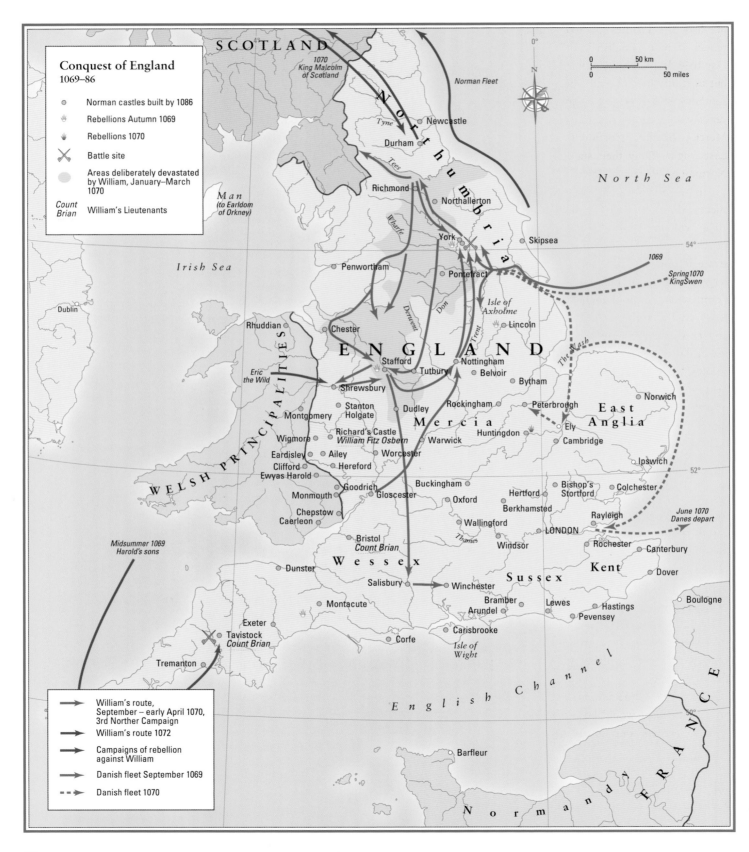

Conquest of England
1069–86

- ● Norman castles built by 1086
- ♆ Rebellions Autumn 1069
- ♆ Rebellions 1070
- ✕ Battle site
- ⬭ Areas deliberately devastated by William, January–March 1070
- *Count Brian* William's Lieutenants

SCOTLAND

1070 King Malcolm of Scotland

Norman Fleet

Tyne ● Newcastle

Durham ●

N o r t h u m b r i a

Tees

Richmond ●

● Northallerton

Wharfe

York ● ✕ ● Skipsea

Man (to Earldom of Orkney)

Irish Sea

● Penwortham

Pontefract ●

Derwent *Don* *Isle of Axholme*

1069

Spring 1070 King Swen

North Sea

54°

Dublin ●

Rhuddlan ●

● Chester

Trent

● Lincoln

The Wash

E N G L A N D

Stafford ●

● Tutbury ● Nottingham

Eric the Wild

● Shrewsbury

● Belvoir

● Bytham

● Norwich

● Stanton Holgate

● Dudley

● Rockingham

● Peterborough

E a s t A n g l i a

W E L S H   P R I N C I P A L I T I E S

● Montgomery

M e r c i a

● Ely

● Wigmore

Richard's Castle William Fitz Osbern

● Warwick

● Huntingdon

● Cambridge

● Eardisley

● Ailey

● Worcester

● Clifford

● Hereford

● Ipswich

52°

● Ewyas Harold

● Goodrich

● Buckingham

● Hertford

● Bishop's Stortford

● Colchester

● Monmouth

● Gloucester

● Oxford

● Berkhamsted

● Chepstow

● Caerleon

● Wallingford

Thames

● Rayleigh

June 1070 Danes depart

● Bristol *Count Brian*

W e s s e x

LONDON ●

● Windsor

● Rochester

● Canterbury

Midsummer 1069 Harold's sons

● Dunster

Salisbury ● ➔ ● Winchester

S u s s e x

K e n t

● Dover

● Bramber

● Lewes

● Hastings

● Boulogne

● Montacute

● Arundel

● Pevensey

● Exeter

Tavistock Count Brian ✕

● Carisbrooke

● Corfe

● Tremanton

Isle of Wight

E n g l i s h   C h a n n e l

● Barfleur

N o r m a n d y   FRANCE

0°

50 km

50 miles

N

— William's route, September – early April 1070, 3rd Northern Campaign

— William's route 1072

— Campaigns of rebellion against William

— Danish fleet September 1069

- - - Danish fleet 1070

north of the Thames followed, forcing the surrender of many English leaders. On Christmas Day 1066, William was crowned King of England but in reality he had only defeated the forces of southern and central England. The next few years would see revolts in the West Country, Mercia, Yorkshire, Northumbria and the fens of East Anglia. Only their suppression would see Norman power consolidated.

Some historians explain eventual Norman success through castle building. At Pevensey in 1066, William built his first castle, clearly shown in the Bayeux Tapestry. Castles were placed at strategic points at road junctions, fords and in large centres of population where they would dominate and intimidate the defeated English. A traditional picture emerges of the early timber and earth fortifications which hoped to make use of natural, if not, man-made features. Often the castle comprised a motte, or mound, topped by a wooden palisade and a surrounding bailey or enclosure. These fortifications could be built rapidly, with William erecting two at York in eight days. However, Norman castles or fortifications were varied in their types.

After 1066, castles were often erected at the sites of Anglo-Saxon burhs. William's companions were rewarded with land and some 600 castles were constructed in the Welsh marches, although many were abandoned after conquest. Generally, early fortifications were enclosures with outer ditches and sheer scarps, the spoil making earth ramparts surmounted with timber palisades. Not all earthen and timber castles were motte and baileys. Many were large baileys enclosed by a ditch, rampart and gate and within this ring would be placed buildings needed by the new lord, his retainers, household and garrison. Sometimes there would be mottes without baileys, baileys without mottes, ramparts topped with palisades, ramparts with masonry walls, multiple ditches, artificial mounds, and sited on cliff tops, promontories or on defensible river banks such as Chepstow Castle in England, built 1067–75. Carisbrooke Castle, on the Isle of Wight, was built on the site of a Roman fort that had defended the Saxon shore.

Resistance to Norman authority began in 1067 with a rising in Herefordshire under Edric the Wild, followed by one in Kent. The next year witnessed Exeter being subdued, followed by the southwest with castles being placed at Trematon, Dunster, Exeter and Montacute. The strength of the Normans there, especially Bristol, prevented King Harold's illegitimate sons from winning support when they mounted an expedition out of Ireland.

In the north of England, a general rising took place headed by Edgar the Atheling, grandson of King Edmund II Ironside. King Swein Estrithson sent a fleet to help, the combined forces capturing York before moving into north Lincolnshire. Edgar eventually swore fealty to William and served him. Resistance stiffened elsewhere and Edric the Wild's rebellion spread towards Chester and Stafford. Other revolts occurred in Dorset and Somerset and Harold's sons launched another expedition.

William retaliated in a brutal and harsh fashion. His forces crushed the south and west while he marched north, cutting a swathe of destruction around York, forcing the rebels to retreat to ships in the Humber estuary. The 'Harrying of the North' followed with systematic destruction in the height of winter. The Norman forces marched north to the Tees, crossing the Pennines to crush Chester and Stafford. The Danish fleet sailed from the Humber to join a Lincolnshire thegn, Hereward the Wake, who conducted a rebellion from the fens in the Isle of Eley. The joint forces sacked Peterborough but 1070 saw the Danes withdraw from the fray and Hereward's island defences were eventually overrun.

In 1086, the Domesday survey took place analyzing landholdings and wealth in a systematic fashion so that William could ascertain his royal revenue and who owned fealty to whom. The book demonstrates the dispossession of the Anglo-Saxon-Scandinavian nobility in favour of the Normans and their allies.

Conquest of England

Within four years of the Battle of Hastings, King William I had secured control over England. The power of the Anglo-Saxon Earls had been broken, replaced by William's feudal kingdom with a greater centralization of power than would exist in any other European state for many centuries.

Normans in Ireland and Scotland

A result of domestic conflict, Diarmit MacMurchada, King of Leinster, was expelled from Ireland in 1166. He sought to regain his throne with the help of foreign knights, allowed by Henry II of England after Diarmit acknowledged Henry as his lord. The year 1171 witnessed Henry's intervention in Irish affairs by preventing an independent Irish–Norman Kingdom being established by Richard (Strongbow) FitzGilbert de Clare, Earl of Pembroke, who was helping Diarmit. Strongbow had seized the Kingdom of Leinster, plus the towns of Waterford, Wexford and Dublin and part of the Kingdom of Meath. Henry II landed with his army at Waterford requiring Strongbow to offer to hold Leinster as a fief. The Kingdom was formally recognised and granted, while Henry kept the city and Kingdom of Dublin and all seaports and fortresses. Henry received submission and hostages from seven Irish kings.

The invading forces followed standard Norman practice in enemy territory constructing castles, such as Clonard. This defensive settlement, like many others, would be the focus for raids upon local Irish chieftains to destroy their power, while rustling their cattle, followed by seizure of the best Irish land. This could then be sequestered and subdivided amongst the fort's minions in a process of sub-infeudation.

The Anglo–Norman zone expanded and all Irish Kings, except in the northwest, recognised Henry II's supremacy. New Norman lordships were created and the 1175 Treaty of Windsor witnessed O'Connor, the High King of Ireland, accepting Henry as overlord, restricting his own title to King of Connacht. The invaders pursued economic exploitation, investing heavily in imported agricultural systems, based upon the English manor. The Irish peasantry was not dispossessed, labour was scarce; hence, English peasants and artisans were recruited to colonize the land. The Irish collapse did not mean that Irish resistance ended. However, savage reprisals deterred armed resistance helping diminish raids against new towns and settlements.

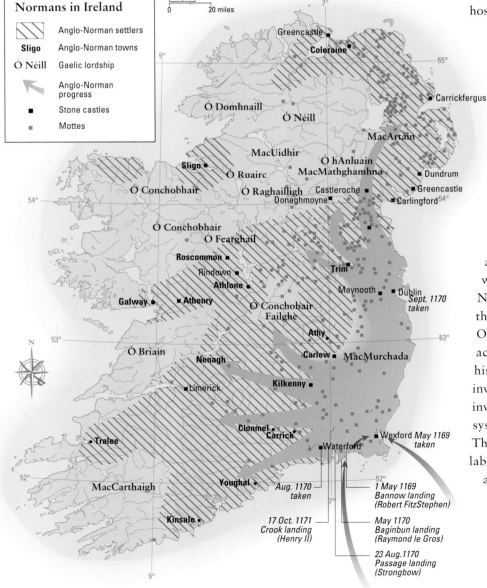

Norman relations with Scotland fluctuated between violence and friendship. King Malcolm III Canmore remembered the past when Scotland controlled Cumbria and parts of Northumberland. His incursions over the border became incessant and, in 1072, William I launched an expedition by land and sea, meeting Malcolm at Abernethy on the Tay. Malcolm performed homage for Scotland yet invaded England again, renewing his homage after William mounted another expedition. Malcolm was eventually killed on his fifth raid in 1093 by the forces of William II Rufus.

English and Norman influence penetrated Scotland in ways other than violence; by stealth. Malcolm III's second wife was Margaret, the sister of Edgar Atheling; three of her six sons ascended the Scots throne. After Malcolm III was succeeded by his brother Donald Ban, Margaret's son, Edgar ousted him with the aid of a Norman army.

Another son, David I (1124–53), supervised a virtual Norman conquest. His reign saw the introduction of a coinage, and motte and bailey castles. Norman infiltration was aided by David spending many of his early years at the Anglo-Norman court where he married in 1113, making friends with his brother-in-law, Henry I, while gaining the Earldom of Huntingdon from his wife. From 1107, with Anglo-Norman aid he acquired from his brother, King Alexander I, the right to rule Cumbria, Strathclyde and Lothian.

In his earldom and his Scottish court, David gathered around himself a number of Anglo–Normans who Normanized southeastern Scotland – Lothian. Many Norman–Scottish barons were used to rule Cumbria. Thus, David ruled with a cosmopolitan knighthood, which feudalized Scotland, providing a basis for more centralised land tenure – feudal knight service.

David's loyalty to Henry I continued to his daughter, Matilda, during the English war of succession on Henry's death. David fought against Stephen hoping to gain Northumberland for himself. In 1136, he made peace with Stephen, gaining Cumberland. Re-entering the fray, David was defeated at Northallerton, the Battle of the Standard, in 1138.

The peace terms gave Northumberland to David's son as a fief from Stephen. Another campaign saw David knighting Matilda's son, Henry Plantagenet, later King Henry II of England.

The Scotland of David I
Scotland was a diverse state, included in its peoples were: Gaelic-speakers in the central Highlands, Scandinavian settlers of the northern and western isles, and the Angles of the south east. Into this mix King David imported Norman lords bringing with them their form of rule.

The Scotland of David I
1124–53

	Kingdom of Galloway
	Teviotdale
	Earldom of Northumberland
	Cumberland and Westmorland
	Kingdom of the Isles

Norman Domination of Country Life

Berkhamsted Castle

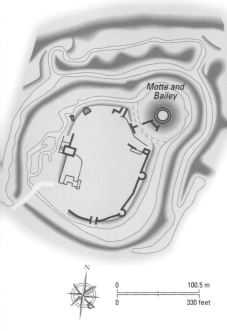

Motte and Bailey

N

0   100.5 m

0   330 feet

William I's intentions towards Wales were made clear when he created counties palatine, whose lords were charged with the burden of defending England against attack in the more remote areas of the Norman–Welsh borders. These Welsh Marches were ordered by the new palatine Earldoms of Hereford (William Fitz Osbern), Shrewsbury (Roger de Montgomery) and Chester (Hugh d'Avranches). These savage, greedy men were diverted from causing trouble in England by being given license to steal and sequester any Welsh lands they could sieze.

The power of the sword ran riot through the Marches and William II Rufus urged the lords and their tenants-in-chief to expand their holdings, which was partly accomplished by castle building and backed up by violence and intimidation. A multiplicity of castles were built, each designed to protect its neighbour in an overlapping network of defences that secured control of important river crossings and passes. These fierce Marcher lords, acting like potentates, dominated and held large areas of eastern Wales, plus the south coast from the major castle at Chepstow to St. David's in Pembrokeshire. The March lands, some 30 to 50 miles in depth, were normally ruled by Norman law, although some Welsh communities were allowed to live according to their own laws and customs. The southern Marcher lords ruled the south-coast Englishry, a virtual Norman colony with castles positioned by sea inlets and rivers so that provisions could be shipped in during times of crisis. Settlers were brought in mainly from the English West Country, protected by the string of castles.

Despite Marcher incursions, a Norman conquest was hindered by numerous factors: the mountainous landscape; the internecine Welsh feuding making it impossible to negotiate; together with badly co-ordinated Norman campaigns. Welsh independence was kept aflame by the Welsh principalities ruled by the princes of Gwynedd, Powys and Deheubarth. Wales awaited heroes to liberate conquered territories such as Llywelyn the Great of Gwynedd.

By 1080, England was under complete Norman control with forbidding castles built at most county towns and strategic points. The Norman influence in Scotland was immense, apart from the Normanisation introduced by David I. For 30 years, following his mother's death, Scotland was a political shambles, with Normans grabbing what they could. Margaret's brother, Edgar Atheling, was given an army by William II 'Rufus', which he used to crush all usurpers and place his nephew Edgar on the Scots throne who obligingly acknowledged William II as his liege lord. Succeeded by Alexander I, Scotland was under some Norman influence, with the future David I being given an independent appendage, enlarged under pressure from Henry I of England.

David I established feudalism in a united Scotland in which Normans and those English who had fled William the Conqueror, and the Scots nobility, inter-married in temporary harmony. David continued the creation of dioceses instigated by his brother, Alexander, and established all the medieval Scots dioceses by the end of his reign. This copying of English methods meant that the Church, like the Anglo-Norman nobility, became a vehicle for the Anglicization or Normanization of Scotland.

David I is also remembered for introducing families into Scotland who became major political participants: the Bruces, the Stewarts and the Comyns. Important, too, was the creation of sheriffs, a royal judge and administrator, and other key officials forming a royal court as a Supreme Court of Law, a proto-parliament. Economically, burghs, incorporated towns, became centres of trade and small scale craft-shops and manufacturers. Yet, despite strengthening Scotland, David left some problems bubbling beneath the surface. His successors had to face regular rebellions from the Celtic north, especially from Moray, a centre of the old Pictland and power base of Macbeth the King, and from Galloway.

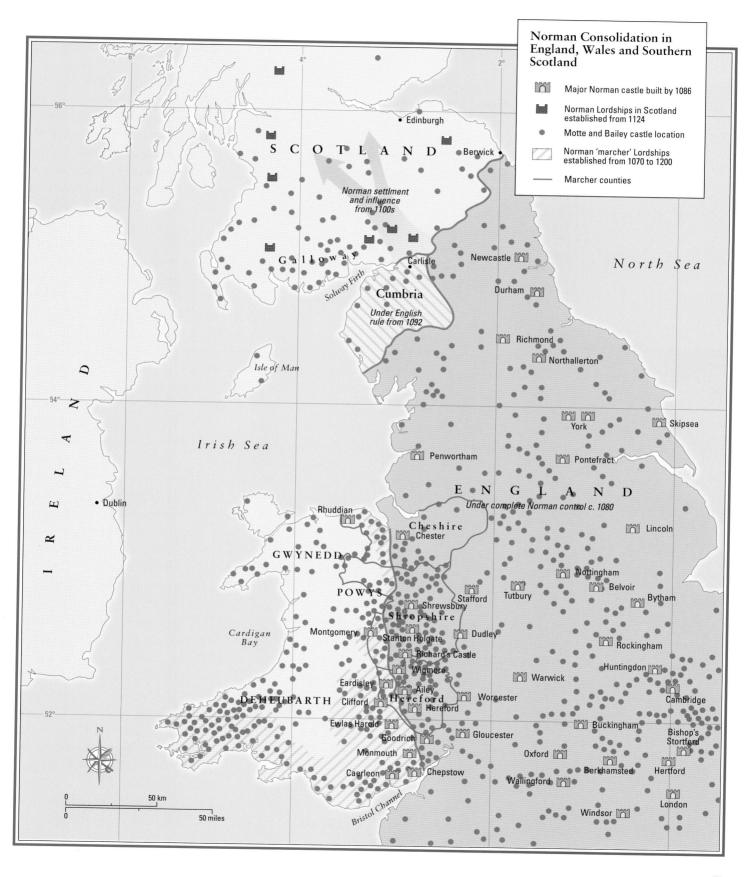

Norman Consolidation in England, Wales and Southern Scotland

- Major Norman castle built by 1086
- Norman Lordships in Scotland established from 1124
- Motte and Bailey castle location
- Norman 'marcher' Lordships established from 1070 to 1200
- Marcher counties

Edinburgh

SCOTLAND

Berwick

Norman settlement and influence from 1100s

Galloway

Carlisle

Newcastle

North Sea

Durham

Cumbria

Under English rule from 1092

Richmond

Isle of Man

Northallerton

York

Skipsea

Irish Sea

Penwortham

Pontefract

ENGLAND

Under complete Norman control c. 1080

Dublin

Rhuddian

Cheshire

Chester

Lincoln

GWYNEDD

Nottingham

POWYS

Belvoir

Stafford

Tutbury

Bytham

Shrewsbury

Shropshire

Cardigan Bay

Montgomery

Stanton Holgate

Dudley

Rockingham

Richard's Castle

Huntingdon

Wigmore

Eardisley

Warwick

DEHEUBARTH

Ailey

Clifford

Hereford

Worcester

Cambridge

Hereford

Ewlas Harold

Buckingham

Goodrich

Gloucester

Bishop's Stortford

Monmouth

Oxford

Caerleon

Chepstow

Wallingford

Berkhamsted

Hertford

Windsor

London

N

0   50 km
0   50 miles

Bristol Channel

The Normans in Britain and Europe

After the Norman Conquest, England looked south to its new connections in France, instead of the North Sea coasts and Scandinavia. The British Islands were reasonably stable: Scotland was a virtual client state while the Welsh, holed up in their mist-filled valleys and mountains, conducted guerrilla warfare with verve and skill, preventing further Norman incursions by using a longbow, a precursor of the English war-bow, keeping the invaders to the lowlands. England became quiescent with the King being itinerant, moving from residence to residence across the country, eating his rents and dispensing justice. This economic and political process was mainly centred in the Thames Valley and Wessex. Henry I linked England to Normandy by two ferry routes: from Southampton and Portsmouth to Dieppe and Barfleur. In Normandy, his peregrinations were mainly focused in the Seine Valley, south of Rouen, in the Vexin and Evrécin, a region threatened by the proximity of the French royal domain.

The major problem facing the Norman monarchy was the inheritance of the Anglo-Norman state when William I died in 1087. Robert, the eldest son became Duke of Normandy. William Rufus, born next, became heir to England, while the youngest Henry received a sum of £5,000 in silver. Rufus was killed in 1100 leaving Henry to seize the treasury at Winchester and be crowned three days later at Westminster Abbey. He was then faced with the prospect of trouble from Robert II of Normandy, who was returning from Crusade and wanted to regain his pawned duchy. Enmity between the brothers led to warfare, with Robert being defeated in 1106 at Tinchebrai. Here Henry's English axe-men helped chop Robert's cavalry to pieces thereby avenging Hastings. Robert was imprisoned for life. His son, William, died in a rebellion, aged 25 years in 1128.

Henry also defeated King Louis VI, the Fat, at Brémule in 1119, and Norman holdings were augmented by bringing Bellême, Maine and Brittany under English control. The dynasty was strengthened by marrying Henry's daughter, Matilda, to the German Emperor and his son, William Atheling, to the heiress of Anjou, while his nephew, Stephen, became Count of Blois and Chartres. However, the Norman male line was extinguished when Henry's heir, William Atheling, was drowned. Henry's death was followed by the Anarchy in which a civil war was fought for the crown between Stephen and Matilda. The situation was resolved with Stephen becoming King but his heir was to be Henry Plantagenet, son of Matilda's second marriage to Geoffrey of Anjou.

The Norman saga does not end here. Norman adventurers became mercenaries recruited to fight in the wars of the southern Italian states, which were controlled by Byzantine Greeks and Lombard principalities, while Sicily was a Muslim emirate. Significant amongst the Normans were the sons of Tancred de Hauteville, Robert Guiscard becoming the strongest. In 1059, at the Investiture of Melfi, Pope Nicholas II granted Guiscard with Calabria, Apulia and Sicily, which he had to wrest from the Byzantines and Muslims. Southern Italy fell by 1071, while a simultaneous campaign was fought by land and sea for Sicily. Guiscard's death in 1085 left the key source of Norman power with his brother, who became Roger of Sicily. He eventually took over the Italian Norman territories and, in 1139, Pope Innocent II confirmed Roger II as King of Sicily with an over-lordship covering Italy south of the River Garigliano.

Like other Normans, Roger II was a skilled ruler and administrator. Heading a multi-lingual state, ruling with the concept of Divine Right, he created a financially efficient state with a civil service based upon Norman, Greek and Arabic methods. Roger's tolerance allowed education to flourish in both Greek and Arabic, the latter being the language of science. Sicily was unique where all faiths, races and cultures could co-exist in almost equality.

Europe, 1095

Europeans observed the gradual centralization of government, especially in Norman England and France. Monarchs became more powerful and displayed their wealth by building monumental castles and cathedrals. Living standards improved owing to land clearance and agricultural innovation, providing enough food for an expanding population.

Europe 1095

- — Holy Roman Empire
- — Border
- --- Probable border
- ▨ Areas under Norman control

Norwegian Sea

NORWAY

• Bergen

S W E D E N

Oslo •

• Stockholm

• Åbo

F I N N S

ESTONIANS

LIVS

60°

56°

SCOTLAND

• Scone

Glasgow • • Edinburgh

North Sea

Aarhus •

Roskilde •

• Malmö

Baltic Sea

DENMARK

Hamburg •

POMERANIA

Vistula

LITHUANIANS

52°

IRISH KINGDOMS

• Dublin

• York

Bremen •

Hanover •

E
L
B
E

• Poznan

POLAND

• Cork

WELSH STATES

ENGLAND

Amsterdam •

Rotterdam •

Cologne •

Rhine

KINGDOM

• Wroclaw

• Cracow

• Hereford

• Oxford

• Wells • London

Mainz •

• Frankfurt

• Prague

KINGDOM OF BOHEMIA

48°

Rouen •

NORMANDY

• Rheims

OF

Vienna •

• Pozsony

• Esztergom

Brittany

• Paris

• Metz

• Strasbourg

GERMANY

• Munich

• Salzburg

• Buda

HUNGARY

ATLANTIC OCEAN

• Nantes • Tours

• Orléans

Dijon •

Geneva •

• Zurich

• Bern

• Innsbruck

• Graz

• Szeged

FRANCE

Limoges •

• Lyon

Milan •

• Verona

Trieste •

• Zágráb

• Temesvár

44°

Aquitaine

Bordeaux •

Gascony

• Toulouse

KINGDOM OF BURGUNDY (ARLES)

• Avignon

• Nice

• Turin

• Genoa

KINGDOM OF ITALY

• Bologna

VENETIAN REPUBLIC

Venice •

• Zara

• Spalato

• Belgrade

• Naissus

BYZANTINE EMPIRE

Corunna •

Oviedo •

Bayonne •

NAVARRE

ARAGON

CATALAN COUNTIES

Marseille

Pisa •

PISA

• Florence

Perugia •

Adriatic Sea

• Mostar

40°

Oporto •

LEÓN-CASTILE

Saragossa •

MUSLIM STATES

• Barcelona

Corsica

Rome •

PAPAL STATES

Salonica •

Salamanca •

CID

• Tuledo

• Naples

• Bari

• Taranto

Janina •

Lisbon •

• Valencia

MUSLIM KINGDOM OF MALLORCA

Sardinia

Caralis •

36°

EMPIRE OF THE ALMORAVIDS

• Qurtubah (Córdova)

Ishbiliyah •

Qadis •

• Malaqah

• Cartagena

M e d i t e r r a n e a n   S e a

Palermo •

NORMAN PRINCIPALITIES

Sicily

• Messana

• Catana

• Algiers

• Tunis

Castles and Estates

Besides being a fortress, a castle was the home of a lord and his family, with the lord providing the focus and rationale for the castle's very existence. The accommodation arrangements reflected a lord's status in medieval society and his needs as the head of a sizeable establishment and lands. The lords required a body of officials to implement and enforce his decisions and a secretariat to support them.

Members of the household were duty bound to cater to the personal needs of the lord and his relations and guests. Additionally, they were required to administer his lands and, in return, gained his patronage. In times of war, they were required to fight for their lord in defence of his rights and lands. Sons of the nobility and of knightly families were expected to serve and train in the households of superiors where they received a military and academic training, as well as education in manners.

During the Norman and Angevin periods, the royal household appointed a chancellor who looked after the royal chapel and the monarch's written records. Henry II of England moved around his diverse Angevin lands followed by a column of carts bursting with records. Eventually, the Chancellor of the Exchequer had a permanent office in England at Westminster.

A lord would tend to build comfortable quarters for his family in the bailey, the keep being used as a final bastion in an attack. The garrison was stationed in the outer bailey. Thus, the majority of castles had two baileys, with the heavily fortified inner bailey containing the lord's rooms, great hall, chapel, other lodgings and domestic units, while the outer bailey housed all other departments and provided the environment for daily work of the garrison. Over the centuries household arrangements changed with the lord and his family increasingly having the use of their own suite of comfortably-appointed rooms.

When the Normans arrived in England, they introduced an administrative unit known as the manor, which was a holding of a feudal lord, being an economic, political and judicial unit. The 'classic' manor comprised: a village, the lord's manor house, the arable, pasture and meadows of the unfree and the free tenants, plus common land, woodland and wasteland. The holder of the manor and its lands was a fief holder of a powerful lord. Several villages might be located on a manor but the peasants were the farmers producing the crops under the direction of the lord's overseer. They farmed the meat and draught oxen, paid taxes in services, were required as forced labour on the lord's lands and were even expected to fight.

A large manor might have a water-driven mill for grinding grain, fish ponds, a bakery, orchards, herb and vegetable gardens, and bee skeps for making honey. The sheep produced wool for yarn and clothes, while linen from flax could make finer clothing or be farmed for its oil. The peasants produced the ordinary food for the castle such as ducks, geese, pigeons, chickens, fish, pork, beef and mutton, as well as a range of vegetables such as carrots, turnips, cabbages, onions and the all important peas and beans (an important part of the staple diet for ordinary people). Fruit was grown and dairy products and alcohol were produced. The lord hunted throughout the year for deer, wild boar and game birds; peasants occasionally poached. During winter, some livestock was slaughtered because there was not enough winter feed. Rich houses even possessed a dovecote and fish ponds. The peasants had only bacon or pickled pork during winter because pigs did not need winter fodder as they could forage in woods for their food.

Hard cheese was a staple food for peasants. Sometimes grated cheese would be mixed with herbs and eggs to make herbolace, a cross between scrambled eggs and an omelette. Eggs were much used in richer households for dishes such as custards, being mixed with cream, saffron and honey. The manor would normally have a blacksmith, carpenter and wheelwright who could make agricultural implements and carts.

The manor utilized a three-field crop rotation system: one field lay fallow, one field grew wheat or rye, sown in autumn; and, another for spring sown barley, rye, oats, beans or peas. Every male householder would obtain about 30 strips divided into good and bad land and would farm under the direction of the lord's overseer; but if he owned his strips he would copy the villager custom. The harvest would use the labour of all men, women and children, and the community's animals could forage on the fields after harvest. The lord's strips, like the peasants', were also distributed through good and bad land. The lord's needs were paramount and only about three days of the week were left for peasants to work their own strips and garden plots. Even the village priest might possess his own strips, which he farmed himself. Woodlands held in common would produce timber and beech mast for pigs and the animals were pastured on the village meadows. Food and agricultural surpluses would be sold at market.

Typical Village Plan

Labels on plan: Woodland, West Fields, Lord's Mill, Stream, South Fields, Village Houses, Village Church, Priest's House, Manor House, Pasture, Fish Ponds, East Fields

Village Plan

Cottagers would receive a number of field strips to till in a three-field system, as well as maintaining a farm yard for chickens and pigs. Labour would be given to the Lord of the manor to farm his land. Oxen and horses might be owned in common for ploughing. Large villages might have a blacksmith, wheelwright and carpenter. Any food surplus would be sold in a local market where salt could be purchased for preserving meat for winter.

Church and State

Society of the Middle Ages witnessed a gradual merging of interests between Church and state as each sought stability. The two relied on each other in operating local government and administration, remembering that the clergy were normally the only literate part of society. A major policy was to keep the peasantry quiescent, since their labour was important in supplying food and profit and to ensure that urban dwellers did not become unruly in times of crisis. A linkage between the two institutions was furthered by the younger sons of the nobility entering the Church as a career, with the hope that the achievement of high ecclesiastical office would benefit the family.

It is important to remember that the islands were populated by churches, cathedrals, monasteries, friaries, abbeys and priories; also, each parish had a priest and every city a bishop. Religious institutions pervaded the British Isles and were often endowed by the rich and powerful. Additionally, many knights and tenants-in-chief held their fiefs from abbeys and monasteries, which were important and powerful landlords. Also significant were the rituals, especially the granting of knighthood in a dubbing ceremony, that secular lords devised for themselves to be carried out in church precincts. Lord and prelate were intertwined politically, socially and economically.

The Normans used this Church as an agent of territorial expansion. Under Papal approval, the Scottish Church was placed under the authority of the Archbishop of York, while new Anglo-Norman-style bishoprics were established in Wales as the Normans occupied Welsh lands. Even some Irish kings sought the aid of Archbishops Lanfranc and Anselm of Canterbury. Thus, the Church spread its clerical wings over the island's various polities. When appointed, Lanfranc established a rigid hierarchy in a territorial organisation, which ensured Canterbury's hegemony over all bishoprics.

Norman rule financed many Benedictine abbeys, with Henry I and Stephen presiding over 100 New Augustinian priories as well as hospitals, hospices and almshouses; most of these were urban. New monastic orders were supported by great landowners and the Cistercians were enabled to spread throughout England, Wales and the northern regions in particular. Yorkshire became a bastion of Cisterican activity with the foundation of Rievaulx, Bylands and Fountains Abbeys. Wales saw Tintern Abbey founded in 1131, becoming a springboard for daughter houses to be established in the Englishry before spreading northwards where many Welsh princes supported and endowed the order. In sum, religion in the islands was organised, rigorously institutionalised and diversified, with the common people benefiting from medical and charitable services.

The Angevins continued Norman policies but were confronted with the developing powers of the Gregorian popes leading to conflict as in the case of Thomas Beckett. While state sought co-existence with a centralizing Church, the islands were facing great changes, ushering in forces that required adaptation by both Church and state.

These social and economic changes derived from rapid urban growth, an expansion in international trade (wool, cloth, wine), the rise of a commercial *burgher* class, and the establishment of international institutions of learning, with universities originally producing well-educated clerics with different degrees of learning.

New institutions of learning were founded throughout Europe, with scholars being peripatetic to hear different renowned teachers. English cathedral schools used quality teachers eventually concentrated on teaching the arts, law and theology at Oxford. They created a scholastic guild, aka university, and enjoyed large attendance figures, especially after Henry II banned students from attending the Parisian university. Cambridge University was founded by a group of dissident Oxford teachers. These two universities provided an educated clerical elite that received top ecclesiastical posts. This left the parishes to languish in the hands of ill-educated priests, little better than the parishioners from whom they often sprang. This differed from the towns, where a literate constituency was there to receive educated clerics.

Rural pastoral care was obliged to seek reform by using innovatory methods. Mendicant friars fulfilled this role: Dominicans, Franciscans, Carmelites and Augustinians. These orders, seen by the Pope as preachers and confessors, eventually established their own theological schools in the English universities and directed themselves to an urban mission rather than a rural one leaving the peasantry increasingly bereft of confessors and spiritual guides.

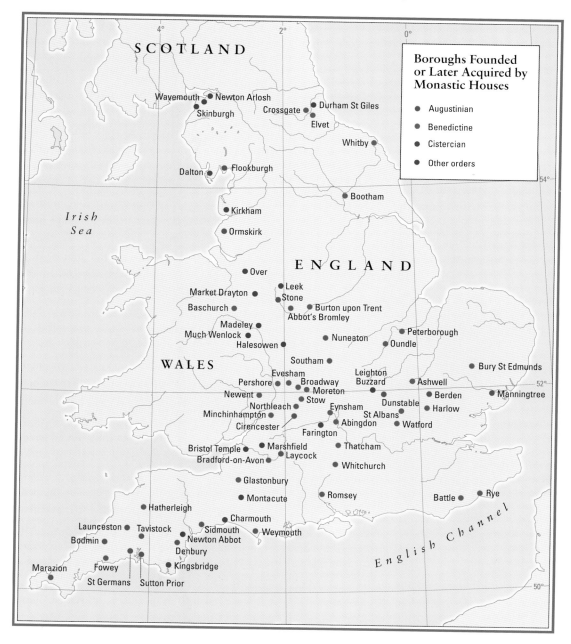

Boroughs Founded or Later Acquired by Monastic Houses

- Augustinian
- Benedictine
- Cistercian
- Other orders

Boroughs Founded or Later Acquired by Monastic Houses

As well as founding and controlling rural estates, monastic houses founded boroughs, the status of which gave enhanced income, administrative advantages and a certain independence from lay interference.

The Angevin Empire 1150–1214

Henry II was an energetic and intelligent King who wanted to improve the condition of England after the Anarchy. He was particularly interested in developing the legal system of common law in the country: that is a uniform legal system administered by royal courts whose authority superseded the jurisdiction of local or baronial courts. He aimed not just at law but justice, with legal decrees grounded in the judge and jury system. The move towards a monarchical bureaucracy transcended the feudal monarchy, especially with the use of scutage and royal courts for private legal suits. Henry was, therefore, a transitional figure in the move towards the early vestiges of a parliamentary system.

In 1164, the Constitutions of Clarendon were promulgated, which reasserted the old rights of the King over the Church in matters such as clerical immunity, appointment of bishops, custody of vacant sees, excommunication and appeals to Rome. Archbishop Becket refused to accept these and battle was drawn. The conflict was ended by the Archbishop's murder in Canterbury Cathedral in 1170 at its very altar, a crime of sacrilege. Becket became a martyr and was soon canonized, with Canterbury becoming a pilgrimage centre. Henry, although innocent of the murder, performed a penance. Nevertheless, Henry won effective control of appointments to Church offices in England, and the end of his reign witnessed royal justice making major inroads on the jurisdiction of Church courts. Hence, centralization was being achieved.

By virtue of his various titles, Henry II had inherited claims over neighbouring territories, which led to several expeditions into Wales to ensure the continuation of homage and fealty to the King of England. Scotland was treated likewise. In Ireland, Henry allowed an expedition by Welsh-based barons to establish Anglo-Norman supremacy in Leinster in 1169, which the King used to extend his own power. Despite these successes, there were distinct weaknesses in this empire stretching from Scotland to the Pyrenées, the empire being a collection of several principalities differing one from another in customs, political government and racial characteristics.

In 1170, the King crowned his eldest son, Henry, as co-regent but gave his son no powers. Young Henry opposed his father's proposals to find territories for John, known as Lackland, at the expense of brother Geoffrey. Richard joined the argument, being supported by his mother. At this point, a general revolt of the baronage in England and Normandy occurred, supported by Louis VII of France and William the Lion of Scotland. Henry re-acted quickly, crushing the rebellions and pardoning his sons but Eleanor remained in custody until his death. A second rebellion broke out in 1181 ending with Henry's death in 1189. The rebellion involved Richard allying with King Philip II of France. Henry was defeated and some say his death in 1189 was hastened when he heard that John had joined his enemies.

Under Richard I (1189–99) and John (1199–1216), the Angevin Empire was attacked by the French King and rebellious barons. When Richard died the baronage of the empire preferred different heirs. In the resultant strife, John fled to England having lost Normandy, Anjou, Maine, Touraine and all of Poitou except La Rochelle. In 1206 and 1214, John led campaigns in Poitou but, ultimately, John's European strategy failed.

The King's defeat caused baronial disquiet in England, and to retain support John was forced to sign the Magna Carta in June 1215. The settlement was made impossible by a group of militant lords and John appealed to the Pope for support. This being granted, John ravaged the northern counties and the Scottish border. Prince Louis of France landed in England at the request of certain barons. John's death in 1216 saw his son become King as Henry III. By 1224, Gascony and the Channel Islands was the only French land England still possessed.

The Angevin Empire

Henry II was King of England, Duke of Normandy and Lord of Aquitaine, Britanny, Poitou, Anjou, Maine and Guienne. However, his empire was a hotch-potch, poorly-knit collection of states gathered together by inheritance, marriage and conquest. Family bickering, a turbulent baronage and French royal interference eventually pulled the empire apart.

The Angevin Empire
1150–1214

Growth

Areas inherited by Henry II in 1150–54

Areas acquired by Henry II's marriage to Eleanor of Aquitaine in 1152

Areas acquired by conquest or diplomacy

Areas acknowledging Henry II as overlord

Areas claimed by Henry II

→ Irish campaign of Richard FitzGilbert de Clare (Strongbow) in 1171

⇢ Henry II's progression in Ireland 1171

Principal castle or stronghold

Castle held against Henry II during the rebellion of 1173–74

Collapse

→ Campaigns of Philip II and his allies 1202–04

→ Campaigns of John and his allies 1214

→ Campaigns of Philip II and his allies 1214

French territory retained by John in 1214

✗ Battle site

Kingdoms and Princes

The mid-thirteenth century saw a degree of political turbulence after the death of King John in 1216. His son, Henry III (1216–72), was aged nine years when he ascended the throne. He spent much of his career in conflict with the barons over his rights under Magna Carta, which ultimately led to a forced 'parliament' in 1264. Henry's reign was characterized by baronial rebellions, failed wars against King Louis IX of France and a totally disgruntled English nobility when Henry appointed his French favourites to positions of power. His political weakness allowed peripheral parts of the islands to seek their own destiny.

In Wales, political leadership devolved upon Llywelyn ap Iowerth, aka Llewelyn Fawr, 'the Great', (1173–1240), Prince of Gwynedd. The year 1201 witnessed a treaty whereby Gwynedd swore fealty and paid homage to John as his liege lord. Llywelyn's main lords were required to follow suit, which begged a future question of where their split loyalties actually lay.

John led two expeditions into Gwynedd in 1211 sometime after Llywelyn had annexed southern Powys in 1208, the first failing as the Welsh retreated into the mountains while the second achieved some success. The English plunged into the depths of Gwynedd and hostilities were concluded by peace terms that involved ceding all Gwynedd east of the River Conwy. However, this plan was abandoned in the face of political pressures in England when the baronage forced John to sign Magna Carta in 1215.

Llywelyn, in company with other Welsh princes, used this opportunity to take back their lands. He allied with former enemies Gwenwynwyn of Powys, Maelgwyn ap Rhys and Rhys Gryg of Deheubarth. Gwynedd now led all the independent princes of Wales and they launched a campaign that seized the castles of Carmarthen, Kidwelly, Llanstephan, Cardigan and Cilgerran. Welshmen were also appointed to the vacant bishoprics of St. David's and Bangor.

In 1216, the lesser princes gave their homage to Llywelyn again but Gwenwynwyn, who had had his Powys lands restored by John, reneged and returned to John, losing his lands to Llywelyn for a second time. When John died, Llywelyn concluded the Treaty of Worcester in 1218 with the new King, Henry III, which confirmed the former in all his Welsh lands. Yet conflict continued, with royal campaigns mounted against Wales in 1223, 1228 and 1231 achieving little except regaining Carmarthen and Cardigan castles.

Llywelyn died in 1240 leading to conflict between his two sons and half-brother Gruffudd. The Marcher lords attacked Gwynedd and the English built and refortified castles throughout Wales. By the Treaty of Woodstock in 1247, Dafydd's heirs, Owain and Llywelyn ap Gruffudd, also submitted and Henry reclaimed the fealty of all barons and nobles in Wales while Gwynedd was divided between the heirs.

In Ireland, chiefs tended to co-operate with the English crown but accommodation failed in the face of a fitful, unplanned English advance into Irish lands. In 1258, the more powerful independent Irish chiefs recognized Brian O'Neill as High-King of Ireland, a move crushed in the Battle of Down in 1260. 1259 witnessed Aed O'Connor, present at the Battle of Down, marrying a Hebridean princess whose dowry included 160 gallowglass, heavily-armoured and well-equipped Gallo-Norse mercenaries from her islands. When these warriors were hired by other Irish chiefs, the English military advantage declined allowing important native dynasties to survive and English settlers were forced onto the defensive.

In Scotland, its kings attempted to project their power into lands owing allegiance to Norway. In 1263, Alexander's forces fought those of King Håkon at Largs in an indecisive battle. Negotiations with a new Norwegian King, Magnus, resulted in the Treaty of Perth in 1266 when Norway ceded its Scots territories to Scotland. In reality, these territories just changed from a Norwegian to a Scots overlord, eventually comprising the Lordship of the Isles.

British Isles, 1250

Llywelyn the Great was key in creating a single code of law and establishing advanced legal principles, generating a spirit of unity amongst the Welsh. In Ireland, failure of the Irish at the Battle of Down in 1260 ensured that there would never be an Irish High-King ever again. The defeat of Håkon at the Battle of Largs in 1263 removed Norwegian sea power from the Irish Sea, allowing English naval operations against Wales, especially Anglesey.

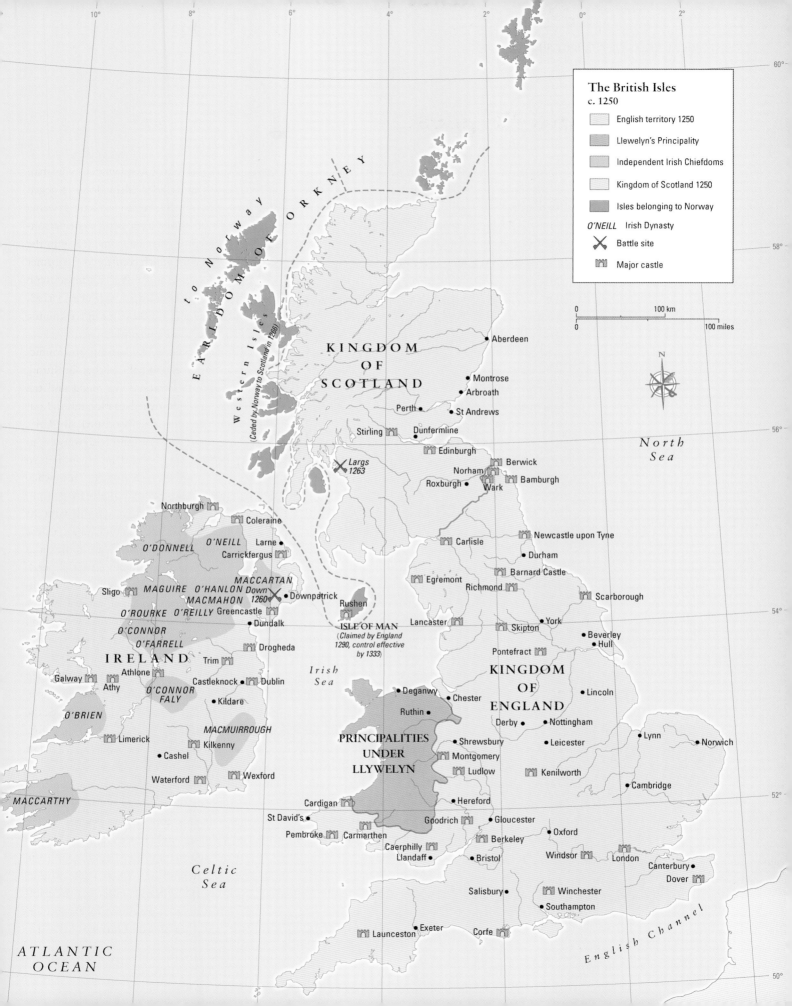

The British Isles
c. 1250

- English territory 1250
- Llewelyn's Principality
- Independent Irish Chiefdoms
- Kingdom of Scotland 1250
- Isles belonging to Norway
- *O'NEILL* Irish Dynasty
- ✕ Battle site
- Major castle

ATLANTIC OCEAN

EARLDOM OF ORKNEY

to Norway

Western Isles
(Ceded by Norway to Scotland in 1266)

KINGDOM OF SCOTLAND

- Aberdeen
- Montrose
- Arbroath
- Perth
- St Andrews
- Stirling
- Dunfermline
- Edinburgh
- ✕ Largs 1263
- Berwick
- Norham
- Roxburgh
- Wark
- Bamburgh

North Sea

- Northburgh
- Coleraine
- *O'DONNELL*
- *O'NEILL*
- Larne
- Carrickfergus
- Sligo
- MAGUIRE O'HANLON *MACCARTAN*
- MACMAHON Down 1260 ✕ Downpatrick
- *O'ROURKE O'REILLY* Greencastle
- Dundalk
- Rushen
- **ISLE OF MAN**
  (Claimed by England 1290, control effective by 1333)
- Carlisle
- Newcastle upon Tyne
- Durham
- Barnard Castle
- Egremont
- Richmond
- Scarborough
- Lancaster
- Skipton
- York
- Beverley
- Hull
- Pontefract

Irish Sea

- *O'CONNOR*
- *O'FARRELL*
- **IRELAND**
- Trim
- Drogheda
- Galway
- Athlone
- Athy
- Castleknock
- Dublin
- *O'CONNOR FALY*
- Kildare
- *O'BRIEN*
- *MACMUIRROUGH*
- Limerick
- Kilkenny
- Cashel
- Waterford
- Wexford
- *MACCARTHY*

KINGDOM OF ENGLAND

- Deganwy
- Chester
- Ruthin
- Lincoln
- Derby
- Nottingham
- **PRINCIPALITIES UNDER LLYWELYN**
- Shrewsbury
- Leicester
- Lynn
- Norwich
- Montgomery
- Ludlow
- Kenilworth
- Cambridge
- Cardigan
- Hereford
- St David's
- Goodrich
- Gloucester
- Pembroke
- Carmarthen
- Berkeley
- Oxford
- Caerphilly
- Windsor
- London
- Llandaff
- Bristol
- Canterbury
- Dover
- Salisbury
- Winchester
- Southampton
- Launceston
- Exeter
- Corfe

Celtic Sea

English Channel

0 — 100 km
0 — 100 miles

Feudal State

Feudalism, developing in early medieval France, was not a new concept but one evolving naturally out of the social conditions that had existed for hundreds of years in western Europe, where settled Christian states were almost always under threat from invasion by hostile Norse from the north or Muslims from the south, or destructive raids by Slav and Magyar tribes from the east. The fundamental two-way contract of feudalism, in which a lord protected his people in exchange for services, was the obvious way to structure a society that was heavily rural and agricultural where there were few towns and 'government' consisted of an agreement between the most powerful noblemen in the land. The obligation of the lord to protect his society containing the people who worked his land and generated his wealth in particular was desirable in such conditions. Just as the peasants were required to work on their lord's lands a certain number of days in the year, the lord himself was required to be a trained warrior, capable of turning out, ready and equipped to fight at the command of the overlord from whom he held his lands. If the lord had an extensive holding, his obligation would extend to the provision of a number of trained fighting men in addition to himself. The wealthier he was, the larger, better equipped and more highly skilled the force he provided had to be.

Every lord held his lands in fief from an overlord who, in turn, held his from a great and powerful noble family, who held their patrimony from the King. Each link in this chain had made an oath to the effect that his tenure of the land was conditional on the service he rendered to his overlord. The relationship was symbolized by the act of homage, in which the lord would kneel and place his hands between the hands of his overlord and swear an oath to serve him. In this way, the relationship between mounted cavalrymen would be between lord and vassal and so on downwards.

In theory, this system enabled a well-regulated kingdom to mobilize an efficient fighting force against a common enemy for the protection of society. However, constant feuding between lords meant destruction of agricultural production and instability. The tenth and eleventh-century legislation known as the Peace and Truce of God was an attempt by the Church to limit the sufferings caused by these wars. Interestingly, the Dukes of Normandy ruled in an autonomous fashion, ignoring their fealty to the French King, but used feudalism to bind their supporters to them, especially when they became Kings of England, there being a small Norman elite in a sea of English hostility.

The year-long research for the Domesday Book may well have been William I's method of establishing and pinning down the patterns of vassalage in his new lands. William had cleverly combined the European system of obtaining information from cohorts of men sworn to tell the truth with the English organization of shire and hundreds across which the survey was instituted. His sons continued this amalgamation of Norman and English methods, notably under Henry I.

However, in England, unlike Europe, the lord owed something other than knightly service. A lord was required to attend the courts of the hundred and shire, to administer customary law in these, the King's courts. A problem troubling the Conqueror's son, King William II Rufus, was that his powerful Norman barons owned land on both sides of the Channel and thus owed fealty to the Kings of England and France and sought to play one off against another, leading to baronial revolts. These ended when Duke Robert II of Normandy, William's elder brother, left on the First Crusade, pawning Normandy to Rufus for a loan of 10,000 marks.

Feudalism

Feudalism describes the political, military and social customs that maintained the power of a military elite. This power originated in the political collapse of the Carolingian Empire. When central power disintegrated, local lords fearing raids from Vikings, Hungarians and Saracens, protected the people in return for their labour and food supply. An alternative term is vassalage.

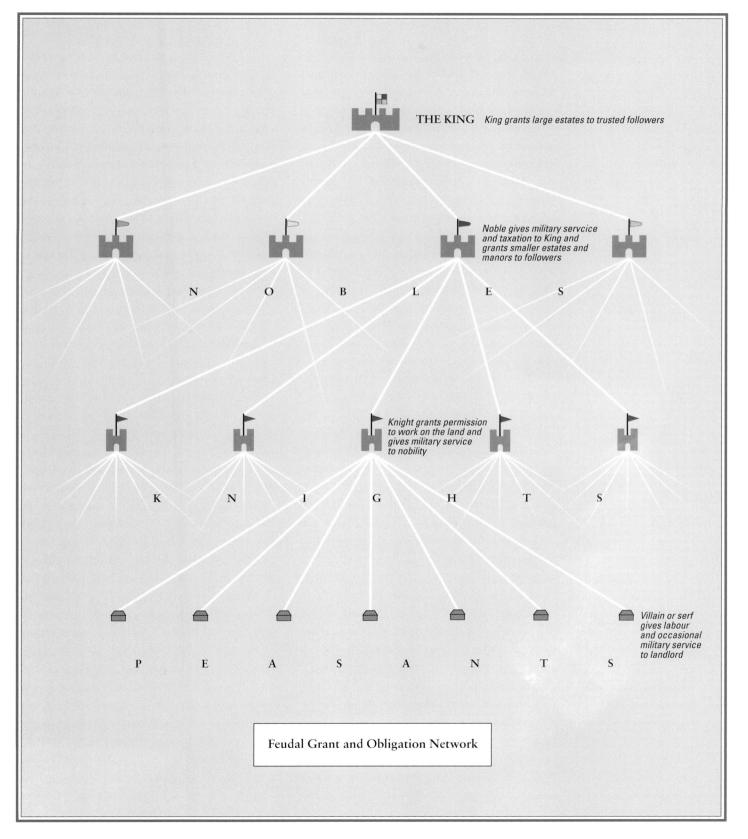

THE KING   *King grants large estates to trusted followers*

N   O   B   L   E   S

Noble gives military servcice and taxation to King and grants smaller estates and manors to followers

K   N   I   G   H   T   S

Knight grants permission to work on the land and gives military service to nobility

P   E   A   S   A   N   T   S

Villain or serf gives labour and occasional military service to landlord

Feudal Grant and Obligation Network

Holy Places and Pilgrimages

The Christian faith changed in nature during the medieval period. Earlier Christianity was based upon awe and mystery, not entirely suited to emotional human beings. Devotional practice altered with the divine judgemental Christ being replaced by the figure of Jesus suffering on the cross, bleeding from his wounds for the sake of humanity's sins. Medieval Christians became increasingly conscious of Christ's redemptive qualities, this taking a firm hold on their minds. People became contemplative of Christ's wounds, pain and suffering, believing that this would lead to salvation. This move towards an emotive portrayal of religion and faith helped draw in the Virgin Mary as a key figure of religious veneration. Medieval people thought she became the compassionate intercessor for sinners. Christianity became a religion of love, hope, compassion and mercy.

However, the average town dweller and peasant, knight and lady were superstitious, requiring something more than a God of love and reason. They needed tangible evidence of religion, especially in an era filled with hunger, pain, disease, rape, murder, war and premature death. Thus, God could be best accessed by praying at a roadside shrine, owning a relic or going on pilgrimage. An important place of pilgrimage was Walsingham in Norfolk. Legend claims that a noblewoman, Richeldis de Faverches, had a vision of the Virgin Mary (1061) who told her to build a replica of her house in Nazareth. This was completed and an alleged phial of the Virgin's Milk was a relic there. Even today, both the Roman Catholic and Anglican Churches celebrate Our Lady of Walsingham with annual cross-carrying pilgrimages.

Other important sites were the shrine of St. Thomas Beckett at Canterbury Cathedral, which houses his bones. St. Joseph of Arimathea is associated with bringing the Holy Grail to Britain and Glastonbury Abbey. He is now linked with the Arthurian legend cycle. Glastonbury Tor remains a place of pilgrimage while the area now also hosts an annual music concert. Other major pilgrimage sites were to venerate St. Hugh of Lincoln while Holy Isle, associated with early British Christianity, has a pilgrim's way, leading across the sands at low tide. Saints also existed to suit every illness or for every occupation. Dentists could offer their devotions to St. Apollonia, fishermen to St. Andrew, cobblers to St. Crispin, soldiers to St. Joan of Arc and bakers to St. Honoratus. All parts of the islands are home to religious and pilgrimage sites. Interestingly, in Cornwall, some people still make offerings at wells and springs to appease the old Celtic water gods but these places now all seem to be associated with Christian Celtic saints. Well water is often associated with healing, the Celts used immersion for curing insanity. Some important wells are St. Nun's, St. Keynes Holy Well and Madron Holy Well.

Despite this popular piety involving hundreds of saints and relics, often encouraged by the lower clergy, other aspects of religion were carefully regulated. The Church has guided religious practice carefully through the sacraments, which were strictly defined at the Fourth Lateran Council in 1215. Births are sanctified by baptism whereby the baptised, normally infants, are cleansed of the taint of original sin and are initiated into the Christian congregation, with the event being witnessed by part of that congregation. Confirmation takes place at puberty, a reaffirmation of church membership. Marriage sanctifies a Christian couple's union. At the end of life's journey, one can be given extreme unction and shriven, allowing the soul to travel to the next world easily. Throughout life one could take the sacraments, once a year according to Pope Innocent III. The sacraments made the Church the intermediary between God and people, giving the Church and priests tremendous power. At its most severe, the Church could cut off people from the Christian fellowship by excommunication.

The Holy Church

Medieval religion appealed visually. The path to God was shown in cathedrals, churches and pilgrimage sites. Skilled craftsmen carved decorations in wood and sculpted stone, creating magnificent sights. The monks penned music and composed songs providing another dimension of worship. Monasteries served communities by practising medicine, especially herbal, in attached hospitals.

The Holy Church
c. 1500

✝ Major pilgrimage site

YORK Archbishopric

⎯ Archdiocesan boundary

Bishopric

⎯ Diocesan boundary

Benedictine House

Cistercian, Carthusian or other new order house

Augustinian canon's house

Town with three or more friaries

Nunnery

University founded by 1500

Kirkwall   Orkney Islands

(to Orkney)

Shetland
Islands

Dornoch
Tain
St Duthus
Fortrose   Elgin
Beauly   Pluscarden

Moneymusk
Brechin
Aberdeen

ST ANDREWS

Lismore   Dunkeld

Iona   Elcho

Dunblane   **ST ANDREWS**
Stirling   Culross
Paisley   Dunfermline
Manuel   Haddington
Glasgow   Berwick
Coldstream
Melrose   Lindisfarne
Dryburgh   Kelso
Jedburgh

Lanercost   Newcastle
Sweetheart   Jarrow
Glenluce   St Ninian   Carlisle   St Cuthbert
Whithorn   Armathwaite   Durham
Shap   **YORK**   Whitby
Coverham   Jervaulx   Rievaulx
Cartmel   Fountains   Byland   Bridlington
Furness   Bolton   Ripon   Watton
Nun   **YORK**   Meaux
Monkton   St John
Hampole   Beverley
Nun Cotham

Macosquin
Raphoe   Derry   Connor
Clogher   Inch   Nendrum
Dromore   Downpatrick
Armagh   **ARMAGH**
St Germans
Rushen

Killala
Achonry   Boyle
Mayo   Elphin   Kilmore
Clare Island   Mellifont   Drogheda
TUAM   **TUAM**   Kells   Grace Dieu
Annaghdown   Athlone   Kilbeggan
Clonmacnoise   **DUBLIN**
Kilmacduagh   Clonfert   Kildare
Kilfenora   **DUBLIN**
St Patrick's
Purgatory
Annaghdown   Leighlin
Monasteranenagh   Kilkenny
Ardfert   Emly   Jerpoint   Glascarrig
Dingle   Abbeydorney   Inishlounaght   Ferns
Innisakken   Fermoy   Lismore   Bergerin
CASHEL   Youghal   Waterford   Wexford
Cork   Cloyne
Ross

ARMAGH

CASHEL

Limerick
Kilmacduagh

*Irish
Sea*

St Asaph   Norton
St Winifred   Vale Royal
Holywell   Sixhills
Bangor   Aberconwy   Chester   St Hugh
Clynnog Fawr   Lincoln   Boston
Beddgelert   Valle   St Guthlac
Crucis   Sempringham   Crowland
Bardsey   Garendon   Virgin Mary
Island   St Chad   Stamford   Walsingham
Llanllugan   Lichfield   Kings Lynn
Leicester   Sawtry   Markham   Norwich
Halesowen   Nuneaton   Ely   Bungay
Wigmore   Northampton   Thetford
Strata Florida   Cambridge   Bury St Edmunds
Hereford   Hailes
St David   St David's   Godstow   Dunstable   Markyate
Carmarthen   Monmouth   St   Waltham
Haverfordwest   Gloucester   Albans   Kilburn   St Bartholomew's
Kidwelly   St Teilo   Tintern   Cirencester   Oxford   Bermondsey
Margam   Llandaff   Reading   London   Rochester
Bristol   Waverley   **CANTERBURY**
St Joseph   Wells   Wilton   St Thomas
Glastonbury   Salisbury   Winchester   Battle
Taunton   Shaftesbury   Romsey   Lewes
Forde   Chichester
Christchurch
Launceston
Bodmin   Exeter
Buckfast
St Germans
St Michael
St Michael's
Mount

CANTERBURY

*North
Sea*

English Channel

0 ___ 100 km

0 ___ 100 miles

N

10° 8° 6° 4° 2° 0° 2°

58°

56°

54°

52°

50°

Borderlands

The death of the ineffective King Henry III ushered in the strong rule of Edward I (1272–1307) who learnt of his father's death while returning from Crusade. Arriving in England, Edward sought to restore the rights of kingship, weakened in the previous reign, and to secure his immediate borders.

Anglo-Norman power in Ireland was weakened, falling back from its greatest extent in the 1270s, where it spread to Galway and Co. Clare, to southeast of a line from Louth to Limerick. English weakness stemmed from a variety of factors. The thirteenth-century population explosion was slowing and peasants no longer had to seek empty land in Ireland, preferring to remain in England and Wales. Around the Pale of Settlement, Gaelic customs, language and hairstyles spread to Anglo-Norman settlers, causing them to blend with the indigenous populations. Irish military tactics copied the invaders, utilized mercenary kerns (*ceithernaigh*) and gallowglass

mercenaries from the Hebrides. Military success is exemplified by Aed O'Connor's victory over the Earl of Ulster at Athankip in 1270. The constant conflict between Irish chiefs and English settlers, meant that the region around Dublin was devastated as Irish lords won back land. Edward was more concerned with Wales and Scotland.

Meanwhile, in the Welsh lands, Llywelyn ap Gruffudd became the sole ruler of Gwynedd in 1255, spreading his power through Wales; the Treaty of Montgomery in 1267 pronouncing his status as overlord of all Wales. Llywelyn ignored summons to the English court on several occasions, refusing homage and thereby being declared a rebel.

Edward conducted two campaigns against the Welsh. Accordingly, Edward's first campaign used forces on land and by sea using a triple pincer movement on Gwynedd. English forces moved out of Carmarthen, Montgomery and Chester and, by 1277, all Llywelyn's Welsh allies

Beaumaris Castle

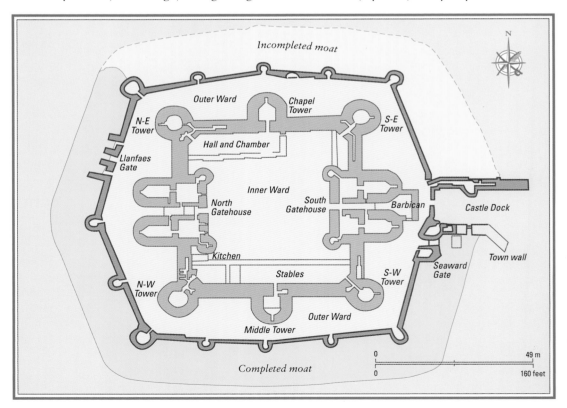

Beaumaris, in Anglesey, was Edward I's last castle to be built and remained unfinished as the funds were needed for campaigns in Scotland. The equivalent of some £8 million was spent in its construction. The population, previously living on the site, were evicted and sent to Newborough, on the other side of Anglesey.

were overrun or had defected. The English also moved into Gwynedd while, simultaneously, troops were landed on Anglesey by sea and this granary of Gwynedd was captured. The 1277 Treaty of Aberconwy fined Llywelyn £50,000, while the Welsh prince was coerced to London to pay homage. The English also built castles that circumscribed Gwynedd with an arc of fortifications in 1282, the whole military establishment being linked by routes through the forests.

The English presence in Wales was brutal and ignorant of Welsh law, with excessive use of privileges by English merchants in the new boroughs surrounding the new castles. Rebellion followed. Edward reprised his earlier strategy and Welsh resistance collapsed with Llywelyn's death. The 1284 Statute of Rhuddlan divided Gwynedd into the counties of Merionethshire, Anglesey, Flint and Caernarfonshire, while a Justiciar of West Wales was appointed to rule Cardiganshire and Carmarthenshire. Castle building began on a grand scale and, in 1301, Edward invested his son, Edward of Caernarfon, with the title of Prince of Wales.

Scotland delivered a potentially damaging problem. Alexander III had owed fealty to Edward but he died in 1286, leaving no male heir with the successor grandchild, the Maid of Norway, also dying. The nearest male claimant, John Balliol, became King, supported by Edward who saw John as a stooge and vehicle for pursuing English interests by undermining Scotland's independence. John rebelled, making an alliance with France. During 1296 saw the English invasion of France and the deposition of King John. William Wallace and Andrew of Moray responded, raising troops and defeating the English at the Battle of Stirling Bridge and leaving Wallace to rule Scotland as Guardian on behalf of John. Edward marched north defeating Wallace at the Battle of Falkirk in 1298, causing Wallace to resign his Guardian-ship. John Comyn and Robert the Bruce were appointed in his place, the intense hostility between the two men leading to another stage in Scotland's history and renewed English invasions.

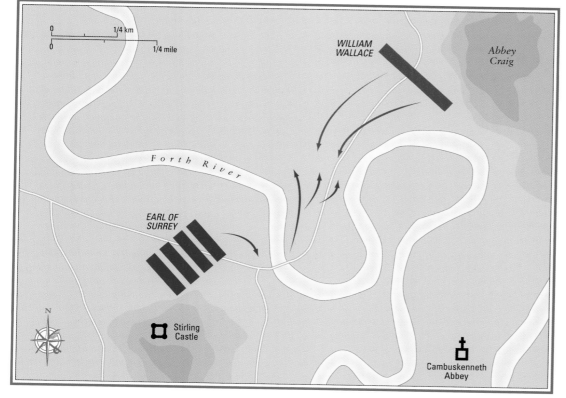

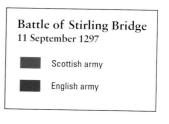

Battle of Stirling Bridge
11 September 1297

Scottish army

English army

The English defeat at Stirling demonstrated the value of Scots pikemen and that Edward I's conquest of Scotland was hollow. Yet, the Scots lost their other leader, Andrew of Moray.

The Woolsack – England's Wealth

The Woolsack is the seat used by the Lord Speaker in the House of Lords in the English Parliament. Originating in the fourteenth century, the sack symbolized the significance of the wool industry to the English economy and symbolized the country's enduring wealth. So important was wool to the well-being of England that, in 1294, Edward I, requiring money for a military campaign in Gascony, impounded all wool and leather, the staples of British export commerce. Sacks of wool could be redeemed on payment of 40 shillings per sack. This extortion worked because there were 50 different grades of wool with prices ranging from £9.37p to £2.50p, so redemption would generally ensure a profit.

Landowners, be they lords, abbots or bishops, reckoned their wealth in sheep and the Cistercian monastic order, in particular, became very important in wool production and in improving flocks by skilled sheep breeding. The Cistercian houses in Yorkshire became iconic in the English wool industry. Wool production benefited the crown, which levied a tax on all exported woolsacks. Sheep flocks roamed the hills from Cumbria and the Pennines, through the Cotswolds to the West Country, across to the South Downs, over to East Anglia. The best wool emanated from the Shropshire and Herefordshire borderlands with the second rank coming from Lindsey and the Cotswolds, However, Cornish wool was counted amongst the poorest.

The various wool markets welcomed Flemish and Italian merchants buying wool for cash. The wool was carried by pack-animals and taken to important ports of the day: Boston, London, Sandwich, Southampton, Hull, Lynn, Ipswich and Yarmouth. Ships would transport the sacks to Antwerp for distribution in Flanders while Genoese vessels sailed for Italy. Wool production was aided by a population explosion whereby poorer and more marginal land was brought into production and peasant labour could be bought very cheaply. Rural wage labour tended the flocks,

washed, combed and spun wool; and manned the fulling industry based on the banks of fast-flowing streams. Some ten per cent of English wool was used in home produced textiles.

Large landowners established trading connections direct with foreign cloth manufacturers, cutting out the middle men upon whom the peasants still relied. The peasant also wore wool-based fustians, which became the sign of the labouring man. The wealth accrued became so important that historians have suggested that Edward III waged war in Flanders to protect English wool interests from a French threat to the Low Countries. The Flemish burghers from the cloth-manufacturing towns certainly lobbied the English King for aid against their French liege lord. The Duke of Brabant and Count of Hainault were keen to help Edward with England's Flemish allies joined in the killing of French sailors who escaped from sinking ships as they staggered ashore at the Battle of Sluys in 1340.

When English export taxes became too high, more cloth was produced in England with the Midlands, Yorkshire and regions around Winchester becoming important. War in Flanders stimulated Flemish weavers to migrate to England, many finding homes in Norfolk and Suffolk. Others travelled to the West Country, the Cotswolds, the Yorkshire Dales and Cumbria. Weaving then developed and a flourishing cottage industry was developed. A supreme example of a medieval wool town is the current tourist destination of Lavenham in Suffolk, allegedly the fourteenth wealthiest town in England and famed for its pastel-shaded timber-framed medieval buildings.

The Black Death posed a problem for wool producers, with the wiping out up to half the population. Cheap labour was wiped out with one biological swoop, then peasants realised their labour was at a premium. Disease and famine retarded the wool industry, which only picked up with the large-scale development of the textile industry during the later medieval period, especially in the West Country.

English Export of Wool

Raw wool was traded in foreign markets through a centre called The Staple, variously at Bruges, Calais or Antwerp. Here, the wool's quality would be ascertained and graded. Prices were then fixed and customs duties collected for the English King. Eventually, woollen textiles made in England superseded the export of raw wool.

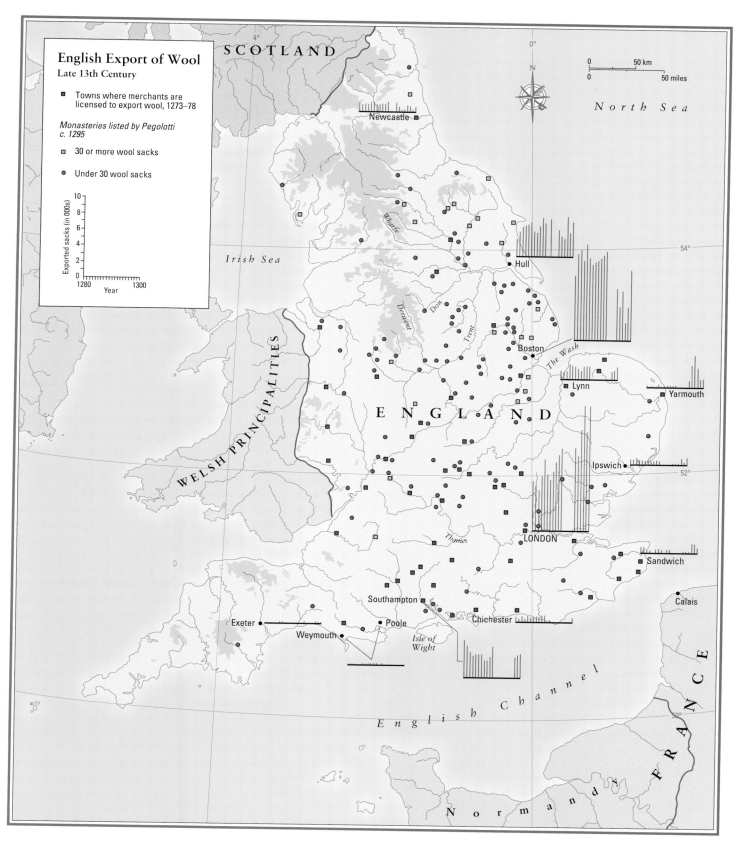

English Export of Wool

Late 13th Century

■ Towns where merchants are licensed to export wool, 1273–78

Monasteries listed by Pegolotti c. 1295

▫ 30 or more wool sacks

● Under 30 wool sacks

Exported sacks (in 000s)

Year

SCOTLAND

Newcastle

North Sea

Irish Sea

Hull

Boston

The Wash

Lynn

Yarmouth

E N G L A N D

Ipswich

WELSH PRINCIPALITIES

Thames

LONDON

Sandwich

Southampton

Chichester

Calais

Exeter

Poole

Weymouth

Isle of Wight

English Channel

FRANCE

Normandy

Wharfe

Derwent

Don

Trent

The Black Death

The Black Death, or bubonic and pneumonic plague, was first noticed in China in 1346 after which it surged along the Eurasian trade routes, appearing in Sicily and Italian ports in 1348. The sickness outwitted quarantine regulations and hit Western Europe in 1348. The disease bacillus is *Pasteurella pestis,* which lives in the blood of the flea, *Xenopsylla cheopis,* which, in turn, lives on the rat, *Rattus rattus.* When the plague killed the rats on shipboard, the fleas jumped on to the crew, who then infected the crowded seaports of Europe. During 1348–49, the plague spread rapidly in Europe killing between a fifth and a third of the populations of France and England, with similar losses in other European countries.

The disease killed nearly half of the clergy, savaging monasteries in particular. Twenty-four cannons of St. Andrews Cathedral were wiped out. So severe was the death rate that, including a recurrence ten years later, over 50 per cent of the Scots population had died by the early fifteenth century. As ploughmen and shepherds died, fallow land turned to waste, flocks roamed freely, crops rotted in the fields and the entire social fabric fractured, damaging the feudal system irrevocably. As people died, rents were not paid, money failed to circulate, slowing down economies. In the winter, famine affected the British Isles with whole villages wiped out.

The Black Death was transported to England from Gascony and arrived at Melcombe in Dorset, sweeping throughout the country in months. Winchester witnessed the death of 40 per cent of its population, some 4,000 souls. New cemeteries were opened in London but many bodies were tossed into the Thames, spoiling the water for those downstream. The population of England in 1400 was probably half of what it had been a century earlier with over 1,000 villages disappearing. One pleasant response to the plague has been the well dressings prevalent in the Peak District of Derbyshire and Staffordshire, where the purity of the water was held to have protected local populations.

In Ireland, the Black Death stalked Dublin, Drogheda and Dundalk, spreading to Louth and Meath before devastating Waterford and moving up the River Nore to Kilkenny. The major feature of the plague was that it flourished mainly in the ports and towns, infecting the English settlers more severely than the rural Irish. Little information exists covering the remoter parts of Ireland and even the *Annals of Ulster* makes only one lonely reference.

Medical knowledge was inadequate to deal with the problem. Jews became scapegoats with pogroms unleashed to such an extent that 2,000 Jews were butchered in Strasbourg and those of Frankfurt and Mainz were exterminated. Those who were born in between plague years died off more rapidly because they had no inbuilt immunity. During the first exposure, young women and children were especially vulnerable, which meant that populations took a long time to recover and sometimes declined; thankfully warfare diminished.

The impact of the Black Death was momentous in other ways. Trade slumped for a while. More fateful, the acreage of land under cultivation was reduced owing to the deaths of so many labourers. Many landowners were ruined. The labour shortage forced many landowners to substitute wages or money rents in place of feudal labour service in an attempt to keep tenants. Labourers knew that they could leave their masters and find work anywhere where new needy employers would protect them. Men left for the towns or went soldiering with Free Companies of mercenary soldiers. Social stratification broke down into a more fluid system.

As landowners could not pay their taxes, manor lands remained unploughed, while national resources and revenues shrank. The shortage of money cut military plans but a well-run war could return a profit as it supplied ransom money, always a good revenue. Fortunately for England, the capture of King John of France at Poitiers solved some of its cash flow problems.

The Black Death

The first symptoms of the Black Death were raised pustules in the armpit and groin. Fever, coma and death followed. The terrible disease killed so many people that mass burials became normal, such as that excavated at the site of the Royal Mint near the Tower of London. Most people thought the plague to be a symbol of God's anger.

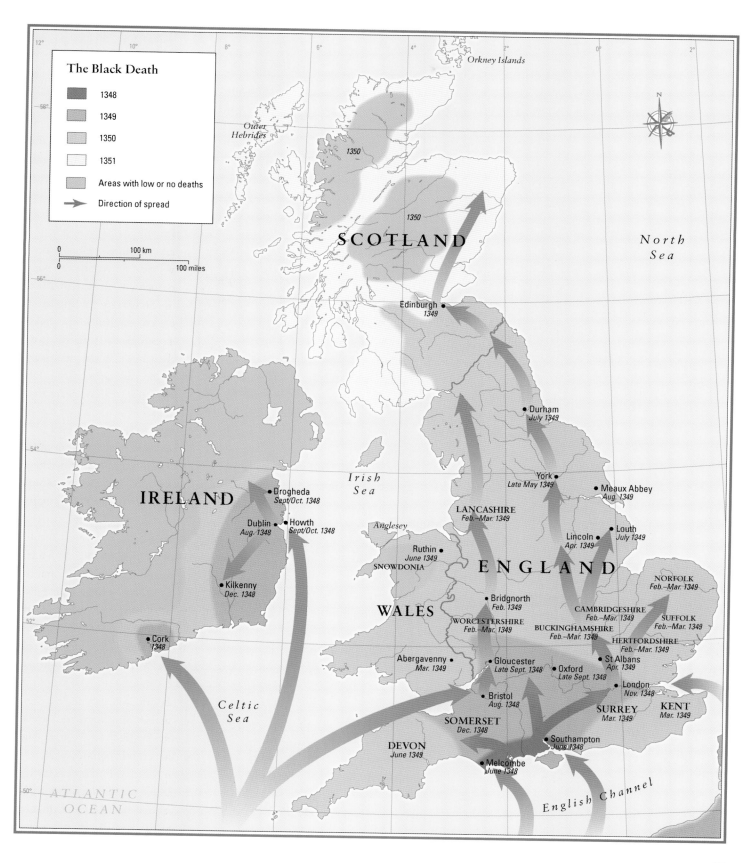

The Black Death

- 1348
- 1349
- 1350
- 1351
- Areas with low or no deaths
- → Direction of spread

0 — 100 km
0 — 100 miles

Orkney Islands

Outer Hebrides

1350

1350

SCOTLAND

Edinburgh
1349

North Sea

Irish Sea

• Durham
July 1349

• York
Late May 1349

• Meaux Abbey
Aug. 1349

IRELAND

• Drogheda
Sept/Oct. 1348

Dublin   • Howth
Aug. 1348   *Sept/Oct. 1348*

• Kilkenny
Dec. 1348

• Cork
1348

LANCASHIRE
Feb.–Mar. 1349

Anglesey

• Ruthin
June 1349
SNOWDONIA

WALES

• Lincoln
Apr. 1349

• Louth
July 1349

E N G L A N D

NORFOLK
Feb.–Mar. 1349

• Bridgnorth
Feb. 1349

WORCESTERSHIRE
Feb.–Mar. 1349

CAMBRIDGESHIRE
Feb.–Mar. 1349

SUFFOLK
Feb.–Mar. 1349

BUCKINGHAMSHIRE
Feb.–Mar. 1349

HERTFORDSHIRE
Feb.–Mar. 1349

• Abergavenny
Mar. 1349

• Gloucester
Late Sept. 1348

• Oxford
Late Sept. 1348

• St Albans
Apr. 1349

• London
Nov. 1348

• Bristol
Aug. 1348

Celtic Sea

SURREY
Mar. 1349

KENT
Mar. 1349

SOMERSET
Dec. 1348

• Southampton
June 1348

DEVON
June 1349

• Melcombe
June 1348

ATLANTIC OCEAN

English Channel

The Reign of Edward I

Chepstow Castle was built by William fitz Osbern to secure the border or March between England and Wales. Constructed along a narrow limestone promontory above the River Wye, the castle could be supplied by ship with goods hauled up by rope and crane.

Plan of Chepstow Castle

Apart from military campaigns in Wales, Scotland and France, the reign of King Edward I (1272–1307) is associated with the evolution of an English Parliament. Edward was significant because he developed and continued existing trends in generating rationality in the royal administration, common law and representation of the people.

Before 1272, Edward had observed his enemy, Simon de Montfort, summoning a great council that included not just the usual great lords but two knights from each shire, and two burghers or merchants from each town. The last two categories had occasionally been called before but now would be called more often, and eventually always. Edward's reign witnessed a constant tinkering with who should attend Parliament, in every permutation of class, ensuring that this assembly participated in royal legislation. The innovation lay in the King-making law rather than interpreting customary law, Thus, Edward would manipulate a Parliament to back him, especially in granting taxes, thereby gaining legitimacy and 'entrapping' the participants. As a result, Parliament was a royal tool bolstering but not limiting monarchy.

Like medieval kings elsewhere, Edward constantly travelled around his realm but his Chancery and Exchequer – the secretariat and treasury – remained at Westminster, while his council and household journeyed with him. The council was his peripatetic judiciary and advisors, while the household became a miniature government in motion. The King only heard very important cases, the remainder being reserved for itinerant judges or a variety of courts in the capital, all staffed by professional lawyers or accountants in the treasury. In conclusion, Edward created a complex and professional royal administration, centralizing law, while stimulating a Parliament that could build consensus through discussion and consultation. Although feudalism continued in being, it was

tempered by modernizing tendencies, displaying the seeds of an early democracy.

Edward's foreign policy aims were always ambitious and required large cash injections to succeed. The Jews were taxed, asset stripped, and expelled to the delight of the Exchequer. Elsewhere, taxes were extracted from the wool industry but also from the important wine trade. English Gascony in France, with its port at Bordeaux, exported wine in vast quantities, England being the largest market. Hence, both Henry III and Edward I were determined to hang on to Gascony and augment their territories. Saintonge, the Agenais and Quercy were acquired in 1279 under the Treaty of Amiens just as lands in the three dioceses of Limoges, Perigueux, and Cahors had been gained in 1259. Unfortunately, the King of France retained domains in Edward's territory and this eventually led to war after Edward's death. Edward was promised lands worth £750 for his rights in Quercy.

Meanwhile, Edward had founded large numbers of bastides in Gascony; these fortified new towns defended Edward's interests and their success enabled the concept to travel to Wales to provide domiciles for the Englishry. The importance of the French possessions can be appreciated by the revenue generated. In 1306–07, the monarch's revenue from the Agenais was some £6,000, 30 per cent of the total Gascon taxes. Also, in the 1240s, revenue from Gascony was estimated at £300 but this rose to nearly £17,000 in 1306–07. The relationship between England and France was wine to England and English merchandize to Gascony. No wonder that Edward sent armies to Gascony in 1294 and 1296.

Elsewhere, Scots politics was turned inside out. Exiled King John Balliol's chief supporter, John Comyn, the Red Comyn of Badenoch, was murdered by Robert the Bruce, Earl of Carrick, in Greyfriars Kirk in Dumfries. Balliol supporters, hitherto Scots patriots, turned against Bruce by joining the English, whereas Bruce, who had

Wales and the March

- ——— Border of shires created by Edward I c. 1284
- ——— Approximate greatest extent of Llewellyn Principality c. 1267
- ——— Border with England
- Edwardian castle
- Other castle
- *LACY* Marcher Lords
- Principality of Gwynedd
- Other Welsh lands
- Area under Marcher Lords
- England

In 1277, Edward I launched a major campaign into northern Welsh territories by land and sea. His ruthless tactics eventually defeated Welsh resistance. He began a scheme of castle building which circumscribed Gwynedd. This, together with other areas of west Wales, became Edward's Principality of Wales which was united to the English crown in 1284, when Edward created a local ruling structure based on new 'counties'. Other parts of the county were administered by the Marcher Lords. Edward made his eldest son, Edward, Prince of Wales, the first heir to the English throne to bear this title.

ANGLESEY
GWYNEDD
Beaumaris
Bangor
CARNARVON
Caernarfon
Criccieth
Dolwyddelan
Deganwy
Conway
Dyserth
Rhuddlan
St Asaph
Denbigh
LACY
Ruthin
FLINT
Mold
WARENNE
Chester
COUNTY PALATINE OF CHESTER
Halton
Hawarden
Malpas
FLINT
Vaille Crucis
Chirk
FITZ ALAN
Oswestry
MERIONETH
Harlech
Bere
POWYS
Welshpool
Montgomery
Shrewsbury
Acton Burnell
ENGLAND
Cardigan Bay
Aberystwyth
Llanbadarn Fawr
MORTIMER
Clun
Stockesay
Ludlow
Wigmore
Radnor
Weobley
CARDIGAN
Cardigan
DEHEUBARTH
CARMARTHEN
Llandovery
Builth
Hay
BRYCHEINIOG
Brecon
Pipton
Llantony
Hereford
BOHUN
Grosmont
Goodrich
St. Davids
Carmarthen
Dynevor
Crickhowell
LANCASTER
Skenfrith
White Castle
Haverfordwest
Narberth
VALENCE
Kidwelly
BRAOSE
Swansea
Neath
Margam
CLARE
MORGANNWG
BOHUN
Abergavenny
CLARE
GHENT
Usk
Caerleon
BIGOD
Newport
Chepstow
Pembroke
Manorbier
Caerphilly
Llandaff
Cardiff
Bristol

0   20 km
0   20 miles

N

Edward I's Campaigns in Scotland

During Edward I's campaigns in Scotland, each side sought to capture Stirling Castle, built on a rock, and guarding the farthest downstream crossing of the Forth. The castle changed hands several times.

Stirling Castle

This has been a fortified site since Pictish times. It has remained possibly the most militarily-important site in Scotland.

Plan of Stirling Castle

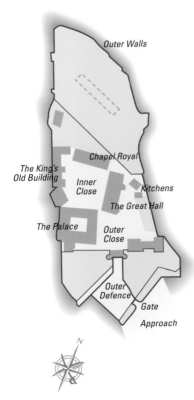

Outer Walls

Chapel Royal

The King's Old Building

Inner Close

Kitchens

The Great Hall

The Palace

Outer Close

Outer Defence

Gate

Approach

N

helped the English hunt down Wallace, became the icon of the fight for Scots independence.

Robert the Bruce was crowned King of Scotland in March 1306. Edward I sent the Earl of Pembroke after him and he successfully beat Robert at Methven but later lost to him at Loudon Hill and Glen Trool in 1307. Bruce's other enemy was the family of Red Comyn, now led by the Earl of Buchan. The latter was defeated at Slioch in 1307 and Barra in 1308 and the MacDougalls, cousins to Comyn, were trounced at the Pass of Brander in 1308.

Meanwhile, Edward I had died in July 1307, leaving a Scots' postscript to his lazy, shiftless son, Edward II. At this point, Scots castles were still mainly in English hands and a determined English campaign could have unseated Bruce, who was still opposed by many Scots. Edward II vacillated, allowing Robert and his brother to win the southwest leaving only a few castles in English control. By the end of 1308, Bruce ruled most of Scotland north of the Tay and much of Fife by early 1309. Edward retaliated in 1310 with an invasion which was so hampered by the Scots' scorched earth policy that the English retreated to Berwick.

Bruce next raided England savaging Coquetdale and Redesdale, even threatening Durham. The Northumbrians paid Bruce £2,000 to not damage their county further. In 1313, raids surged into Tyndale, Durham was marauded, and Hartlepool looted. This time, Bruce was given £10,000 to leave. Elsewhere, Dundee Castle was taken and all the English castles in the south-west. The royal castles were now reduced: Perth, Dumfries, Lochnaben, Roxburgh, Edinburgh and Linlithgow. However, the key castle at Stirling remained under the command of English Sir Thomas Mowbray, who promised to surrender the castle if he was not relieved by June 1314.

Edward II was stirred into activity deploying a large invasion force that marched, virtually unopposed, from Wark to Stirling where Bruce was

waiting at Bannockburn. An English detachment, some 700 strong, attacked and fell foul of two schiltrons who killed most of them. Next day, the English charged, crashed into the schiltrons, and were pushed back into marshy ground. The English archers were dispersed by the Scots cavalry as their own Scots cavalry was crushed by pikes. The camp followers also entered the fray, pulling men off their horses before killing them. The English broke and fled. The losses that day are unknown but the English probably lost 200 knights and thousands of infantry. Some seventy knights were captured including two Earls.

The Bruce now launched raids into England, incinerating Appleby and Durham and looting Hartlepool again. He defeated a force at Myton-on-Swale in 1319, captured Berwick and torched Northallerton, Boroughbridge and Knaresborough. In 1322, Bruce avoided an English invasion force and raided through Allerdale, burning Lancaster and Preston. The English returned towards Yorkshire where Bruce met them near Byland Abbey. The Earl of Moray's forlorn hope pinned down the English, while Bruce sent a large detachment of Highlanders over surrounding crags and these mountain men then launched an outflanking attack that totally defeated the English. Edward II took no part in the battle "being ever chicken-hearted and luckless in war", as stated in the *Lanercost Chronicle*. In September 1327, Edward II was murdered at Berkely Castle, the crown being taken by the young Edward III who recognized Robert the Bruce as the King of Scotland. On 1 March 1323, a thirteen-year truce was agreed. In 1329, Robert died of leprosy.

To summarize, Edward I bled the country of wealth for his wars, created an efficient administration, held on to Gascony and subdued Wales. However, his Scots ventures were turned to nothing, by his son, a total poltroon influenced by favourites, unstable politically, and a Plantagenet blot on the landscape between Edwards I and III.

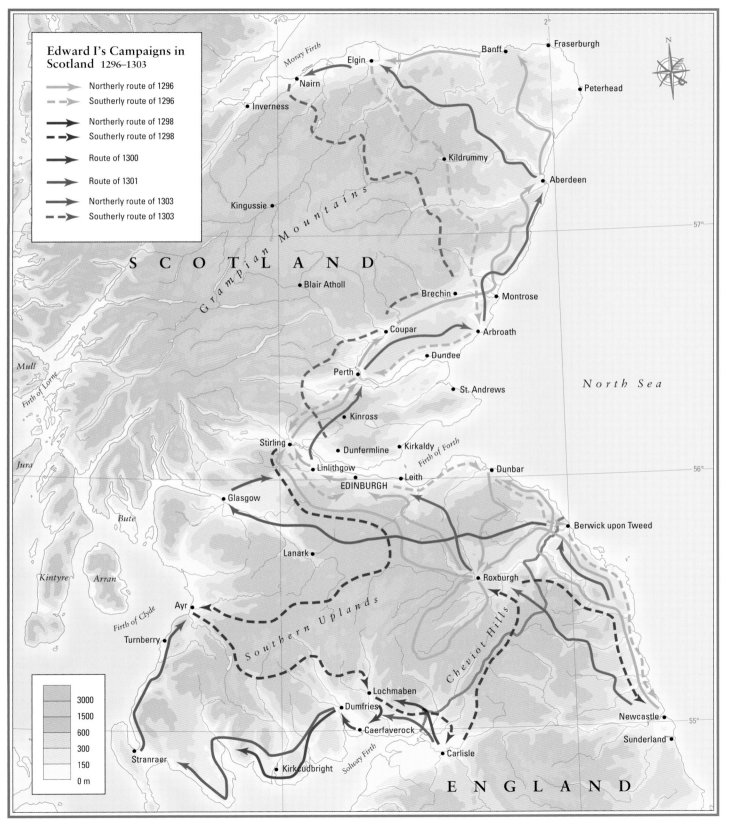

Edward I's Campaigns in
Scotland 1296–1303

→ Northerly route of 1296
⇢ Southerly route of 1296
→ Northerly route of 1298
⇢ Southerly route of 1298
→ Route of 1300
→ Route of 1301
→ Northerly route of 1303
⇢ Southerly route of 1303

3000
1500
600
300
150
0 m

SCOTLAND
Grampian Mountains
Moray Firth
Fraserburgh
Banff
Elgin
Nairn
Inverness
Peterhead
Kildrummy
Kingussie
Aberdeen
Blair Atholl
Brechin
Montrose
Coupar
Arbroath
Dundee
Perth
St. Andrews
Kinross
Stirling
Dunfermline
Kirkaldy
Linlithgow
Leith
EDINBURGH
Dunbar
Firth of Forth
North Sea
Glasgow
Berwick upon Tweed
Lanark
Roxburgh
Ayr
Southern Uplands
Cheviot Hills
Turnberry
Lochmaben
Dumfries
Caerfaverock
Newcastle
Stranraer
Kirkcudbright
Carlisle
Sunderland
Solway Firth
ENGLAND
Mull
Firth of Lorne
Jura
Bute
Kintyre
Arran
Firth of Clyde

57°
56°
55°
2°
4°

N

Usurper: Richard II and Bolingbroke

When Richard II acceded to the throne in 1377, he faced an England bedevilled by the aftermath of the Black Death and its social and economic repercussions. Ploughmen and labourers were in such demand that they formed unions of labourers to safeguard their interests against landlords who wished to revive the old ties of forced labour and serfdom. This domestic upheaval occurred in the aftermath of Edward III's dotage in which campaigns in France were profitless, French ships were raiding the south coast and maritime trade was suffering as control of the Channel was lost. Taxation still lay heavily upon those surviving the plague and the parliamentary Commons, shire knights and merchants questioned the skill of leading politicians and forced them from their posts in 1371.

The year 1376 witnessed the 'Good Parliament' demanding accountability of parliamentary Lords and held them publicly responsible. In this scenario began the Peasants' Revolt, led by Wat Tyler and John Ball. Manorial and taxation records were burnt and members of the King's Council beheaded. The insurrection spread from the east and southeast (which had the worst death-rate from the plague) to townspeople and Londoners. The rebels converged on London where the young King confronted their leaders. Tyler was killed, the rebels lost their nerve and finally dispersed. Authority regained its nerve and government vengeance followed.

The country now entered a period of fragmentation of the ruling class, which allowed a self-willed King to impose an unpopular government and engage in conspicuous royal consumption. In 1387, five great lords (Warwick, Arundel, Gloucester, Bolingbroke and Mowbray), the Lords Appellant, pointed the finger of treason at key figures of the royal administration. They convoked the Merciless Parliament after defeating royalist forces at Radcot Bridge in 1387, forcing the King to submit. The King was not deposed, thus allowing Richard to reassert his authority in 1389. He restored his sympathisers and bolstered his power by establishing a power base in Ireland and marrying the six-year-old Isabelle of Valois, the marriage contract providing French support against English domestic opponents of the King.

The five Lords Appellant were either exiled, executed or murdered, with Bolingbroke, son of John of Gaunt, a son of Edward III, fleeing to France. In 1399, Richard returned to Ireland after disinheriting his cousin, Bolingbroke, whose father had just died, leaving him huge domains in Lancashire and lands all over the north of England. This was a threat to every landowner in the country. Bolingbroke, now Henry of Lancaster, returned, landing at Ravenspur in Yorkshire. Richard returned via Wales but failed to raise forces that would now confront a Henry supported by most important feudal families. He submitted to Henry at Flint Castle, was deposed and died in captivity in 1400, perhaps starved to death.

Henry IV Lancaster spent the rest of his reign fighting to retain his usurped crown. The Scots immediately reneged on their truce with England, invading Earl Henry Percy's Northumberland. In 1402, a Scots army was decimated by Percy at Homildon Hill, English archers performing their normal slaughtering function. Hostility between the Percies and Henry broke out in 1403 over monies spent in royal service and over ransoms of prisoners taken at Homildon Hill. Northumberland's son, 'Hotspur', raised a rebellion and was defeated and killed near Shrewsbury. A further outbreak in the north of England ended in 1405 with the execution of the Scrope, Archbishop of York. These rebellions had been accompanied by a plot with Owain Glyndŵr of Wales, which envisaged dividing England between Owain, the Percies and Mortimer, another heir of Edward III. This Welsh conflict lasted until 1412 when Glyndŵr disappeared. This usurpation commenced the Wars of the Roses, only ended when Henry Tudor defeated Richard III at Bosworth Field in 1485.

British Isles, 1399–1488

The usurpation by Henry of Lancaster was followed by numerous plots against him. The conflict with Henry Percy (Hotspur) ended at the Battle of Shrewsbury in 1403 with Hotspur's death. His father continued the struggle but was killed at the Battle of Bramham Moor in 1408. This eradicated Welsh Owain Glyndŵr's last English ally.

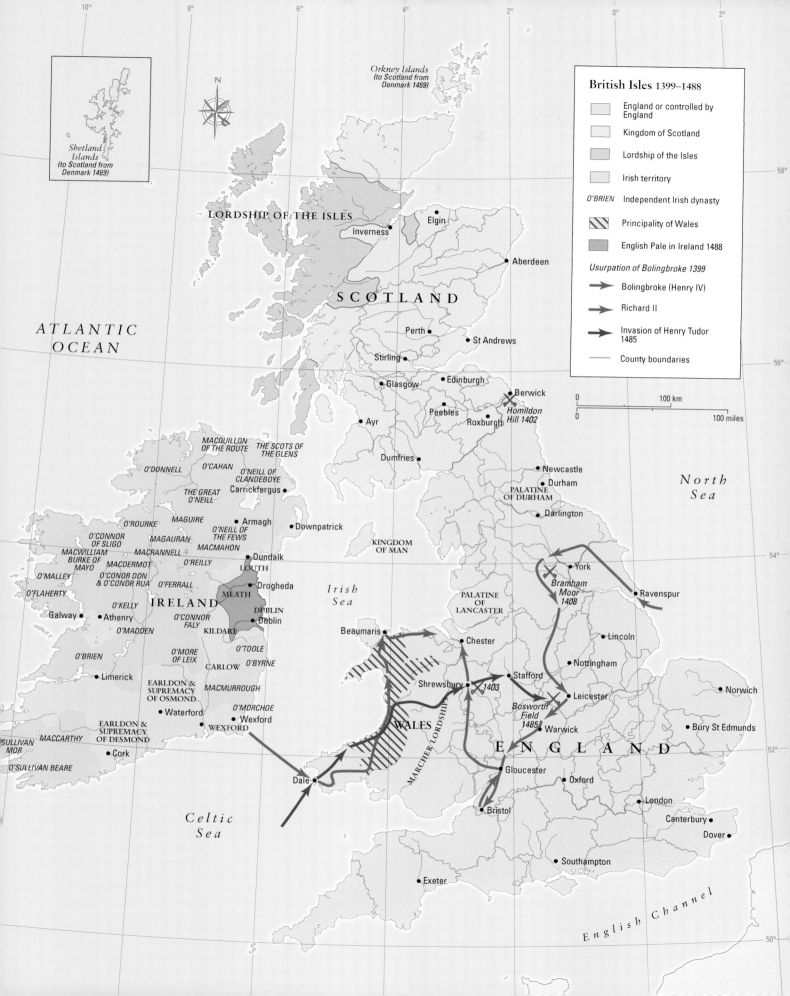

10° 8° 6° 4° 2° 0° 2°

Shetland Islands
(to Scotland from Denmark 1469)

ATLANTIC OCEAN

Orkney Islands
(to Scotland from Denmark 1469)

LORDSHIP OF THE ISLES

Elgin

Inverness

Aberdeen

SCOTLAND

Perth
St Andrews

Stirling

Glasgow · Edinburgh

Ayr
Peebles
Berwick
Roxburgh · Homildon Hill 1402

Dumfries

Newcastle
Durham
PALATINE OF DURHAM
Darlington

MACQUILLON OF THE ROUTE
THE SCOTS OF THE GLENS
O'DONNELL
O'CAHAN
O'NEILL OF CLANDEBOYE
THE GREAT O'NEILL
Carrickfergus

O'ROURKE
MAGUIRE
Armagh · Downpatrick
MAGAURAN
O'NEILL OF THE FEWS
MACMAHON
O'CONNOR OF SLIGO
MACWILLIAM BURKE OF MAYO
MACRANNELL
MACDERMOT
O'REILLY
Dundalk
LOUTH
O'CONOR DON & O'CONOR RUA
O'FERRALL
Drogheda
O'MALLEY
O'KELLY
MEATH
O'FLAHERTY
IRELAND
O'CONNOR FALY
DUBLIN
Galway · Athenry
Dublin
O'MADDEN
KILDARE
O'BRIEN
O'MORE OF LEIX
O'TOOLE
O'BYRNE
Limerick
CARLOW
EARLDON & SUPREMACY OF OSMOND
MACMURROUGH
Waterford
O'MORCHOE
MACCARTHY
EARLDON & SUPREMACY OF DESMOND
Wexford
WEXFORD
SULLIVAN MOR
O'SULLIVAN BEARE
Cork

KINGDOM OF MAN

Irish Sea

KINGDOM OF MAN

PALATINE OF LANCASTER

Beaumaris
Chester
WALES
Shrewsbury · 1403
Stafford
MARCHER LORDSHIP
Bosworth Field 1485
Warwick
ENGLAND
Gloucester
Oxford
Bristol

York
Bramham Moor 1408
Ravenspur
Lincoln
Nottingham
Leicester
Norwich
Bury St Edmunds

London
Canterbury
Dover

Southampton

Exeter

Dale

Celtic Sea

English Channel

North Sea

N

0   100 km
0   100 miles

58°
56°
54°
52°
50°

The Hundred Years' War

Château Gaillard

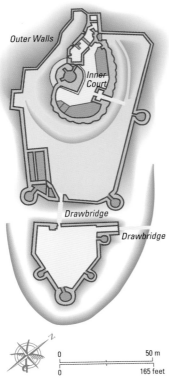

Outer Walls

Inner Court

Drawbridge

Drawbridge

0   50 m

0   165 feet

The Hundred Years' War began in 1337 and lasted until 1453. It involved patches of vicious warfare with long periods of peace. The wars sapped the wealth out of the English state and ravaged France, the major arena. The war was occasioned by no large issue but rather a series of small causes combining to see English armies despatched across the Channel to wreak havoc upon French lands.

In some ways, the war was a continuation of previous hostilities involving the loss of most of the Angevin Empire. England's continued claims to French territory, even though only Gascony remained to England, was reinforced by a disagreement over the French royal succession began in 1328. Charles IV died without issue leaving Edward III with the best claim through his mother but Philippe of Valois laid claim through his father. Fearful of an English monarch, the French passed a law allowing inheritance to the throne only through a man. The Valois became Philippe VI and Edward used the situation as a *casus belli* in 1337. In reality, Edward wished to protect and expand the trade in English textiles and wool for Bordeaux wine.

In May 1337, Philippe formally confiscated Aquitaine, sending troops across the border to seize his vassal, Edward's, castles. The threat to Aquitaine trade was serious; commerce was also pertinent to Flanders, coveted by Philippe of France, the English wool trade with Flanders forming the staple of English exports. France desired to turn a political lordship over Flanders into an assault on English economic dominion there.

Initial English attacks achieved nothing territorial despite Edward's naval victory at the Battle of Sluys in 1340. However, a French invasion was now rendered impossible but a succession war in Brittany allowed England to intervene and win a base in that duchy. Eventually, in other campaigns, the English archers and their war-bows devastated French forces in crushing English victories at Crécy in 1346 and Poitiers in 1356. However, the French mounted a campaign led by the Eagle of Brittany, Betrand du Guesclin, which avoided pitched battles and instead engaged in skirmishes and attrition, gradually pushing back the English to minor outposts defending Bordeaux and Calais.

A virtual truce extended through the reigns of Kings Richard II and Henry IV but English eagerness for foreign adventures recommenced with the succession of Henry V (1413–22). His extraordinary victory over the French at Agincourt in 1415 won him Normandy, Brittany, Maine and the Champagne, and the hand of a French princess. His unexpected death led to the reign of his feckless son, Henry VI, who managed to lose France. The career of St. Joan of Arc witnessed a revival of French fortunes and the coronation of Charles VII.

In 1449, the French invaded Normandy, clearing the duchy of the English by 1450. French forces then assaulted Gascony, this being lost to England by 1453, a telling blow since these lands had been held by the English from the twelfth century. French victories at Formigny in 1450 and at Castillon in 1453, the latter won with the use of French cannon, ensured that England was powerless in France, apart from the remnant of Calais. By 1471, Henry VI had lost his English realm too in dynastic clashes with the House of York and he was murdered later that year in the Tower of London.

In a final burst of ambition, Edward IV invaded France in 1475, only advancing as far as Amiens before being bought off with a lump sum and an annual payment that enabled him to be virtually independent of Parliamentary finance. In 1492, Henry VII acted likewise, his annual stipend being one fifth of crown revenues. Finally, in 1558, the French retook a neglected Calais, much to the dismay of the English Queen, Mary I.

War of the Roses
1455—85

Area supporting the House of Lancaster

Area supporting the House of York

GREY Family supporting the House of Lancaster

GREY Family supporting the House of York

✗ Battle sites with dates

SCOTLAND

PERCY

✗ Hedgeley
1464 Moor

PERCY

DACRE

✗ Hexham
1464 • Durham

PERCY

CLIFFORD

TUDOR

Richmond • *NEVILLE*

BEAUFORT

Isle of Man

North Sea

• Scarborough

MOWBRAY

Lancaster • Ripon •

CLIFFORD York •

Irish Sea

PERCY 54°

Towton ✗ *1461*

• Hull

Wakefield ✗ *1460*

• Ravenspur

Isle of Anglesey

Derwent *Don*

Trent • Lincoln

TALBOT

• Chester

GREY

Blore Heath ✗ *Trent* ✗ Stoke on Trent ✗ Stoke Field *1487*

1459 *1487*

FITZALAN *STAFFORD*

The Wash

Shrewsbury • *MOWBRAY* *STAFFORD* ✗ Stamford

• Lynn *MOWBRAY* • Norwich

TALBOT ✗ Bosworth Losecote Field

Ludlow • *1485* *1470*

Gloucester ✗ • Lutterworth • Ely • Bury St Edmunds

Warwick ✗ *1460* ✗ Northampton *DE LA POLE*

Mortimer's Cross ✗ *STAFFORD* ✗ Edgecote Field *TIPTOFT*

1461 *1469*

✗ *1471* *ENGLAND* 52°

NEVILLE • Tewkesbury *VERE* *BOURCHIER*

Milford Haven • *TUDOR* Gloucester • Oxford • St Albans ✗ *1455*

• Pembroke Barnet ✗ *1471*

STAFFORD ● LONDON

BEAUFORT • Bristol • Canterbury

• Bath *STAFFORD* • Dover

Thames

Salisbury • *MOWBRAY*

COURTENAY • Winchester

FITZALAN

• Southampton • Hastings

• Exeter • Dorchester *Isle of Wight*

• Launceston *COURTENAY*

Plymouth • • Dartmouth

English Channel 50°

FRANCE

Channel Islands

N

0 ____ 50 km
0 ____ 50 miles

95

The War of the Roses

The Wars of the Roses began with the First Battle of St. Albans in 1455 and ended at Bosworth Field in 1485, with a postscript at Stoke Field in 1487. Fought between the competing houses of Lancaster and York, the wars did not rage through the entirety of this period; in fact, the actual campaigning lasted barely two years. Shakespeare hyped up the bloodletting and gore in his plays but what occurred were brief outbreaks of aggression and violence in a normally peaceful society. Armies were small and casualties light, with certain families suffering from summary executions. The notion of medieval sieges, vast battles and a devastated countryside simply did not happen. Most lords seemed quite happy to endure an incompetent King, Henry VI, rather than rebel.

Perhaps, the birth of the wars occurred when Henry Bolingbroke usurped the crown from Richard II. However, England became used to Henry IV's (1399–1413) rule and was proud of Henry V (1413–22) seizing vast chunks of northern France. However, that monarch's early death led to the reign of the incompetent and weak-minded Henry VI (1422–61). His ineffectual rule presided over the loss of territories in France and failure to curb lords building up private armies and engaging in local warfare. His incompetence in controlling greedy aristocratic families, and misunderstanding of the issues of the poor was related in Jack Cade's Kentish revolt in 1450. Henry VI dissolved into a catatonic state at the loss of Bordeaux in 1453, leaving him incapable of communication for more than a year.

The wars can be divided into three separate conflicts. The first lasted from 1455–61, wherein Richard Duke of York acted as the country's Protector during the King's madness, showing soundness in administration and policy making. Henry's recovery saw York pushed aside leading him to raise a rebellion in fear that his life and property were threatened. Supported by the earls of Salisbury and Warwick, he defeated the Lancastrians at the First Battle of St. Albans but was forced to flee the country in 1459. York returned from exile and faced the combined forces of the heirs of Lancastrians killed at St. Albans with the support of Margaret of Anjou, the King's wife. The Yorkists were defeated at Wakefield in 1460 and Richard was killed. The Earl of March, Richard's eldest son, responded by defeating Welsh Lancastrian forces at Mortimer's Cross and their main army at Towton in 1461. Henry was deposed and March crowned as Edward IV (1461–83).

The second war witnessed the Earl of Warwick, jealous that Edward needed his advice less now he was King, sulking and making cause with Edward's treacherous brother, the Duke of Clarence. Defeats at Edgecote in 1469 and Lose-Coat Field in 1470 saw Warwick's flight to France where he was enticed by King Louis XI, the Spider King, to join with Margaret of Anjou, his former enemy. They combined and, with French troops, landed in England and pushed Edward into exile. He returned quickly and destroyed Warwick at Barnet in 1471, eradicating the whole Lancastrian house at Tewkesbury in 1471.

Edward died unexpectedly, maybe from appendicitis, in April 1493. This situation led his brother, Richard of Gloucester, to seize the legitimate heirs, eliminate all opposition and declare Edward's marriage to Elizabeth Woodville illegal. The two Woodville princes vanished and Gloucester was crowned Richard III. A rebellion by Buckingham was crushed and supporters persecuted. The Yorkists were split and Richard's support diminished. A new Lancastrian pretender was found, Henry Tudor, Earl of Richmond, a descendent of Edward III. He landed in Wales, raised an army, marched and defeated Richard at Bosworth Field in 1485. Crowned as Henry VII, Tudor married Elizabeth, Edward VI's eldest daughter, thereby uniting the feuding houses.

War of the Roses
The dismissal of Richard of York from the King's Council, and dictatorial powers being assumed by Queen Margaret and the Duke of Somerset, prompted a revolt by Richard and his adherents. England was thrown into a 30-year period of alternating violence, political manoeuvring and wildly-fluctuating personal fortunes.

War of the Roses
1455—85

Area supporting the House of Lancaster

Area supporting the House of York

GREY Family supporting the House of Lancaster

GREY Family supporting the House of York

Battle sites with dates

SCOTLAND

Hedgeley Moor
1464

Hexham
1464

Durham

PERCY

DACRE

PERCY

CLIFFORD

TUDOR

NEVILLE

Richmond

BEAUFORT

Lancaster

Ripon

CLIFFORD

York

Towton *1461*

Wakefield *1460*

Hull

MOWBRAY

PERCY

Scarborough

Ravenspur

North Sea

Isle of Man

Irish Sea

Isle of Anglesey

Chester

GREY

Blore Heath *1459*

FITZALAN

Shrewsbury

STAFFORD

Stoke on Trent *1487*

Stoke Field *1487*

TALBOT

MOWBRAY

STAFFORD

Stamford

Losecote Field *1470*

Lynn

MOWBRAY

Norwich

TALBOT

Ludlow

Bosworth *1485*

Lutterworth

Mortimer's Cross *1461*

STAFFORD

Gloucester

Warwick

1460

Northampton

Edgecote Field *1469*

Ely

TIPTOFT

DE LA POLE

Bury St Edmunds

1471

Tewkesbury

ENGLAND

VERE

BOURCHIER

TUDOR

Milford Haven

Pembroke

NEVILLE

STAFFORD

Gloucester

Oxford

St Albans *1455*

Barnet *1471*

LONDON

Canterbury

Dover

BEAUFORT

Bristol

Bath

Thames

STAFFORD

Winchester

FITZALAN

Southampton

MOWBRAY

Salisbury

Hastings

COURTENAY

Exeter

Dorchester

Isle of Wight

Launceston

COURTENAY

Plymouth

Dartmouth

English Channel

FRANCE

Channel Islands

Lincoln

Derwent

Don

Trent

The Wash

97

Revolts and Risings

Henry Tudor's victory at the Battle of Bosworth Field did not mean that the new Tudor dynasty was firmly entrenched in the volatile English political environment. Every Tudor monarch faced popular uprisings of a political or religious background, while each royal needed to contemplate aggression from France or its ally, Scotland.

Henry VII faced two pretenders supported by Margaret, Dowager Duchess of Burgundy and brother to Richard III. Lambert Simnel, a mere child-puppet, was backed by Flemish mercenaries and an Irish force that landed in Lancashire, only to be defeated at the Battle of Stoke Field in 1487. The second imposter, Perkin Warbeck, claimed to be the younger of the two princes murdered in the Tower. Financed by Burgundy and backed by some Yorkist rebels in Ireland, Flemish troops and some Scottish support, his career lasted seven years, with three invasion attempts, the final effort being linked to the Cornish Revolt of 1497. This particular popular uprising responded to extra taxation demands to raise monies to finance war against Scotland, which engaged in border skirmishes in support of Warbeck.

Cornish tin miners felt their Stannary rights were being ignored and marched on London where they were defeated at the Battle of Blackheath. Elsewhere, Warbeck was captured and eventually executed.

Henry VIII faced the Pilgrimage of Grace in 1536, a rising by northern lords concerned over inheritance rights and other economic grievances together with anger over the treatment of Catherine of Aragon and the expulsion of monks and nuns from their religious houses. This was supported by Bigod's 1537 Rebellion in Cumberland and Westmoreland; Henry's revenge exacted the death penalty upon knights and abbots alike. However, the rebels did occasion some retreats in the monarch's religious policy, and a new Statute of Wills.

Henry's policy towards Scotland was coloured by the Old Alliance between that country and France, which saw the Scots King James IV invade England to help France. The crushing English victory at Flodden in 1513 ushered in a period of conflict, with James V dying after a Scots' defeat at Solway Moss in 1542. Henry wished to marry his son Edward to the week-old, orphaned Mary Queen of Scots. A period of military wooing resulted with an English defeat at Ancrum Moor in 1545, followed by a massive defeat of the Scots at Pinkie in 1547 shortly after Henry's death.

In 1536 and 1543, 'Acts of Union' incorporated Wales into England, with Welsh law being replaced by English laws.

Edward IV suffered two risings: one in Devon and Cornwall, the other in Norfolk. The Western Rebellion was a conservative religious reaction against the growth of Protestantism leading to Western rebels being defeated at various battles, ending at Sampford Courtenay in 1549. The government reprisals eradicated Catholicism in the West. Kett's Rebellion was an anti-enclosure movement leading to a six-week-long control of Norwich before the Earl of Warwick crushed the dissidents at Dussindale in 1549.

Mary Tudor confronted Wyatt's Rebellion, which commenced as an attempt to replace Catholic Mary with her Protestant sister Elizabeth, most probably because Mary sought to marry Philip of Spain. The conspiracy was betrayed and risings in Devon, Leicestershire and Herefordshire fizzled out, leaving Wyatt cut off in Kent. His advance upon London caused great fear but was defeated, with Wyatt and companions executed. Elizabeth escaped any penalty but was challenged by the Northern Rebellion where the Earls of Westmoreland and Northumberland attempted to depose Queen Elizabeth in favour of Mary, Queen of Scots. The rebels raised troops and marched south, about turned when larger forces confronted them and their leaders later retreated across the border to Scotland.

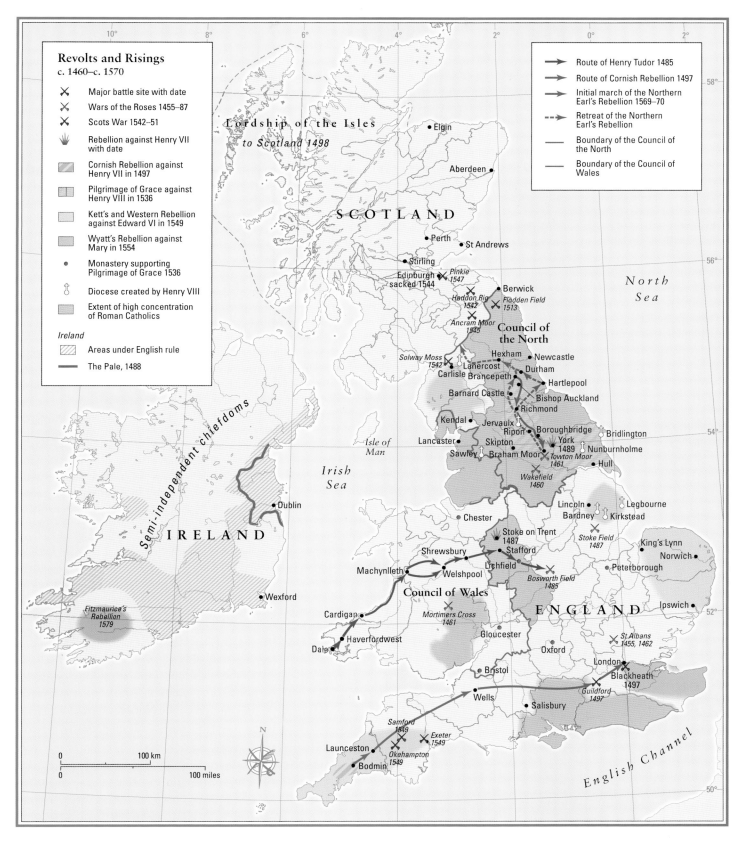

Revolts and Risings
c. 1460–c. 1570

✕   Major battle site with date

✕   Wars of the Roses 1455–87

✕   Scots War 1542–51

   Rebellion against Henry VII with date

   Cornish Rebellion against Henry VII in 1497

   Pilgrimage of Grace against Henry VIII in 1536

   Kett's and Western Rebellion against Edward VI in 1549

   Wyatt's Rebellion against Mary in 1554

●   Monastery supporting Pilgrimage of Grace 1536

   Diocese created by Henry VIII

   Extent of high concentration of Roman Catholics

Ireland

   Areas under English rule

   The Pale, 1488

→   Route of Henry Tudor 1485

→   Route of Cornish Rebellion 1497

→   Initial march of the Northern Earl's Rebellion 1569–70

⇢   Retreat of the Northern Earl's Rebellion

   Boundary of the Council of the North

   Boundary of the Council of Wales

Lordship of the Isles
to Scotland 1498

● Elgin

● Aberdeen

SCOTLAND

● Perth   ● St Andrews

● Stirling

Edinburgh sacked 1544   *Pinkie 1547*

Haddon Rig 1542   ● Berwick   *Flodden Field 1513*

Ancram Moor 1545

North Sea

Solway Moss 1542   ✝ Lanercost   Hexham ● Newcastle

Council of the North

Carlisle   Brancepeth   ● Durham

Barnard Castle ●   ● Hartlepool

● Bishop Auckland

Richmond

Kendal ●   Jervaulx   ✝ Bridlington

● Ripon   ● Boroughbridge

Lancaster ●   Skipton   York   1489   Nunburnholme

Sawley ●   Braham Moor   *Towton Moor 1461*

Isle of Man

Irish Sea

Wakefield 1460

● Hull

Lincoln ●   ● Legbourne

Bardney   ● Kirkstead

Semi-independent chiefdoms

● Dublin

IRELAND

Chester ●

Stoke on Trent 1487   *Stoke Field 1487*

Shrewsbury ●   ● Stafford   ● King's Lynn

● Norwich

Machynlleth ●   ● Welshpool   Lichfield

Council of Wales   *Bosworth Field 1485*

● Peterborough

Cardigan ●   *Mortimers Cross 1461*   **ENGLAND**

● Wexford

● Ipswich

Fitzmaurice's Rebellion 1579

Haverfordwest ●   ● Gloucester   *St Albans 1455, 1462*

Dale ●   ● Oxford   ● London

● Bristol   *Guildford 1497*   Blackheath 1497

● Wells   ● Salisbury

Samford 1549

Launceston ●   *Exeter 1549*

Okehampton 1549

● Bodmin

English Channel

0   100 km

0   100 miles

N

Economies and Populations 1200–1400

Unification of Wales and
England

After 1284, the Welsh economy
became increasingly integrated
with that of England. Landlords
from the fertile Welsh valleys
were eager to export wool and
cattle, usually through England.

Unification of Wales and England 1536

Principality of Wales shired by Edward I in 1284

Marcher Lordships shired in 1536

Approximate area of marcher lordships added to English shires

—— Administrative border 1542–1830

—— Boundary area subject to the council in the marches

The economic mainstay of all parts of the islands was agriculture. There was little in the way of technology to expand production into poor or marginal land to support a growing population. Before the Black Death struck, in 1348, some historians claim that the population of the British Isles had reached some five to seven million inhabitants. The plague struck the young and old in particular, with those in their twenties and thirties displaying the greatest immunity. However, population figures failed to move back to pre-plague numbers. The plague ran riot again in 1361, severely pruning the nobility and young men, thereby distorting sex ratios and regeneration rates. Added to the plague were at least two famine years plus a range of infectious diseases such as cholera, typhoid, tuberculosis and the pneumonic plague. These islands were a laboratory for bacteria, with high mortality and low fertility reducing the population by half in England during the reign of Richard II.

Despite demographic damage, the islands' people were creating a rich economic life with internal markets developing due to road links and waterways. Bustling ports attached the islands to the various trading networks working out of European trading areas. Venetian and Genoese trade routes reached Southampton and London, with Genoese merchants travelling inland to York, Carlisle and Berwick. Elsewhere, the North German and Baltic Hanseatic League partially controlled trade on England's east coast and possessed an extra-territoriality area in the Steelyard in London. Thus, the islands were linked to the Orient via the Mediterranean and to the important Baltic herring fisheries, such food being essential for religious days and salted winter food.

Apart from wool and textiles, England sold wheat to Scandinavia, Gascony and occasionally to Italy, while butter and cheese were exported across the Channel. As far as vegetables were concerned, surprisingly, England imported cabbages, garlic, onions and onion seeds from France and the Low Countries and apples from Normandy. Other major imports were bow staves from Portugal and Baltic ports. Elsewhere, Scotland was trading with Scandinavia and the Low Countries as well as France and Spain. Newcastle coal was sold in Germany, the Low Countries and France. The islands were most strongly tied to relatively densely populated manufacturing – textiles, metalwork, ceramics – of north-eastern France, the Low Countries and north-western Germany, from where skilled craftsmen of every kind were drawn into south-eastern England before percolating through the islands, operating in the major fairs at Northampton, Boston and Winchester, spreading the name of Fleming everywhere.

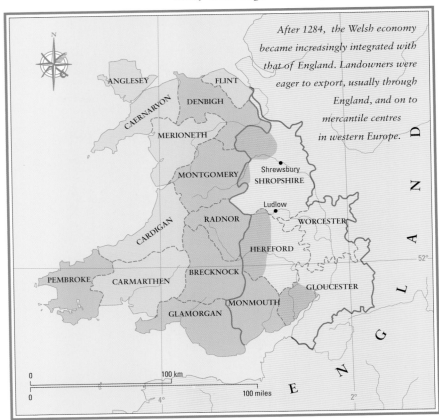

After 1284, the Welsh economy became increasingly integrated with that of England. Landowners were eager to export, usually through England, and on to mercantile centres in western Europe.

Economy and Population
1200–1400

Economy and Population

All Scotland engaged in mixed of farming, with cattle raising in the Highlands and sheep rearing in the Lowlands. The two regions were separated by language. Wales was rich in wool, many sheep farms being run by Cistercians.

Towns and Cities

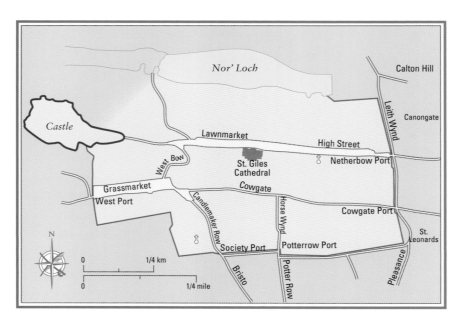

Medieval Edinburgh

- ☐ City area with wall
- ▬ Castle walls
- ⛪ Churches

Towns and Cities

Towns grew and their records show charters granting market privileges and freedom from rolls and exempted inhabitants from feudal dues. Merchant guilds organised a banking system and administered justice according to guild courts and laws.

Medieval lords found it beneficial to help develop communities near their castles in order to service the castle and improve revenues from commerce, often by providing charters for fairs and markets. Towns-people were provided with land grants, low rents, trading monopolies, collection of their own taxes and, in London, the chief magistrate became the mayor. Some towns and cities were protected by walls and these aided the maintenance of law and order by checking entrants at the city gates and bars. Urban communities created guilds where members of common trades or crafts (mercers, grocers, stone-masons etc.) established mutual protection societies to maintain high standards of work. Normally, affiliated to a local saint or monastery, the guilds ran the cities and provided local government.

By the fourteenth century, cities such as York, Edinburgh, Norwich, Lincoln and Bristol probably had 20,000 inhabitants each, with a London population of some 120,000 that spread outside the walls into suburbs stretching towards the royal courts at Westminster, with lawyers congregating around The Temple. Urban society organised social care through orphanages, hospitals, old peoples' homes and social clubs.

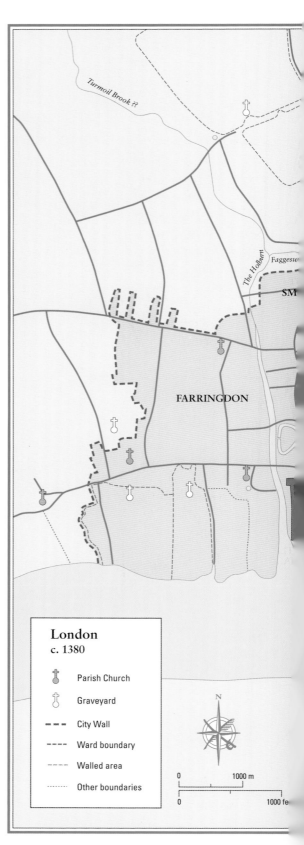

London
c. 1380

- ⛪ Parish Church
- ⛪ Graveyard
- – – – City Wall
- – – – Ward boundary
- – – – Walled area
- ········· Other boundaries

Holy Well

The Moor

Lollesworth
Field

CRIPPLEGATE

Deep Ditch

ALDERSGATE

FARRINGDON

CRIPPLEGATE

Hounds Ditch

BISHOPSGATE

COLEMAN
STREET

PORTSOKEN

FARRINGDON

CHEAP

BROAD
STREET

BISHOPS

BREAD
STREET

St Paul's
Cathedral

CORNHILL

LIME
STREET

CORDWAINER

WALBROOK

GATE

QUEEN
HITHE

LANG-
BOURNE

LANGBOURNE

ALDGATE

VINTRY

CANDLEWICK

PORTSOKEN

DOWGATE

TOWER

BRIDGE

BILLINGSGATE

Tower
Hill

Tower
Hill

River Thames

London
Bridge

The Tower
of London

Bishop of Winchester's Park

BOROUGH OF
SOUTHWARK

Border Lordships

The Anglo-Scottish border region remained a disputed and poorly demarcated land over which the various local clans or families fought and rustled livestock as a way of life. The frontier was the key factor generating the political and social character of the north where feuding and raiding remained a threat to local economies, life, and homes. The problem was exacerbated by the English monarchy when it gave responsibility for guarding the frontier to a group of families who Parliament characterized as 'the Marcher lords of the North' in 1388.

Border wars constantly occurred from the thirteenth to sixteenth centuries with monarchs seeking to control their subjects who had wills of their own and regarded their local issues as being of paramount importance and not those of the state. Even so, Border soldiers were involved in invasions on both sides generally being used as cavalry suitable for scouting and skirmishing, riding light, agile horses particularly suited to the terrain. Interestingly, contemporary horse shows in the Borders demonstrate the particular affection that the populace still has for the horse.

To police the Borders, both sides built numerous castles and pele towers, originally a palisaded enclosure. These developed into a fortified tower-house with an entrance at first floor level, being accessed by an easily withdrawn ladder. Two such remaining fortifications are at the Vicar's Pele in Corbridge, Northumberland and at Sizergh Castle in Cumbria, which boasted 90 pele towers. The Border soldiers, sometimes known as reivers, were armed with a sword, dagger and light lance, and armoured with leather jacks, occasionally with steel plates stitched on, and steel helmets, from whence their name of the Steel Bonnets emerged.

The Kings of Scotland and England found the Borders so ungovernable that they agreed to exert some control by creating the West, Middle and East Marches on each side of the border. State salaried officials would be appointed as Wardens in each march by their respective monarchs with administrative and judicial powers over their charges. The wardenships tended to become hereditary in a few important families who realised the power that could accrue from their posts. Truce days were held periodically when disputes were tried by Scots and English wardens in concert but they never really controlled the Debateable Lands of the West March. Here, the Graham and Armstrong families engaged in such hostility that the Grahams were transported to Ireland and not allowed to return on pain of death.

Border families were gradually deprived of power. In 1530, James V imprisoned various lords, including the famed and notorious Scott of Buccleuch and hanged Johnnie Armstrong of Gilnockie, a reiver leader, and thirty-one others at Carlanrig Chapel in 1530. As late as 1606, the Earl of Dunbar hanged 140 miscreants. A major problem in handling Borderers was that families often lived on both sides of the border so loyalties remained uncertain except, of course, loyalties to themselves. At the Battle of Ancrum Moor in Scotland in 1545, where a large English force ran into a prepared Scots ambush, the 700 'assured' Scots on the English side switched allegiance, killing or capturing more English than their supposed opponents. In 1547, an English observer at the Battle of Pinkie saw English and Scots borderers conversing in the battle, only engaging in mock combat when they knew they were seen.

The difference between Highland clans and Border families is not obvious, except that the Highlanders lived in a more feudal society tied by the payment of rents whereas the Border families were linked by kinship and a notion of collective self-interest and self-defence. When Scots King James VI of Scotland became James I of England, major grounds of conflict diminished and the Borders subsided into a more peaceful mutual reiving rather than state warfare.

The Anglo-Scottish Borders
The way of life in both English and Scots Marches was similar. Cross-border raiding was endemic and populations defended themselves by lords living in strongly fortified castles while the lesser gentry and farmers inhabited tower-houses, pele towers and fortified farmsteads. Pele towers and tower-houses were not designed to withstand a siege. Research has listed 426 tower-houses, mainly throughout Lowland Scotland. Northumberland also saw the unique bastle house, which held both livestock and people.

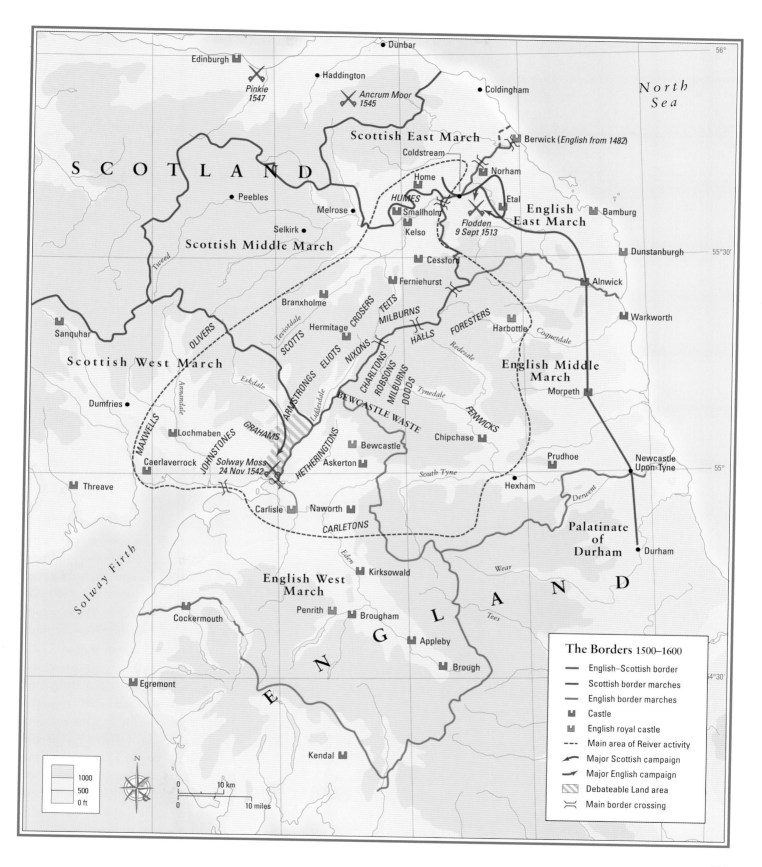

North
Sea

• Dunbar

Edinburgh ⚔
Pinkie
1547

• Haddington

Ancrum Moor ⚔
1545

• Coldingham

S C O T L A N D

Scottish East March

Berwick (*English from 1482*)

Coldstream

Norham

• Peebles

Home

Etal

English
East March

Bamburg

Melrose •

HUMES

Smallholm

Selkirk •

Kelso

Flodden
9 Sept 1513

Dunstanburgh

Scottish Middle March

Cessford

Tweed

Alnwick

Ferniehurst

Branxholme

CROSERS
TEITS
MILBURNS

Warkworth

Hermitage

Teviotdale

SCOTS
ELIOTS
NIXONS
HALLS
FORESTERS

Harbottle

English Middle
March

Sanquhar

OLIVERS

CHARLTONS
ROBSONS
MILBURNS
DODDS

Coquetdale

Scottish West March

Eskdale

ARMSTRONGS

BEWCASTLE WASTE

Redesale

Morpeth

Dumfries •

Liddesdale

Tynedale

FENWICKS

Annandale

GRAHAMS

Chipchase

Lochmaben

JOHNSTONES

Bewcastle

Prudhoe

Newcastle
Upon-Tyne

MAXWELLS

Solway Moss
24 Nov 1542

HETHERINGTONS

Askerton

South Tyne

Caerlaverrock

Threave

Carlisle

Naworth

Hexham

Derwent

CARLETONS

Palatinate
of
Durham

• Durham

Eden

E   N   G   L   A   N   D

Kirksowald

Wear

English West
March

Tees

Solway Firth

Cockermouth

Penrith

Brougham

Appleby

Brough

Egremont

N

Kendal

1000
500
0 ft

0   10 km

0   10 miles

The Borders 1500–1600

— English–Scottish border
— Scottish border marches
— English border marches
⬓ Castle
⬓ English royal castle
----- Main area of Reiver activity
⤙ Major Scottish campaign
⤚ Major English campaign
▨ Debateable Land area
⧓ Main border crossing

56°

55°30'

55°

54°30'

Elizabethan Rule

Elizabeth's reign (1558–1603) was characterized by a high flowering of the Northern Renaissance, seen in the plays and sonnets of Shakespeare, the architecture and music, with a counterpoint of relative poverty in the bulk of the population made up of agricultural labourers. Importantly, Elizabeth was able to: ameliorate religious divisions; preside over exploration and trading ventures and, survive conspiracies and plots, often surrounding Mary Queen of Scots; support Protestantism internationally; and survive a Spanish onslaught in the form of the Armada and Spanish invasion forces in Cornwall and Ireland.

In the field of religion, Elizabeth took a moderate line unlike her father who persecuted Catholics and her pro-Catholic sister who burned Protestants. She managed to enact the Acts of Supremacy and Uniformity, the first confirming her as Supreme Governor of the Church of England. The Act of Uniformity in 1559, after much debate in Parliament and amongst bishops, allowed Roman Catholicism to exist providing Catholics paid a fine for non-attendance at a local Protestant parish church. Simultaneously, she removed all bishops but one, appointing her supporters in their place and ousted all Catholics from her Privy Council. Her middle way promoted the Anglicans in faith who were antipathetic to Protestants but did not support the Papacy. Religion was quiescent until mutually hostile positions developed under the Jacobeans.

A major problem for Elizabeth was the fate of her deposed cousin, Mary Queen of Scots, imprisoned in England for years. A focus of Catholic plots to remove Elizabeth in favour of Mary, Elizabeth was uncertain what to do. Her policy not to marry and provide an heir meant Mary was next in line to the throne. After years of prevarication, evidence provided from the Babington plot ensured that Mary was beheaded in 1587. A collective sigh of relief was exhaled by the Privy Council, which knew that Mary's, and now Elizabeth's, heir James VI of Scotland, was safe in Calvinist hands.

1588 witnessed Elizabethan England confronting the might of King Philip II of Spain. He felt obliged to: avenge the execution of Mary Queen of Scots; restore England to the Catholic Church; prevent further English commerce-raiders attacking Spanish ships; and, end Elizabeth's financial and military support of both French Huguenots in the French Wars of Religion and the Protestants in the Spanish Netherlands who sought independence under William the Silent and his warrior sons, Maurice and Justin. Philip II's Grand Design involved sailing a huge armada, under the Duke of Medina Sidonia, up the English Channel to the Netherlands where the Duke of Parma's formidable army would be escorted across to England. Parma's military expertise and infantry *tercios* would then conquer England.

Elizabeth's first line of defence was an expert navy, capable of engaging Spanish vessels at long range. Should the fleet prove inadequate, shore defences encompassed a chain of coastal signal beacons, refurbished forts guarding potential landing places, together with trained bands of the militia. Ultimately, the Spanish expedition failed owing to harrying attacks by the English fleet, fire-ships and tempest causing many shipwrecks on the Scots and Irish coasts.

Elizabeth's reign is notorious for her support of enterprising seamen, such as Drake, Hawkins, Frobisher and Cavendish who preyed on Spanish vessels and captured treasure ships from the Americas. This seamanship extended further with the backing of the Merchant Adventurers of the Muscovy Company, which became a virtual diplomatic link between Muscovy and England to the extent that Tsar Ivan IV made a proposal of marriage. Support was also given to the Levant Company and the East India Company was founded in 1600; trade was aided, too, by the expulsion of the Hanseatic League from London, weakening a competitor in Northern waters.

Elizabethan Rule

As well as coping with internal intrigue, Queen Elizabeth faced huge external threats, including the Spanish Armada, launched against her by Philip II. Her government mobilized the revenues of the nation to equip and deploy its fleet and the army. The Queen could rely on the resourcefulness and experience of her naval commanders, like Drake and Hawkins.

Elizabethan Rule

- Under direct rule of Elizabeth I
- Areas of Ireland subject to limited or fluctuating control
- Owing fealty to Elizabeth I
- Route of the Armada 1588
- Ships blown off-course
- Risings against English rule in Ireland

Shetland Islands

Orkney Islands

Outer Hebrides

North Sea

SCOTLAND

Aberdeen

Edinburgh

Berwick-on-Tweed

Naworth Hexham Newcastle
Northern Rising 1569–70 Durham

Richmond

Rippon

York

Irish Sea

Glenshesk

Yellow Ford
Clontibret

Ardinaree

IRELAND

The Pale
Dublin

Glenmalure

Monasternenagh

Fitzmaurice's Rebellion 1579

Affane

Anglesey

WALES

ENGLAND

Kings Lynn Riots 1597 Kings Lynn

Cambridge

Oxfordshire Rising 1596 Oxford

London

Bristol

Dover

Exeter

Portsmouth

Isle of Wight

Plymouth

Calais

English Channel

ATLANTIC OCEAN

FRANCE

0 — 100 km
0 — 100 miles

Scottish Reformation

Scottish Reformation

*"Madam, as right religion receive
not its origin nor authority from
princes but from the eternal God
alone, so are not subjects bound
to practise their religion
according to the tastes of their
princes, for oft it is that princes
are the most ignorant of God's
true religion ..."*
(John Knox to Queen Mary)

The Scots reformation reinforced a sense of Scots identity, just as it had in England during the conflict with Spain. Pressure built up in Scotland for reform and the Scottish Parliament felt so under threat that the import of Lutheran books was banned to dampen its influence; this failed. Lutherans were executed and persecuted during the 1530s and 1540s, beginning with Patrick Hamilton being burnt at the stake in 1528.

The pre-Reformation Church attempted some reforms to alleviate criticism by educating its clergy; however, this had little effect. Outside influences also bore upon Scotland: the English invasion during the Rough Wooing, 1544–48, helped make it known that Henry VIII allowed the reading of the Bible in English, seemingly making priests superfluous. Cardinal Beaton's attempts to attack reformers, including the execution of George Wishart, a Calvin-educated preacher, incited John Knox and others to murder Beaton. English occupation, following the Battle of Pinkie in 1547, ensured the circulation of English Bibles, with Scots earls moving into the Protestant camp. The Scots gained French help when their young Queen was betrothed in France and French hegemony in Scotland angered both patriots and reformers alike.

The Queen Mother, Mary of Guise, had been involved in ensuring Queen Mary had, as part of her marriage agreement in 1558, stated that should she die without producing a son, Scotland would go to France. These assurances made to King Henry II of France, engendered anti-French feeling and a Protestant grouping, abetted by England, formed the Congregation of the Lord and signed the first National Covenant in 1557.

The accession of Queen Elizabeth in England in 1588 boosted the Protestants' morale. Knox, returning from captivity in France, fired up crowds with his sermons in

Dundee, whose population then looted religious houses. A period of civil war followed which Mary, the Queen Regent, lost leading to the Treaty of Edinburgh, which called for the withdrawal of both French and English troops and the right of the Scots to summon a parliament.

The 1560 Reform Parliament abolished the Catholic Mass and ended the authority of the Pope. Thus, the Scottish Reformation was proclaimed by Parliament and not by a monarch as in most other countries. Reform was promulgated by John Knox and others who wrote a *Book of Discipline* in 1561 requesting the state to punish sins like blasphemy and idolatry with death. Knox wished to establish a theocracy along Calvinist lines established in Geneva. With William Maitland of Lethington and Lord James Stewart, the Queen's illegitimate half-brother, he formed the triumvirate, ruling Scotland until the Queen Mother's death. Despite Knox's fanaticism, many Lords of the Congregation were more interested in grabbing ecclesiastical lands than their immortal souls.

Queen Mary opposed the reformers but was deposed in 1567 during a civil war. Her flight to England led to her imprisonment by Elizabeth. The Scottish throne passed to King James VI who was raised as a Protestant. Some reformers hoped that the Scottish Church or Kirk would adopt a church organization ruled by elders, or presbyters (thus, Presbyterianism). However, an adult James refused and appointed new bishops ensuring that radical reformers, as in England, were disappointed. Yet, James was a moderate man and allowed the continuation of church courts, sessions of the kirk, presbyteries, synods and a General Assembly – as long as he controlled the bishops who were brought into Parliament in 1600; thus, James compromised to ensure domestic stability.

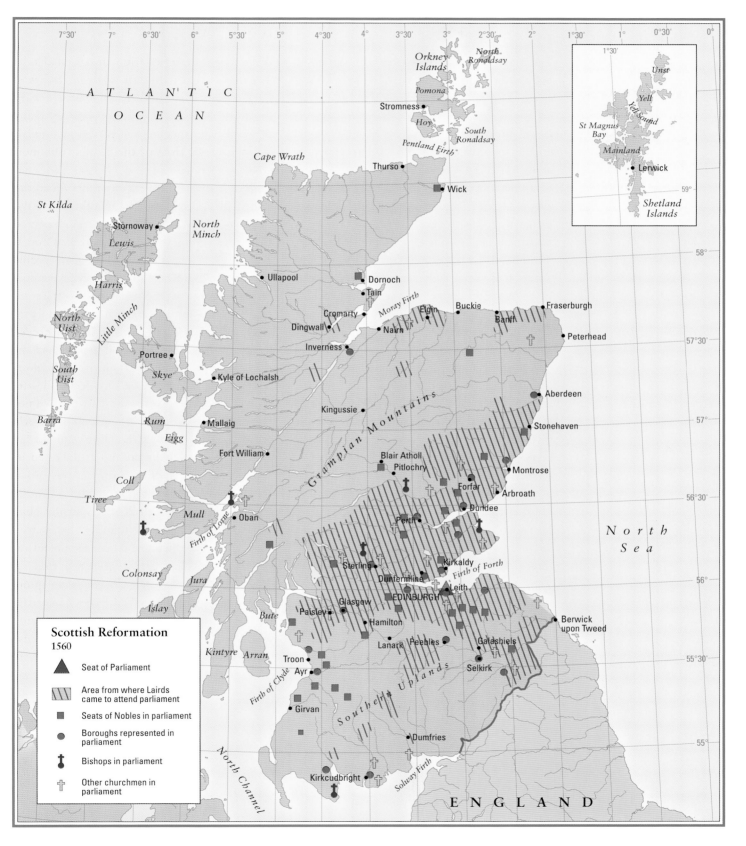

Scottish Reformation
1560

▲   Seat of Parliament

▨   Area from where Lairds came to attend parliament

■   Seats of Nobles in parliament

●   Boroughs represented in parliament

♰   Bishops in parliament

✝   Other churchmen in parliament

Reformation in Europe 1520–1600

Reformation in Europe
The Reformation denotes the division of Latin Christendom into Protestant and Catholic churches. This movement gathered pace, especially in northern Europe and the British Isles, transforming the religious landscape by 1600.

Printing in the British Isles
William Caxton established his printing press in 1470. Within thirty-five years, this innovative technique had spread across the British Isles. Thousands of new books circulated among an eager audience taking with them new ideas, both religious and secular.

Printing in the British Isles

- ■ 15th Century centres
- ■ 16th Century centres
- ■ 17th Century centres

The Protestant Reformation occurred in a time of political and religious flux in the late fifteenth and sixteenth centuries. A transformation was generated by: an increased religious awareness and the spread of the *devotio moderna*, a more individual attitude towards belief and religion, especially strong in the Low Countries; and the Renaissance, which enhanced the interests of princely power and also increased intellectual curiosity, spread by the humanism of key figures such as Erasmus of Rotterdam and Sir Thomas Moore in England. The intellectual ferment was located in the fast changing economic and social networks produced by an emergent capitalist system, new banking methods and increased urbanization. The corrupt Catholic Church came under close inspection in terms of ideas and organization.

Humanism required an improvement in scholarship with a rejection of non-biblical superstition and an individual and personal commitment to the concept of personal salvation, which eschewed the need for an intermediary priest to intercede between mankind and God. Simultaneously, free thinkers argued for an end to church taxation and tithes, demanding improved standards of religious practice and obligation. Anti-clericalism reached a high point when Martin Luther, outraged over the sale of papal indulgences, nailed his ninety-five theses to the door of All Saints Church in Wittenberg in October 1517. His demands and those of the Swiss Zwingli and Frenchman, John Calvin, supported the emergence of centralized and absolutist states in confrontation with more radical Dissenters, such as the Anabaptists and Millenarian movements.

Germany was an especial home to virulent anti-clericalism and hostility to church abuse and corruption. Many princes, imperial knights and city councils seized upon the new ideas to legitimize curtailing the powers of the Holy Roman Emperors Maximilian I and Charles V, as well as the papacy. The Dissenters appropriated Church property, and Protestant churches became subor-dinate to temporal rulers, such as England's Henry VIII who developed the early Anglican Church.

Protestantism never managed to unite its various elements despite the attempts made by Philip of Hesse who sought to mend fences between Lutherans and Zwinglians, to no avail, since they continued to differ upon conflicting interpretations of the Mass. A most important Protestant was Calvin, whose ideas on developing the Reformed Faith, spread from the city state of Geneva to France, the Netherlands, the German states and parts of eastern Europe, notably Poland, and Transylvania under Calvinist princes owing fealty to the Ottoman Sultan.

In 1531, German Protestant leaders formed the Schmalkaldic League against Emperor Charles V to defend their faith, fighting against the Emperor in 1546–47 and losing at the Battle of Mühlberg in 1547. However, Charles was so beset by other foreign policy issues that he could not prevent the spread of Protestantism and its firm establishment. Wars with Valois France, the Dutch, the Turks and a difficult Spain kept him too occupied. Tired of some 30 years of war, in the Treaty of Augsburg in September 1555, the Emperor agreed that each subject of the Holy Roman Emperor should follow their prince's faith. Consequently, some 40 per cent of Europeans accepted a form of reformed religion. However, religion became a major factor in the Thirty Years' War (1630–48), which was ended by the Treaty of Westphalia, a major theme being that all parties should recognize and uphold the Treaty of Augsburg.

Reformation in Europe 1520 – 1600

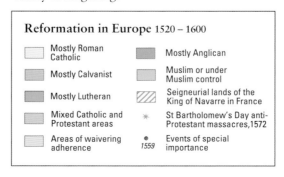

□ Mostly Roman Catholic	▨ Mostly Anglican
▨ Mostly Calvinist	▨ Muslim or under Muslim control
▨ Mostly Lutheran	▨ Seigneurial lands of the King of Navarre in France
▨ Mixed Catholic and Protestant areas	✳ St Bartholomew's Day anti-Protestant massacres,1572
□ Areas of waivering adherence	● *1559* Events of special importance

0   200 km

0   200 miles

N

**ATLANTIC
OCEAN**

*North
Sea*

NORWAY

SWEDEN

FINLAND

DENMARK

Baltic Sea

COURLAND

SCOTLAND

● Edinburgh
1559

IRELAND

Dublin

Mecklenburg

Pomerania

● Stettin

● Danzig

● Bremen   ● Hamburg

BRANDENBURG

KINGDOM
OF
POLAND

Wales   ENGLAND

NETHERLANDS

Brunswick

● Berlin

London
1559

● Münster
1535

● Magdeburg
Religious violence 1631

Saxony
● Leipzig   Dresden

Silesia

● Breslau

● Cologne

⚔ *Battle of
Mühlberg
1547*

Moravia

FRANCE

⚹ Rouen

● Frankfurt

● Prague 1618

BOHEMIA

Paris ⚹ ⚹ Meaux

● Worms
1521

Alençon

⚹ Troyes

Strasbourg ●

Würt-
temberg
1517

● Regensburg

● Augsburg 1530, 1555

Vienna ●

KINGDOM
OF
HUNGARY

● Ulm

● Salzburg

Bavaria

⚹ Bourges

Basel
●

● Zürich 1522

Innsbruck ●

AUSTRIA

Freiburg
●

SWISS CONFED.

● Bern

La Rochelle ●

● Limoges

Lyon ⚹

Geneva
1536, 1555

Savoy

● Trent
1545–63

REP. OF
VENICE

OTTOMAN
EMPIRE

Bordeaux ●

● Périgueux
● Bergerac

● Rodez   ● Orange

Montauban ●

Albi ● Millau ●

⚹ Nîmes

Gaillac ⚹
Toulouse

● Montpellier

● Bologna

REP.
OF
GENOA

PAPAL STATES

*Adriatic
Sea*

● Pamplona
NAVARRE

Corsica

Tuscany

ARAGON

S P A I N

NAPLES

CASTILLE

SARDINIA

Mediterranean Sea

SICILY

Messina ●

Elizabethan Ireland

In Tudor England, in 1486, Henry VII's accession to the crown was legitimized by Parliament. In 1534, Henry VIII appealed to that institution to validate his break with Rome and appoint him head of the Church of England. Hence, edicts sanctioned by Parliamentary approval constituted the foundation for the basis of the modern English state and sovereignty was vested not solely in the monarchy but by the 'King-in-Parliament'. Hence, the Crown and Parliament were omnicompetent, with neither side pressing too far to ascertain how the powers would actually be divided. Queen Elizabeth I showed how a monarch could rule, living within its financial means, while treating religion as a political issue where Catholics could worship privately, providing they were loyal to the crown.

Tudor policies towards Ireland were partially a response to England becoming entangled in European affairs with French Protestants and in support of Protestants fighting for independence from Spain in the Low Countries. Ireland seemed to be an Achilles heel in England's fragile security perimeter, thereby requiring some strengthening of English rule there. Henry VIII sought to destroy Catholicism and tie the Church to state institutions, while enforcing English legal customs by restructuring Gaelic and Anglo-Irish lordships.

Attempts to govern Ireland in line with Wales by centralizing and establishing administrative uniformity clashed with the kaleidoscope of differing cultures present in Ireland. Old English Catholic settlers controlled the Pale between Dublin and Dundalk while another Anglo-Irish enclave existed around Galway from when the Anglo-Normans had advanced into Connacht. Drawing an irregular line from Limerick to Dundalk, regions to its northwest were controlled by Gaelic chieftains with outlying bastions in the Wicklow Mountains and the far southwest. Elsewhere, powerful Anglo-Norman lords dominated the south between the Pale and Cork;

amongst these were the Butler earls of Ormond and the Fitzgerald Earls of Desmond and Kildare. These Gaelicised earls were used to being their own masters until faced by Tudor centralization.

The Protestant Reformation in England legislated for an Anglican state Church and this religious policy caused disquiet amongst the Irish Gaels and amongst the Old English Roman Catholic lords who found themselves disqualified from serving a Protestant state and could be fined or suffer legal and social penalties for recusancy. This exclusion drew the Old English ruling class and the Gaels closer together when they witnessed the monarchy relying upon imported administrators and Protestant New English planters who colonized Laois, Offaly, Kerry and Limerick. Given this situation, Elizabeth faced three major uprisings: the O'Neill Wars; the Desmond Rebellion; and the Nine Years' War.

Shane O'Neill was an Ulster chieftain, posing as a defender of Catholicism, who, nevertheless, attacked fellow Gaels who stood in the way of his Irish ambitions. He hated the MacDonalds of Antrim and the O'Donnels of Tyrconnel. He attacked and defeated the MacDonalds at Glentaise (Glenshesk) in 1565 only to be beaten by the O'Donnells at Farsetmore in 1567. Despite escaping, O'Neill was murdered by a contingency of Scots during peace negotiations.

The Desmond Rebellion witnessed Catholic Dissenters seeking papal support against Elizabeth I. In 1570, Pope Gregory XIII excommunicated Elizabeth and backed armed forces against her in Ireland. Some sixty Papal troops landed on the Dingle peninsula in Autumn 1579, inspiring revolts in Munster and Wicklow, sucking in the Earl of Desmond. The Desmonds were defeated at Monasternenagh in 1579 but defeated Lord Grey of Wilton at Glenmalur in 1580. A second papal expeditionary force of some 600 Italian troops landed at Smerwick; Lord Grey defeated them, then hunted down Desmond who was killed by Irishmen in 1583.

Elizabethan Ireland

ORIEL Chiefdoms
● Cities, towns and sites
■ Forts
□ Garrisons
⌐ Castles
✕ Battles

0   20 km
0   20 miles

3280   500
1320   400
990   300
660   200
330   100
0 ft   0 m

INISHOWEN

Dunluce
Coleraine ROUTE ✕ Ballycastle
Glenshesk Cushendun
GLYNNS

Derry
Lifford Strabane OIREACHT-UI ANTRIM
CHATHAIN Larne
DONEGAL CLANDEBOYE Carrickfergus
Ulster
Donegal TYRONE Belfast ARDS
Omagh (TIR EOGAIN) Comber
Ballyshannon Dungannon Yellow DUFFERIN
Bundrowes Belleek Ford Ardkeen
CARBURY Benburb Blackwater KINELARTY
FERMANAGH Armagh DOWN
Sligo Enniskillen ✕ Clontibret IVEAGH LECALE
Collooney ARMAGH Ardglass
Ardnaree ✕ SLIGO ORIEL Newry
Ballymote LEITRIM MONAGHAN FEWS
MACWILLIAM Boyle CAVAN ORIOR
BURKE WEST FARNEY
Burrishoole BREIFNE Carrickmacross Dundalk
Castlebar MAYO EAST
Hag's Castle BREIFNE LOUTH
C o n n a c h t ROSCOMMON LONGFORD Drogheda
Roscommon ANNALY MEATH
Shrule Athleague M e a t h
GALWAY Mullingar
HYMANY WEST MEATH
Athenry Athlone DUBLIN
Galway CLANRICARD Philipstown □ KILDARE Dublin
Meelick ■ KING'S COUNTY CLANMALIER Naas
IREGAN WICKLOW
UPPER QUEEN'S Kildare MOUNTAINS
Lemenagh OSSORY COUNTY Ballymore-
INCHIQUIN Ballyadams □ Eustace Newcastle
Ennis CLARE Maryborough Athy GABHAL
THOMOND Disert Mullaghmast RAGHNAILL
Bunratty Castleconnell Carlow ✕ Glenmalure
Carrigaholt Limerick TIPPERARY IDRONE
Askeaton Kilkenny Leighlinbridge
Carrigafoyle ✕ Monasternenagh KILKENNY WEXFORD
LIMERICK Cashel L e i n s t e r Ferns
LIXNAW Kilmallock Cahir
Tralee Clonmel New Ross
Smerwick □ Kilcolman Carrick on Suir Wexford
Dingle Castlemaine Mitchelstown Waterford
KERRY WATERFORD Youghal
M u n s t e r DECIES
BEARE Affane
MUSKERRY ✕ Castlemartyr
Cork Tallow Dungarvan
CARBERY Carrigaline Cloyne
Tracton IMOKILLY
Kinsale

9° 7° 55° 54° 53° 52°

The final but most dangerous rebellion was led by Hugh O'Neill, Earl of Tyrone, who opposed New English administrators and joined Gaelic and Old English Dissenters together. Rebellion ensued and the English suffered various defeats, notably at Yellow Ford in 1598. O'Neill raised and paid standing troops of horse and

O'Neill's Rising

The future King, James I of England, obsessed about Divine Right, probably as a partial response to knowledge of O'Neill's rebellion and treason, when O'Neill took the title of Ard Righ or High-King of Ireland.

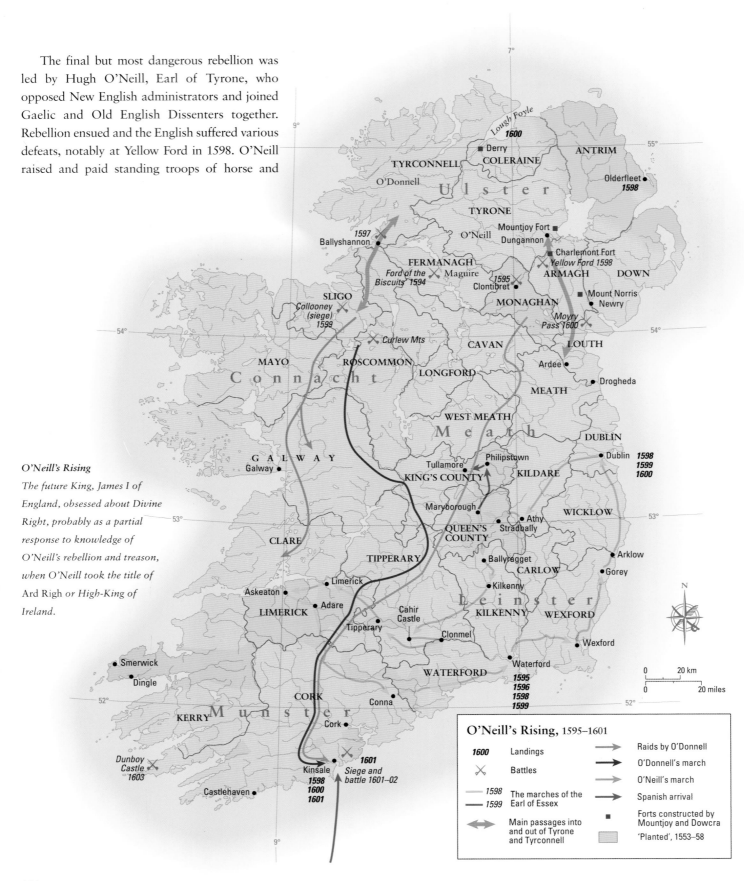

O'Neill's Rising, 1595–1601

1600	Landings	→	Raids by O'Donnell
✕	Battles	→	O'Donnell's march
—— *1598*	The marches of the Earl of Essex	→	O'Neill's march
—— *1599*		→	Spanish arrival
↔	Main passages into and out of Tyrone and Tyrconnell	■	Forts constructed by Mountjoy and Dowcra
			'Planted', 1553–58

arquebusiers and also employed Spanish soldiers in 1601, when 3,500 men landed at Kinsale, the other end of Ireland from O'Neill. The Spanish were besieged in the south, while English Lord Mountjoy brought O'Neill to battle. The advancing Irish and allies fought in the unfamiliar Spanish formations and were overwhelmed, losing a good quarter of their forces, which caused O'Neill to surrender at Mellifont on 30 March 1603, six days after Queen Elizabth's death.

Elizabeth was the last of the Tudors, dying in 1603, allowing James VI of Scotland to become King James I of England. James was well-read and an author of some note, sometimes dubbed 'the wisest fool in Christendom'. He lacked common sense, authority, presence, tact, and owned no notion of conciliation. He certainly possessed no economic sense and was continuously insolvent, wasting money in courtly extravagance. He was the direct opposite to Elizabeth and, being dropped into the English political pond, made ripples everywhere, swamping its banks.

The political philosophy of James I was encapsulated in various tomes, especially the *Basilicon Doron*, where he demanded absolute royal rule based on a powerful ecclesiastical hierarchy, which was the sole authority for law and order, and prosperity in the realm. His other notable work, *The True Law of Free Monarchies*, created an ideological basis for monarchy. He lays out the Divine Right of Kings, sustaining his views by alluding to the Bible where kings are thought, he said, to be higher beings than other people. Yet, he did admit that sitting on a throne was a dangerous business. His works propose a theory of absolute monarchy, which allowed him, by royal prerogative to propose laws. However, the King must heed tradition and not thwart God's will, because God would punish wicked kings, just as Saul was punished for disobeying God's wishes. In the *Basilikon Doron*, written as a guide for kingship to his son, Henry, he advised that Parliament was his chief court,

but also suggested that his son should not hold Parliaments except to validate new laws. In the *True Law*, James argued that the King possessed his kingdom like a feudal lord owns his fief, but to God, because kings were historical personages before Parliaments were ever devised or classes of men developed. Kings handed out land that was theirs to distribute, and laws were theirs.

Whereas Elizabeth had listened to skilled ministers, like Cecil, James antagonized some of the best minds in the country and used inconsequential advisors. The notion of Divine Right certainly goes back to Charlemagne when Christianity stated that kings held their position by the grace of God; hence, kings were anointed with Holy oil much like Saul and David. Such an attitude was reinforced by the survival of Roman law with its tenet that what pleased a prince had the force of law. However, kings might think they ruled by Divine Right but they were circumscribed by institutions and custom, whereby kings entered into a covenant with, say, feudal lords who subordinated their rights to a public, royal set in a mutual bond between ruler and ruled. His administration was venal, and Parliament penalised Lord Chancellor Bacon for bribery. Hence, James and his favourite, the Duke of Buckingham, ignored Parliament, raising money anyway possible, including selling titles. Constantly strapped for cash, the monarchy caused economic confusion in the country. Also, the monarchy stood for an old organic state where the social orders were to co-operate. However, modern capitalism, combined with the Protestant work ethic, where profit was Godly, clashed with the old order. Modern capitalists became industrialists or commercial farmers enclosing land, thereby establishing a conflictual social and economic order. These new men were best represented in Parliament representing the new modes of economic production whereas the Jacobean monarchy represented the past.

English Emigration

English Emigration to America 1620–42

→ Pilgrim migration 1620

→ Puritan migration 1630s

▬ Main area of emigration during English Civil War

▬ Secondary area of emigration during English Civil War

● Main port of embarkation

Inhabitants of the British Isles sought new homes in North America in response to the issues of religion and economic dispossession. A colony in Virginia failed under Raleigh in 1554, with a successful second attempt in 1607. Other colonies were founded in Massachusetts, at Plymouth in 1620, with other settlements founded in that colony. New colonies followed in Maryland in 1632, Rhode Island in 1636 and Connecticut in 1636. Migrants from Massachusetts moved to New Haven in 1638 and New Hampshire in 1638. An important Royal Charter had been granted to the Massachusetts Bay Company in 1629 and John Winthrop was elected Governor, his views being that he was to form a communal endeavour establishing the submission of the individual to the collective good. Charity and friendship were to be the guiding pillars of the colony with a covenant agreeing that all should live under God's law. After the Massachusetts' Charter only Maryland received one in 1632 as a sanctuary for Roman Catholics, while other new colonies were administered and organized by proprietory charters. The inhabitants of these received certain legislative privileges, but authority over the new colonies was delivered to the owners.

English colonists flooded into Massachusetts between 1630 and 1642 during the Great Migration. East Anglia and the West Country supplied the bulk of the families, seeking new opportunities no longer available in England. Enclosing landlords were commercializing agriculture in their counties, driving their tenants and labourers off the land. These business interests were largely those supporting Parliament against King Charles I during the English Civil War.

Disputes over the parameters between religious idealism and secular materialism soon surfaced. In 1638, Anne Hutchinson, who believed in direct communication with God rather than through ministers, thus threatened men's roles and was banished, moving to Aquidneck Island, later Rhode Island, founding Portsmouth, followed later by Newport in 1639. Others said church and state should be separated and supported religious toleration, or were interested solely in commerce. Settlements followed in Providence, Fort Saybrook, Hartford, Windsor and Wethersfield. The latter three became Connecticut founding an annual assembly with representatives from each town and an elected governor.

By the 1650s, English settlers competed with Swedish colonists along the Delaware, Dutch around New Amsterdam, with French to the north and Spaniards to the south. To complicate issues, relations with Native American nations disintegrated, with European weapons and disease decimating the tribes while the 1637 Pequot War virtually destroyed the Pequot and Narragansett tribes. In the southern colonies, the James River settlements had fought off the native Powhattan confederacy in 1622.

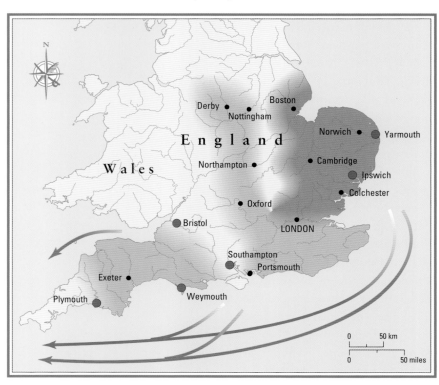

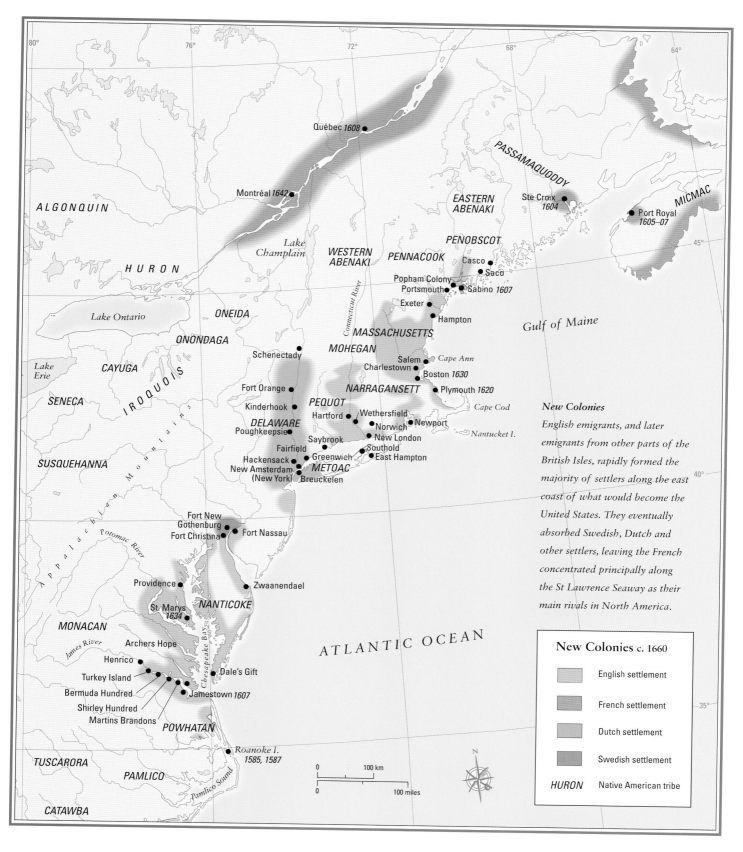

80°   76°   72°   68°   64°

Québec *1608*

Montréal *1642*

PASSAMAQUODDY

ALGONQUIN

Ste Croix *1604*

Port Royal *1605–07*

MICMAC

EASTERN ABENAKI

PENOBSCOT

45°

Lake Champlain

WESTERN ABENAKI

PENNACOOK

HURON

Casco

Saco

Popham Colony

Portsmouth   Sabino *1607*

Gulf of Maine

Exeter

Hampton

Lake Ontario

ONEIDA

ONONDAGA

Schenectady

MASSACHUSETTS

MOHEGAN

Salem   *Cape Ann*

Lake Erie

CAYUGA

Charlestown

Boston *1630*

SENECA

Fort Orange

NARRAGANSETT

Plymouth *1620*

IROQUOIS

Kinderhook

PEQUOT

Cape Cod

Hartford   Wethersfield

Newport

DELAWARE

Poughkeepsie

Norwich

Nantucket I.

Saybrook

New London

Fairfield

Southold

SUSQUEHANNA

Hackensack

Greenwich

East Hampton

New Amsterdam

(New York)

METOAC

Breuckelen

40°

Fort New Gothenburg

Potomac River

Fort Christina

Fort Nassau

New Colonies

English emigrants, and later emigrants from other parts of the British Isles, rapidly formed the majority of settlers along the east coast of what would become the United States. They eventually absorbed Swedish, Dutch and other settlers, leaving the French concentrated principally along the St Lawrence Seaway as their main rivals in North America.

Providence

Zwaanendael

St. Marys *1634*

NANTICOKE

MONACAN

James River

Archers Hope

ATLANTIC OCEAN

Henrico

Turkey Island

Dale's Gift

Bermuda Hundred

Shirley Hundred

35°

Martins Brandons

Jamestown *1607*

POWHATAN

TUSCARORA

Roanoke I. *1585, 1587*

PAMLICO

Pamlico Sound

N

CATAWBA

	New Colonies c. 1660
	English settlement
	French settlement
	Dutch settlement
	Swedish settlement
HURON	Native American tribe

0   100 km

0   100 miles

King or Parliament – Civil Wars

Tradition stated that the King was subject to the law and he could not raise taxes nor pass legislation without the consent of Parliament. However, Charles I had taken his father's absolutist ideas and tendencies to heart. He confronted Parliament, imprisoned members and ruled for eleven years without Parliament. Denying the ship tax for more than one year and, strapped for cash, he raised money in various ways, using old laws and acting illegally according to his critics. In the subsequent civil war, fought in England, Scotland and Ireland, the King faced an alliance between a group of aristocrats and the prosperous middle-class. The latter were often innovating landlords, using experimental agricultural techniques and efficient business management, who were enclosing land and dispossessing small farmers and cottagers, turning them into rural wage labour; the victims of agricultural capitalism. In the landlords' eyes, the King championed old economic modes of production, making him an obstacle to progress. Additionally, support for the Parliamentary Army, the Roundheads, developed strongly among Calvinists and other dissenting sects, such as the Levellers. The Protestant faith was adopted by numerous middle class, artisan and merchant families, who saw in the King the personification of Roman Catholicism, an old enemy recalling Marian burnings and the Tudor wars with Spain.

Reinforcing constitutional resistance to absolutist monarchy, associated with the notion of Divine Right, was hostility towards centralization: against the diminution of county and urban radicals and borough representation in Parliament; and, hatred of High Church Anglicanism, a blink away from Rome, that supported privileges of monarchy and the principles of clerical authority over the laity. Furthermore, the intellectual stimuli of the Renaissance and the Reformation, together with a growth in the knowledge of science and reason, was the spread of secular education in England and Scotland, resulting in the rise of an independent-minded and self-confident social grouping often influenced by the growth of English Puritanism. These questioning classes, rooted in early capitalism, at the time of population growth, wished to remove the last vestiges of feudalism and constrain the monarchy.

Charles was first seriously questioned by the Scots National Covenant, which successfully resisted the political and Church reforms that the King sought to impose from London. The Covenant's General Assembly abolished episcopacy, settled the liturgy and canons and gave the final shape to the Scots Kirk. The King sought a military solution but the Scots scattered his forces and occupied the North of England. To buy off the Scots, the King was forced to summon Parliament, the Long Parliament (1640–60), which now had the monarch over a barrel. A compromise over Parliamentary-demanded reforms might have been negotiated except that an Irish rebellion broke out in 1641, bringing to London news of the murder of 30,000 Protestants in Ulster.

Negotiations between King and Parliament collapsed and Charles raised his standard at Nottingham on 22 August 1642, inaugurating the Civil War. The King's support was based in the North and West of England with support in Wales and amongst Catholics. Parliament's strength lay in London and the south-eastern counties, as well as cloth-working areas. The Scots Covenanters were eventually drawn into the conflict on Parliament's side. The military organizations devised were that associations of individual counties would have forces based in them while the counties were responsible for billeting and logistics. In practice, the Eastern Association for Parliament was the only efficient example providing the wherewithal for Cromwell's New Model Army. The war was characterized by skirmishes, ambushes, patrol actions, cattle rustling and guerrilla warfare, with each side seeking to destabilize the other's base regions and supplies. Although areas controlled varied over time, military supplies

English Civil War

The Royalist base in Oxfordshire saw its troops and garrisons distributed from the Chilterns to the Berkshire Downs and Cotswolds. Troops at Donnington Castle would raid Warwickshire and Buckinghamshire. Considering the small sizes of armies, a very large area was needed for supplies, forage and food. This region was a constant target for Parliamentarian raids.

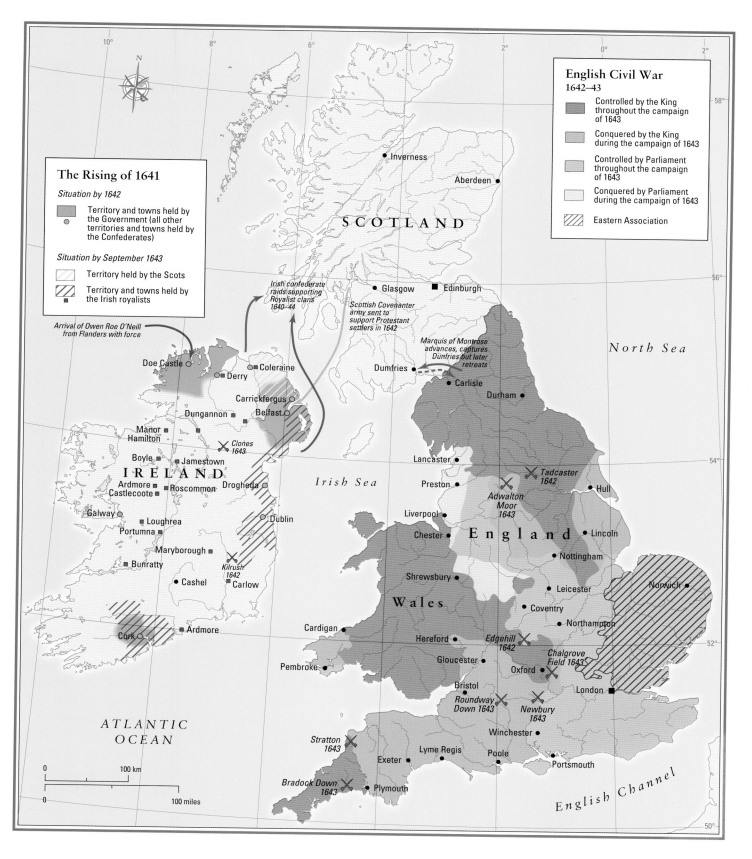

English Civil War
1642–43

- Controlled by the King throughout the campaign of 1643
- Conquered by the King during the campaign of 1643
- Controlled by Parliament throughout the campaign of 1643
- Conquered by Parliament during the campaign of 1643
- Eastern Association

The Rising of 1641

Situation by 1642

- Territory and towns held by the Government (all other territories and towns held by the Confederates)

Situation by September 1643

- Territory held by the Scots
- Territory and towns held by the Irish royalists

Arrival of Owen Roe O'Neill from Flanders with force

Irish confederate raids supporting Royalist clans 1640–44

Scottish Covenanter army sent to support Protestant settlers in 1642

Marquis of Montrose advances, captures Dumfries but later retreats

North Sea

Inverness

Aberdeen

S C O T L A N D

Glasgow   Edinburgh

Dumfries

Carlisle

Durham

Doe Castle

Derry   Coleraine

Carrickfergus

Dungannon   Belfast

Manor Hamilton

Clones 1643

Boyle   Jamestown

Irish Sea

Lancaster

Preston

Adwalton Moor 1643

Tadcaster 1642

Hull

I R E L A N D

Ardmore   Roscommon   Drogheda

Castlecoote

Galway

Loughrea   Dublin

Portumna

Maryborough

Bunratty

Kilrush 1642

Cashel   Carlow

Liverpool

Chester   E n g l a n d   Lincoln

Nottingham

Shrewsbury

Leicester   Norwich

W a l e s   Coventry

Northampton

Cardigan

Hereford   Edgehill 1642

Chalgrove Field 1643

Ardmore

Cork

Gloucester   Oxford

London

Pembroke

Bristol

Roundway Down 1643   Newbury 1643

A T L A N T I C   O C E A N

Stratton 1643

Winchester

Lyme Regis   Poole

Exeter   Portsmouth

Bradock Down 1643   Plymouth

English Channel

0   100 km

0   100 miles

for the King arrived from the Midlands and, after their capture in 1643, from Bristol and the western ports. The Parliamentary war effort received much help from the commercial centre of London.

Parliament's major advantage lay in its access to the chief ports, the sea and the navy. Its army was helped by sound administration, good communications and a unified command. Financed by a solid taxation system and access to the more populous regions of the country, the Parliamentary army also benefited from religious and puritanical zeal, discipline, training and the development of a numerically superior cavalry under Oliver Cromwell. His professionalism and that of the New Model Army meant that troops obeyed orders rather than dash off in an ill-disciplined rabble like Cavalier Rupert's cavalry.

In 1642, the Battle of Edgehill was drawn and Parliament suffered heavy losses in the southwest, which were not made good by some small gains in the northwest. Rupert captured Bristol but Parliament's Commander, Essex, relieved a siege of Gloucester. The King looked to be in a superior position in 1643 but then Parliament won the support of the Scots Covenanters. The Scots marched south and joined Parliament at the battle of Marston Moor in 1644. The Scots suffered from Rupert's cavalry but victory went to the Roundheads who secured the North by this crucial battle, with York and Newcastle surrendering. Elsewhere, the Marquis of Montrose slipped into Scotland and raised some Highland clans for Charles and scored notable victories over the Covenanters until Parliament sent Scots General Leslie north. He finally defeated Montrose at Philiphaugh in 1645, who fled to Europe.

The year 1645 saw the Battle of Naseby, giving the New Model Army a decisive victory over Charles who surrendered to the Scots after the last battle at Stowe-on-the-Wold. The war would continue for a year and a half until Parliament had secured the entire country. The King was handed to Parliament, which attempted negotia-

English Civil War
In 1644, Parliamentary forces comprised the New Model Army and seven regional armies. The new force possessed an establishment of 22,000 men: 11 regiments of 600 horses; one regiment of dragoons (1000); and 12 of foot (1,200 each). This army was liable for service anywhere in the country and its officers were selected for professionalism not birth. This force knocked the Royalists out of the war in just two hours at the Battle of Naseby.

tions, presenting the Four Bills reform suggestions in December 1647. Meanwhile, Charles, who had been play-acting, had signed a secret treaty with the Scots who feared the rising toleration in England. The Scots agreed to restore Charles to his throne by force.

This Second Civil War between Scotland and England broke out after Charles escaped incarceration in the Isle of Wight. Cromwell crushed the Scots at the Battle of Preston and sundry Royalist uprisings were broken at St. Fagans near Cardiff and at Maidstone, with a final Royalist force defeated at Colchester. The Royalist commanders, Lucas and Lisle, contrary to convention were, by General Fairfax's orders, shot after surrendering. Charles was seized by the army who now controlled parliament. A show trial was held and Charles refuted all accusations using the law and Constitution. Those watching the trial backed Charles but the army wanted his death, and so it happened. On 30 September, demonstrating remarkable courage and dignity, the King was sacrificed in the interests of the army, being beheaded at the Banqueting Hall in London on 30 January, 1649.

Charles I stands out as a believer in absolutism. However, he fearlessly confronted the Army, which had destroyed all Parliamentary government by 1648, a Parliament about to plunge England into a military dictatorship and tyranny which was restrictive in political, religious and social terms. Ultimately, he died for English liberties and for the English Church, even though he failed to defend them. The Army failed to realize that the death of the man did not end the past because all Charles' prerogatives and visions now devolved upon his son and heir, Charles II. To secure Army control, Cromwell was now faced by an 11 years' war in Ireland, conflict in Scotland, and the hostility of most people who did not support military political extremism. The country would suffer cant, hypocrisy and social suffering until the Restoration.

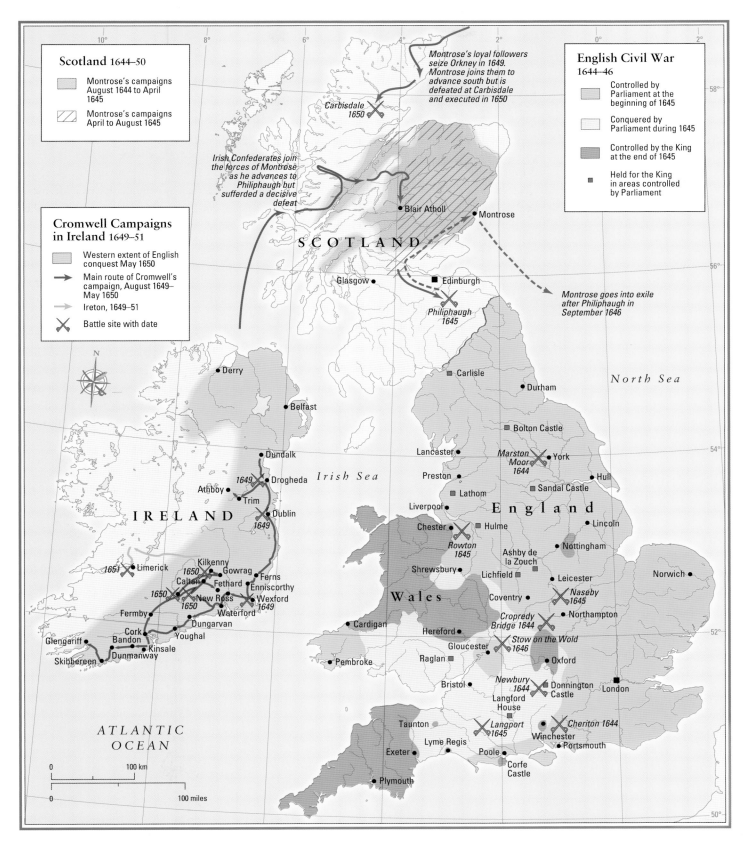

Scotland 1644–50

- Montrose's campaigns August 1644 to April 1645
- Montrose's campaigns April to August 1645

Cromwell Campaigns in Ireland 1649–51

- Western extent of English conquest May 1650
- Main route of Cromwell's campaign, August 1649–May 1650
- Ireton, 1649–51
- Battle site with date

English Civil War 1644–46

- Controlled by Parliament at the beginning of 1645
- Conquered by Parliament during 1645
- Controlled by the King at the end of 1645
- Held for the King in areas controlled by Parliament

Montrose's loyal followers seize Orkney in 1649. Montrose joins them to advance south but is defeated at Carbisdale and executed in 1650

Irish Confederates join the forces of Montrose as he advances to Philiphaugh but suffered a decisive defeat

Montrose goes into exile after Philiphaugh in September 1646

Carbisdale 1650

Blair Atholl

Montrose

S C O T L A N D

Glasgow

Edinburgh

Philiphaugh 1645

North Sea

Derry

Belfast

Carlisle

Durham

Bolton Castle

Lancaster

Marston Moor 1644

York

Dundalk

Irish Sea

Preston

Hull

1649 Drogheda

Lathom

Sandal Castle

Athboy

Trim

E n g l a n d

I R E L A N D

1649 Dublin

Liverpool

Lincoln

Chester

Hulme

Limerick 1651

Kilkenny

Gowrag

Rowton 1645

Nottingham

Ferns

Ashby de la Zouch

Calton 1650

Fethard

Shrewsbury

Lichfield

Leicester

Norwich

1650

New Ross

Enniscorthy

Coventry

Naseby 1645

1650

Waterford

Wexford 1649

W a l e s

Northampton

Fermby

Dungarvan

Cropredy Bridge 1644

Cork

Youghal

Cardigan

Hereford

Stow on the Wold 1646

Glengariff

Bandon

Kinsale

Gloucester

Oxford

Skibbereen

Dunmanway

Pembroke

Raglan

Newbury 1644

Donnington Castle

London

Bristol

Langford House

Taunton

Langport 1645

Cheriton 1644

Lyme Regis

Winchester

ATLANTIC OCEAN

Exeter

Poole

Portsmouth

Corfe Castle

Plymouth

0   100 km

0   100 miles

Cromwell's Republic

The execution of King Charles I ushered in the Commonwealth (1649–60), a republican form of government. Strictly speaking, legislative power remained in the Rump Parliament, comprising some fifty Independent members of the Long Parliament. Executive power was vested in a council of state of forty-one, these being three judges, three army officers, five peers and thirty members of the Commons. The title of King was abolished, as was the House of Lords. However, real power resided in the army and Oliver Cromwell, its leader.

In February 1649, the Scots proclaimed Charles II in Edinburgh and the Irish rose on his side under Ormonde. Cromwell, a pious man believing God was on his side and that the Irish were pagans, descended on Ireland in a burst of fury and suppressed the rebellion with extreme violence and cruelty, leaving scars on the Irish psyche which still exist today. Drogheda was stormed, as was Wexford, with massacres of the garrisons and innocent citizens following. Cromwell returned to England leaving Ireton to mop up remaining rebels by 1653. The settlement that followed abolished the Irish Parliament; confiscated land that was given to veterans of the Parliamentary Army, including a coastal strip of Connacht; created government reservations; and, reserved land for transplanted Irish in Connacht. Scotland saw the return of Montrose, his defeat and execution after the Battle of Carbisdale. Charles II arrived in 1650. Leslie and the Scots army faced Cromwell at the Battle of Dunbar, being defeated and leaving the successful Cromwell to pursue Charles and another Royalist army that had invaded England. King Charles was crushed at Worcester in 1651 and fled to France, hiding along the way in an oak tree near Boscobel House.

The Commonwealth was a government of generals and Cromwell overthrew the Rump Parliament because it was becoming anti-military and dissolved the council of state. He established a new council and a nominated parliament (Little Parliament), which resigned its powers to Cromwell who established the Protectorate in 1653 with Cromwell as Lord Protector of England, Scotland and Ireland. Between sessions of parliament, Cromwell and his council could issue edicts but this was balanced by parliament granting supplies and levying taxes, the power of the purse.

Cromwell's rule was characterized by freedom of religion for Protestants but not for Catholics and Quakers, and a nationalistic and militaristic foreign policy. The English Navy was strengthened and fought the Dutch over the 1651 Navigation Act, which forbade the importation of goods into England unless in English ships or in ships of the country producing the goods. War with Spain erupted after the English capture of Jamaica in 1656 and saw a treasure fleet seized off Cadiz and a naval victory at Santa Cruz in 1657. Dunkirk, the port of privateers, was surrendered to the English and retained by treaty. Elsewhere, the Navy cleared the Channel of pirates and damped down Royalist privateering. Further afield, Admiral Blake entered the Mediterranean, assaulting the Barbary pirate bases to sound effect.

Domestically, in 1655, the rising of Penruddock at Salisbury was suppressed and England divided into twelve military districts, each with military forces supported by a tax of ten per cent on Royalist estates. The Puritans weakened the Poor Law believing that poverty should be punished and not relieved. Socially, gambling and swearing were banned and subject to fines. Ale houses were closed, Christmas Day discouraged, maypoles cut down, walking on Sunday except to church was punishable and all types of athletic sports banned. Laws attempted to ban all types of male and female adornment and elaborate clothing. However, this system of petty repression generated hostility but this was tempered by a respect for property, the opening up of England to Jews and the protection of English commerce but Cromwell's vision collapsed following his death in September, 1658.

Cromwell's Republic

Noted for its harshness, the Cromwellian Republic butchered 3,500 people at Drogheda and more elsewhere. After the Battle of Dunbar, Scots prisoners were so badly treated in a march south that some 2,000 died before reaching Durham. In England, unable to regulate the publication of political and religious tracts, Cromwell established a commission to censor the press. This nightmare offended some but others saw the defeat of the Dutch and the seizure of Spanish Jamaica as God's work.

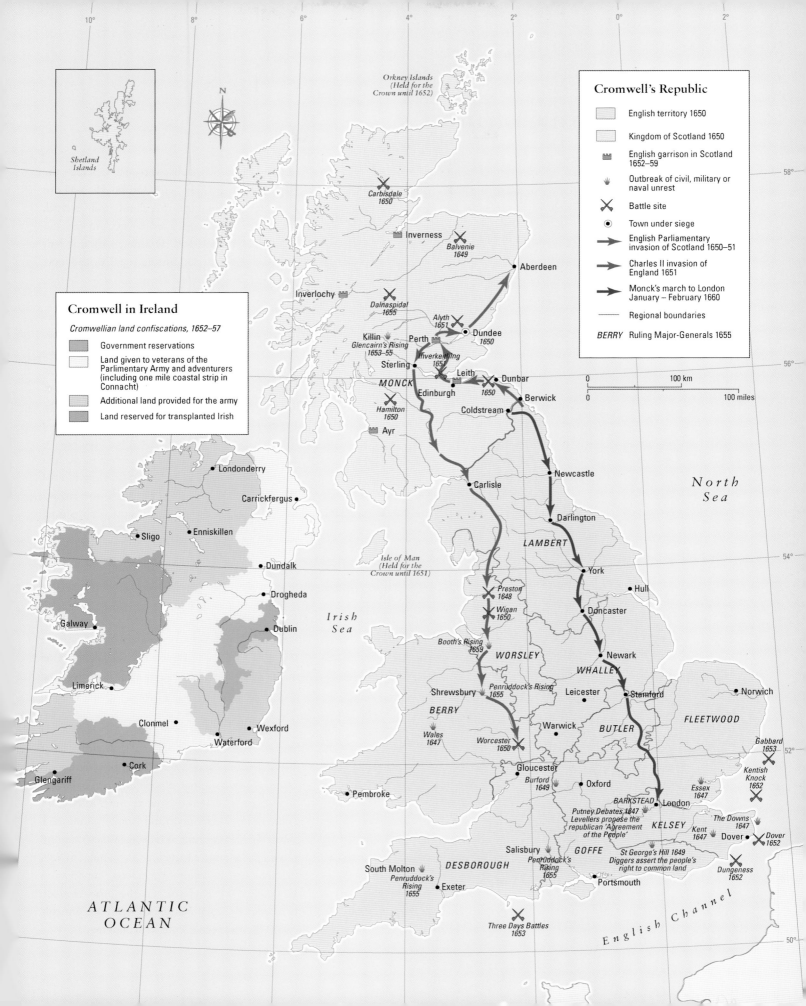

Shetland Islands

Orkney Islands
(Held for the
Crown until 1652)

N

Cromwell's Republic

	English territory 1650
	Kingdom of Scotland 1650
♚	English garrison in Scotland 1652–59
⚘	Outbreak of civil, military or naval unrest
✗	Battle site
⊙	Town under siege
→	English Parliamentary invasion of Scotland 1650–51
→	Charles II invasion of England 1651
→	Monck's march to London January – February 1660
—	Regional boundaries
BERRY	Ruling Major-Generals 1655

Cromwell in Ireland

Cromwellian land confiscations, 1652–57

	Government reservations
	Land given to veterans of the Parlimentary Army and adventurers (including one mile coastal strip in Connacht)
	Additional land provided for the army
	Land reserved for transplanted Irish

✗ Carbisdale 1650

♚ Inverness

✗ Balvenie 1649

● Aberdeen

Inverlochy ♚

✗ Dalnaspidal 1655

Killin
Glencairn's Rising 1653–55

Perth

Alyth 1651

● Dundee 1650

Sterling

Inverkeithing 1651

MONCK

Leith

● Dunbar

Edinburgh

Dunbar 1650

● Berwick

✗ Hamilton 1650

♚ Ayr

Coldstream

0   100 km
0   100 miles

● Newcastle

● Carlisle

● Darlington

LAMBERT

● York

● Hull

Isle of Man
(Held for the
Crown until 1651)

✗ Preston 1648

✗ Wigan 1650

● Doncaster

● Londonderry

● Carrickfergus

● Sligo   ● Enniskillen

● Dundalk

● Drogheda

● Dublin

*Irish
Sea*

Booth's Rising 1659

WORSLEY

● Newark

WHALLEY

● Leicester

● Stamford

● Norwich

● Galway

● Limerick

● Clonmel

● Wexford
Waterford

Shrewsbury

Penruddock's Rising 1655

BERRY

⚘ Wales 1647

● Gloucester

Worcester 1650 ✗

● Warwick

BUTLER

FLEETWOOD

✗ Gabbard 1653

Kentish Knock 1652

● Glengariff

● Cork

*ATLANTIC
OCEAN*

● Pembroke

Burford 1649 ⚘   ● Oxford

BARKSTEAD

Putney Debates 1647
Levellers propose the
republican 'Agreement
of the People'

● London

Essex 1647

KELSEY

Kent 1647

The Downs 1647

● Dover   ✗ Dover 1652

● Salisbury

South Molton ⚘
*Penruddock's
Rising
1655*

● Exeter

DESBOROUGH

Penruddock's Rising 1655 ⚘

GOFFE

St George's Hill 1649
Diggers assert the people's
right to common land

● Portsmouth

Dungeness 1652 ✗

Three Days Battles 1653 ✗

*North
Sea*

English Channel

The American Colonies

In 1607, the foundation of Jamestown began the British colonization in the Americas. The settlement becoming a lodestone for young unmarried men travelling to work the tobacco and sugar plantations of the South and West Indies. Between 1630 and 1642, a Great Migration took place to the Massachusetts Bay Colony with some 20,000 settlers arriving. Whole families migrated to North America, the Bermudas and the Caribbean islands of Nevis, Antigua and Montserrat.

Migration from the British Isles occurred for a variety of reasons. Those from England sailed from Yarmouth and Ipswich in East Anglia; from Southampton in the south; or, from Bristol, Weymouth and Plymouth in the West Country. Thus, most migrants originated in the south and east of England from low-lying lands or those with gentle hills. Norfolk, Suffolk and Essex provided the greatest percentage of colonists, leaving the heartland of where Cromwell recruited his soldiers for the Roundhead Puritan army from the Eastern Association of those counties during the Civil War. During the sixteenth and seventeenth centuries, Puritanism spread through East Anglia into Northamptonshire and Rutland. Some historians argue that these migrants sought religious freedom while others held a desire for land from those being dispossessed of land by land enclosures and the reduction in jobs in the textile industry during the 1640s depression.

Later arrivals to the colonies, after the virtual ending of migration during the Commonwealth dictatorship under Cromwell, were motivated often by different reasons. Stuart monarchs of the Restoration period rewarded their supporters with vast tracts of territory in New York, New Jersey, Pennsylvania and the Carolinas. Some proprietors successfully recruited settlers causing New Jersey and New York to expand rapidly, then incorporating a Dutch population from the former New Amsterdam, renamed New York. A small Swedish population on the Delaware River was also absorbed. Elsewhere, William Penn, a Quaker, was

granted Pennsylvania, viewed as a sanctuary for co-religionists. Likewise, Maryland became a haven for Roman Catholics. The Carolinas developed differently. North Carolina became a virtual economic colony of Virginia, while South Carolina was founded by white Barbadians quitting their overpopulated island and bringing their slave-owning culture with them.

The origins of migration are an intertwined mixture of economic, political and economic factors, occasionally linked to religion and slavery. North Carolina is a case in point, with its rich ethnic mix. In 1730, the population was approximately 30,000 white and 6,000 blacks on the Coastal Plain. By 1775, the population had spread through the Piedmont to the Blue Ridge Mountains with over 265,000 inhabitants. The original settlers boasted English descent but the 1740s saw Scots Highlanders begin to arriving, mainly via Wilmington. Persecution of the clans drove them from Scotland, but, ironically, they generally remained loyal to Britain during the Revolution. The Scots-Irish from Ulster were another migrant group. These Presbyterian dissenters provided Washington with large numbers of recruits during the Revolution. Other migrants were German Lutherans and members of the German Reformed Church, and they peopled the backcountry. One highly coherent German group were the Moravians, whose unique community at Salem was neutral during the Revolution.

Other groups establishing themselves in America were Welsh Quakers who occupied a Welsh Tract in Pennsylvania accounting for a third of the colony's estimated population of 20,000. In 1654, Sephardic Jews arrived in America to New Amsterdam (later New York), some moving elsewhere and prospering as merchants and traders. French Protestants, Huguenots, fled France following intense persecution after King Louis XIV's Revocation of the Edict of Nantes in 1685, bringing their craft skills with them and enriching America just as they had other Protestant countries.

Settlers from the British Isles and Europe

European settlers from Sweden and Finland bought land from the Lenni-Lenape (Delaware) nations intending to engage in agriculture and trade for fur with the Native Americans. Eventually, New Sweden was captured by the Dutch but Swedish immigration continued. The Dutch settlement of New Netherlands was a trading centre rather than a colony. England acquired the Dutch settlements in 1664. English speaking immigrants formed the largest European group by far along the American seaboard.

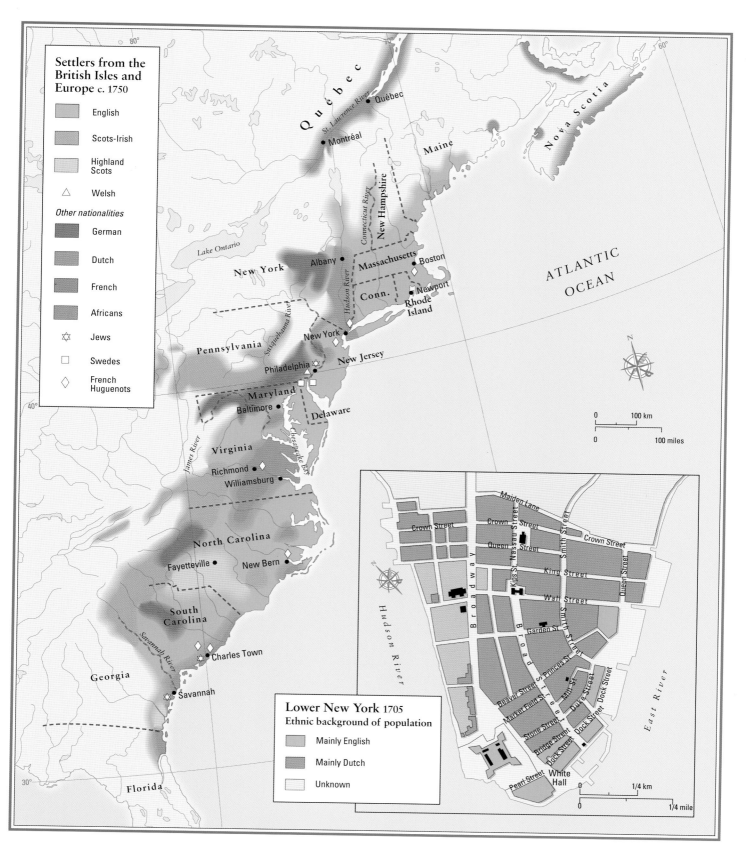

Settlers from the British Isles and Europe c. 1750

- English
- Scots-Irish
- Highland Scots
- △ Welsh

Other nationalities
- German
- Dutch
- French
- Africans
- ✡ Jews
- □ Swedes
- ◇ French Huguenots

Québec

St. Lawrence River

Québec

Montréal

Quebec

Nova Scotia

Maine

New Hampshire

Connecticut River

Lake Ontario

New York

Albany

Hudson River

Massachusetts

Boston

Conn.

Newport

Rhode Island

ATLANTIC OCEAN

New York

Pennsylvania

Susquehanna River

New York

New Jersey

Philadelphia

Maryland

Baltimore

Delaware

James River

Chesapeake Bay

Virginia

Richmond

Williamsburg

North Carolina

Fayetteville

New Bern

South Carolina

Savannah River

Charles Town

Georgia

Savannah

Florida

0 — 100 km
0 — 100 miles

Lower New York 1705
Ethnic background of population

- Mainly English
- Mainly Dutch
- Unknown

Hudson River

East River

Maiden Lane

Crown Street

Crown Street

Crown Street

Queen Street

Nassau Street

Smith Street

Queen Street

Broadway

Kips St.

King Street

Wall Street

Broad Street

Smith Street

Garden St.

Beaver Street

Princes St.

Market Field St.

Mill St.

Duke Street

Dock Street

Dock Street

Stone Street

Bridge Street

Dock Street

Pearl Street

White Hall

0 — 1/4 km
0 — 1/4 mile

The Great Fire and Reconstruction 1666

Great Fire of London
1666

- Area of fire on Sunday 2 September
- Area of fire by Wednesday 5 September
- Parks
- Parish Church
- Graveyard
- City Wall
- Ward boundary
- Walled area
- Other boundaries

In September 1666, a fire broke out at 2 am in the premises of the King's baker, Thomas Farynor, in Pudding Lane, near London Bridge. The overhanging timber buildings and narrow streets proved to be a tinder box allowing flames to spread rapidly. By morning, London Bridge was afire but a large gap separating two groups of buildings acted as a firebreak, preventing the conflagration spreading over the Thames into Southwark.

The fire became largely confined to the City

of London. King Charles II and his brother, James, Duke of York, were immediately involved in fire-fighting, Charles ordering houses to be demolished as firebreaks but to no avail. Ultimately, houses were blown up stopping the flames spreading and blowing out fires. Three days of devastation saw St. Paul's Cathedral burnt, together with 13,200 houses, 84 churches and 44 livery company halls. However, luckily there were few deaths recorded. The ground was too hot to walk on for several days afterwards. In

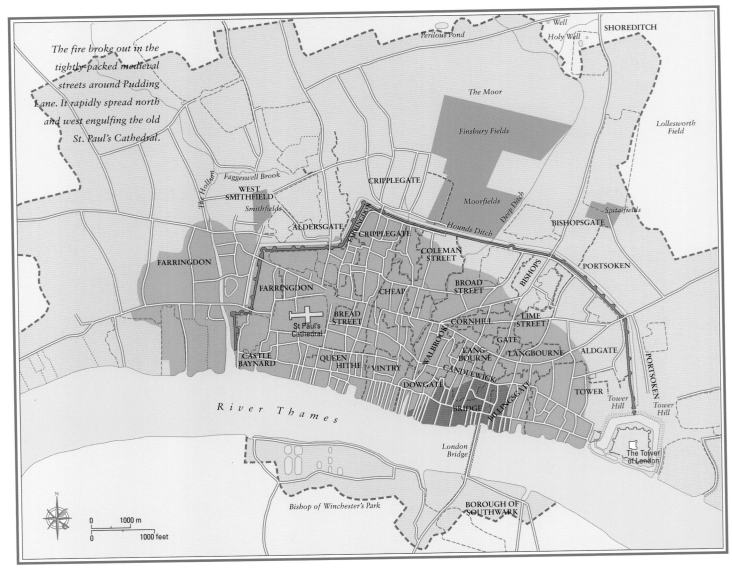

The fire broke out in the tightly-packed medieval streets around Pudding Lane. It rapidly spread north and west engulfing the old St. Paul's Cathedral.

a state of shock, Londoners felt the need to blame someone for this disaster that had befallen them. With religious bigotry and xenophobia recurring they attacked Roman Catholics, the French, the Dutch and almost any other suitable minority group. A French Protestant watchmaker confessed to arson and was hanged at Tyburn. The Monument commemorating the conflagration was inscribed, wrongly accusing a 'Popish frenzy' for setting London alight.

The King appointed Commissioners, including Sir Christopher Wren, to regulate the rebuilding of London. One proposed grid plan was discarded but subsequently adopted by the American planners of Philadelphia. Numerous churches were rebuilt, as was the Cathedral under the aegis of Wren. The opportunity to create public squares with new public buildings was swamped by vested interests. By 1670, 6,000 new houses had been built, with the city rebuilt by 1676. However, many merchants had lost their stock and were ruined, there being virtually no fire insurance. There was one benefit from the Great Fire. It seemed the city was cleansed of the causes of the plague, which lasted from 1664–66 and left 68,000 of its citizens dead.

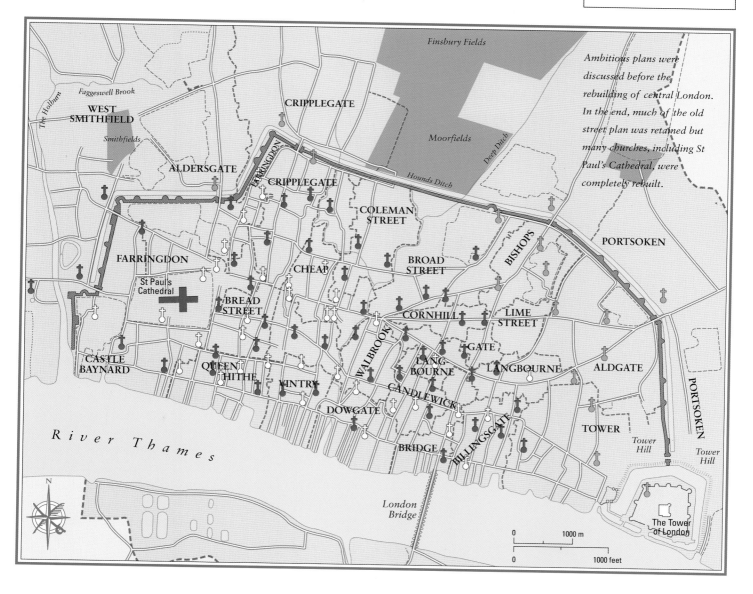

London's Spiritual Rebuilding 1666

- Church surviving the fire
- Church destroyed not rebuilt
- Church rebuilt (some subsequently destroyed)
- – – – City Wall
- – – – Ward boundary
- – – – Walled area
- ········· Other boundaries

Ambitious plans were discussed before the rebuilding of central London. In the end, much of the old street plan was retained but many churches, including St Paul's Cathedral, were completely rebuilt.

'Glorious Revolution' to the Act of Union

Glorious Revolution

The Revolution of 1688–89 resulted in the forced abdication of James II and the succession of William III and Mary II.

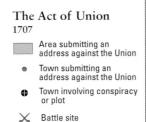

The Act of Union
1707

☐ Area submitting an address against the Union

● Town submitting an address against the Union

⊕ Town involving conspiracy or plot

✕ Battle site

Greeted with public outpourings of joy, Charles II's Restoration in 1660 was marked by moderation whereby he sought to pardon enemies in the Act of Indemnity and to advocate religious toleration. However, Parliament was harsher in excluding religious dissidents and two thousand parish priests lost their livings. The 1670s witnessed a royal move towards absolutism, which was countered by a recurrence of left-wing and republican ideas. From now on adherents of the two ideological stances were Tories and Whigs respectively. Charles settled for ruling without Parliament from 1681 until he died in 1685, having successfully outwitted campaigns to exclude his Catholic brother, James, from the succession. Whigs and Non-conformists experienced persecution after this Tory victory.

As King, James II alienated every powerful elite group in the land and when his second Catholic wife gave birth to a son, fears grew of his absolutism continuing. His position grew stronger when the Duke of Monmouth, an illegitimate son of Charles II, led a rebellion that was defeated at the Battle of Sedgemoor in 1685. The Bloody Assizes run by Judge Jefferies saw 333 alleged rebels given the death sentence and 814 transported to the Caribbean. James then increased the size of the army to improve his personal security. He proceeded to appoint Catholics to important positions, attacked the authority of the Established Church, and meddled with officials in local government; his enemies grew in number, including important Tories.

Consequently, William of Orange, husband of James' Protestant daughter, Mary, was invited to depose the King. A successful invasion saw William and Mary crowned in a 'Glorious Revolution' in 1688 in a regime which was politically moderate and pragmatic. William's major interest was in using England's wealth and troops against Louis XIV of France, a war in which John Churchill, Duke of Marlborough, achieved fame and fortune. William's financial needs required regular meetings with Parliament and inaugurated the unbroken annual Parliaments ever since.

The Act of Settlement in 1701 stated that Mary's death should be followed by the accession of her sister Anne and then go to her closest Protestant relative, which was the Dowager Electress Sophia of Hanover or her issue. Queen Anne (1702–14) presided over Whig and Tory political conflicts and the 1707 Act of Union with Scotland, which saw that country disappearing as a self-governing unit in the new Great Britain. Seemingly, Scots elites had been bought off with economic inducements in the best of all possible bad deals for Scotland. Meanwhile, the Tories' right-wing became so virulently old fashioned that it regarded the Old Pretender to be the true heir. This incompetence pushed the Tories into the political wilderness for the next forty-five years.

In 1706 the Scots agreed to send 16 Peers and 45 MPs to the English Parliament in return for full trading privileges and the equalisation of customs duties with England and its possessions.

Orkney Islands

Shetland Islands

Inverness
✕ *Cromdale 1690*
● Peterhead

S C O T L A N D

Stonehaven

✕ *Massacre of Glencoe 1692*
✕ *Killiecrankie 1689*
● Forfar
✕ *Dunkeld 1689*
Perth ⊕
— Magus Muir
Archbishop of St Andrews murdered by Convenanters 1679

Inveraray ●
St Andrews
Stirling ●
Edinburgh
Glasgow
Dunbar
Paisley
✕ *Bothwell Brig 1679*
✕ *Rullion Green 1666*
Drumclog 1679 ✕
Airds Moss 1680 ✕

North Sea

Campbeltown ●
Earl of Argyll's landing May 1685
Ayr ●
⊕
Convenanters' Sanquhar Declaration 1680
● Lochmaben
● Annan

● Kirkcudbright

0 ___ 100 km
0 ___ 100 miles

N

'Glorious Revolution'
1660–91

✗ Battle site

✛ Town involving conspiracy or plot

➔ Duke of Monmouth's route to Sedgemoor 1685

➔ Invasion route of William of Orange in 1688

The Williamite War in Ireland

Kingdoms recognising James II

➔ Campaign of 1690

➔ Campaign of 1691

✳ Siege town with date

Orkney Islands

Inverness •

✗ *Cromdale 1690*

• Peterhead

S C O T L A N D

• Stonehaven

S C O T L A N D

✗ *Killiecrankie 1689*

• Forfar

Magus Muir
Archbishop of St Andrews murdered by Convenanters 1679

Inveraray •

✗ *Dunkeld 1689*

Perth •

✛ St Andrews •

Stirling •

Edinburgh •

North Sea

Glasgow •
Paisley •

✗ *Bothwell Brig 1679*

• Dunbar

✗ *Rullion Green 1666*

Drumclog 1679

Campbeltown •
Earl of Argyll's landing May 1685

✗ *Airds Moss 1680*

Ayr •

✛ *Convenanters' Sanquhar Declaration 1680*

• Annan

• Newcastle

Londonderry
✳ *1689*

• Kirkcudbright

William III lands in Ireland 1690 • Carrickfergus
Bangor
Williamite forces under Schomberg land 1689

Mugglesweick ✛
Derwentdale Republican Plot 1663

Enniskillen ✳ • Armagh
1689

✗ Dromore
1689

✗ *Newtownbutler 1689*

• Dundalk

Isle of Man

I R E L A N D

Ballymore • Mullingar •
Aughrim 1691 ✗

• Drogheda

✗ *Boyne 1690*

Irish Sea

Harrogate ✛ • York
Yorkshire Republican Plot 1663

Galway •
Athlone *1691*

Dublin •
James II convenes the 'Patriot Parliament' May–July 1689

• Liverpool

• Sheffield

• Banagher

Denbigh •

• Chester

Limerick ✳
1690

Caherconlish •

• Carlow
Bennetsbridge •

• Derby

• Carrick-on-Suir

W A L E S

• Leicester

• Birmingham

E N G L A N D

Norwich •

• Cambridge

Kinsale ✳
1690

Cork ✳
1690

• Gloucester

• Carmarthen

Abingdon •
• Oxford

Rye House
'Popish Plot' 1678 ✛

✛ *Plot 1683*

• London

Cardiff •

• Bristol

'Secret' Treaty of Dover

Bath •
Sedgemoor 1685 Monmouth's army of West Country religious dissenters defeated 5–6 July

Wells •

• Newbury

Dover ✛
1670

Charles II lands 25 May 1660

Bridgwater ✗
Taunton •

Shepton Mallet •
Frome •

Ilminster •

• Sherborne

• Portsmouth

Exeter •

Lyme Regis •
Duke of Monmouth lands 11 Jan. 1685

Plymouth •

• Brixham
William of Orange lands 5 Nov. 1688

English Channel

0   100 km
0   100 miles

N

129

Ireland and Scotland 1690 – 1715

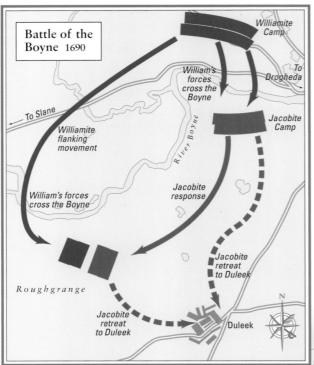

Battle of the Boyne 1690

Galway and Limerick fell, leaving William in control of Ireland.

The Presbyterian dominance in the Convention of Scottish Estates guaranteed William's rule south of the Tay, though here Viscount Dundee raised troops on behalf of James. The Scots government army was beaten at the Battle of Killikrankie by a Highland charge, yet Dundee lost a third of his men to volley fire, dying himself. The Jacobites were defeated at Dunkeld and finished off at the Haughs of Cromdale in May 1690. The clans were quiet until 1715 when a brief rebellion occurred led by James Edward Stuart, known as the Old Pretender.

Britain's new King, William of Orange, faced rebellions in both Scotland and Ireland. In 1689, James landed in Ireland and besieged Derry, which was filled with Protestant refugees. The city held out, starving until relief ships broke through the siege lines and boom across the River Foyle and landed food. Shortly afterwards, William landed at Carrickfergus to campaign against James who was sponsored by William's enemy, Louis XIV of France. James retreated to Dublin and decided to hold the line of the River Boyne. William advanced, defeating James' army, which retreated, covered by a skilled French rearguard ensuring that three-quarters of the Jacobite army survived. It was later to be defeated at Aughrim, losing nearly 8,000 men.

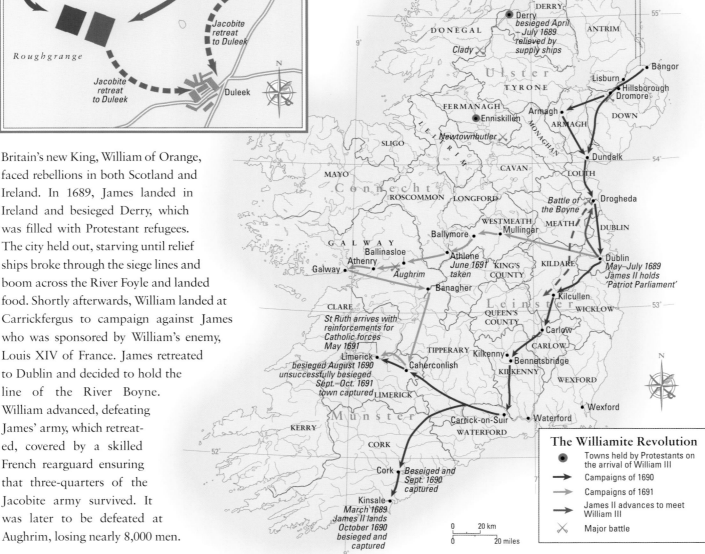

The Williamite Revolution

- ⊙ Towns held by Protestants on the arrival of William III
- → Campaigns of 1690
- → Campaigns of 1691
- → James II advances to meet William III
- ✕ Major battle

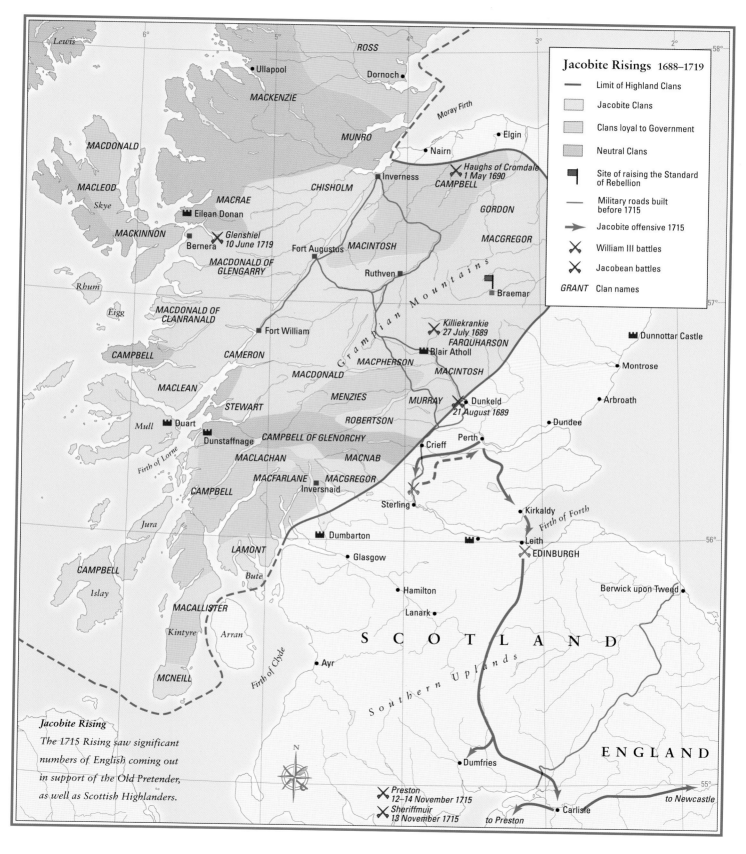

Jacobite Risings 1688–1719

- Limit of Highland Clans
- Jacobite Clans
- Clans loyal to Government
- Neutral Clans
- Site of raising the Standard of Rebellion
- Military roads built before 1715
- Jacobite offensive 1715
- William III battles
- Jacobean battles

GRANT Clan names

Lewis

Ullapool

Dornoch

ROSS

MACKENZIE

Moray Firth

MUNRO

Elgin

Nairn

Inverness

Haughs of Cromdale
1 May 1690

CAMPBELL

CHISHOLM

MACDONALD

MACLEOD

Skye

MACRAE

Eilean Donan

MACKINNON

Bernera

Glenshiel
10 June 1719

*MACDONALD OF
GLENGARRY*

Fort Augustus

MACINTOSH

Ruthven

GORDON

MACGREGOR

Braemar

Rhum

Eigg

*MACDONALD OF
CLANRANALD*

Fort William

CAMERON

MACDONALD

MACPHERSON

G r a m p i a n   M o u n t a i n s

Killiekrankie
27 July 1689

FARQUHARSON

MACINTOSH

Blair Atholl

Dunnottar Castle

Montrose

CAMPBELL

MACLEAN

STEWART

Mull

Duart

Dunstaffnage

MENZIES

ROBERTSON

CAMPBELL OF GLENORCHY

MURRAY

Dunkeld
21 August 1689

Arbroath

Dundee

MACLACHAN

MACNAB

Crieff

Perth

Firth of Lorne

MACFARLANE

MACGREGOR

Inversnaid

CAMPBELL

Jura

Sterling

Kirkaldy

Firth of Forth

Dumbarton

Leith

EDINBURGH

Glasgow

LAMONT

Bute

Hamilton

Berwick upon Tweed

Lanark

CAMPBELL

Islay

Kintyre

Arran

MACALLISTER

S C O T L A N D

E N G L A N D

MCNEILL

Firth of Clyde

Ayr

S o u t h e r n   U p l a n d s

Jacobite Rising
The 1715 Rising saw significant
numbers of English coming out
in support of the Old Pretender,
as well as Scottish Highlanders.

N

Preston
12–14 November 1715

Sheriffmuir
13 November 1715

Dumfries

Carlisle

to Newcastle

to Preston

Global War

Great Britain was involved in numerous wars in the first half of the eighteenth century: the War of the Spanish Succession; the Jacobite Rebellions; the 1739 War of Jenkins Ear; and the War of the Austrian Succession (1740–48). These and inter-colonial wars were all part of a struggle for the balance of power in Europe where Britain saw itself as curbing French and Spanish ambitions. The last war had seen a European war turn into an Anglo-French conflict, ranging from North America to India and the West Indies. The 1748 Treaty of Aix-la-Chapelle failed to resolve imperial tensions, with France building a series of forts down the Ohio River in North America in an attempt to prevent British-American colonies expanding westwards.

All issues surfaced again in the Seven Years' War (1756–63). Here, British fleets stopped France from reinforcing its empire by controlling sea communication routes. In the Caribbean, the British captured nearly every French and Spanish sugar-producing island. These were kept by the 1763 Treaty of Paris in which the British exchanged Guadeloupe for Canada. Admirals Albermarle and Pocock captured Havana in 1762, occupying the city for six months. British naval victories at Lagos and Quiberon Bay were vital in securing British sea power.

In India, Anglo-French rivalry continued, with each side supporting native rulers to protect both the French and British East India Companies. British sea power enabled reinforcement of its forces led by Robert Clive, who stemmed French advances by seizing Arcot in 1751 and defeating the French-backed claimant to the throne of the Carnatic. This unofficial war merged into the Seven Years' War, during which the British seized French Chandernagore in 1757, while victory at Plassey in 1757 secured Bengal, with victories in the south and the capture of French Pondicherry in 1761 eliminating French influence. Britain was now the world hegemon, resented by all countries.

Global War

Britain's use of sea power effectively sealed off France from its overseas possessions. Between 1756 and 1763, Britain became the dominant global power with possessions stretching across North America, the Caribbean, trading posts in Africa and a developing Empire in India.

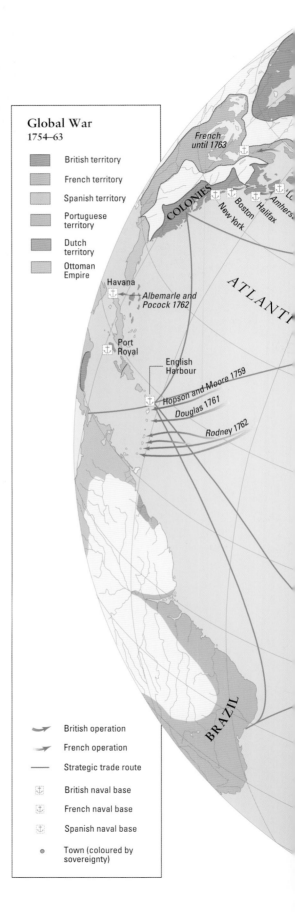

Global War
1754–63

- British territory
- French territory
- Spanish territory
- Portuguese territory
- Dutch territory
- Ottoman Empire

⚓ British operation
→ French operation
— Strategic trade route
⚓ British naval base
⚓ French naval base
⚓ Spanish naval base
● Town (coloured by sovereignty)

RUSSIAN EMPIRE

GREAT
BRITAIN

Hugh and Bligh 1758

ven

Hawke

Keppel 1761

Hawke and Mordaunt 1757

HOLY
ROMAN
EMPIRE

FRANCE

MANCHU
EMPIRE
(CHINA)

Rochefort

Azores

Toulon

Le Galissonnière

1756

OCEAN

PORTUGAL   SPAIN

Lagos 1759

Gibraltar

Cadiz

Byng

Cartagena

La Clue

PERSIA

Panipat 1761   Buxar 1764

Plassey 1757

OTTOMAN EMPIRE

INDIA

Canary Is.

1780–81

Bay of
Bengal

Goa

Madras

S

a   *h*   *a*   *r*   *a*

Gorée   St. Louis

Albredo

ape Verde Is.   Ft. James

Laccadive Is.

Maldive Is.

A   *f*   *r*   *i*   *c*   *a*

INDIAN OCEAN

Assinie   Accra

Elmina   Cape Coast Castle

Chagos
Archipelago

ZANZIBAR

Seychelles

Loanda

ANGOLA

PORTUGUESE
EAST AFRICA

Ste Marie   Mauritius

Bourbon

Madagascar

Fort-Dauphin

Delagoa Bay

133

Cape Town

Britons Abroad

The Treaty of Paris in 1763 ending the Seven Years' War gave Britain territorial control of: Canada, Spanish Florida and all French territories east of the Mississippi. Britain sought to create an imperial policy rather than letting its colonies look after themselves. However, the Thirteen Colonies had developed similar patterns of government with governors, councils, elected legislative assemblies and a system based on English law.

A Royal Proclamation in 1763 prohibited the colonists from establishing settlements west of an imaginary line running down the crest of the Appalachian Mountains. This decree acknowledged that Native Americans possessed the land where they were living and that encroaching white settlers must be removed. The edict sought to avoid warfare with the native nations and concentrate British settlement abroad in the coastal regions and the immediate hinterland where they could be tied in closely to the British mercantile system, making the Britons abroad even more of an economic adjunct of Britain itself. Colonial land speculators and frontier families were angered and ignored the line believing that it would be moved. The adjustment of the line in 1768 and 1775 witnessed white incursions westwards bedevilling relations with the Native Americans.

The British government's high-handed actions and perceived creeping aggression provoked violence among the labouring class, whereas professional classes wished to resolve issues by political debate. A mixture of opposition activity developed, one method feeding off the other in the face of new British demands of its colonial 'subjects'. Inexpedient laws were enacted in 1764 with the Sugar and Currency Acts. The first attempted to stop the smuggling trade in molasses, an important American product. The second banned colonial issuance of paper money, which slowed down trade by diminishing the medium of exchange. That these acts occurred during a slump causing immense distress occasioned petitions against the Sugar Act by eight colonial assemblies; these were rejected.

The 1765 Stamp Act required a tax stamp on most printed material, paid in Sterling. Violators would be tried in an admiralty court without a jury. The colonies claimed that they taxed themselves and the British Parliament could not impose taxes because the Britons abroad were not represented in that institution. 1776 saw the Act repealed in the face of opposition from both American and British merchants. Yet the 1776 Declaratory Act stated that the British Parliament possessed the authority to tax and enact laws for America in all cases.

The 1767 Townshend Act sought to extract colonial taxes by placing levies on glass, paper, tea, lead, and painters' colours. Revenues thus extracted would pay fixed salaries to royal officials in the colonies. A two-year colonial campaign was waged against the Townshend Acts ranging from colonial non-importation agreements to riots. In 1770, the acts were repealed except that on tea. The 1773 Boston Tea Party resulted, which pushed the new British Ministry of American Affairs to demand the Coercive Acts. The Boston Port Act closed that port, generating fears that others might be shut down. The Massachusetts Government Act deprived that colony's citizens of most rights while increasing the governor's powers. The Justice Act allowed people accused of a capital crime to be tried in Britain or another colony while the 1774 Quartering Act gave British officers authority to requisition uninhabited houses, out-houses, barns and other structures to be occupied by troops.

Finally, the Québec Act extended that province's boundary to include territory east of the Mississippi and north of the Ohio River thereby truncating some colonies' claims to what now became Indian Territory. Roman Catholicism was also extended into the enlarged Québec, upsetting Protestants. In response to the acts, the first Continental Congress met at Philadelphia from 5 September to 26 October 1774.

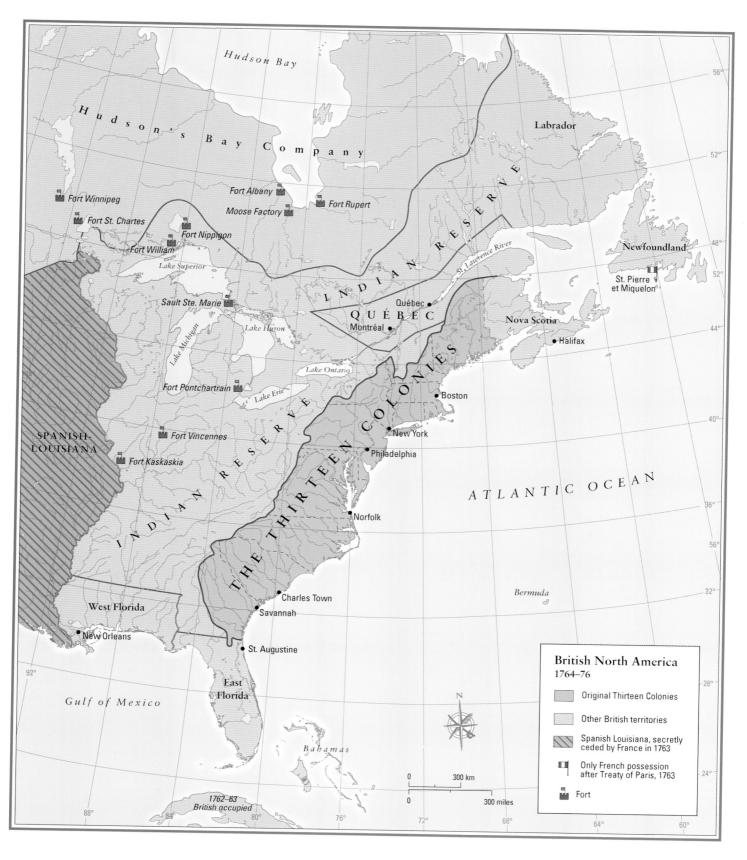

Hudson Bay

Hudson's Bay Company

Labrador

Fort Winnipeg

Fort Albany

Fort Rupert

Fort St. Chartes

Moose Factory

Fort Nippigon

Newfoundland

Fort William

Lake Superior

INDIAN RESERVE

St. Pierre
et Miquelon

Sault Ste. Marie

QUÉBEC

Québec

St. Lawrence River

Lake Michigan

Lake Huron

Montréal

Nova Scotia

Halifax

Lake Ontario

Fort Pontchartrain

Lake Erie

Boston

SPANISH
LOUISIANA

Fort Vincennes

THE THIRTEEN COLONIES

New York

Philadelphia

INDIAN RESERVE

Fort Kaskaskia

ATLANTIC OCEAN

Norfolk

Bermuda

West Florida

Charles Town

Savannah

New Orleans

St. Augustine

Gulf of Mexico

East
Florida

N

Bahamas

1762–63
British occupied

British North America
1764–76

Original Thirteen Colonies

Other British territories

Spanish Louisiana, secretly
ceded by France in 1763

Only French possession
after Treaty of Paris, 1763

Fort

0   300 km

0   300 miles

Colonies in Rebellion

Raids on Trade

Privateers gave America two benefits during the Revolution. They imported arms and gunpowder. They attacked West Indian and British shipping, forcing British warships to police the Caribbean while reducing the numbers of ships available for the blockade of American ports. By 1783, 2,000 privateers were operating and captured 3,386 British vessels. The American ship Rattlesnake *was extremely successful and took prizes worth $1 million on a single cruise in the Baltic Sea.*

The American Revolution began with the ambush of British troops on the Lexington-Concord road in April, 1775, and saw the first major conflict at Bunker Hill in June, 1775 where the British eventually won, though at a terrible cost in casualties. During the ensuing war, the Americans were benefited by numerous factors that ensured their ultimate success.

France, Spain and the Dutch Republic entered the fray on the American side, thereby putting extreme strain upon British naval resources through their national battle fleets and the numerous privateers who joined the Americans in damaging British commerce and thus increasing insurance rates. The Americans possessed two military strategists in George Washington in the northern

The Battle of "Bunker" Hill

This battle was the first major engagement between British troops and American Revolutionary forces. British professional forces evenutally won the battle leaving them in possession of the battlefield, though at a terrible cost with almost half their men becoming casualties.

The Battle of "Bunker" Hill

17 June 1775

———	British forces
←——	British advance
‹- - -›	British retreat
━━━	American forces
‹- - -›	American retreat
🚢	British ship

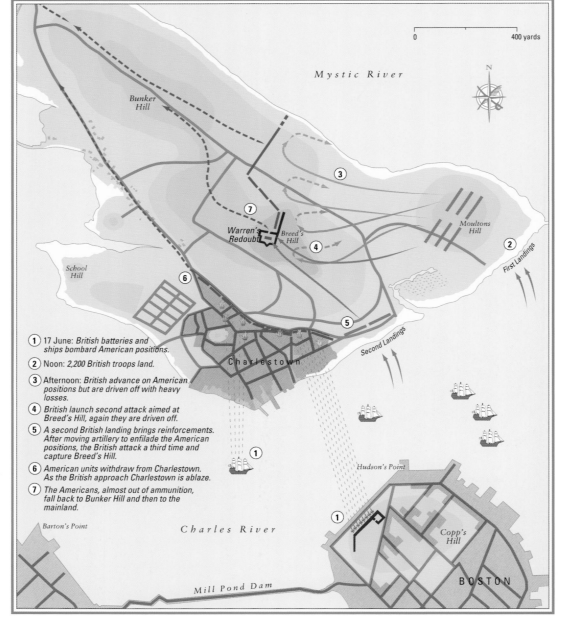

1 17 June: British batteries and ships bombard American positions.

2 Noon: 2,200 British troops land.

3 Afternoon: British advance on American positions but are driven off with heavy losses.

4 British launch second attack aimed at Breed's Hill, again they are driven off.

5 A second British landing brings reinforcements. After moving artillery to enfilade the American positions, the British attack a third time and capture Breed's Hill.

6 American units withdraw from Charlestown. As the British approach Charlestown is ablaze.

7 The Americans, almost out of ammunition, fall back to Bunker Hill and then to the mainland.

colonies and Nathaniel Greene in the southern colonies. Both used guerrilla tactics, seldom seeking formal battle. A war of attrition ensured British forces were constantly weakened and losses were difficult to replace. Britain constantly won Pyrrhic victories in the south with such losses that they ended up holding only coastal enclaves.

As other countries helped America, Britain was forced to defend worldwide interests, like combating the brilliant Admiral Suffren in the Indian Ocean. Nevertheless, British forces became increasingly mobile and the final Virginia campaign, with its scorched-earth policy, opened up possibilities for the British.

However, the British could never guess where the French might land troops to aid the Americans. Eventually, the French landed an expeditionary force that led to the siege and surrender of British-held Yorktown in October 1781. The war lingered in a desultory fashion, being ended by the Treaty of Paris in 1783. Britain recognized the independence of the Thirteen Colonies and each European country basically exchanged captured territories, except Spain retained Minorca. Britain appeared to have been weakened in the world and the successful American revolt caused men of affairs to study the causes of this disaster and demand political reform.

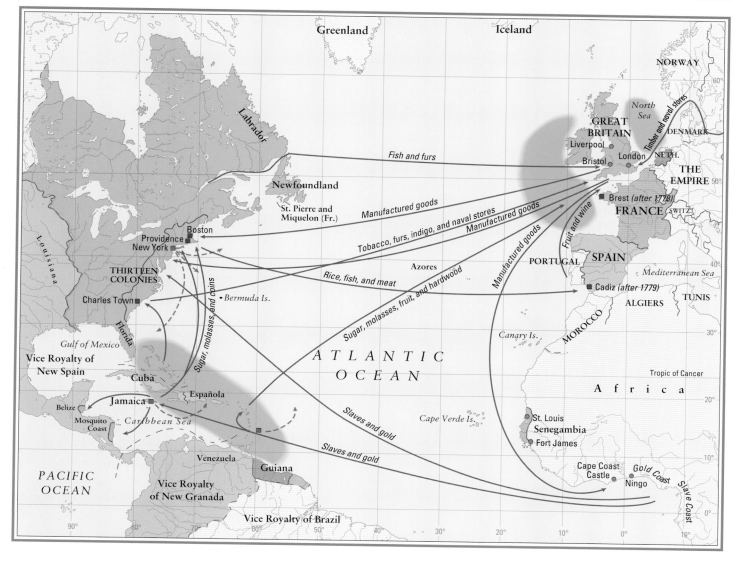

Raids on Trade c. 1778

Privateers

- Trade route with goods named
- British colonies

American allies by 1780

- French colonies
- Spanish colonies
- Dutch colonies
- Major American privateer base
- Loyalist privateer base
- Major hunting grounds for American privateers
- Loyalist privateer

The Risings of 1715 and 1745

In 1714, when the Crown passed to Hanoverian, George I's son, Prince James Edward Stuart, would be deprived of any chance of succession. A civil war erupted between supporters of Prince James Edward Stuart, James II's son, and the new monarchy. In England, MP Thomas Forster raised a Northumbrian force joined by 1500 Scots, who were later defeated at the Battle of Preston.

The next battle was at Sheriffmuir on 13 November 1715. On 10 November, James Erskine, Earl of Mar, marched an army of some 6,000 men to join Jacobite forces south of the border, increasing his force. The Duke of Argyll had the thankless task of opposing him with a smaller force of 3,500, most of George I's troops being abroad. Outnumbered nearly three to one, the Hanoverians faced Mar and lost nearly three times as many men as the Jacobites. Mar did not follow up on his victory, showing his incompetence, and the 1715 uprising began to fizzle out.

While Britain was engaged with France during the War of the Austrian Succession (1740–48), the Old Pretender's son, Bonnie Prince Charlie, landed at Arsaig in Scotland, raising 2,500 clansmen. His troops swept away British forces at Prestonpans on 21 September 1745. Prince Charlie then led 5,500 Jacobites into England, marching down the west coast, reaching Derby on 4 December. Owing to the lack of French support, the Scots retreated; had the Scots pushed on, London was virtually undefended.

Meanwhile, the Hanoverians reoccupied Edinburgh. A penultimate battle occurred at Falkirk on 17 January 1746, where Generals Hawley and Huske faced Prince Charles and Lord Murray. Although technically defeated at Falkirk, the Hanoverians were soon able to reform themselves while the Jacobites withdrew their forces into the Highlands. The Jacobite rebellion ended at the bloody Battle of Culloden on 16 April 1746 where the Young Pretender suffered a crushing defeat; he then fled the country. Cumberland's victory sent his troops throughout the Highlands in punitive searches burning homes and crops, leading to the devastation of the southern Highlands. New laws banned Highlanders from owning weapons, wearing traditional dress, or playing the bagpipes.

The Rising of 1715

- Area of Jacobite clan support with clan name
- Jacobite sympathisers
- 'Old Pretender' supporters
- → Earl of Mar's Jacobean forces Sept. 1715 – Jan. 1716
- → Other Jacobite advances Oct. – Nov. 1715
- → Government advance under Duke of Argyll Nov. 1715 – Jan. 1716
- → Other Government (Hanoverian) movements
- ✕ Battle site

An army made up of largely Catholic Highlanders was raised together with Lowland support. As they marched south they also attracted the support of a few English Jacobites.

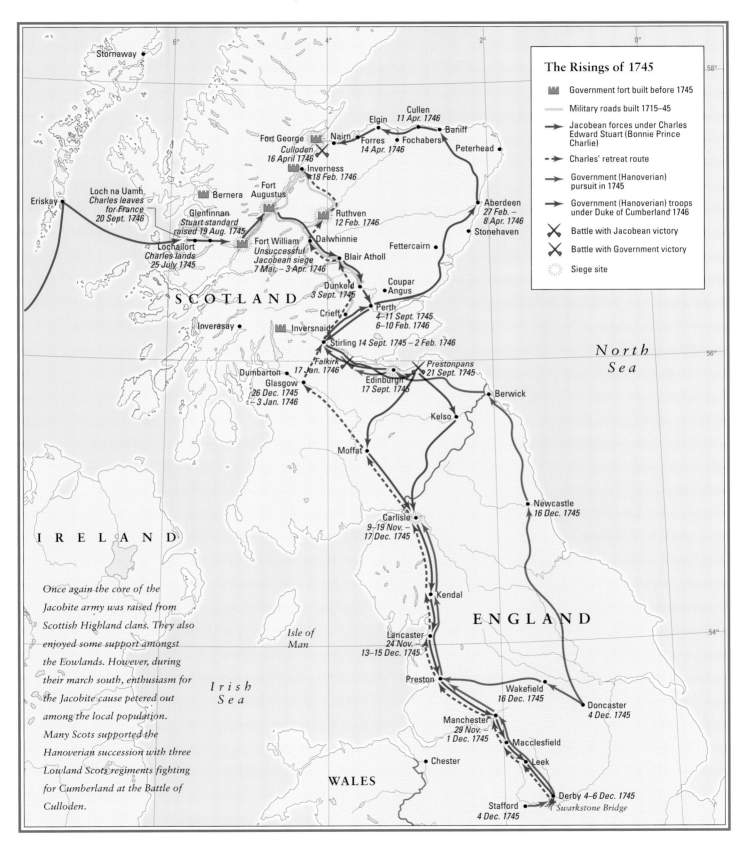

The Risings of 1745

- Government fort built before 1745
- Military roads built 1715–45
- Jacobean forces under Charles Edward Stuart (Bonnie Prince Charlie)
- Charles' retreat route
- Government (Hanoverian) pursuit in 1745
- Government (Hanoverian) troops under Duke of Cumberland 1746
- Battle with Jacobean victory
- Battle with Government victory
- Siege site

Stornaway

Eriskay

Loch na Uamh
Charles leaves for France
20 Sept. 1746

Lochailort
Charles lands
25 July 1745

Bernera

Fort George
Culloden
16 April 1746

Inverness
18 Feb. 1746

Glenfinnan
Stuart standard
raised 19 Aug. 1745

Fort Augustus

Fort William
Unsuccessful Jacobean siege
7 Mar.–3 Apr. 1746

Dalwhinnie

Ruthven
12 Feb. 1746

Nairn

Elgin
Forres
14 Apr. 1746

Cullen
11 Apr. 1746

Banff

Fochabers

Peterhead

Blair Atholl

Dunkeld
3 Sept. 1745

Fettercairn

Aberdeen
27 Feb.–8 Apr. 1746

Stonehaven

S C O T L A N D

Crieff

Coupar Angus

Perth
4–11 Sept. 1745
6–10 Feb. 1746

Inverasay

Inversnaid

Stirling *14 Sept. 1745 – 2 Feb. 1746*

Falkirk
17 Jan. 1746

Dumbarton

Glasgow
26 Dec. 1745
– 3 Jan. 1746

Edinburgh
17 Sept. 1745

Prestonpans
21 Sept. 1745

Kelso

Berwick

North Sea

Moffat

Newcastle
16 Dec. 1745

I R E L A N D

Carlisle
9–19 Nov. –
17 Dec. 1745

Kendal

E N G L A N D

Isle of Man

Irish Sea

Lancaster
24 Nov. –
13–15 Dec. 1745

Preston

Wakefield
16 Dec. 1745

Doncaster
4 Dec. 1745

Manchester
29 Nov. –
1 Dec. 1745

Macclesfield

Chester

Leek

WALES

Stafford
4 Dec. 1745

Derby *4–6 Dec. 1745*
Swarkstone Bridge

Once again the core of the Jacobite army was raised from Scottish Highland clans. They also enjoyed some support amongst the Lowlands. However, during their march south, enthusiasm for the Jacobite cause petered out among the local population. Many Scots supported the Hanoverian succession with three Lowland Scots regiments fighting for Cumberland at the Battle of Culloden.

139

The British Empire in 1707

Prior to the 1707 Act of Union, the English Empire, which was closed to Scots trade, virtually left its possessions to govern themselves. Ireland was in a mid-way political position, being neither a colonial dependency nor fully self-governing. Its own Parliament needed approval from the English Privy Council for its decisions to become laws. Even in the Thirteen Colonies in North America, the colonial legislatures were seen as subordinate assemblies by the English government.

England lacked a clear direction in imperial government. Settlements were established in St. Kitts in 1624, Barbados in 1627 and Nevis in 1628, with these colonies developing slave-run sugar plantations considered to be worth more commercially than New England. So concerned was England with its commodity driven colonial system that it led to a series of Anglo-Dutch Wars fought mainly for reasons of trade. Elsewhere, English settlements at Belize and the Mosquito Coast, with former buccaneers turning loggers, the settlers were left to their own devices. More important was the 1670 charter, granted to the Hudson's Bay Company with its monopoly of trade in the vast area of Rupert's Land in Canada though its forts were often subject to French attack.

Founded in 1672, the Royal African Company was granted the monopoly of supplying slaves to the English West Indies. To facilitate this trade, English traders built forts on the West African coast at places like James Island, Accra, Bunce Island and Whydah. In Asia, the English challenged the Dutch and Portuguese for a portion of the spice trade but real success occurred in India where a factory was established at Surat in 1613, Fort St. George in Madras, 1640, and Bombay, which was granted to Charles II as Catherine de Braganza's dowry in 1661 and Calcutta, where Fort William was built in 1702. Britain had to wait until 1714 to enlarge its Empire.

British Empire in 1707

From 1707, with the union of England and Scotland, the English Empire became the British Empire. Increasing numbers of British people settled overseas. In the West Indies and southern American states, black slaves were used on plantations producing sugar, cotton, tobacco, tea, coffee and spices. Some traders exported manufactured goods to Africa, then transported slaves across the Atlantic and then carried colonial goods to Britain. In India, so much money could be made that British immigrants returned to Britain nicknamed nabobs.

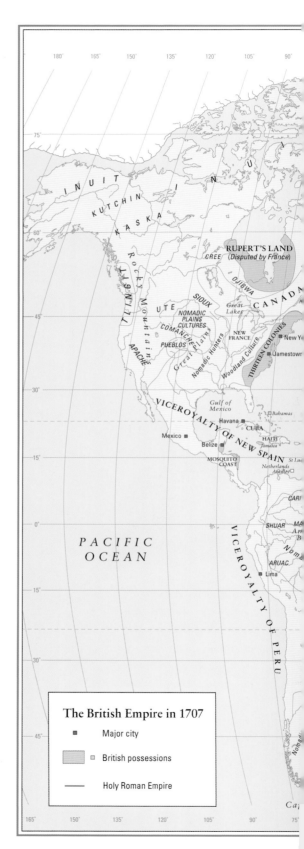

Greenland

ARCTIC OCEAN

Iceland

Siberia

CHUKCHI

RUSSIAN EMPIRE

KORYAKS

NORWAY
SWEDEN
• Stockholm

SCOTLAND
DENMARK
Copenhagen
NETHER-
LAND
IRELAND ENGLAND
London •
COURTLAND
PRUSSIA
• Warsaw
POLAND-
LITHUANIA

Nerchinsk •

K Z A K H S

KHANATE OF
THE DZUNGARS

EWFOUNDLAND

Paris •
FRANCE
SWISS
CONFEDERATION
Vienna •
Hungary
MOLDAVIA
ZAPOROGIAN
COSSACKS
KHANATE
OF CRIMEA

KHIVA
TURKMENS

BUKHARA

Gobi Desert

QING
EMPIRE

Beijing •

KOREA

JAPAN

• Kyoto
• Nagasaki

PAPAL
STATES
PORTUGAL SPAIN
Lisbon • Madrid •
SARDINIA
NAPLES
SICILY

VENETIAN REPUBLIC
WALLACIA
Black Sea
• Constantinople

Caspian Sea

Azores ○

Madeira ○
Canary Islands

Ceuta ○
Melilla ○ Oran ○
ALGIERS
TUNIS
MOROCCO

Mediterranean Sea
OTTOMAN EMPIRE

SAFAVID
EMPIRE
• Isfahan

KHANATE OF
THE DZUNGARS

Himalayas
TIBET

Delhi •
NEPALESE
PRINCIPALITIES
BHUTAN ASSAM
MANIPUR

BURMA
CHIENGMAI
Macao

**A T L A N T I C
O C E A N**

TRIPOLI
FEZZAN
(Vassal of Tripoli)

BEDOUINS

Sahara Desert
TUAREGS

Africa
NILO-SAHARANS

FUNJ

Arabian Peninsula
OMAN

Cambrey
Diu □
Damão
Bombay
Bassein
Chaul

MUGHAL
EMPIRE
ARAKAN
Bay of Bengal

TRAN NINH

ISLANDS

Antigua
Dominica
Barbados

Cape Verde
Islands
St Louis •
Fort James Island
Albreda □ Cacheu
KAABU
WALO
KAARTA
SEGU
MOSSI
KINGDOMS
BORGU
KINGDOMS
FUTA
TORO
BORNU
HAUSA
STATES
WADAI DARFUR
ETHIOPIA
YEMEN

Arabian Sea

Mangalore
Calicut
Goa □
Bhatkal □
Cannartore
Cochin □
Quilon
Tuticorin
Pulicat
Madras □
Pondicherry
Negapatam
Tranquebar
CEYLON
KINGDOM
OF KANDY

SIAM
LAOS
ANNAN

• Manila
PHILIPPINE
ISLANDS

**PACIFIC
OCEAN**

Tobago
RARA
BERBICE
Cayenne

SIERRA LEONE
FUTA
JALLON
MAMPRUSI
BONO
BANDA
ASANTE
DENKYERA
GOLD COAST
DAHOMEY
ALLADA
SAO TOME
GONJA
NUPE KWARARAFA
OYO IGALA
BENIN
SMALL STATES

SMALL
OROMO
STATES
HARAR
KUSHITES

Masulipatam

CAMBODIA
(to Annan)

MALAY
STATES
Malacca
ATJEH
BRUNEI SULU

KUTI

Moluccas

BRAZIL

• Bahia

LOANGO
KAKONGO
NGOYO
KONGO
MATAMBA
ANGOLA
NDONGO
KASANJE
UPPER BEMBE
Fernando Po ○

BANTUS
TEKE
KUBA
KALUNDE
LUBA
KIKONJA
KANIOK
LUNDA
XINJE
SONGO
LOWER BEMBE

BUNYORO
TORO
ANKOLE
RWANDA
BURUNDI
KARAGWE
BUGANDA
BUSOGA
Lake Victoria

Mombasa
(To Oman)
Zanzibar
(To Oman)
Kilwa
(To Oman)

POLYGAR
KINGDOMS

Sumatra
Benkulen
Silebar
Batavia □
MATARAM

MAMPAVA
BANDJAR
MASIN

MALAYS

MALAY
STATES

East Indies

MALAY
STATES

PAPUANS
New
Guinea

PORTUGUESE
TIMOR

WILA
MUZUMBO
A KALUNGA
LOZI
ROZWI
LUNDI
LUNDU
KAEONGA
MERINA
KINGDOM

MALATS

**INDIAN
OCEAN**

Australia
ABORIGINES

*Kalahari
Desert*

Delagoa Bay

□ Mauritius
Réunion

KHOISAN
PEOPLES

DUTCH
SOUTH AFRICA

*Cape of
Good Hope*

onia do Sacramento

**New
Zealand**
MAORIS

SOUTHERN OCEAN

Radicalism and Rebellion – Ireland 1790s

By the 1790s, Ireland was riven by sectarian loyalties, driven by the penal laws, which fuelled political sentiments among Catholics. Armagh witnessed Catholic vigilantism with the birth of the Catholic Defenders protecting Catholics against Protestant violence. A growing population created land hunger. Meanwhile, some Protestants and Presbyterians enjoyed a more philosophical view of events. They looked to the American War of Independence and the French Revolution as inspirations behind a campaign to reform the representative system. They built an organisation known as the United Irishmen in 1791, led by the charismatic Wolfe Tone, who saw a vision of Catholic, Protestant and Dissenters unifying, and destroying links with England. Catholic emancipation was another aspiration.

Catholics were given the franchise in 1793 but this originated with Westminster rather than pressure from the United Irishmen. After war broke out between England and Revolutionary France, the French sent an invasion force to Bantry Bay but bad weather in December 1796 prevented a landing. Given a breathing space, the Protestant-controlled Irish Parliament armed paramilitary groups to coerce the United Irishmen with torture and bullying. Some rebels fought back but they were suppressed in Dublin, Meath and Kildare, while incurring heavy casualties in 1798.

Elsewhere, County Wexford saw United Irishmen victorious in several large skirmishes but an Ulster rising was crushed at Antrim and Ballynahinch. General Lake was reinforced by British troops and continued advancing in a concentric ark on Wexford. The insurgents' army was divided into northern and southern armies, which failed to join up and Lake's force confronted the northern army at Vinegar Hill in June 1798. The British advanced, protected by hedges and fences, and brought light field artillery into play while facing some 15,000 United Irishmen. The insurgents were compressed on Vinegar Hill proving to be an easy target for artillery. A British victory

ensued and the Irish dispersed, several hundred falling to British cavalry. Total Irish casualties are unknown. Some went home while others were pursued by flying columns that destroyed the last insurgent formation at Ballyboghil on 14 July.

Some 1,000 French, commanded by Humbert, landed at Kilala in August 1798 and enjoyed a victory at Castlebar but failed to promote a rebellion in Connacht. He was chased by British troops, who brought him to bay at Ballinamuck on 8 September. The French troops were outmanoeuvred and surrendered, while their Irish allies were shot and ridden down. Those that were captured were generally hanged. Another French incursion was attempted at Lough Swilly. Admiral Bompart left Brest with a squadron of ten vessels carrying 2,800 men and stores. They were intercepted and attacked, losing seven ships captured. The victorious Admiral Warren found Wolfe Tone on a French vessel but he cut his own throat before being tried for treason.

The British troops used in Ireland were a mixture of Irish militia battalions with Protestant officers and Catholic soldiers, Irish Protestant Yeomanry, Fencibles (a sort of home-guard) and some regulars. In combination, they engaged in random butchery to the consternation of British generals Cornwallis and Moore, thereby causing even more bitter resentment amongst Catholics.

The outcomes of the 1798 rebellion were a discredited Irish Parliament and rebel disunity. The Irish Catholic middle-classes had strived to be heard and failed in pushing the Westminster government into making wide-ranging reforms. The pressure on the land and tennants remained while rents and tithes increased as wages fell. Resentment remained amongst ordinary people, at least 20,000 people had died in the rebellion, many murdered by militia. The ensuing 1801 Act of Union closed the Irish Parliament and failed to provide Catholic emancipation. Prime Minister Pitt was prevented from delivering this owing to pressure from Protestants across the kingdoms.

Radicalism and Rebellion in the 1790s

Wolfe Tone and Napper Tandy were unsupported by French forces' failure to arrive as planned. After 1798, leaders of the United Irishmen informed the government the plan of the revolution. Seizure of power would be based upon a French alliance and a well-controlled mass-uprising. What happened was untried leaders generating not a revolution but a peasant revolt. Many peasants were tried and transported to Australia where in fact they had a better economic chance in life.

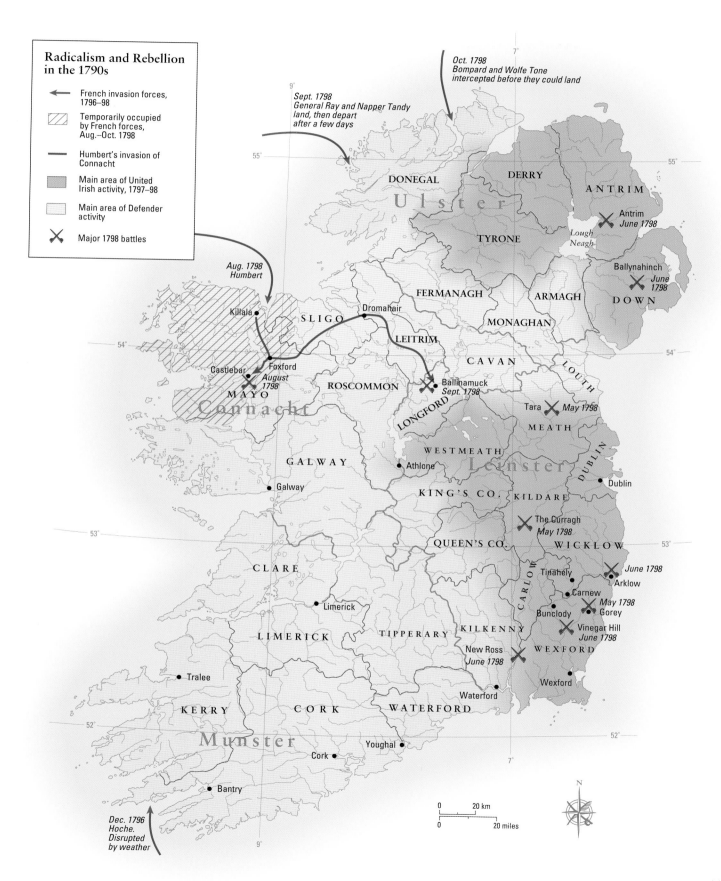

Radicalism and Rebellion in the 1790s

- → French invasion forces, 1796–98
- ▨ Temporarily occupied by French forces, Aug.–Oct. 1798
- — Humbert's invasion of Connacht
- Main area of United Irish activity, 1797–98
- Main area of Defender activity
- ✕ Major 1798 battles

Oct. 1798
Bompard and Wolfe Tone intercepted before they could land

Sept. 1798
General Ray and Napper Tandy land, then depart after a few days

Aug. 1798
Humbert

DONEGAL

Ulster

DERRY

ANTRIM

Antrim
June 1798

TYRONE

Lough
Neagh

Ballynahinch
June
1798

FERMANAGH

ARMAGH

DOWN

Killala

SLIGO

Dromahair

MONAGHAN

LEITRIM

CAVAN

LOUTH

Castlebar
MAYO
Foxford
August
1798

ROSCOMMON

Ballinamuck
Sept. 1798

Connacht

LONGFORD

Tara May 1798

MEATH

WESTMEATH

Leinster

DUBLIN

GALWAY

Athlone

Dublin

Galway

KING'S CO.

KILDARE

The Curragh
May 1798

QUEEN'S CO.

WICKLOW

CLARE

Tinahely
Arklow June 1798

CARLOW

Carnew

Bunclody

May 1798
Gorey

Limerick

Vinegar Hill
June 1798

LIMERICK

TIPPERARY

KILKENNY

New Ross
June 1798

WEXFORD

Tralee

Wexford

KERRY

CORK

WATERFORD

Waterford

Munster

Youghal

Cork

Bantry

Dec. 1796
Hoche.
Disrupted
by weather

0   20 km
0   20 miles

N

Industrial Revolution – Canals

British Canal System

Animal pack trains were entirely unsuitable for carrying heavy or fragile goods. Canals not only carried lumber and coal but fine porcelain. The Trent and Mersey Canal helped carry goods through the Potteries at Stoke-on-Trent.

The Grand Union Canal

The canal system, stretching from the north and the industrial Midlands, connected its regions' products to the great, wealthy metropolis of London. Raw materials and comsumer products could be cheaply transported to the booming population of London and the southeast.

The eighteenth century witnessed an industrial expansion, with an increase in spinning mills and steam-powered factories used engines that were coal-fired. Increasingly important were the iron forges of the Midlands, central Scotland and South Wales. The potteries, in the West Midlands, were increasing production, and all the products of industry needed power, namely coal and then routes to market. Additionally, the agricultural revolution, with its new mechanization created surpluses, that needed to be moved to growing cities and to feed their industrial citizens.

Initially, early years had seen rivers made navigable with 1,160 miles of such waterways by the 1720s. The road network was inadequate and expensive to maintain and the 143 turn-pike trusts, maintaining 3,386 miles of road, were insufficient. Although people and light goods were moving round the country, means did not exist to transport the ever growing demands to shift large volumes of bulky, heavy commodities like coal. The favoured solution was to cut dead-water canals after businessmen saw the commercial success of the Duke of Bridgewater's Canal halving the costs of delivering coal from his Worsley coal mines to Manchester. James Brindley, the engineer concerned, was then asked to build a canal linking Manchester with the port of Liverpool. The cost of transporting coal and agricultural products was so reduced that 'canal mania' swept the country.

A network of canals was constructed across the country in England, Scotland, Wales, and Ireland and, by the end of the building period (c. 1830), some 4,000 miles of navigable waterways existed compared with the 1,400 miles in 1760 (in England and Wales). Vast amounts of private capital had been mobilized, as had Parliamentary Acts which compelled the construction of canals on other people's properties. However, the canal network was built in a haphazard fashion, with construction companies using different widths and standards, making navigation more complex than it needed to be.

The canal system, together with other modes of transport, was fundamental to decreasing costs without which Britain's industrial Revolution would have been slower. Eventually, the slow canal transport was partially overtaken by railway development, which substantially aided the second phase of the industrial revolution. Interestingly, the requirements of the Second World War saw female directed labour helping run the canal system as part of the war effort. Today, these canals are being revamped to provide ecological benefits and leisure activities.

The Grand Union Canal

British Canal System

—— Major canal

① Grand Union
② Trent & Mersey
③ Manchester Ship Canal
④ Leeds & Liverpool
⑤ Kennet & Avon
⑥ Shropshire Union
⑦ Forth & Clyde
⑧ Coventry & Oxford
⑨ Bridgewater
⑩ Calder & Hebble
⑪ Royal Canal
⑫ Grand Canel
⑬ Caledonian

—— Other canals and waterways

North Sea

Irish Sea

Atlantic Ocean

English Channel

SCOTLAND

Inverness
Loch Ness
Fort William
Glasgow
Edinburgh

IRELAND

Belfast
Dublin
Limerick
Waterford
Wexford
Cork

ENGLAND

WALES

Kendal
Lancaster
Ripon
York
Hull
Preston
Leeds
Manchester
Sheffield
Liverpool
Lincoln
Ellesmere Port
Stoke-on-Trent
Nottingham
King's Lynn
Norwich
Welshpool
Leicester
Birmingham
Coventry
Stratford-upon-Avon
Northampton
Cambridge
Ipswich
Brecon
Bishop's Stortford
Gloucester
Oxford
Bristol
LONDON
Cardiff
Reading
Guildford
Taunton

The British Empire in 1800

The original English and, from 1707, British Empire was based upon piracy, plunder and plantations with the intention of making commercial profits. The Treaty of Utrecht, signed in 1714, rewarded Britain with Newfoundland, Acadia, Minorca and Gibraltar, the latter providing a powerful naval base controlling entry into the Mediterranean from the Atlantic. At the end of the Seven Years' War in 1763, Britain became the world's strongest naval power as well as acquiring Canada and Spanish Florida. This expanding empire saw Britain coping with governing foreign, non-Christian peoples and developing the notion that British rule, based on justice, sound administration and Protestantism, was good for everyone, while still not forgetting profit.

By 1800, Britain had accumulated vast territories around the world, despite suffering defeat when the Thirteen American Colonies gained independence, recognised in 1793. Each war, including the French Revolutionary and Napoleonic Wars, generated new opportunities for loot and aggrandizement.

The loss of the American colonies encouraged Britain to find an alternative depository for convicts. The Pacific proved the answer after James Cook discovered the eastern coast of Australia in 1770. The government was persuaded that Botany Bay in New South Wales would be an ideal penal settlement. Cook also claimed the islands of New Zealand in 1769 and 1770, respectively, which would eventually become British colonies.

In India, the East India Company became a British agency. Various Anglo-Mysore wars witnessed Mysore becoming a protectorate, with half its territory seized. In 1797, a new Governor-General of India, Lord Mornington, pursued aggressive and expansionist policies at the expense of Indian rulers. Elsewhere, British sea power snapped up strategic islands and territories to increase markets, protect commerce and gain naval bases as stepping stones to the Far East.

The British Empire in 1800

Whereas the British went to Asia to trade, and America for land, Australia was deemed fit for convicts. A quarter of the felons were Irish. A supreme irony was that convicts who were supposed to be deprived of liberty actually found freedom. New South Wales prospered. As far as New Zealand was concerned, the Maoris were dispossessed and received treatment akin to Native Americans.

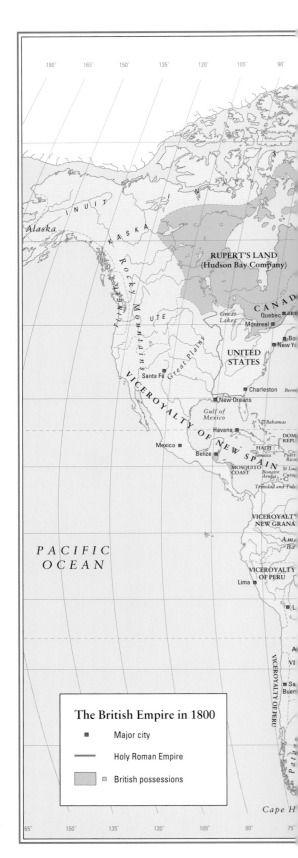

The British Empire in 1800

■ Major city

— Holy Roman Empire

▨ British possessions

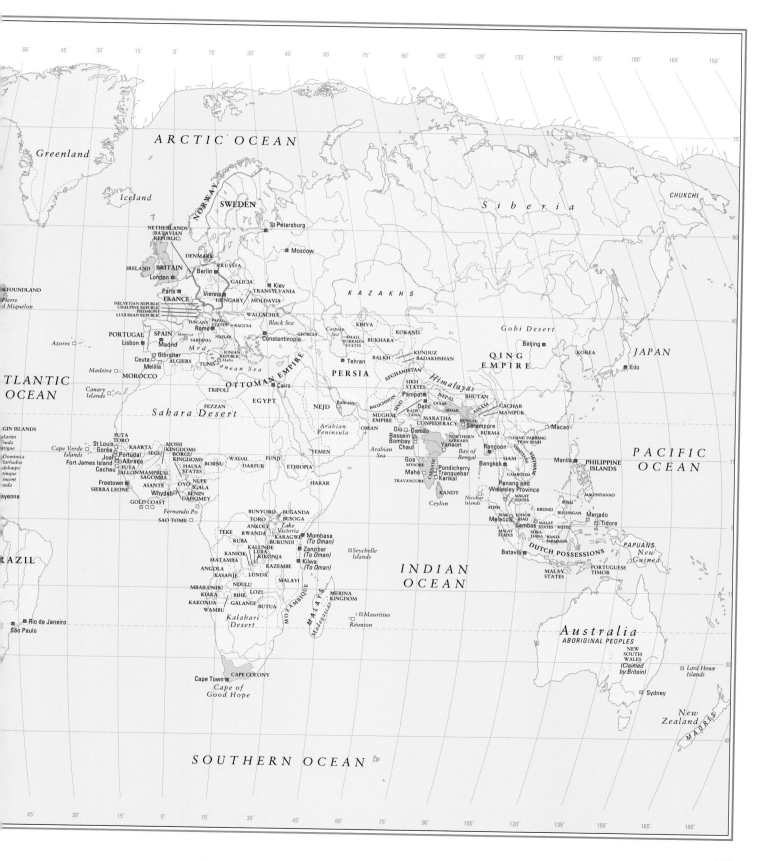

Eastern Imperial Ambitions 1798–1815

When Lord Mornington (later Marquis of Wellesley) was appointed Governor-General in India, he visualised a massive expansion of the British presence and the need to curtail French influence. Arriving one year before Bonaparte became a Consul in France, Wellesley developed a system of subsidiary alliances with Indian rulers by which Britain provided troops in exchange for territory or financial tribute. Britain would acquire control of a state's foreign policy but would not interfere in internal government and would secure the exclusion of other foreign powers from the state's service.

Wellesley's imperialism was given legitimacy by fear of France. The Fourth Anglo-Mysore War served Britain's purposes by first compelling the Nizam of Hyderabad to disband his French-trained troops in return for protection against the Marathas. Mysore was defeated in 1799, becoming a protectorate, while half of its lands were shared between Britain and the Nizam. Sequestrations next occurred in the Carnatic, Tanjore, Surat and Oudh, where half the state was annexed providing a base against the Marathas. Wellesley's policies were changing from acquiring defensive alliances to direct aggressive, expansionist action. His brother, later of Waterloo fame, defeated the Maratha princes of Bhonsle and Sindhia at Assaye in 1803, leaving that confederacy shattered, disunited and ripe for British pillaging later.

Another notable Governor-General, Lord Minto, curbed potential French expansion by making treaties with Sind, Persia and Afghanistan. He was also determined to destroy French naval bases in the Indian Ocean, used as refuges for frigates preying on East Indiamen. Île Bonaparte and Île de France were captured in 1810 and Java was taken to prevent forays against British ships in the Sunda Straits as they returned from China.

A border dispute with Nepal (1814–16) was settled and the period of 1816–18 saw Pindari tribes and remaining hostile Maratha leaders broken. Only Nepal, the Sikh state, and Afghanistan were free from direct or indirect British control.

Eastern Imperial Ambitions

Most histories recount Arthur Wellesley (later the Duke of Wellington) fighting Maratha hordes at Assaye. In fact, there was a high degree of integration between the original British immigrants and Indian society. The armies of Daulat Scindia of Gwalior were trained in European techniques by Anthony Pohlman, a deserter from a Hanoverian regiment serving the East India Company in Madras and Benoît de Boigne, a French adventurer, who commanded 100,000 Marathas. Also present in Scindia's army was James Skinner, of Anglo-Rajput origin, eventually famous for his regiment of light cavalry.

Eastern Imperial
Ambitions c. 1800

■ British territory
■ French territory
■ Spanish territory
■ Portuguese territory
■ Dutch territory
■ Ottoman Empire
□ United States

— Strategic trade route
⚓ British naval base
⚓ French naval base
⚓ Spanish naval base
● Town (coloured by sovereignty)

GREAT
BRITAIN

PRUSSIA

RUSSIAN EMPIRE

HOLY
ROMAN
EMPIRE

FRANCE

Rochefort

Toulon

PORTUGAL SPAIN

1756

QING
EMPIRE
(CHINA)

OCEAN

Cadiz Cartagena

Gibraltar

OTTOMAN EMPIRE

PERSIA

Panipat 1761 Buxar 1764
Plassey 1757

INDIA

Canary Is.

NEJD

1780-81

Goa

Bay of Bengal

Madras

Gorée St. Louis
Albredo
Ft. James

Cape Verde Is.

S a h a r a

Laccadine Is.

Maldive Is.

A f r i c a

INDIAN OCEAN

Assinie Accra
Elmina Cape Coast Castle

Chagos
Archipelago

ZANZIBAR

Seychelles

Ste Marie

Loanda

Mauritius

ANGOLA

PORTUGUESE
EAST AFRICA

Madagascar

Bourbon

Fort-Dauphin

Delagoa Bay

Cape Town

Naval Engagements 1793 – 1815

Britain's naval superiority complex was shattered by the big American frigates between 1812–14. The USS *Constitution dismasted* HMS *Guerriere and the* USS *United States captured* HMS *Java and* HMS *Macedonian.*

Naval Engagements
1793 – 1815

■ Squadron or Fleet action

● Other Naval action

▨ British possessions

The immense economic-industrial investment made by Britain in its navy during this period not only sustained her growing industry at home, but was instrumental in supporting her ambitions abroad.

After France declared war against Britain in 1793, with Holland following in 1795 and Spain in 1796, the world witnessed British naval power being exercised and exerted in all oceans in a bid to defeat enemy fleets; prevent invasion; protect trade routes; destroy privateers; intercept enemy merchantmen; conquer enemy colonies; and carry the small British army to whatever theatre of war the British government deemed fit.

Certain key fleet actions were significant to the survival of Britain. The 1794 Glorious First of June saw a French fleet defeated, with the capture of seven warships but the grain fleet the French were escorting from the United States reached its destination. The 1797 Battle of Cape St. Vincent contained a Spanish threat seeing remaining Spanish warships blockaded in Cartagena and Cadiz and allowing Admiral Jervis to send Nelson, with a squadron, into the Mediterranean Sea the following year. The year 1797 also resulted in a Dutch defeat at the hands of Admiral Duncan at Camperdown, which gave Britain naval superiority in the North Sea by destroying a significant Dutch fleet. The Dutch were so demoralized that they surrendered an entire fleet

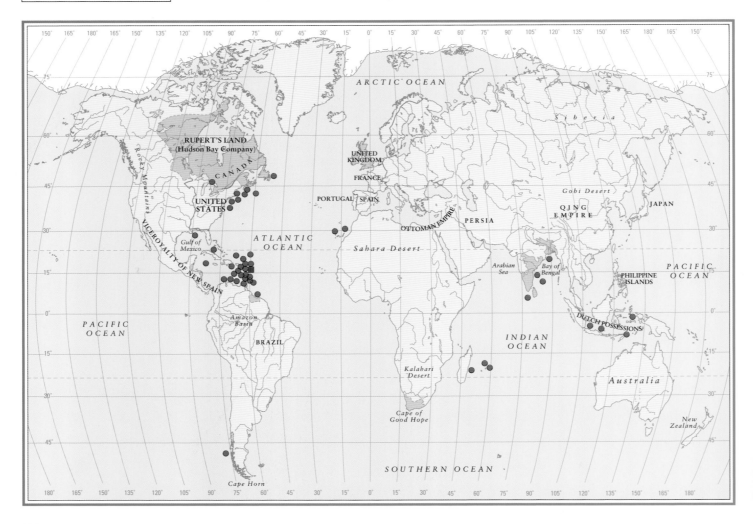

in 1799 at the Vlieter incident. Nelson's intervention in the Mediterranean ended with British superiority there after a French fleet was destroyed at Aboukir Bay on the Egyptian coast. This flurry of victories was completed in 1801 when Nelson defeated the Danes at Copenhagen, with the Peace of Amiens following in 1802.

With Napoleon in power in France, the fear of Britain being invaded resurfaced so French and Spanish ports received a close blockade. However, when those enemy fleets managed to merge, they suffered complete defeat at Trafalgar in October 1805, thereby reinforcing and confirming Britain's naval advantage over its enemies. Yet, enemy squadrons occasionally slipped past blockades and were hunted down. More dangerous were privateers and commerce raiding frigate squadrons,

especially in the Caribbean Sea and Indian Ocean. Britain built more powerful frigates and vastly increased numbers of small warships to contain these types of enemy operations. Many lesser engagements took place such as the Battle of Lissa in 1811, fought in the Adriatic Sea between a British frigate squadron under Hoste and a much larger losing French and Venetian force.

The other enemy faced by Britain in this period was the United States in the War of 1812–14. Occasioned by high-handed naval searches of American vessels, the war was famed for a few frigate actions but American victories there could not counter a blockade. The British burned down Washington but lost at New Orleans and a land war in Canada stalemated. The war fortunately fizzled out, with honour satisfied on both sides.

Despite the British Navy's professionalism and success, it was quite willing, indeed eager, to use captured vessels, especially French-built ships which became influential in the design of subsequently built British ships.

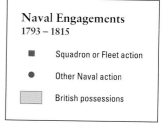

Naval Engagements
1793 – 1815

■ Squadron or Fleet action

● Other Naval action

British possessions

Napoleonic Wars

Britain's confrontation with Napoleon emerged seamlessly out of the French Revolutionary Wars. Here, naval victories confirmed Britain's rsupremacy at sea and prevented any French invasion plans from being put into practice. Britain's major military effort had been spent securing French sugar islands in the West Indies, while an expedition to Holland secured nothing except the capture of a Dutch fleet. A fierce engagement with Napoleon's troops at the second Battle of Abukir was a postscript to a French campaign in Egypt, which threatened Britain's route to India. Napoleon had already returned to France to seize power in a coup d'état orchestrated by Lucien, his brother, and certain members of the ruling Directory in 1799.

During Napoleon's Egyptian campaign, Britain helped create and finance the Second Coalition against France in alliance with Austria and Russia. However, Austro-Russian campaigns in Switzerland and Italy fell apart and Russia withdrew from the war. Austria suffered various defeats and sought peace in 1801. Britain was forced into isolation when Russia, Denmark and Sweden formed the League of Armed Neutrality in 1800 against Britain. However, Britain attacked the Danish fleet at Copenhagen in 1801, thereby breaking the League but later needed to make peace with France at Amiens in 1802.

The peace was a mere breathing space while each side prepared for future conflict. Napoleon envisaged invading Britain but any attempt to gain control of the Channel after war resumed in 1804 was negated by Nelson's victory at the Battle of Trafalgar in 1805. Also, Napoleon wished to crush the Third Coalition, he achieved this in December 1805 when his enemies were defeated at Austerlitz. Prussia was assaulted next, losing at Jena-Auerstadt in 1806, followed by Russia. The French victories at Eylau and Friedland in 1807 pushed Tsar Alexander I into seeking an armistice.

By now, the war had spawned a more virulent economic dimension. When dictating peace terms to the Prussian King in Berlin after the 1806 defeat, Napoleon issued a decree demanding that all European ports under French control should cease trading with Britain. The Emperor maintained that the British Order in Council in May 1806 declaring a blockade on the entire coast of Europe was illegal. Two further Orders in Council followed: the first forbade all neutral shipping from trading between French ports or its allies, or ports observing the Berlin Decree, under pain of capture and confiscation of ship and cargo; the second stated that neutrals were only to trade with France after paying customs in England. A tit-for-tat followed with economic measures damaging both sides, which contributed to a British recession in 1810–11. Meanwhile, the lack of trade at Bordeaux was so severe that grass grew between the cobbles because no transportation was keeping the streets weed free. Some British merchants were helped by the seizure of Heligoland in 1807, turning that island into a vast smuggling emporium.

A Napoleonic error was to invade France's former ally, Spain, in 1808, ostensibly to enforce his economic Continental System in Iberia. After Napoleon installed his brother, Joseph, as the Spanish King and attacked the Church, the Spanish rose and regional juntas waged a guerrilla war. A British expeditionary force, under Sir John Moore, landed in Spain but he died at Corunna after being chased there by the French. His successor was Sir Arthur Wellesley, fresh from India, who waged a long war in Spain, marching backwards and forwards without managing to deliver a knockout blow to the French.

Wellesley was helped when Napoleon made the most remarkable mistake of his career when he invaded Russia in 1812 with his Grande Armée. A drawn battle at Borodino sapped French strength but not as much as hunger owing to the Russian scorched earth policy and the harsh winter. Forced to leave Moscow, the French

The Napoleonic Empire

Although unequal peace treaties forced upon defeated Prussia and Austria instigated military reforms and patriotic movements in those countries, parts of the Empire seemed happy under French rule. Naples thrived under Murat's administration and propertied and commercial classes praised him for lifting the Continental System. In 1814, the Dutch merchants supported French rule. Likewise, departments in the Rhineland were loyal to France, especially business interests in Crefeld, Cologne and Aachen.

The Italian Campaigns, 1796–97
The Marengo Campaign, 1800–01
Ulm–Austerlitz Campaign, 1805
Jena Campaign, 1806
Eylan–Friedland Campaign, 1807
Spanish Campaigns, 1808
The Aurtian Campaign, 1809

The Napoleonic Empire c. 1809

Ruled directly by Napoleon
Ruled by members of Napoleon's family
Dependent state

ARCTIC
OCEAN

Arctic Circle

Faeroe Is.
to Denmark

Shetland Is.

Bergen
Christiana

SWEDEN

Finland
1809 to Russia

Helsingfors
St. Petersburg
Åland Is.
Revel
Novgorod
Stockholm

Scotland

North
Sea

Gothenburg

Gotland

Baltic Sea

Riga

Smolensk

Edinburgh

DENMARK–NORWAY
United until 1814

Copenhagen

REP. OF
DANZIG

Königsberg
East
Prussia

Vilna

UNITED KINGDOM
OF GREAT BRITAIN
AND IRELAND

Dublin
Ireland

Helgoland
1807–14 to Br.

Hamburg

to Sweden

PRUSSIA

Bialystok
1807 to Russia

RUSSIAN
EMPIRE

Wales   England

Amsterdam
1810 to Fr.
Antwerp

Bremen
1807–10
to Fr.

Brandenburg
Hannover Berlin

WESTPHALIA

GR. DUCHY
OF WARSAW Warsaw

London

Brussels
Cologne

Silesia

Cracow

Galicia

Ternopol

ATLANTIC
OCEAN

Channel Is.

Erfurt

Frankfurt

Bohemia
Prague

AUSTRIAN
EMPIRE

1809 to Russia

Bessarabia

Paris

CONFEDERATION
OF THE RHINE

Vienna

Orléans
Tours

Munich

Styria

Buda
(Ofen) Pest

Moldavia

FRANCE

Bern
HELVETIA

Carinthia   Hungary

Transylvania

occupied by Russia

Lyon
Geneva
1798–1814 to Fr.

Milan

Venice

Illyrian Provinces

Banat

Bucharest

Bordeaux

Turin

ITALY

Belgrade

Wallachia

OTTOMAN   EMPIRE

Bulgaria

Toulouse

Marseille

LUCCA

Florence

Adriatic Sea

Sofia

Tuscany

MONTENEGRO

Cataloña
1808–13 to Fr.

Barcelona

Corsica

Papal
States
Rome

Macedonia

Oporto

Balearic Is.

Minorca
1798–1802 to Br.

SARDINIA

NAPLES
Naples

Aegean
Sea

Corfu
1807–14 to Fr.

Thessaly

Lisbon

PORTUGAL

Madrid

SPAIN

Mediterranean   Sea

Palermo

SICILY

Ionian Is.

occupied by Britain

Athens

Gibraltar
to Spain

Ceuta
to Spain

Oran

Algiers

Bona

Tunis

Malta   1798 to Fr.
1800 to Br.

Crete

MOROCCO

ALGERIA
ALGIERS

Tunisia

N

0   200 km
0   200 miles

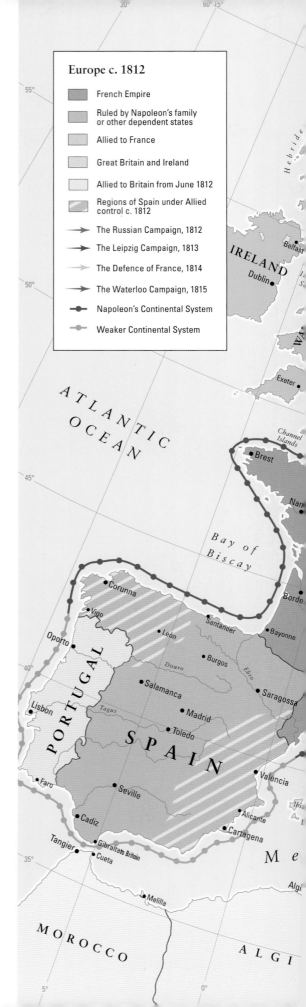

were blocked at the Battle of Maloyaroslavets and also prevented from wintering in Lithuania. Napoleon lost some half a million men. French troops were ordered from Spain to Central Europe to fight the Fourth Coalition.

The British used the French distraction to advance into Spain from Portugal yet again. Joseph Bonaparte was defeated at Vitoria in 1813 and the French expelled from Spain. Wellesley then fought his way across the Pyrenées into France where he scored a further victory at Toulouse, four days after Napoleon had surrendered to Allied forces.

He had suffered a number of reverses at Leipzig and on the French borders. Britain's Foreign Minister, Lord Castlereagh, had kept the Coalition together, which enabled the Prussians, Russians, Austrians and Swedes to push Napoleon back into France where he capitulated.

Wellesley has gained the most publicity owing to his victories but British forces were also engaged outside Spain. The French West Indies were recaptured and Cape Colony and Java seized from the Dutch, as were French Indian Ocean possessions. Sicily was defended from invasion and the Ionian Islands seized. Forays into Italy proper were made, that resulting in a British victory at Maida in 1806. Failed expeditions were those attempting to seize the Spanish River Plate colonies and Montevideo and the catastrophe on the island of Walcheren when Flushing was momentarily occupied.

The final throw in the Napoleonic game was the Waterloo campaign, mounted after Napoleon fled his exile in Elba. Wellesley, now the Duke of Wellington, led an allied army of British, Belgian, Dutch and German troops and won at Waterloo with the aid of Prussians under Blücher, and Napoleon ended in exile at St. Helena. The determination and discipline of British soldiers had proved their worth again as they had in Spain, fighting together with equally fine Portuguese troops, as displayed when Marshall Beresford defeated the French at Albuera in 1811.

Europe c. 1812

Arguably, the French Empire was an Empire of laws. Attempts were made to abolish feudalism, notably in the German states and southern Italy. Everywhere, the French tried to introduce their system of government, the legal Code Napoleon and the Concordat with the Pope. The imperial regime sought to establish the benefits of the French Enlightenment, ideas present in the French Revolution.

Trade and Industry

Britain reacted to failure in the American Revolutionary War by a psychological compensation, which argued that Great Britain was the home of commerce and cutting edge business, working with the benefits of an increasing manufacturing base. This could be used to exploit and dominate world markets, with cheaply produced, mass-produced goods, with the maritime commercial routes protected by the might of the British navy. War had stimulated the iron industry, especially those factories that produced goods for the war effort. Highly noticeable was the Carron works near Falkirk, which produced the naval carronade, a deadly weapon used at close quarters.

Levels of production were increasing in all industries. Coal production rose from 2.5 to 10 million tons between 1700 and 1800. Woven cotton cloth production increased from 5 million pounds weight to 100 million between 1775 and 1815. Yorkshire worsteds and the Scots and Irish linen industry also saw vast increases, as did pig iron output. War had diminished sales but military and naval uniform production helped.

The continued increase in production resulted from numerous factors. Very important was the division of labour where making an item could be subdivided into various activities with one person at each task. Factory work discipline became harsh with workers closely supervised. Textile factories kept windows closed to keep a correct humidity despite the heat; workers could be fined for whistling; disobedience might result in wages being docked; and lateness for work was often subject to a harsh fine. Such work discipline improved production, with the workers being treated as just one more resource to be used.

Technology and the financial investment for the development and testing of machines became highly important. Machines gradually replaced some workers and their labour could then be placed elsewhere or turned on to the street. The machinery used was commonly the redesign or improved version of machinery invented earlier.

Newcomen's seventeenth-century steam engine, used to pump out water from coal mines, was improved by James Watt. His engines were used in coal mining, blast furnace blowing, flour mills, malt mills, sugar refining and stone mills. The cotton industry developed cotton spinning machines, the first factory containing these being built at Cromford in Derbyshire by Sir Richard Arkwright. The workers endured 13-hour shifts, the machine running 24 hours a day; the female and child workforce was paid less than men.

Women became the dominant labour force in the cotton spinning regions of Lancashire and central Scotland. Industrialists needed a labour force and competition for available labour drove up agricultural wages. A noticeable feature of industrialization was the concentration of factories and mines in certain areas. The textile industry was prevalent in contemporary Ulster, the Paisley/Glasgow to Edinburgh lowlands, and a broad swathe from Lancashire into the Midlands. The mechanised woollen and worsted textile industry became focused in the West Riding of Yorkshire. Iron and steel production was focused in central Scotland, Yorkshire, Birmingham and south Wales.

The Black Country and the area around Sheffield became a home of clothing, soap making, glass making, steam engine manufacture and a new gas-producing industry was created, with a gaslight company being established in London in 1812. Britain was also aided both by the geographical availability of raw materials, which could be moved by canal and by rich agricultural land.

Massive production required skilled marketing and British goods were exported creating a demand for developing ports at Edinburgh, Glasgow, London, Bristol and Liverpool. Shipbuilding became increasingly important with the demands for the navy, the merchant fleet and the need to replace the shortfall caused by privateering; Greenock, Aberdeen, Belfast, Newcastle, Southampton and Plymouth were all important centres.

Industry

An important aspect of industrialization and urbanization was an accompanying agricultural revolution. Farmer landlords improved farming methods, developed livestock breeds, tried a wider range of crops. They also enclosed lands which dispossessed tenants but increased crop yields, making the rural sector capable of feeding an expanding urban population. More fodder meant more livestock could be kept over winter. Thomas Coke of Holkham, Norfolk, improved breeds of sheep, cattle and pigs.

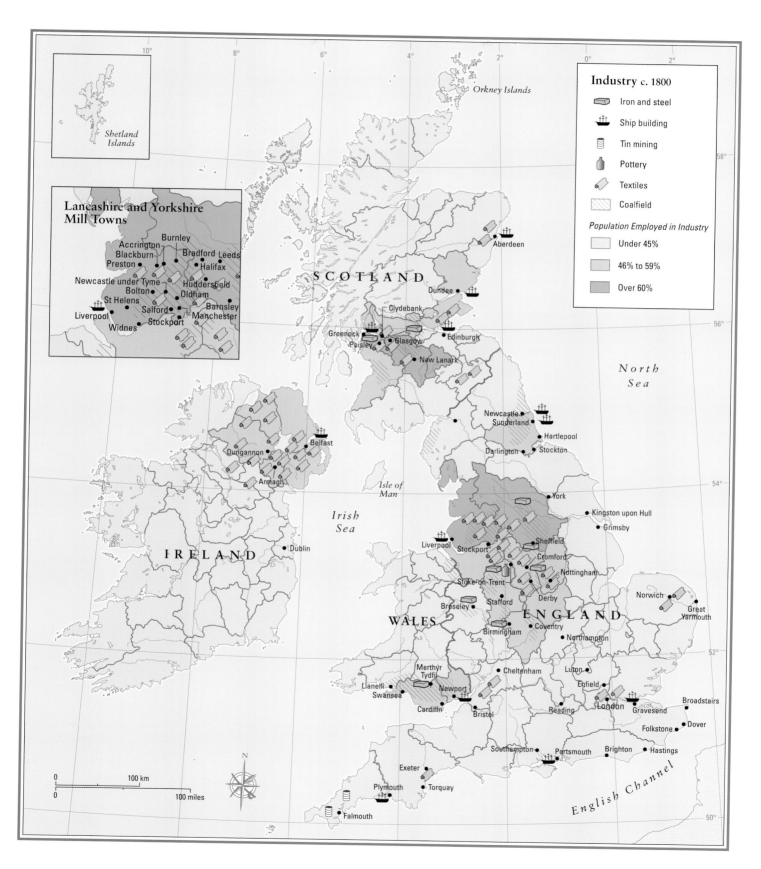

Orkney Islands

Shetland Islands

Industry c. 1800

Iron and steel
Ship building
Tin mining
Pottery
Textiles
Coalfield

Population Employed in Industry

Under 45%

46% to 59%

Over 60%

Lancashire and Yorkshire Mill Towns

Burnley
Accrington
Blackburn   Bradford   Leeds
Preston   Halifax
Newcastle under Tyme   Huddersfield
        Bolton   Oldham
St Helens   Barnsley
Liverpool   Salford Manchester
        Widnes   Stockport

SCOTLAND

Aberdeen

Dundee

Clydebank

Greenock
Paisley   Glasgow   Edinburgh

New Lanark

North
Sea

Newcastle
Sunderland
        Hartlepool
Darlington   Stockton

Belfast

Dungannon

Armagh

Isle of
Man

York

Kingston upon Hull

Grimsby

Irish
Sea

IRELAND   Dublin

Liverpool   Stockport   Sheffield
        Cromford
Stoke-on-Trent   Nottingham

Broseley   Stafford   Derby

Norwich

WALES   Coventry   Great
        Birmingham   Yarmouth
                ENGLAND   Northampton

Merthyr
Tydfil   Cheltenham   Luton
Llanelli   Newport   Enfield
Swansea   Reading   London   Gravesend
        Cardiff   Bristol   Broadstairs
                                Folkstone   Dover
        Southampton   Portsmouth   Brighton   Hastings
Exeter
        Torquay
Plymouth   English Channel

Falmouth

0   100 km
0   100 miles

N

157

The British Empire in 1850

The imperial period following the loss of the Thirteen Colonies, referred to as the Second Empire, was characterized by the development and strengthening of the lands, eventually to be known as the Dominions: Australia, New Zealand and Cape Colony. Captain Cook's expeditions to the Pacific eventually led to the first attempt to establish a colony at Botany Bay in 1788. The convicts transported there, and its successor colony in Sydney Cove, served their time before purchasing land and becoming small farmers. A route was found across the mountains into the hinterland allowing agricultural settlements to flourish there. The discovery of gold in Victoria in 1851 occasioned a huge influx of immigrants, most peopling the cities.

Settlement in New Zealand was facilitated by the Treaty of Waitangi in 1840 with the Maori inhabitants. Many Scots arrived in New Zealand and formed the back-bone of a wool industry. An 1852 New Zealand Constitution Act developed a New Zealand Parliament, meeting in 1854, the colony becoming self-governing two years later. After 1815, Canada benefited from massive migrations of English, Irish and Scots. The years 1825 to 1846 saw over 600,000 migrants from Europe who differed significantly from populations of French and British Empire Loyalists there. A Canadian Confederation was proclaimed in 1867.

After the British seized control of Cape Colony in 1814, they regularized that conquest by a cash payment later. Relations between the British and Dutch Boers deteriorated so badly that 3,000 Boers trekked north under Pieter Retief's leadership in 1835. Defeating Zulus at the Battle of Blood River in 1838, the Boers established independent settlements in Natal but encroaching British stimulated them to move to the High Veldt. By 1860, the Boers established free republics: the Transvaal and in the Orange Free State which would later conflict with Cape Colony and Natal when diamonds were discovered in the disputed territory of Griqualand West.

The British Empire in 1850
Various reasons explain the expansion of the British Empire. Commerce and its protection were probably paramount but technological change, with ships powered by steam instead of driven by sail, was important. Coaling stations were required in strategic places: Gibraltar, Cape Town, Aden and elsewhere. Christian Missionaries were significant in opening up new lands which then became markets requiring defence and communication. Not everything went Britain's way; 1842 witnessed the loss of an army in the first Anglo-Afghan War.

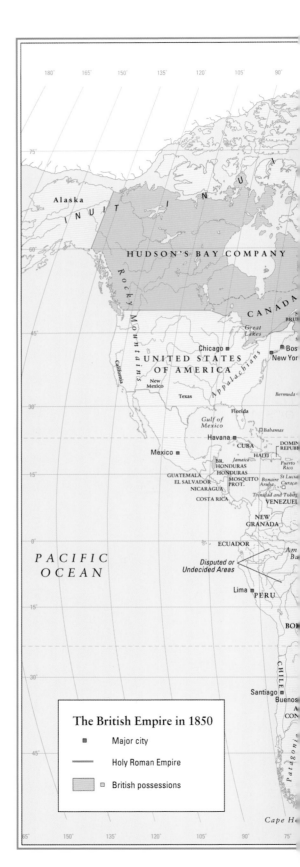

The British Empire in 1850

- ■ Major city
- — Holy Roman Empire
- British possessions

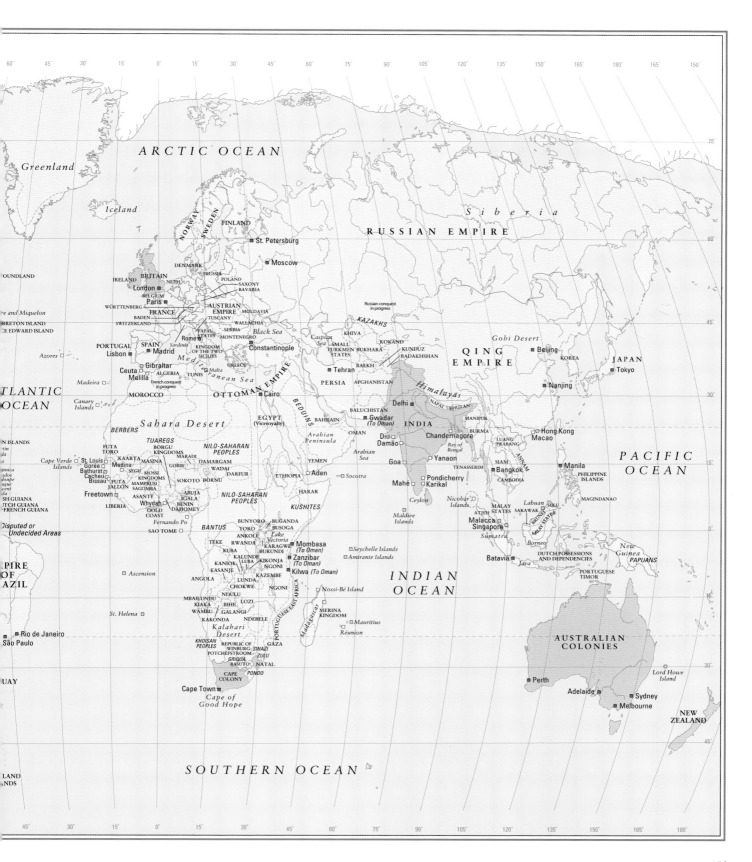

Reform

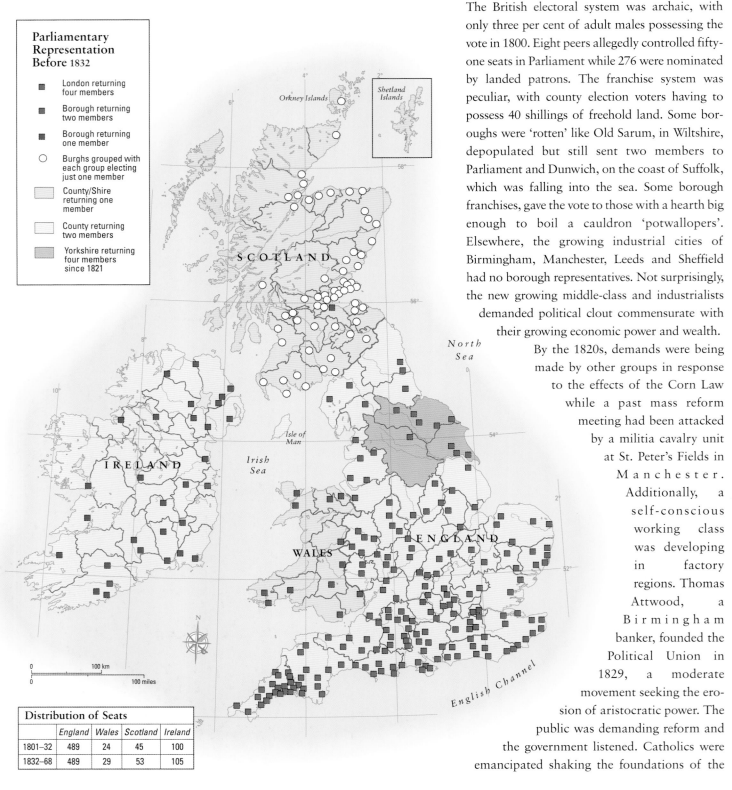

Parliamentary Representation Before 1832

■ London returning four members

■ Borough returning two members

■ Borough returning one member

○ Burghs grouped with each group electing just one member

County/Shire returning one member

County returning two members

Yorkshire returning four members since 1821

Orkney Islands

Shetland Islands

SCOTLAND

North Sea

IRELAND

Irish Sea

Isle of Man

WALES

ENGLAND

English Channel

0		100 km
0		100 miles

Distribution of Seats

	England	Wales	Scotland	Ireland
1801–32	489	24	45	100
1832–68	489	29	53	105

The British electoral system was archaic, with only three per cent of adult males possessing the vote in 1800. Eight peers allegedly controlled fifty-one seats in Parliament while 276 were nominated by landed patrons. The franchise system was peculiar, with county election voters having to possess 40 shillings of freehold land. Some boroughs were 'rotten' like Old Sarum, in Wiltshire, depopulated but still sent two members to Parliament and Dunwich, on the coast of Suffolk, which was falling into the sea. Some borough franchises, gave the vote to those with a hearth big enough to boil a cauldron 'potwallopers'. Elsewhere, the growing industrial cities of Birmingham, Manchester, Leeds and Sheffield had no borough representatives. Not surprisingly, the new growing middle-class and industrialists demanded political clout commensurate with their growing economic power and wealth.

By the 1820s, demands were being made by other groups in response to the effects of the Corn Law while a past mass reform meeting had been attacked by a militia cavalry unit at St. Peter's Fields in Manchester. Additionally, a self-conscious working class was developing in factory regions. Thomas Attwood, a Birmingham banker, founded the Political Union in 1829, a moderate movement seeking the erosion of aristocratic power. The public was demanding reform and the government listened. Catholics were emancipated shaking the foundations of the

Protestant Glorious Revolution, and 1830 saw the death of George IV. The old British state was in flux and an election was due.

The year 1832 ushered in the Great Reform Act, which wiped out political anomalies and abuses, but not totally. Fifty-six small English boroughs were disenfranchised and thirty-one others were reduced by one Member of Parliament. Forty-one towns were granted representation adding sixty-three new borough MPs to the Commons while sixty-two new county seats were created. Wales gained five new MPs, while Scotland and Ireland had their own reform acts. Most men of the middling sort could now vote, as could most farmers but very few members of the working class, industrial or agricultural, could meet the £10 voting franchise. The electorate was increased but inadequately, but the principle of representation was established and the Westminster political classes realized that they must be more responsive to public opinion.

The bones of a reformed British state were being created, symbolized, perhaps, by the burning of Parliament in 1834. In 1833, a Factory Act limited child labour to nine hours a day while an 1834 Poor Law Amendment Act introduced a uniform national system, designed to keep the poor and unemployed from starving while not boosting rates. However, political reform was inadequate and further acts would promote democracy: the 1867 Second Reform Act, the 1884 Third Reform Act, and the 1918 Representation of the People Act.

Parliamentary Representation after 1832

Population changes caused by industrialization necessitated reform so factory towns could be represented in Parliament.

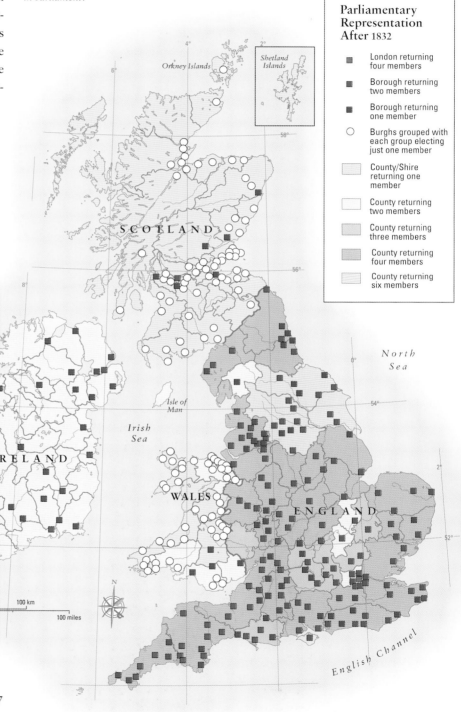

Parliamentary Representation After 1832

- ■ London returning four members
- ■ Borough returning two members
- ■ Borough returning one member
- ○ Burghs grouped with each group electing just one member
- County/Shire returning one member
- County returning two members
- County returning three members
- County returning four members
- County returning six members

Irish Famine and Emigration

Ireland has been perceived as the home of an emigrant people but this movement has been a comparatively recent phenomenon beginning in the mid-nineteenth century. Before 1845, Ulster Scots left for North America in the eighteenth century and considerable populations concentrated in some English cities by 1800. However, the Irish potato famine occasioned a population exodus from a country that had been increasing its population.

The potato comprised the basis of Irish peasant agriculture in the early-nineteenth century. The smallest tenants inhabited shacks on tiny plots with little or no security of tenure while often tennants of absentee landlords; this existence prevailed in western Ireland. In contrast, the regions of Ulster and around Dublin developed a thriving wheat farming system and textile production. So, successful was agriculture that Ireland's population grew from approximately 5,000,000 in 1800 to over 8,000,000 in 1841. Then, English competition shattered the cotton and wool industries,leaving only linen to survive. The English demand for wheat took that product from local markets while a growing population subdivided their already meagre plots amongst children, leaving virtually unviable economic units. Then the potato famine caused by blight, struck from 1845–49.

The blight, originating in Europe, spread rapidly generating a food crisis far worse than others between 1800 and 1845. The impact of the 1845 famine was exacerbated by three more years of blight in the next four years. Malnutrition, starvation, and epidemic diseases followed with at least 1,000,000 people dying, the worst affected areas being Connacht and Munster. The poorest areas suffered most as death and then migration took their toll. The reduction of population to some 6,500,000 meant that, between 1841 and 1851, the proportion of landholdings of less than five acres fell from 35 to 20 per cent while those of 15 acres or more rose from 31 to 48 per cent. Such was the result of reduced rural population pressure.

Next emigration caused a population decline, so great that nothing like it was witnessed anywhere in contemporary Europe, despite similar massive famines in the German states. The population movement affected all regions, classes, and religious communities in Ireland with the largest outflows emanating from Munster, Connacht and Antrim. Many migrants travelled to England and Scotland, some to stay but others to leave from their ports, like Liverpool, to arrive in North America, especially the United States. Vast numbers of the migrant Irish flocked to the big cities, such as Pittsburgh, Detroit, Chicago, St. Louis, Missouri and San Francisco. Once Irish communities were emplaced, they acted as reception centres for future migrants and staging posts to move migrants westwards to other regions. By 1860, the Irish had a large presence in the Northeast and comprised over half the migrants to the United States during the famine years.

Whereas many migrants arriving in the United States were concerned with acquiring land to become or continue as farmers, the Irish Catholic migrants became urban dwellers, the men earning their keep as manual labourers working on public and private building projects such as railroads, canals and sewers. Many more worked in the mills in Massachusetts while many women became domestic servants. Generally, the Irish migrants were at the bottom of the social order on arrival but, by the early 1900s, they were no different from other members of the community, contributing much to social service jobs, police and fire services.

Death and migration slowed the marriage rate in Ireland but with some counties flouting the trend; the numbers of female migrants outnumbering their male counterparts partially explains this occurrence. Increases in average age and people who never married also contributed to this. Economically, agriculture developed with larger landholdings and a switch to dairy farming.

Famine and Emigration

By 1860, the Irish had a large presence in the northeastern United States and constituted over half the immigrants to the country. During the American Civil War, some 50,000 Irishmen joined the Union army, the Irish Brigade being one famous unit, which lost 4,000 officers and men during the war. The 69th Infantry Regiment, the Fighting 69th, was known for its ferocity and valour.

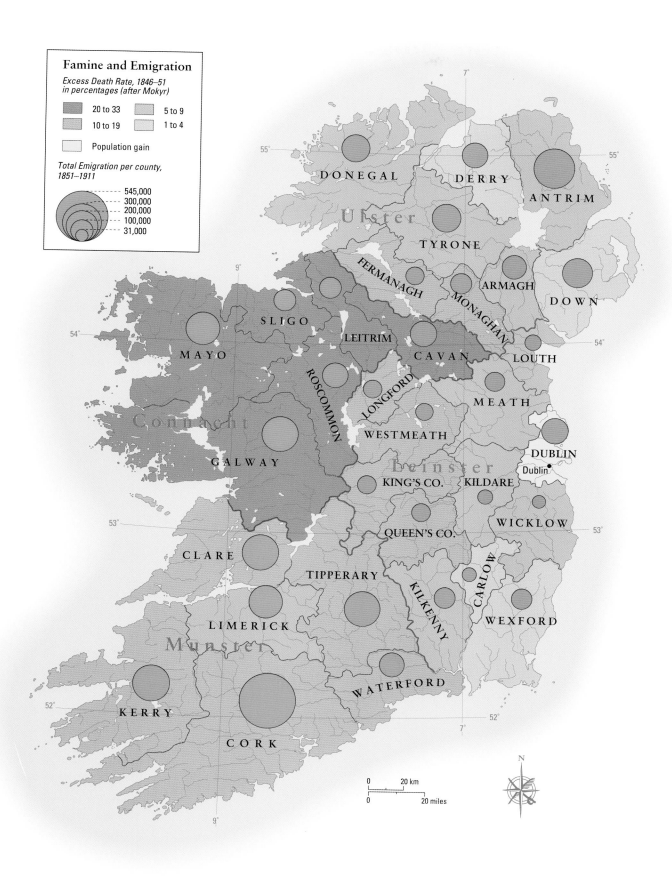

Famine and Emigration

*Excess Death Rate, 1846–51
in percentages (after Mokyr)*

- 20 to 33
- 10 to 19
- 5 to 9
- 1 to 4
- Population gain

*Total Emigration per county,
1851–1911*

- 545,000
- 300,000
- 200,000
- 100,000
- 31,000

DONEGAL

DERRY

ANTRIM

Ulster

TYRONE

FERMANAGH

ARMAGH

DOWN

MONAGHAN

SLIGO

LEITRIM

CAVAN

LOUTH

MAYO

Connacht

ROSCOMMON

LONGFORD

MEATH

WESTMEATH

GALWAY

Leinster

KING'S CO.

KILDARE

DUBLIN

Dublin

QUEEN'S CO.

WICKLOW

CLARE

TIPPERARY

KILKENNY

CARLOW

LIMERICK

WEXFORD

Munster

WATERFORD

KERRY

CORK

N

0   20 km
0   20 miles

Britain's Asian Empire

British Conquest of India

The Indian Mutiny was marked by atrocities on both sides and the rebellion led to the dissolution of the East India Company and the foundation of the British Raj.

In the last half of the nineteenth century, an aggressive scramble for colonies ensured the pace of imperialism increased, the main beneficiary of its formal and informal modes being Britain. Changes occurred in British imperialism as compared with the first half of the century: Britain then preferred not to have authority over territo-

ries in order to secure trade routes, but was prepared to use military and naval forces to preserve its commercial interests, and when these were threatened, to annex the area concerned. Essentially, Britain assumed control of foreign countries for commercial and economic reasons, or because they guarded a trade route, or to gain a

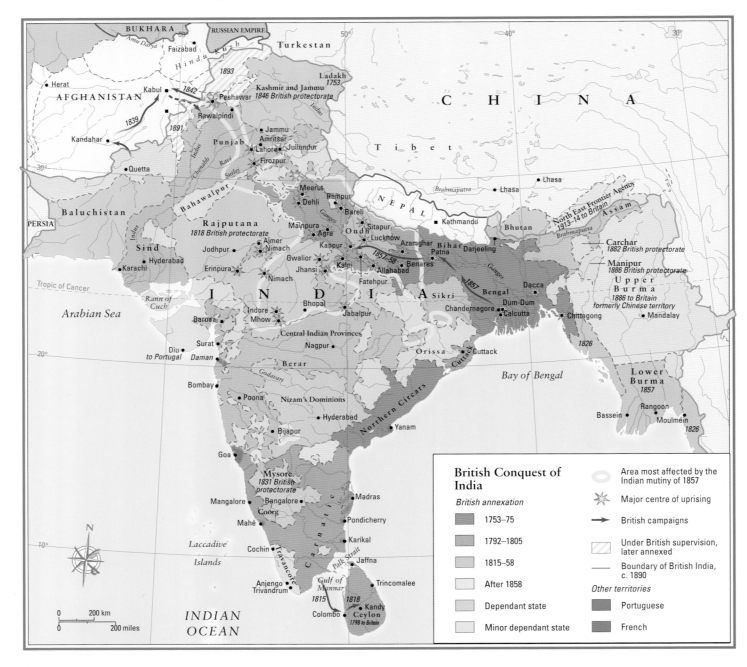

British Conquest of India

British annexation

- 1753–75
- 1792–1805
- 1815–58
- After 1858
- Dependant state
- Minor dependant state

Area most affected by the Indian mutiny of 1857

Major centre of uprising

British campaigns

Under British supervision, later annexed

Boundary of British India, c. 1890

Other territories

- Portuguese
- French

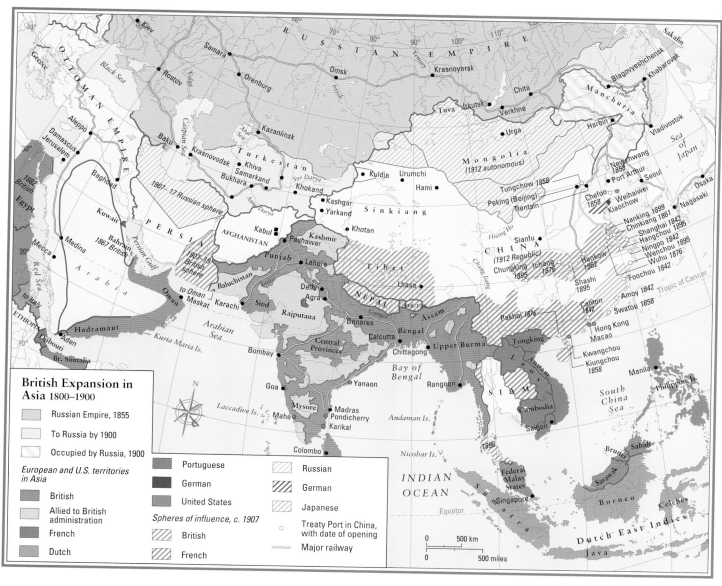

British Expansion in Asia 1800–1900

Russian Empire, 1855

To Russia by 1900

Occupied by Russia, 1900

European and U.S. territories in Asia

British

Allied to British administration

French

Dutch

Portuguese

German

United States

Russian

German

Japanese

Spheres of influence, c. 1907

British

French

Treaty Port in China, with date of opening

Major railway

new market for manufactured goods or to acquire raw materials. Also, a major drive in British imperialism was occasioned by the need to protect their Indian trade.

After the Napoleonic Wars, Britain subjugated the Maratha and Rajput states. In the 1850s, Britain fought the Sikhs, annexed the Punjab and acquired other states on the death of native rulers (the doctrine of lapse). British attempts at modernization and failure to consider the culture of their Indian troops led to the Indian Mutiny in 1857–58, whereby Indian troops rallied around the flag of the last Moghul, Bahadur Shah II, as

Emperor of India. Hostility to British rule continued, leading Indian nationalists to form the Indian National Congress in 1885.

French and British competition in Asia, with France hegemonic in south-east Asia, resulted in the British annexation of Burma in 1886 and then a Franco-British partition of areas of Siam.

The entire British Asian imperium was a result of British world domination, dependent upon unchallenged naval supremacy, an Indian army paid for by Indians, and the garrisoning of strategic sites, such as Gibraltar, Malta, Cyprus, Aden, Hong Kong and Cape Colony.

British Expansion in Asia

British trade with China gained extra-territoriality rights in Treaty Ports and a sphere of influence in the entire Chang Jiang River basin.

The Railways 1829–1890

The beginning of the railway system saw coal being hauled from Stockton to the sea in 1820 and then Darlington in 1825. The first passenger train ran from Liverpool to Manchester in 1830. In 1830, Britain possessed 400 miles of track and 6,600 in 1852, the rapid development being fuelled by railway mania, with two waves of construction in the 1830s and 1840s. A skeletal railway system grew, connecting major cities and, by the 1870s, over 13,000 miles of track were open and the major network completed. Yet, one third of the track was still to be built comprising branch and local lines, feeder lines and shunting facilities, while some small villages possessed their own stations. By 1846, railway construction employed some 200,000 men and, by 1900, the railways' staff reached 600,000 (95 per cent men).

Railway development involved considerable financial investment with a far wider range of shareholders than in previous industries, with the middle classes being significant, attracted by high rates of interest, some 10 per cent up to 1846. The spread of railways benefited an expanding economy, as the steel and associated industries fed off the demand for their products. Also, engineering thrived with the construction of bridges and rolling stock.

Suburban and urban development was promoted around towns and cities. The centres of many cities were flattened, displacing tens of thousands of people in Manchester and London. Underground railway systems were built, notably in London, commencing in the 1860s. Such electrified, rapid transport systems allowed workers to travel easily and helped business development. Travel restrictions were eased allowing mobility with businesses and the middle-class to move to the suburbs, leaving city centres to the working class where they could be more easily controlled and policed. A complementary transport system was the extensive tramway network, employing horses, steam and then electricity. Thus, city internal transport complemented the railway system.

As well as integrating counties in an economic and spatial sense, railways intensified social differences. Carriages were divided into first-, second-, and third-class services; the more costly the class, the greater the luxuries, although these were initially only foot-warmers in the first-class. Third-class passengers originally travelled in little better than open wagons, subject to all weather conditions. Cheap travel opened up tourism and holiday destinations with seaside resorts enticing the upper and middle classes. The York to Scarborough line arrived in 1845 bringing a large influx of visitors to the emerging seaside resort. To cope, the Grand Hotel was completed in 1867, housing 365 bedrooms.

The railway age developed some oddities. The Bridgnorth Funicular Railway linked the Low Town in the River Severn valley with the High Town, the original settlement with its castle. For those desiring an incredible view, the Snowdon Mountain Railway links Llanberis, Wales, with the mountain summit. Another innovation was the cable tramway, opened in 1902, linking Llandudno with the Great Orme and its vistas.

The railways were linked to two other major institutions: the Army and the Post Office. The Army could use the railway system in times of war during mobilization and for logistics. However, the Army also built its own lines to facilitate movements of munitions in armaments depots and ordnance factories, such as Chatham Dockyard and the Royal Arsenal Railway, Woolwich. Post office collaboration with the railways was needed to cope with the increase in written correspondence after the introduction of the 1840 Penny Post. The increase in literacy, due to Sunday Schools and improvement in education, increased newspaper sales and newspaper deliveries were physically impossible on a large scale without railways. In sum, railways were a catalyst for social, industrial and general economic development in Britain, with military and tourist applications.

Victorian Railways
The locomotive, the Iron Horse, could carry loads faster and farther than any other mode of transport. Railways destroyed stage-coach travel and made canals largely redundant. Train stations became symbols of Victorian architecture at its most monumental, with iron girders and glass roofs, as at Paddington and St. Pancras Stations. The latter 'cathedral of railways' has a Victorian Gothic frontage on Euston Road, London.

0   100 km
0   100 miles

N

Wick

Stromferry

Mallaig

Aberdeen

Oban

Edinburgh
Glasgow
Kilmarnock   Berwick
Ayr   Hawick

Carlisle   Newcastle

Whitehaven   Darlington   Stockton
                              Whitby
Barrow   Scarborough
            Skipton   York
Preston   Bradford   Leeds   Hull
            Manchester   Doncaster
Liverpool   Sheffield   Gainsborough
            Chester   Lincoln
            Crewe   Newark   Boston
                  Derby   Nottingham   Fakenham
Shrewsbury   Stafford   Beeston   Yarmouth
        Wellington   Leicester   Peterborough   Norwich
        Birmingham   Rugby   Ely
Ludlow   Cambridge
        Worchester   Ipswich
Carmarthen   Gloucester   Oxford   Colchester

Cardiff   Swindon   Reading   LONDON   Strood
    Bristol   Red Hill   Deal
                Salisbury   Horsham   Dover
                Southampton   Brighton
Exeter   Dorchester   Portsmouth
Bodmin
Truro   Plymouth

Holyhead
Carnarvon

Dublin

Imperial Rivals 1899 – 1914

The decade before the First World War witnessed the culmination of the New Imperialism and its rush to carve up the world into European, American and Japanese spheres of interest. The Far East was divided and Britain and Russia competed in Afghanistan while France completed the acquisition of Indo-China in the 1880s. Elsewhere, Germany and the USA split Samoa, with the US grabbing its own empire after winning the Spanish American War in 1898: Puerto Rico, Guam and the Philippines, Hawaii having been incorporated for different reasons.

In Africa, Franco-British competition in the Sudan culminated in the Fashoda Incident in 1898, almost leading to war. Germany's acquisition of Tanganyika blocked the British Cape to Cairo plan, while German occupation of South-west Africa threatened Cape Colony and Bechuanaland. The German Kaiser's aggression in the Moroccan Crises of 1905–06 also served to highlight his ambitions.

Once the world was divided into imperial possessions, the former British supremacy was challenged in naval terms by Germany and France, while military and diplomatic European alliances isolated Britain. Britain's vulnerability was highlighted by the 1889 Naval Defence Act, which adopted a two-power standard: the British fleet should exceed the combined strength of the next two largest naval powers.

Armed camps appeared in Europe with the Dual Alliance of France and Russia being potentially anti-German and anti-British. The 1894–95 Sino-Japanese War brought Japan into Asian affairs as a major power, later restated by Japan's victory over Russia in 1905. The 1902 Anglo-Japanese Alliance contained Russia in the Orient and allowed Japan to protect British naval interests. The 1904 Anglo-French Entente Cordiale settled imperial disputes and removed the probability of a Franco-British rule. Finally, the 1907 Triple Entente between France, Britain and Russia ended Anglo-Russian rivalries, leaving Britain to face Germany in the North Atlantic and Channel.

Imperial Rivals

When General Kitchener campaigned up the Nile to avenge Gordon of Khartoum's death and regain control of the Sudan, he met French Captain Marchand who had trekked from Congolese Brazzaville to Fashoda. Here, Marchand claimed the headwaters of the Nile for France. Hugely outnumbered, he was eventually compelled to retreat, after gaining no support from Paris.

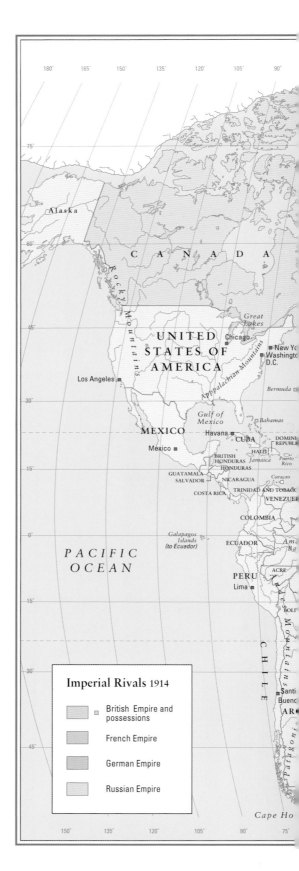

Imperial Rivals 1914

British Empire and possessions

French Empire

German Empire

Russian Empire

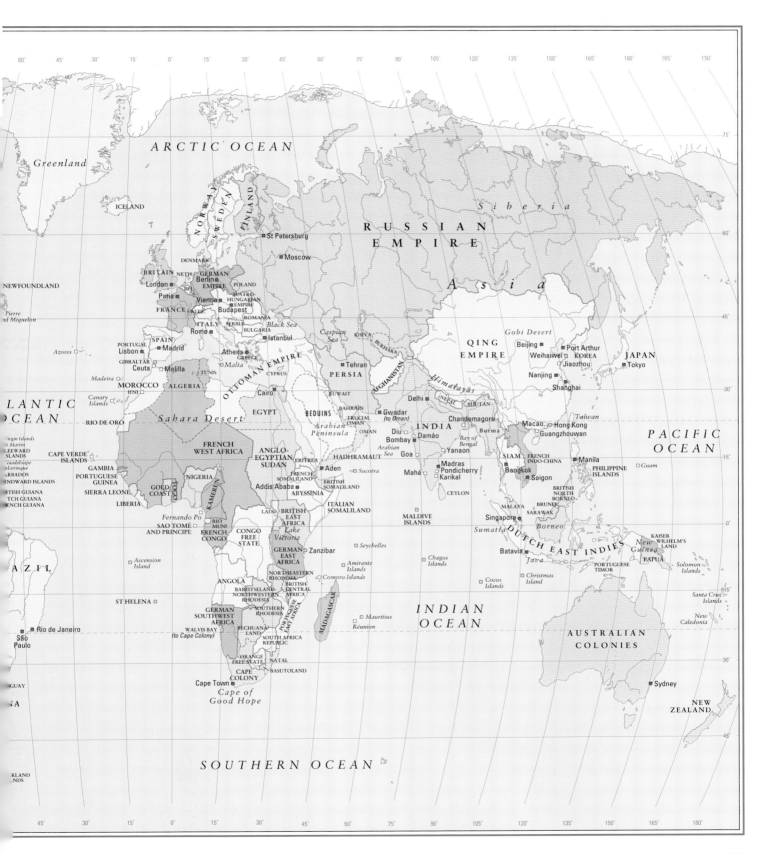

ARCTIC OCEAN

Greenland

ICELAND

NORWAY SWEDEN FINLAND

RUSSIAN
EMPIRE

Siberia

Asia

■ St Petersburg

■ Moscow

DENMARK

BRITAIN NETH. GERMAN
EMPIRE
London ■ ■Berlin POLAND
Paris ■ BEL. ■Vienna
FRANCE SWITZ. AUSTRO-
HUNGARIAN
EMPIRE
■Budapest
ITALY SERBIA ROMANIA
Rome ■ BULGARIA
■ Istanbul
Black Sea

PORTUGAL SPAIN
Lisbon ■ ■Madrid
GIBRALTAR
Ceuta ■ ■Melilla
Malta
Madeira ☐ TUNIS
MOROCCO
IFNI ALGERIA
*Canary
Islands*

NEWFOUNDLAND

*Pierre
and Miquelon*

Athens ■
GREECE
CYPRUS
*Caspian
Sea* KHIVA
BUKHARA

OTTOMAN EMPIRE

PERSIA
■Tehran

Cairo
EGYPT

BEDUINS
*Arabian
Peninsula*
KUWAIT
BAHRAIN
TRUCIAL
OMAN
■Gwadar
(to Oman)

AFGHANISTAN

Himalayas

QING
EMPIRE

■Beijing
Weihaiwei ■ ■Port Arthur
KOREA
■Jiaozhou
Nanjing ■

JAPAN
■Tokyo

■Shanghai
Taiwan

Gobi Desert

Delhi ■
NEPAL BHUTAN
Chandemagore ■
INDIA
Macao ■ ☐Hong Kong
☐Guangzhouwan

PACIFIC
OCEAN

Sahara Desert

RIO DE ORO

ATLANTIC
OCEAN

Virgin Islands
St Martin
LEEWARD
ISLANDS
Guadeloupe
BARBADOS
WINDWARD ISLANDS
ITISH GUIANA
TCH GUIANA
ENCH GUIANA

CAPE VERDE
ISLANDS ☐

GAMBIA
PORTUGUESE
GUINEA
SIERRA LEONE
LIBERIA

FRENCH
WEST AFRICA

ANGLO-
EGYPTIAN
SUDAN

ERITREA
FRENCH
SOMALILAND
Addis Ababa ■
ABYSSINIA

BRITISH
SOMALILAND
■Aden
☐ *Socotra*

ITALIAN
SOMALILAND

HADHRAMAUT

Diu ☐ Damāo
OMAN
Bombay ☐
Arabian
Sea
Goa ■ Yanaon

*Bay of
Bengal*
Burma

Madras ■
Pondicherry ■
■ Karikal
Mahé ■

SIAM
Bangkok ■

FRENCH
INDO-CHINA

■Manila

PHILIPPINE
ISLANDS
☐ *Guam*

CEYLON

MALDIVE
ISLANDS

Saigon ■

BRITISH
NORTH
BORNEO
MALAYA BRUNEI
Singapore ■ SARAWAK

DUTCH EAST INDIES

Sumatra
Batavia ■ *Borneo*
Java

KAISER
WILHELM'S
LAND
New
Guinea
PAPUA

Solomon
Islands

NIGERIA
GOLD
COAST
TOGO

KAMERUN
Fernando Po
SAO TOME
AND PRINCIPE
FRENCH
CONGO
RIO
MUNI

CONGO
FREE
STATE

LADO
BRITISH
EAST
AFRICA
*Lake
Victoria*
■Zanzibar

GERMAN
EAST
AFRICA

☐ *Seychelles*

*Amirante
Islands*
☐ *Comoro Islands*

*Chagos
Islands*

*Cocos
Islands*

*Christmas
Island*

INDIAN
OCEAN

AUSTRALIAN
COLONIES

*Santa Cruz
Islands*

*New
Caledonia*

*Ascension
Island* ☐

AZIL

ANGOLA

ST HELENA ☐

■ Rio de Janeiro
São
Paulo

NORTHEASTERN
RHODESIA
BAROTSELAND
NORTHWESTERN
RHODESIA
GERMAN
SOUTHWEST
AFRICA
WALVIS BAY
(to Cape Colony)

BRITISH
CENTRAL
AFRICA
SOUTHERN
RHODESIA
PORTUGUESE
EAST AFRICA

BECHUANA-
LAND
SOUTH
AFRICA
REPUBLIC
ORANGE
FREE STATE
CAPE
COLONY
Cape Town ■
*Cape of
Good Hope*

MADAGASCAR

☐ *Mauritius*
Réunion

NATAL
BASUTOLAND

■ Sydney

GUAY
A

SOUTHERN OCEAN

NEW
ZEALAND

KLAND
NDS

Cities 1800 – 1900

The population of the British Isles rose rapidly during the nineteenth century. The population has been estimated at 9.5 million in 1700, rising to 10.5 million in 1750. The 1801 census showed a population of 15.75 million and 27.5 million in 1841. 45 million was reached in 1911. The last half of the nineteenth century saw demographic growth focusing on the industrial regions of Central Scotland, North-east England, West Yorkshire, South Lancashire, Birmingham and the Black Country, South Wales and London. Ireland differed, losing population to the potato famine of 1845 and mass migration. A rural-urban drift was another major tendency throughout the nineteenth century; many Irish people moved to Merseyside, Clydeside and London.

Between 1841 and 1911, the urban share of the population rose from 37 to 74 per cent. London dominated urban life, accommodating 2 million in 1841 and 6.5 million in 1911, but there was vast growth in Liverpool, Glasgow, Birmingham and Manchester where populations approximated 1 million each. The urban sprawl emerged around such regional centres with towns like Bolton and Wolverhampton growing and complete industrial shipbuilding conurbations like Tyneside. Other areas seeing high population increases were mining areas in Derbyshire, Cornwall and Durham.

The treatment of the urban population was sometimes unusual. Gang-masters from specific factories were known to recruit labour in East Anglia and ship them north on the canal system, sometimes breaking up families, leaving younger children behind because there were age restrictions to work in the mills. As towns and cities developed, increasing pressure was placed on scarce urban resources. In London, rivers turned into fluvial sewers and cholera was rife. Terraced housing near factories were subject to the smoky pollution of blast furnaces and mill towns often developed a yellow tinge to the sky. Back-to-back housing round a courtyard was common with water supplied only on certain days with maybe a single earth closet for twenty or more families. Health was constantly at risk with disease and alcohol problems common.

Cities were divided between rich and poor areas. The West End of London possessed wide streets and public gardens while the East End was a different country together with languages hardly understood 'up West', like cockney, Irish and Yiddish. In Glasgow, one third of the families lived in just one room as Highlanders flooded in. Sometimes one toilet served 120 people so courtyards and stairways would be filled with piles of excrement several feet high until contractors cleansed them at intervals. Urban problems excited reformers. Joseph Chamberlain, mayor of Birmingham (1873–75), ensured the City Council bought gas and waterworks, cleared slums and built new streets. This sense of civic pride, complete with new civic buildings, helped urban dwellers. Certain industrialists were keen to alleviate the conditions of their workers. The Quaker Cadbury family, chocolatiers, built the Bournville model village near Birmingham, while the Quaker Rowntrees, in the same business, constructed the model village of New Earswick at York, the Foundation still running today. Another model village was built for employees of Lever Brothers, soap manufacturers, at Port Sunlight in the Wirral, showing that philanthropy and workers' care were highly important. In Nottingham, Jesse Boot, founder of the chemist chain, was noted for his concern for his workers and for philanthropy in the city.

Cities brought certain benefits like public baths, libraries and educational institutions whether primary schools or mechanics' institutes, which began in 1823, eventually numbering hundreds across the British Isles. Social mobility developed and lower middle-class occupations grew to run the urban infrastructure and communications systems, as well as governmental functions as tax collectors, postal workers and general clerical assistants.

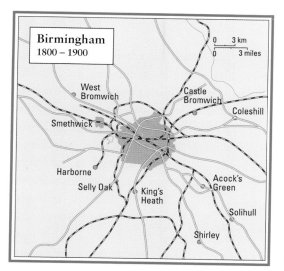

Birmingham
1800 – 1900

0 3 km
0 3 miles

West Bromwich
Castle Bromwich
Coleshill
Smethwick
Harborne
Selly Oak
King's Heath
Acock's Green
Solihull
Shirley

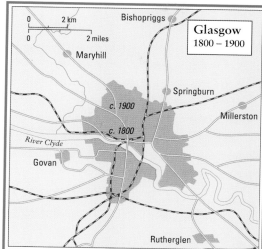

0 2 km
0 2 miles

Bishopriggs
Glasgow
1800 – 1900

Maryhill
Springburn
c. 1900
Millerston
c. 1800
River Clyde
Govan
Rutherglen

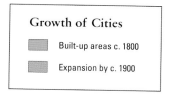

Growth of Cities

Built-up areas c. 1800

Expansion by c. 1900

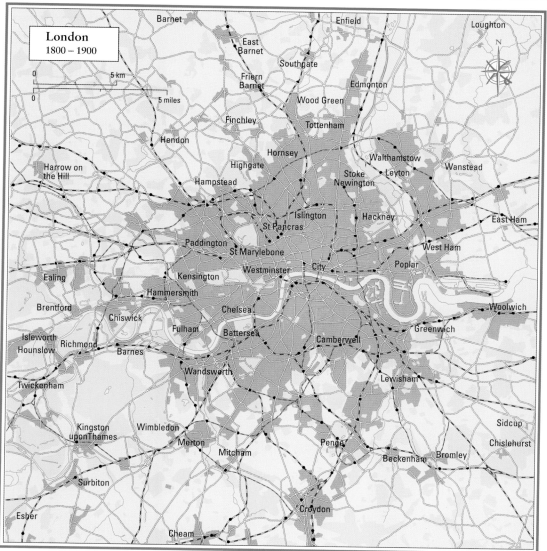

London
1800 – 1900

0 5 km
0 5 miles

Barnet
Enfield
Loughton
East Barnet
Southgate
Friern Barnet
Edmonton
Wood Green
Finchley
Tottenham
Hendon
Hornsey
Walthamstow
Highgate
Leyton
Wanstead
Stoke Newington
Hampstead
Harrow on the Hill
Islington
Hackney
St Pancras
East Ham
Paddington
St Marylebone
West Ham
Ealing
Kensington
Westminster
City
Poplar
Hammersmith
Woolwich
Brentford
Chelsea
Chiswick
Fulham
Battersea
Isleworth
Hounslow
Richmond
Barnes
Greenwich
Camberwell
Wandsworth
Lewisham
Twickenham
Kingston uponThames
Wimbledon
Sidcup
Merton
Chislehurst
Mitcham
Penge
Surbiton
Beckenham
Bromley
Croydon
Esher
Cheam

Cities

*Urbanization generated poor
health conditions with typhus
and tuberculosis endemics.
Terrible epidemics, too, swept
the country. Bacteria had not
been identified and medicines
were not always effective.
Reformers, like Edwin
Chadwick, campaigned for
improved conditions and a Public
Health Act was passed in 1848
and an 1869 Act divided the
country into health districts.
Health dangers were gradually
limited and water supplies
improved resulting in a decline in
death rates.*

On the Eve of War

Before the First World War, Britain remained an elite controlled country despite the huge strides made towards democracy in the nineteenth century. Ten per cent of the population owned ninety-two per cent of all property. Yet, this wealth was under threat as Britain's labour intensive, export-driven industries, often family financed, came into competition with the corporate giants developing in the USA. Additionally, Germany was surpassing Britain in heavy industry and capturing many export markets.

The British Empire was no longer a subservient market; the Dominions wished to develop their own fledgling industries. The Empire could only be defended by British naval superiority. which was now challenged by German industrial might; competing with this threat stretched imperial finance. Furthermore, the debts incurred during the Boer War required servicing. The old order was being questioned with the 1911 Parliament Act hamstringing the House of Lords, while socialist voters returned Labour MPs to the House of Commons.

Industries

As the Edwardian Age moved along, British industry, becoming increasingly outmoded, the country suffered a growing annual trade deficit. By 1910, the profits normally accruing from invisible exports like insurance, banking and other services no longer covered the country's trading losses. Britain could not pay for itself out of its own skill and manufacturing base. Foreign investment was needed for survival.

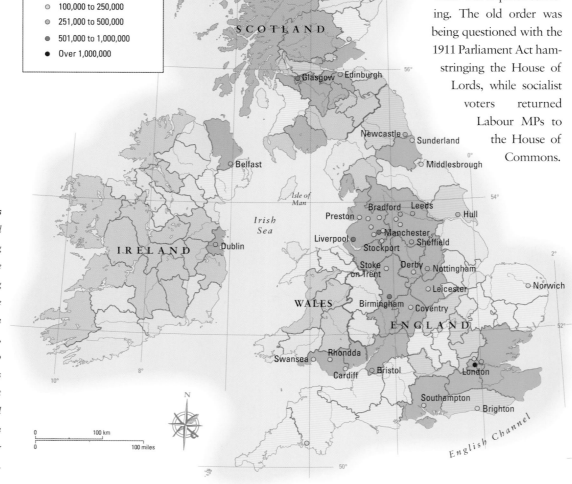

Population c. 1911

per square mile		per square kilometre
0		0
52		20
104		40
208		80
336		130
518		200

Cities and Towns

○ 100,000 to 250,000
◉ 251,000 to 500,000
● 501,000 to 1,000,000
● Over 1,000,000

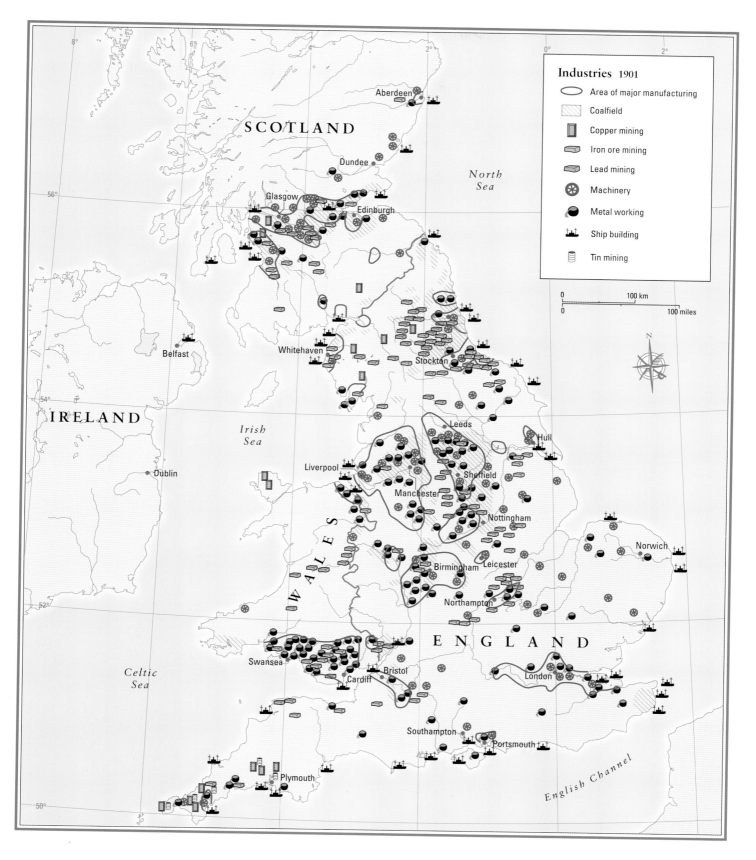

Industries 1901

⬭ Area of major manufacturing

▨ Coalfield

▢ Copper mining

▱ Iron ore mining

▭ Lead mining

⊛ Machinery

● Metal working

⚓ Ship building

⬚ Tin mining

0 ____ 100 km
0 ____ 100 miles

SCOTLAND

Aberdeen

Dundee

Glasgow

Edinburgh

North Sea

Belfast

Whitehaven

Stockton

IRELAND

Irish Sea

Dublin

Leeds

Hull

Liverpool

Sheffield

Manchester

Nottingham

W A L E S

Norwich

Birmingham

Leicester

Northampton

E N G L A N D

Swansea

Bristol

London

Cardiff

Celtic Sea

Southampton

Portsmouth

Plymouth

English Channel

World War I – Battlefronts 1914–16

On 28 July 1914, Austria-Hungary declared war on Serbia, triggering a whole series of established alliances. Russia, in support of Serbia, declared war on Austria-Hungary followed by a German declaration against Russia and then against France, with Britain declaring war on Germany to allegedly protect Belgian neutrality, together with its French ally.

Germany's *Schlieffen Plan* envisaged a holding operation against Russia while its armies swept through neutral Belgium and Luxembourg, thus enveloping the French forces and driving and pinning them against prepared defences in Alsace-Lorraine. Despite the Germans' speed, the *Schlieffen Plan* failed as the German 1st Army lost its nerve. Instead of enveloping Paris to the west, it drove south-east of the city. The Battle of the

Marne ensued with French forces, with the help of the small British Expeditionary Force, preventing the Germans from completing their amended plan. The Germans retreated northwards and both sides settled down for four years of trench warfare, with lines stretching from the Channel to Switzerland.

Elsewhere, Turkey joined Germany and Austria-Hungary occasioning the Allies to land mainly Commonwealth troops during the disastrous Gallipoli campaign, which failed to force the Dardanelles and restore the sea route to Russia. During 1915, sundry Allied offensives achieved little with the alliance suffering manpower losses of over 1.5 million. 1916 observed two titanic battles on the Western Front. The Germans launched an offensive

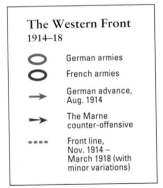

The Western Front
1914–18

⬭ German armies

⬭ French armies

→ German advance, Aug. 1914

→ The Marne counter-offensive

···· Front line, Nov. 1914 – March 1918 (with minor variations)

The Western Front

The Schlieffen Plan scheduled thirty-nine days for the conquest of Paris, with France to be defeated four days later. Belgium's and Luxembourg's neutrality would be violated. However, the plan failed with the extreme western German army failing to envelop Paris and the Allies rallying their forces at the Battle of the Marne. The front line eventually settled down to a line that stretched from the Swiss border to the North Sea.

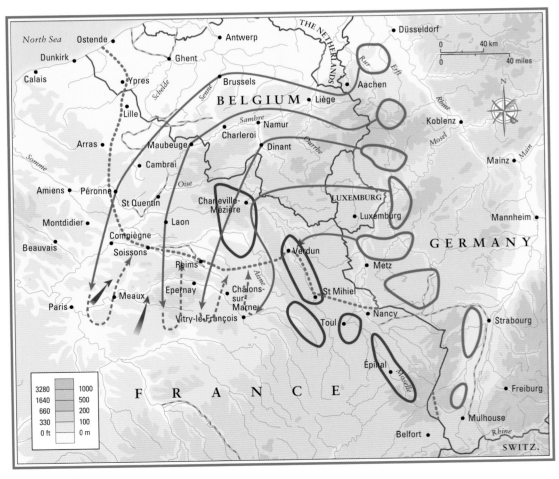

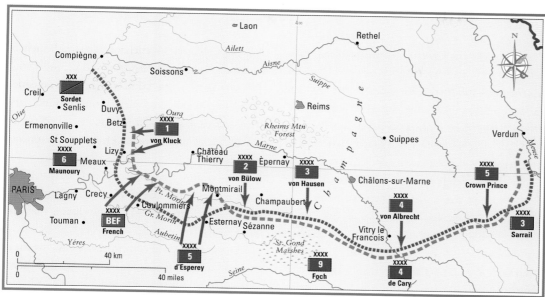

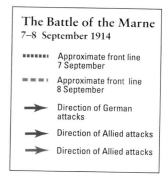

The Battle of the Marne
7–8 September 1914

- - - - - Approximate front line
7 September

– – – Approximate front line
8 September

→ Direction of German attacks

→ Direction of Allied attacks

→ Direction of Allied attacks

The Allies were driven back towards Paris but the Germans exposed their right-flank and were attacked along the Marne River, being forced to retreat some 65 kilometres.

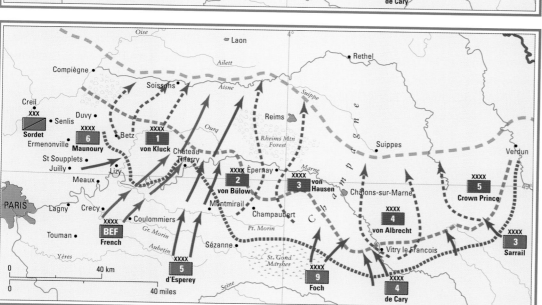

The Battle of the Marne
9–13 September 1914

- - - - - Approximate front line
9 September

– – – Approximate front line
10 September

– – – Approximate front line
13 September

→ Direction of Allied attacks

→ Direction of Allied attacks

- - → Direction of German retreat

around Verdun intending to 'bleed France white …' the offensive savaged both armies. As this horrific battle was fought, the British attacked in the First Battle of the Somme, losing 60,000 men on the first day. The battle lasted from July to November, with the British and French only advancing a few miles. Counter-attacks followed and, by the battle's end, the Germans had lost 650,000 men, the British 427,000 and the French 195,000. This must be added to the Verdun carnage where the French lost some 544,000 and the Germans 434,000 soldiers.

At sea, German unrestricted submarine warfare caused the US government to end diplomatic relations on 3 February 1917. March witnessed the publication of the Zimmerman note which proposed a German-Mexican alliance, with German assistance to aid Mexico in regaining the lands lost in the American-Mexican war of 1846–47, territories stretching from the Atlantic to the Pacific. On 6 April, the Americans declared war on Germany and Austria-Hungary and US mobilization followed, with a planned three million men in Europe by 1918.

Irish Easter Rising 1916

Politically, the Irish responded in the nineteenth century with the renaissance of nationalism. The Gaelic League tried to defend its language in the face of the increasing use of English while Young Ireland instigated a failed rebellion in 1848 in Tipperary. The Irish Republican Brotherhood, the Fenians, was another revolutionary group that wanted to create an independent Irish Republic. Their insurrection in 1867 failed but their bombings in mainland Britain highlighted the Irish issue to be debated by William Gladstone. In Parliament, Protestant Charles Stewart Parnell ran the Irish Parliamentary Party. Although he was a Protestant, in reality Irish nationalism was increasingly defined by its militant Catholic majority support. Protestants tended to support the continuation of the Union of 1800. In 1905, Sinn Féin was founded, demanding independence and a strong economic agenda. Gladstone attempted on two occasions to pass a Home Rule Bill in 1885 and 1893 but was defeated by the Conservatives and Unionists.

Before the First World War, Unionist support became concentrated in Ulster with strong, aggressive hostility towards the issue of Home Rule. A Protestant Ulster Volunteer Force was created and taken with the Curragh 'mutiny' and the foundation of an opposing Catholic National Volunteer grouping, the Ulster situation created the possibility of civil war. A Parliamentary bill proposing Home Rule was tabled with the point that most, or all, of the nine Ulster counties would be left out of the equation. John Redmond, leader of the Irish Parliamentary Party, seemed willing to concede this principle just to secure the passing of the bill as a whole.

The Great War of 1914–18 prevented this Act of Parliament from being implemented, the Act being postponed until the end of the war. Despite Irish nationalist fervour, forty per cent of the adult male Irish population served in the British armed forces during the First World War.

Easter Rising

The competing private armies, independence or pro-union in Ireland received arms from abroad. The Clydevalley *delivered a cargo of guns to the Ulster Volunteer Force at Larne. The author and politician, Erskine Childers, sailed his* Asgard *to Hamburg where a consignment of 1,000 rifles awaited him. He returned through the ships of the British Home fleet and made landfall at Howth Harbour, five miles south of Dublin.*

For example, the 36th Ulster Division fought at Messines Ridge and Cambrai and the 16th Irish Division at Roncroy. Additionally, large numbers of Irish people worked in the munitions industry. Irish troops incurred heavy losses, especially at the Battle of the Somme in July 1916. Many nationalists enlisted hoping their support for Britain would guarantee Home Rule, while members of the Ulster Volunteer Force who served felt their actions would ensure the survival of the Union.

The Irish Republican Brotherhood envisaged the war as a golden opportunity to overthrow British rule. They infiltrated into the 10,000-strong National Volunteers who refused to join the British armed forces but they hid their plans from the majority of the Volunteers, including its Commander-in-Chief, Eoin MacNeill. Contacts were made with Germany, which considered that a postulated uprising at Easter 1916 would be a great embarrassment to Britain and accordingly shipped 20,000 rifles to Ireland, which the Royal Navy intercepted off County Kerry in Tralee Bay. The same day witnessed Sir Roger Casement, the Brotherhood's international agent, being arrested at nearby Banna Strand as he landed from a German U-boat.

These blows to the Brotherhood's cause created confusion in its plans which were to hold National Volunteer manoeuvres on Easter Sunday, which would be used as a launch-pad for a general rising against British rule. Learning of the plans at the last moment, MacNeill cancelled the manoeuvres but Pádraig Pearse, a nationalist poet, issued orders secretly for a more limited uprising on Monday, to be started in Dublin. Contradictory orders confused the Volunteer membership, many of whom remained at home on Monday. Pearse was not concerned, feeling that even failure would keep the Irish nationalist cause burning bright by a 'blood sacrifice', creating martyrs for the cause.

The Easter Rising seized key points on both

sides of the River Liffey, which were mutually supporting. Ultimately, some 2,000 rebels joined the uprising, including 220 trade unionists of James Connolly's Irish Citizen Army. Armed with rifles and revolvers, the insurrection lasted until Saturday with extremely fierce fighting. On Wednesday, seventeen riflemen held up an entire brigade for hours inflicting 234 casualties. The rebel headquarters at the General Post Office was the major British target being battered by two 18-pounder artillery pieces. Pearse evacuated the GPO on Friday and surrendered on Saturday afternoon. British forces had incurred 532 casualties and the insurgents 196, but 2,300 civilians were killed and wounded.

The general Dublin population had greeted British troops with tea and biscuits and regarded the rebels as wartime slackers who deserved the white feather. This attitude was short-lived. The failed insurrection was followed by a bloody aftermath with Ireland under martial law and the execution of dissidents. Nationalism was strengthened by the rhetoric of Pádraig Pearse, the failed leader, and by the execution of James Connolly, a wounded rebel who was shot while being tied to a chair. Fifteen rebel leaders were executed including Sir Roger Casement.

These harsh reprisals and the internment of suspected nationalists, combined with fears about possible conscription, generated a sea change in public opinion. The executions caused revulsion and latent nationalist sympathy venerated the fallen leaders and admired the bravery of the insurgents in the face of the British Army. The Volunteer movement became known as the Irish Republican Army, while Sinn Féin became extremely radical. US pressure saw some prisoners released for Christmas. The 'khaki elections' of November 1918 saw Redmond's constitutional Nationalist Party wiped out by Sinn Féin, its MPs refusing to sit in Westminster. The Anglo-Irish War followed fought by unconventional means: hunger strikes, Michael Collins' selective terrorism, murder and ambush.

Dublin

"… you cannot conquer Ireland, you cannot extinguish the Irish passion for freedom. If our deed has not been sufficient to win freedom, then our children will win it with a better deed."
(Pádraig Pearse)

Easter Rising, Dublin
24–29 April 1916

- ◼ Rebel garrisons
- - - - Intended British cordon
- —— Actual British cordon

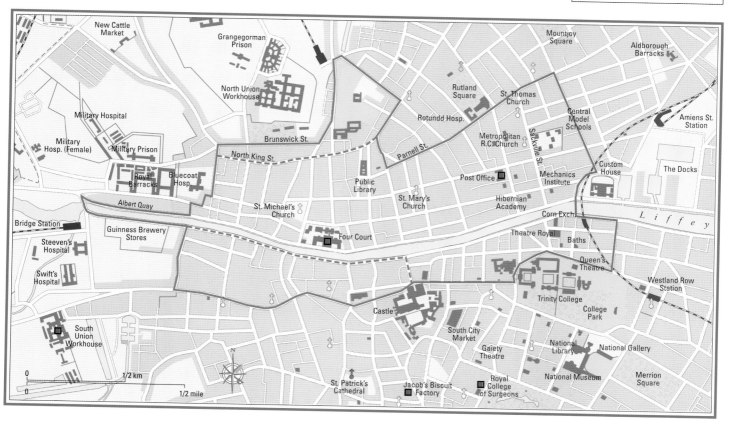

Battlefronts 1917–18

Messines, a pre-cursor action to Passchendaele, saw a German salient eradicated. Their position on a ridge was undermined and exploded, killing thousands of Germans and allowing the British to advance. The Battle of Passchendaele was an offensive designed to breakthrough German lines and outflank German defences. This battle of attrition gained a few miles at enormous human cost and the Germans held their line and won back their losses five months later.

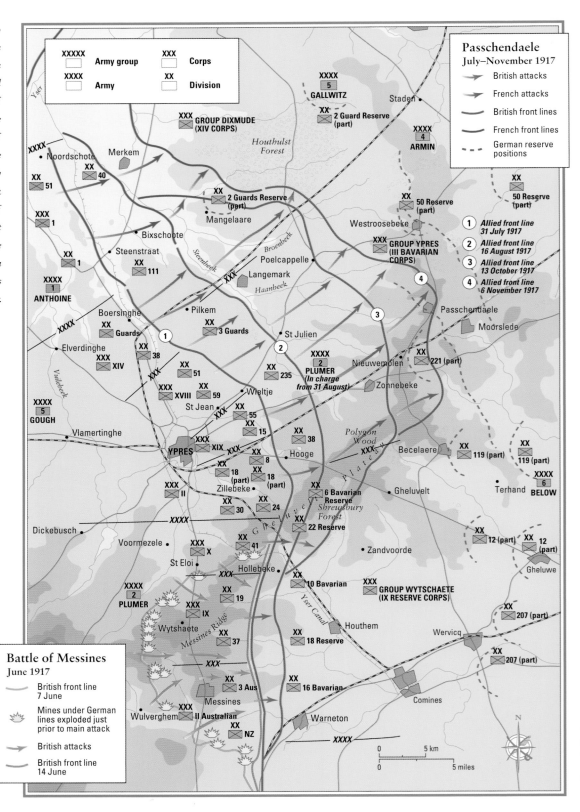

Passchendaele
July–November 1917
- British attacks
- French attacks
- British front lines
- French front lines
- German reserve positions

1. *Allied front line 31 July 1917*
2. *Allied front line 16 August 1917*
3. *Allied front line 13 October 1917*
4. *Allied front line 6 November 1917*

Battle of Messines
June 1917
- British front line 7 June
- Mines under German lines exploded just prior to main attack
- British attacks
- British front line 14 June

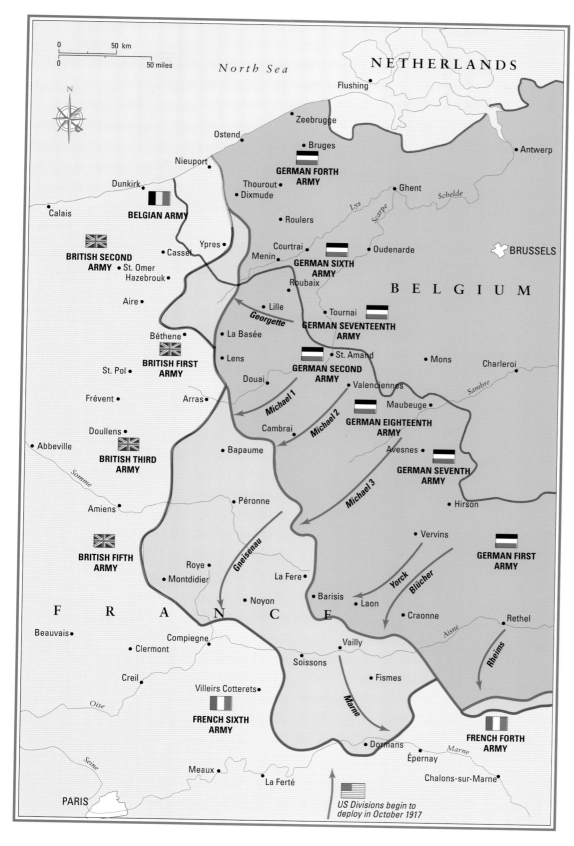

Final German Offensives
21 March – 17 July 1918

Front held by Belgians
Front held by British
Front held by French
Front held by Germans

In December 1917, Bolshevik Russia made peace with Germany at Brest-Litovsk, terminating the war of the Eastern Front. The German High Command decided on a new offensive before American divisions arrived. Troops transferred from the East spearheaded attacks from the Channel southwards. Initially successful, this strategy was defeated when American divisions arrived. July saw Americans arriving at the rate of 300,000 a month. The exhausted German army gradually disintegrated and an armistice was declared on 11 November 1918.

Europe 1919–22

By the end of the First World War, the Allies imposed a series of peace treaties upon the defeated powers. These were the Versailles Treaty with Germany, Trianon with Hungary, St. Germain with Austria, Neuilly with Bulgaria and Sèvres with Turkey.

Commencing in January 1919, the Versailles Conference sought to emulate the Congress of Vienna in 1814 in redrawing the map of Europe. Taking certain principles into consideration, nationalist demands for independence in eastern and central Europe and the Balkans would receive attention applying the principles of democracy, freedom, self-determination and US President Wilson's 'Fourteen Points'. Wilson wanted to create a new open diplomacy, not the machinations of traditional European behaviour with decisions made behind closed doors. However, Clemenceau of France and Lloyd George of Britain, were ruthless realists consumed by their own national interests and driven by public opinion, sought revenge.

Lloyd George viewed Britain as a naval and imperial power, seeing Germany as a bastion against France and Bolshevik Russia, and he also desired Germany's African colonies. Clemenceau sought revenge, a weakened Germany and four Allied military-controlled Rhine bridgeheads, to be established by treaty. Conflicting interests condemned President Wilson's idealism to virtual oblivion. Ultimately, Germany lost territory to Poland, France, Belgium and Denmark, and was virtually disarmed as well as suffering a war-guilt clause and massive reparations, estimated at one third of Germany's GNP. German colonies were seized as League of Nations' mandates, Britain acquiring Tanganyika, half the Cameroons and one third of Togoland. The Saarland was occupied by French troops and Germany was separated from East Prussia by the Danzig Corridor, simultaneously losing millions of people to Polish rule.

The Russian Empire was destroyed in a bloody civil war, turning Communist and losing land to the newly independent Poland, Lithuania, Latvia and Estonia. Austria-Hungary was fragmented, its successor states giving birth to Austria, Hungary, Czechoslovakia, and with its Balkan lands going to the new Yugoslavia, with some territory being awarded to Romania. These new national divisions cut across railway lines and formerly viable economic units were sundered. Austria, with most of its population in Vienna, was cut off from key agricultural areas; and industrial areas were blocked from access to raw materials. Vienna had been the focus of the railway systems and had possessed the central European banking system. All this was gone and many nationalities lived under alien sovereignty.

The Ottoman Empire was penalized by losing all its non-Turkish areas, leaving a rump state of Turkey in Anatolia. Its Empire was divided with Britain being mandated with Mosul, Mesopotamia and Palestine, the first two being rich in oil. France received Syria and the Lebanon

The new states sometimes fought for their survival with a virulent civil war between Whites and Reds in Finland and the other Baltic states fought for their existence. Poles fought Ukrainians and Czechs over border adjustments. Elsewhere, the Hungarians resented the loss of Slovakia, whose population, in turn, was subordinated to dominant Czechs. Slovenia lost people to Austria and feared their assimilation by German language speakers.

In the Far East, during the war, Japan had seized Qingdao, the German coaling station in the Shandong Peninsula and was awarded a mandate over German Pacific islands north of the Equator. The USA became wary of Japanese imperialism and Australia feared an extension of Japanese influence in the Pacific, while Britain viewed Japan as a potential threat to India.

The fragmentation of Europe generated much resentment resulting in regimes seeking to revise the Versailles Treaty. The Second World War was fought initially to destroy the decisions imposed at Versailles.

Europe 1919–22
Postwar Settlements

ICELAND
● Rekjavik

*Norwegian
Sea*

ATLANTIC
OCEAN

Faroe Is.

N O R W A Y

S W E D E N

FINLAND

● Helsinki

Oslo ●

● Stockholm

● Leningrad

Tallinn ●

ESTONIA

Riga ●

LATVIA

Shetland Is.

*North
Sea*

Baltic Sea

LITHUANIA

● Kaunas

USSR

Orkney Is.

Glasgow ● ● Edinburgh

DENMARK

Copenhagen ●

Danzig
*(free city under
League of Nations)*

Königsberg ●

East
Prussia

● Minsk

UNITED

● Dublin

IRELAND

● Liverpool

KINGDOM

● Birmingham

Amsterdam ●

Hamburg ■

● Berlin

NETHERLANDS

Warsaw ●

● Brest Litovsk

P O L A N D

Bristol ●

■ London

Calais ●

Brussels ●

BELGIUM

GERMANY

Cracow ●

● Lvov

● Vinnitsa

Rhine

Brest ●

■ Paris

LUX.

● Frankfurt

SAARLAND
*(autonomous under
League of Nations)*

Prague ●

CZECHOSLOVAKIA

F R A N C E

Lyon ●

L.

● Bern

SWITZ.

Vienna ■

AUSTRIA

● Budapest

HUNGARY

R O M A N I A

Bordeaux ●

● Milan

Trieste ●

Genoa ●

MONACO

Venice ●

Belgrade ■

Danube

● Bucharest ■

Marseille ●

ANDORRA

Zara ●

Y U G O S L A V I A

SAN
MARINO

Adriatic Sea

BULGARIA

Corsica

I T A L Y

Rome ■

● Sofia

● Barcelona

Naples ●

ALBANIA

G R E E C E

*Aegean
Sea*

PORTUGAL

● Madrid

S P A I N

Balearic Is.

Sardinia

Mediter

Sicily

r a

Athens ●

*(Italian
occupied)*

bon ●

Cádiz ●

● Gibraltar
(British)

Tangier ●
*International
one in 1923*

*Algeria
(French)*

*Tunisia
(French)*

*Malta
(British)*

n   e   a   n

Morocco

Irish Separation 1918–23

The Volunteer movement became designated the Irish Republican Army while Sinn Féin became extremely radical, with a tremendous electoral victory in the 1918 General Election. The party dominated the vote outside Ulster, creating pressure for Irish separatists.

This nationalist impetus caused Sinn Féin MPs to found their own republican assembly, the Dáil Éirann, in January 1919. That month, the IRA undertook a guerrilla war against the British. This War of Independence saw the violence of Bloody Sunday in 1920 with the deaths of twenty-three soldiers and civilians. Cork City was burnt and the Dublin Customs House was destroyed. British intelligence officers established a network of informants in Dublin. Michael Collins decided that these spies should be eliminated lest the IRA be prevented from operating. He devised the strategy of selective terrorism: the IRA would attack British intelligence operatives and armed units knowing that the IRA could not win. However, if the British government felt it could not win either, then both sides would need to negotiate. These tactics were so successful that they were used by independence movements in Algeria and Kenya.

The British retaliated by using special militias known as the 'Black and Tans'. Their violence was so excessive that they succeeded in turning public opinion even more against the British. World opinion turned against Britain, especially in the USA, which possessed a vocal Irish population. A truce evolved with both sides negotiating in July 1921, after the formal partition of the country, by the Government of Ireland Act in December 1920, with six counties in Ulster remaining a British political division but the south was left to its own devices. A republican negotiating team visited London, headed by Arthur Griffith and Michael Collins. On 6 December 1921, the 26 counties of the south became known as the Irish Free State with the Dáil as its parliament, the country having Dominion status like Canada and remaining within the British Commonwealth.

Éamon de Valera and his Sinn Féin did not accept this situation and a civil war ensued with guerrilla warfare and the killings of leaders on both sides, including the charismatic Michael Collins in an ambush at Bealnablath, County Cork in August 1922. The government retaliated with a harsh policy of reprisal executions. Emergency Powers were enacted that established martial law, with carrying arms without a legal license being made a capital offence. Erskine Childers, the secretary-general of the Irish delegation, which had negotiated the Anglo-Irish Treaty but opposed the oath of allegiance to the King, was arrested. He possessed an unlicensed semi-automatic pistol given to him by Michael Collins when they were friends. He was accordingly executed. The guerrilla opposition to the treaty ceased resistance on 24 May 1923.

This ceasefire predated elections to the Dáil. In 1923, the Irish Free State joined the League of Nations and the 1931 British Statute of Westminster stated that the British government would not overturn legislation passed in its Dominions' legislatures. De Valera ended his boycott of the Dáil in 1927 and entered it leading his new party, Fianna Fáil, founded in 1926. He feared that the Cumann na nGaedhal government wished to exclude him after the assassination of a prominent minister, Kevin O'Higgins, killed in retaliation for his support of the Dáil's reprisal executions. In 1932, Fianna Fáil formed the government and De Valera's work, carrying out radical policies, led to a new constitution in 1937, approved by referendum. A new state came into being, Éire. This term applied to all Ireland but common parlance saw it as an expression of the twenty-six counties. The country was ruled by a President as Head of State, Uachtarán na hÉireann, with the Prime Minister known as An Taoiseach.

Separation

Irish determination to resist repression and win freedom is symbolized by the sacrifice of Terence MacSwiney, Lord Mayor of Cork, who endured a 75-day hunger strike, dying in the process. The IRA probably never had more than 15,000 men while facing 43,000 British troops, the Royal Irish Constabulary and 7,000 Black and Tans. Michael Collins' military genius confounded his enemies.

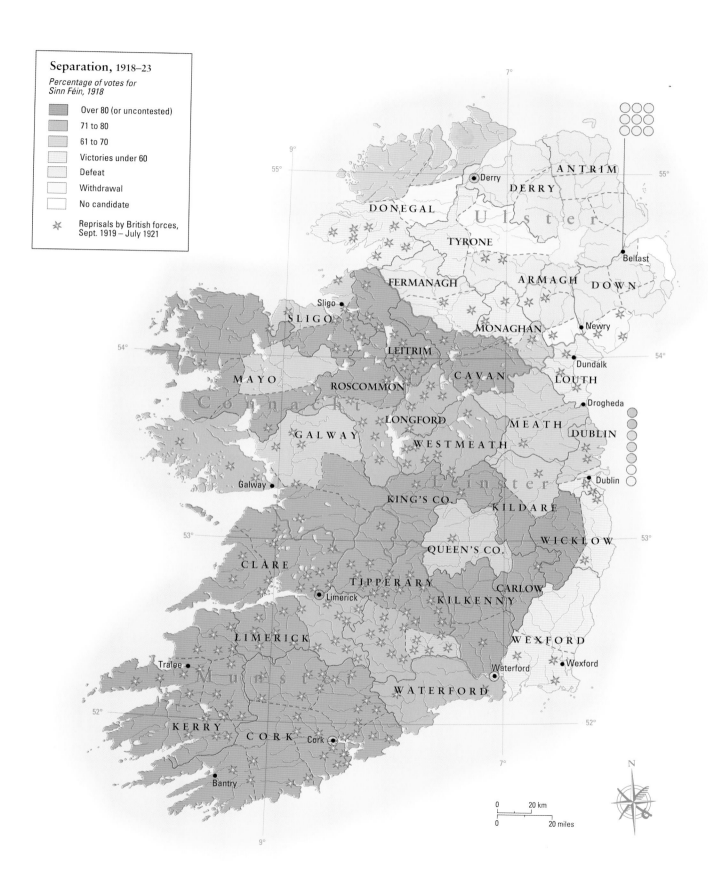

Separation, 1918–23

Percentage of votes for Sinn Féin, 1918

- Over 80 (or uncontested)
- 71 to 80
- 61 to 70
- Victories under 60
- Defeat
- Withdrawal
- No candidate

✳ Reprisals by British forces, Sept. 1919 – July 1921

ANTRIM
DERRY
Derry
DONEGAL
Ulster
TYRONE
Belfast
FERMANAGH
ARMAGH
DOWN
Sligo
MONAGHAN
Newry
SLIGO
LEITRIM
Dundalk
MAYO
ROSCOMMON
CAVAN
LOUTH
Connacht
Drogheda
LONGFORD
MEATH
GALWAY
WESTMEATH
DUBLIN
Galway
Leinster
Dublin
KING'S CO.
KILDARE
WICKLOW
QUEEN'S CO.
CLARE
TIPPERARY
CARLOW
Limerick
KILKENNY
LIMERICK
WEXFORD
Tralee
Munster
Waterford
Wexford
WATERFORD
KERRY
CORK
Cork
Bantry

0   20 km
0   20 miles

N

The 1926 General Strike and the Great Depression

The inter-war years brought hardship to Britain, with poor industrial relations and the socio-economic problems exacerbated, in 1929–30, by the world wide Depression. A General Strike bedevilled the country from 3–12 May 1926. The root of the strike was the coal industry, facing the problems of falling markets, the ending of a subsidy to coal miners and the end of a temporary wage agreement. The miners' refusal to accept this brought on a strike, with other trade unionists persuaded to join in. Little violence occurred with volunteers maintaining essential services while emergency plans were enforced. Special constables were enrolled. Three million trade unionists struck until 12 May when only the miners persisted. They struggled for six months until a conciliatory Baldwin ended the situation This was followed by the 1927 Trade Disputes and Trade Union Act, which made sympathetic strikes illegal and restricted the use of strike action funds.

In 1929, the Great Depression, as it became known, spread out from the United States after the Wall Street Crash, affecting every country in the world, whether industrial or agricultural producers. Additionally, American economic growth outstripped Britain's, which experienced a relative decline in its share of world trade. After Versailles, US loans to Germany helped it to make reparation payments to Britain and France. The Crash saw these loans recalled, causing severe hardship in Germany; unemployment peaked at over six million. In the British Isles, the despair of out-of-work men expressed itself in hunger marches, notably from Jarrow to London.

The British government ended its 86 years of free trade by the 1932 Import Duties Act and the Ottowa Imperial Conference, which granted preferential treatment to agricultural products from the British Dominions, while British manufactured goods received reciprocal treatment in Dominion markets. Budgetary control was adopted and the revival of domestic consumer demand, provided with cheap money, helped private enterprise and gradually turned round the economy. That southern England's manufacturing was concentrated in newer industries, such as automobile manufacturing, meant that the Midlands and North, with traditional heavy industry, bore the brunt of unemployment.

Many European countries suffered more than Britain, experiencing governmental crises as in the French Third Republic. The development of fascist leagues, the Croix de Feu, in turn, led to Léon Blum's Popular Front government to combat the extremist right-wing. Britain became home to various rightist movements, the most notorious being Oswald Mosley's British Union of Fascists. In response to its violence, the government passed the 1936 Public Order Act.

Moderate politics faced this and international events by mothballing the normal single-party government and creating a multi-party National Government. Britain followed the economic orthodoxy of the day and came off the gold standard and introduced deflationary measures, reducing government spending, cutting unemployment benefits and restricting credit. John Maynard Keynes, the radical economist, argued for the government to spend its way out of trouble with public works but was largley ignored. In 1934 and 1935, the government decided to increase unemployment benefits and restore government salaries to pre-Depression levels. This policy generated an increase in consumer spending and a modest economic recovery, supporting Keynes' approach to economics. Subsidised house construction also pumped money into the economy and raised tariffs on industrial imports increasing prosperity; unemployment levels fell. Real wages rose. Import quotas on agricultural imports helped British farmers.

Elsewhere, support for right-wing extremist parties grew, from the Lapua movement in Finland to the Hungarian Arrow Cross. The middle-class voters in Germany brought Adolf Hitler to power in 1933.

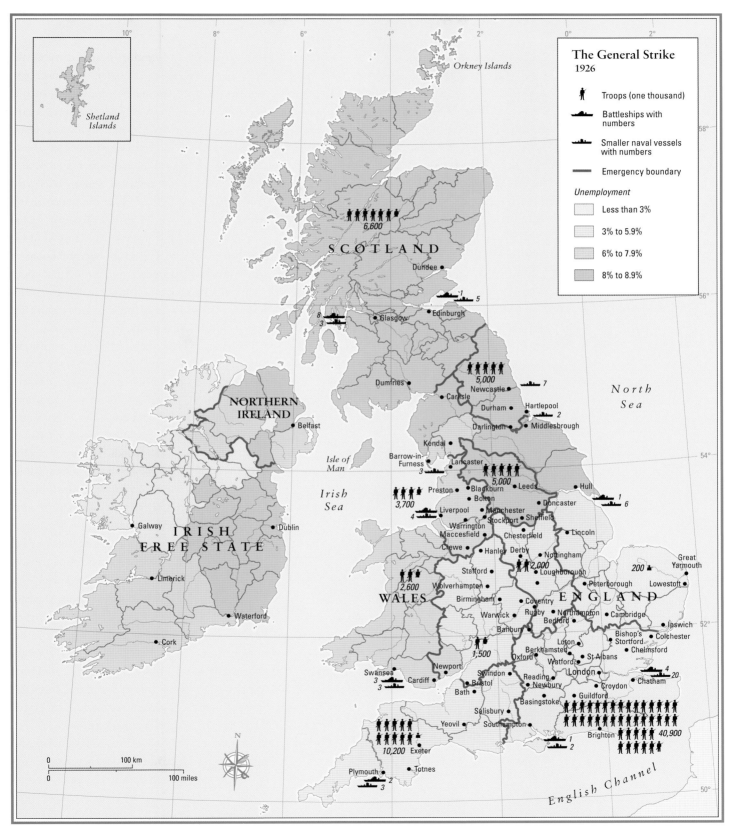

The General Strike
1926

Troops (one thousand)

Battleships with numbers

Smaller naval vessels with numbers

Emergency boundary

Unemployment

Less than 3%

3% to 5.9%

6% to 7.9%

8% to 8.9%

Shetland Islands

Orkney Islands

SCOTLAND

6,600

Dundee

1
5

8
3

Glasgow

Edinburgh

North Sea

NORTHERN IRELAND

Dumfries

Belfast

5,000

Newcastle

7

Carlisle

Durham

Hartlepool

2

Darlington

Middlesbrough

Kendal

IRISH FREE STATE

Isle of Man

Irish Sea

Barrow-in-Furness

3

Lancaster

5,000

Leeds

Hull

Galway

Dublin

3,700

Preston

Blackburn

Bolton

Doncaster

1
6

Liverpool

Manchester

Stockport

Sheffield

4

Warrington

Maccesfield

Chesterfield

Lincoln

Limerick

Crewe

Hanley

Derby

Nottingham

WALES

2,600

Stafford

2,000

Loughborough

200

Great Yarmouth

Waterford

Wolverhampton

Peterborough

Lowestoft

Birmingham

ENGLAND

Coventry

Warwick

Rugby

Northampton

Cambridge

Cork

1,500

Banbury

Bedford

Ipswich

Bishop's Stortford

Colchester

Luton

Chelmsford

Oxford

Berkhamsted

St Albans

Watford

Newport

Swindon

Reading

London

Croydon

4
20

Swansea

3

Cardiff

Bristol

Newbury

Chatham

3

Bath

Basingstoke

Guildford

Salisbury

Brighton

40,900

Yeovil

Southampton

1
2

10,200

Exeter

Plymouth

Totnes

2

3

N

100 km

100 miles

English Channel

Re-armament 1936–37

Political Agreements
1938–39

◼ British and French guarantees for Poland, Greece, Romania and Turkey, 1939

◻ Copenhagen declaration of neutrality, July 1938

◼ Axis, May 1939

◼ German-Soviet Non-Aggression Pact, 23 August 1939

In 1933, Adolf Hitler became the German Chancellor adding one more extreme right-wing regime to the European political scene. Together with Italy's Mussolini, Germany sought to revise the Versailles Treaty, which restrained the aspirations of the Nazi and Fascist states. European politics now became increasingly dominated by repressive, authoritarian regimes highlighted by the extremely traditionalist, militarist regime of Franco, created in the aftermath of the Spanish Civil War in 1939. The Far East, too, witnessed a political sea change as Japanese aggression established the puppet state of Manchukuo (Manchuria) under the last Manchu Emperor, Puyi in 1933. The seizure of the Chinese province of Jehol rounded off Japan's conquests before the Sino-Japanese War broke out in 1937, an event causing intense concerns about British and US possessions in India and the Pacific Ocean.

On 7 March 1936, German troops occupied the de-militarized Rhineland although their gen-erals claimed they only had enough ammunition for one day's fighting. However, the French and British did not respond to this breach of the Versailles Treaty. German ambassadors claimed that the move was intended to protect their country against the Franco-Soviet Pact ,which destroyed the existing Locarno agreements. This Franco-British appeasement boosted Hitler's prestige and accelerated German re-armament. Meanwhile, an expansionist Italy defeated Abyssinia, thereby enlarging its African Empire while placing British-run Egypt under threat from the south and west.

German re-armament meant that its arsenals built up the most modern weaponry: new, fast aeroplanes, surface ships and submarines, and tanks practiced the new *Blitzkrieg* tactics. By 1938, Germany was spending fifty-two per cent of state expenses and seventeen per cent of its gross national product on armaments production. Britain was forced to modernize its armed forces and 1934 to 1937 saw military expenditure doubled. All major states began spending more on weaponry but still hoped that diplomacy would remove the heat from international tensions.

Hitler allied with Italy and Japan in 1936. In March 1938, German forces occupied Austria, which was absorbed into the Third Reich by the *Anschluss*. Next year, the Germans, having incorporated the Czechoslovak Sudetenland by international agreement in 1938, then annexed the rump of the Czech state, creating a Protectorate of Bohemia and Moravia and the puppet state of Slovakia, allowing Hungary and Poland to take some Slovak land. Lithuania lost the Memelland in 1939 and then Hitler and Stalin stunned the world with the Nazi-Soviet Pact. Britain and France accepted the occupation of Austria and Czechoslovakia during the much-maligned appeasement process but maybe the British government, as some evidence suggests, was buying time to re-arm more adequately.

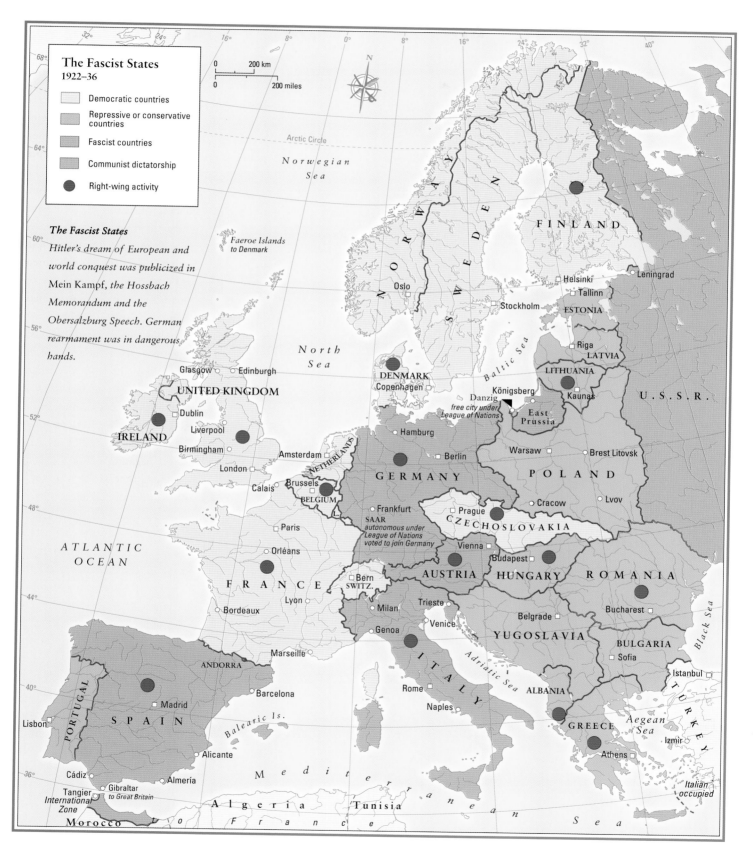

The Fascist States
1922–36

- Democratic countries
- Repressive or conservative countries
- Fascist countries
- Communist dictatorship
- Right-wing activity

The Fascist States

Hitler's dream of European and world conquest was publicized in Mein Kampf, *the Hossbach Memorandum and the Obersalzburg Speech. German rearmament was in dangerous hands.*

0   200 km

0   200 miles

N

Arctic Circle

Norwegian Sea

Faeroe Islands to Denmark

North Sea

NORWAY

SWEDEN

FINLAND

Oslo

Stockholm

Leningrad

□ Helsinki

□ Tallinn

ESTONIA

□ Riga

LATVIA

Baltic Sea

LITHUANIA

□ Kaunas

Königsberg

Danzig *free city under League of Nations*

East Prussia

U.S.S.R.

DENMARK

Copenhagen □

Glasgow □

Edinburgh □

UNITED KINGDOM

□ Dublin

IRELAND

Liverpool

Birmingham □

Amsterdam □

NETHERLANDS

London □

Calais □

Brussels □

BELGIUM

Hamburg □

□ Berlin

GERMANY

POLAND

Warsaw □

□ Brest Litovsk

○ Cracow

□ Lvov

Frankfurt □

SAAR *autonomous under League of Nations voted to join Germany*

□ Prague

CZECHOSLOVAKIA

Vienna ○

Budapest ○

HUNGARY

ROMANIA

AUSTRIA

Bucharest □

Paris □

FRANCE

Orléans ○

ATLANTIC OCEAN

Bern □ SWITZ.

Lyon ○

Bordeaux ○

Milan □

Trieste □

Venice ○

Genoa ○

ITALY

Belgrade □

YUGOSLAVIA

BULGARIA

Sofia □

Adriatic Sea

Black Sea

Marseille ○

ANDORRA

Barcelona □

PORTUGAL

□ Madrid

SPAIN

Balearic Is.

Rome ○

Naples ○

ALBANIA

Istanbul □

TURKEY

Izmir □

GREECE

Aegean Sea

Athens □

Lisbon □

Cádiz ○

Almería ○

Alicante ○

Gibraltar *to Great Britain*

Tangier *International Zone*

Mediterranean Sea

Algeria   Tunisia   *France*

Morocco

Italian occupied

World War II

On 1 September 1939, German forces invaded Poland thereby triggering World War II in its initial European stage. Soviet forces invaded Poland from the east, thus destroying Poland. While the USSR occupied the Baltic states and attacked Finland, Germany occupied Denmark and major Norwegian ports and, then, on 10 May 1940, unleashed the *Blitzkrieg* offensive in the west, sweeping through the Netherlands and Belgium into France.

By 19 May, Guderian's tank forces arrived at the English Channel, having advanced 200 miles. The majority of the Allies' best combat units were now surrounded in a pocket in northern France and Belgium, with scant chance of escape and facing probable destruction. To his generals' consternation, Hitler halted his Panzer units, instead relying on Goering's *Luftwaffe* to destroy the British Expeditionary Force by aerial bombardment. The BEF established a perimeter to defend the coastline near Dunkirk, where an evacuation was planned, codenamed Operation Dynamo. The RAF surpassed itself by stemming the German air attacks, allowing the British Navy and many private vessels to lift 338,226 men, a third foreign Allied troops, in eight days. However, the BEF lost most of its equipment but remained defiant, forming the corps of a new and better army.

Left in France were other British forces, mainly the 51st Highland Division and some RAF units who joined the French as they all faced renewed German attacks. The French army fought fiercely but the Germans eventually broke through French lines with armoured spearheads, supported by the *Luftwaffe*, constantly bombarding points of allied resistance. By 17 June, the last British forces withdrew from France and 20 June witnessed the French government signing an armistice at Compiègne. The new French government, under Marshall Pétain, established a free zone with its capital at Vichy while German forces occupied the rest of France, with Alsace-Lorraine ceded to Germany.

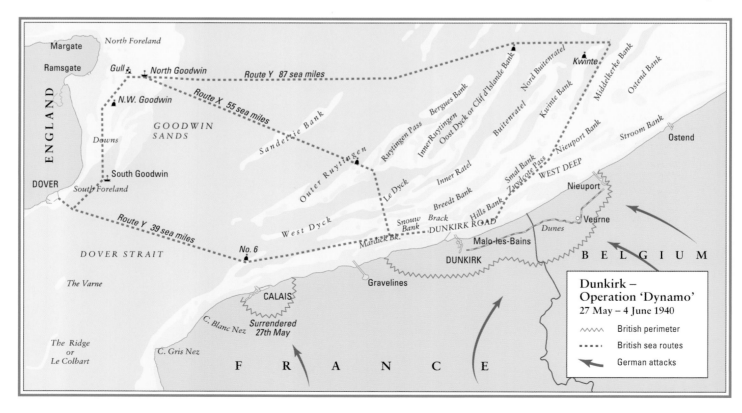

Dunkirk – Operation 'Dynamo'
27 May – 4 June 1940

〰〰〰 British perimeter
· · · · · British sea routes
➤ German attacks

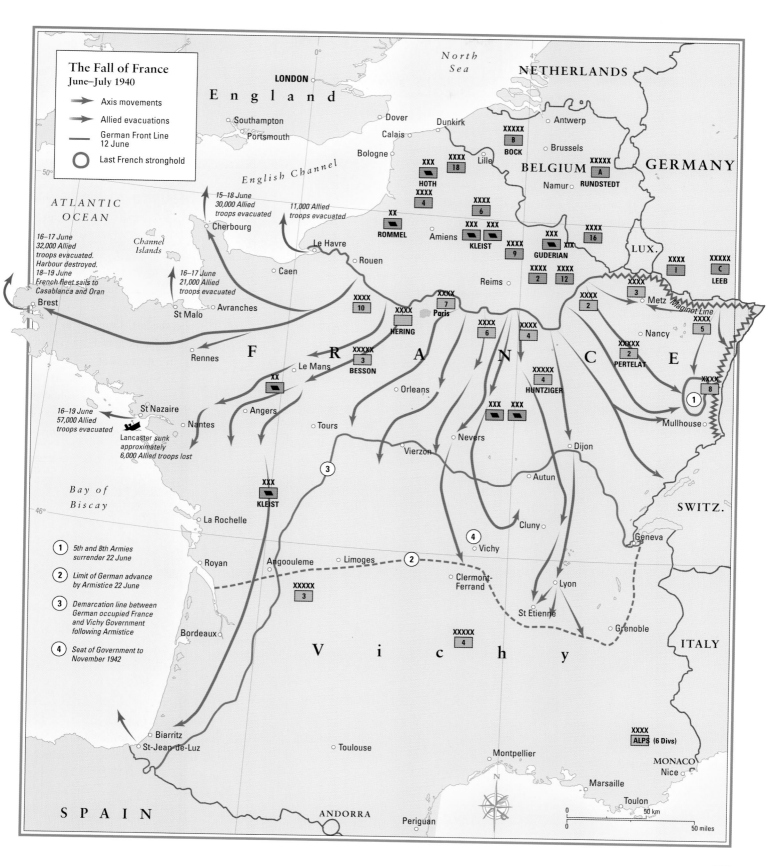

The Fall of France
June–July 1940

→ Axis movements

→ Allied evacuations

— German Front Line 12 June

◯ Last French stronghold

England

LONDON

Southampton
Portsmouth
Dover

English Channel

ATLANTIC OCEAN

Channel Islands

50°

16–17 June
32,000 Allied troops evacuated. Harbour destroyed.
18–19 June French fleet sails to Casablanca and Oran

Brest

15–18 June
30,000 Allied troops evacuated

11,000 Allied troops evacuated

Cherbourg

Le Havre

16–17 June
21,000 Allied troops evacuated

Caen

Rouen

North Sea

NETHERLANDS

Antwerp

Dunkirk

Calais
Bologne

Lille

Brussels

XXXXX B **BOCK**

BELGIUM

Namur

XXXXX A **RUNDSTEDT**

GERMANY

XXX HOTH
XXXX 18

XXXX 4

XX ROMMEL

Amiens

XXXX 6

XXX XXX KLEIST

XXXX 9

XXX GUDERIAN

XXX 2 **XXX** 12

XXXX 16

LUX.

XXXX 1 **XXXXX** C **LEEB**

XXXX 2

XXXX 3

Metz *Maginot Line*

Nancy

XXXX 5

XXXXX 2 **PERTELAT**

XXXXX 10

XXXX HERING

Paris

Reims

XXXX 7

XXXX 6

XXXX 4

XXXXX 4 **HUNTZIGER**

XXXX 8

◯ 1

Mullhouse

E

Rennes

F   **R**   **A**   **N**   **C**

St Malo

Avranches

XXXXX 3 **BESSON**

Le Mans

XX

Angers

Orleans

Tours

Nevers

Vierzon

XXX XXX

Dijon

Autun

SWITZ.

16–19 June
57,000 Allied troops evacuated

St Nazaire

Lancaster sunk approximately 6,000 Allied troops lost

Nantes

Bay of Biscay

XXX KLEIST

La Rochelle

③

Cluny

Lyon

Geneva

46°

① 5th and 8th Armies surrender 22 June

② Limit of German advance by Armistice 22 June

③ Demarcation line between German occupied France and Vichy Government following Armistice

④ Seat of Government to November 1942

Royan

Angoouleme

Limoges

②

Clermont-Ferrand

St Etienne

④ Vichy

XXXXX 3

Bordeaux

V   i   c   h   y

XXXXX 4

Grenoble

ITALY

Biarritz
St-Jean-de-Luz

SPAIN

Toulouse

ANDORRA

Periguan

Montpellier

Marseille

Toulon

XXXX **ALPS** (6 Divs)

MONACO
Nice

N

0   50 km
0   50 miles

The Battle of Britain

Battle of Britain

Spitfires and Hurricanes comprised the backbone of Royal Air Force Fighter Command, though some of the 704 fighter planes at the start of the Battle of Britain were older and slower, such as the Gloster Gladiator bi-plane.

Fighter Command and Control

The radar directed fighter control system was the instrument of the country's survival in the summer of 1940.

May to June 1940 saw the German conquest of France followed by a likely invasion of Britain, which could only occur if the *Luftwaffe* obtained air superiority over the combat zone. This was only achievable by the destruction of the Royal Air Force Fighter Command.

To fight the *Luftwaffe*, Air Vice Marshal Hugh Dowding had constructed a detection and command system capable of outwitting the German campaign. British airspace was divided between four Groups with 11 Group, under Air Vice-Marshal Keith Park, defending the air approaches to London and southeast England. Information from observers and radar stations poured into HQs like II Group's at RAF Uxbridge.

Radar could estimate the strength, height and route of enemy bombers and fighters and then call Sectors to scramble fighter squadrons and

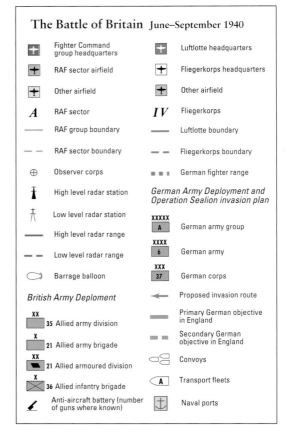

The Battle of Britain June–September 1940

⊞	Fighter Command group headquarters	⊞	Luftlotte headquarters
✚	RAF sector airfield	✚	Fliegerkorps headquarters
✚	Other airfield	✚	Other airfield
A	RAF sector	*IV*	Fliegerkorps
—	RAF group boundary	—	Luftlotte boundary
– –	RAF sector boundary	– –	Fliegerkorps boundary
⊕	Observer corps	▪▪▪	German fighter range
⊺	High level radar station		*German Army Deployment and Operation Sealion invasion plan*
⊼	Low level radar station	XXXXX A	German army group
—	High level radar range	XXXX 6	German army
– –	Low level radar range	XXX 37	German corps
▱	Barrage balloon	←	Proposed invasion route
British Army Deployment		▬	Primary German objective in England
XX 35	Allied army division	▬ ▬	Secondary German objective in England
X 21	Allied army brigade	⊂⊃	Convoys
XX 21	Allied armoured division	⟨A⟩	Transport fleets
X 36	Allied infantry brigade	⚓	Naval ports
⤙	Anti-aircraft battery (number of guns where known)		

vector them by radio-telephone to intercept enemy forces. Each Group area was split into Sectors with commanding officers in charge of two to four squadrons of fighters.

In mid-August, the *Luftwaffe* attacked forward airfields and radar stations, the latter were difficult to destroy and were soon on stream again. The battle of the airfields severely stretched II Group's Sector stations but also exhausted the *Luftwaffe*. The later stages of the struggle were fought over London, giving the RAF the advantage and final victory.

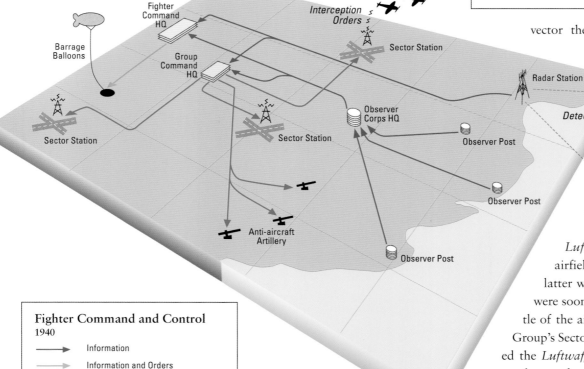

Fighter Command HQ

Interception Orders

Barrage Balloons

Group Command HQ

Sector Station

Sector Station

Radar Station

Observer Corps HQ

Detection

Sector Station

Observer Post

Anti-aircraft Artillery

Observer Post

Observer Post

Fighter Command and Control
1940

→ Information

→ Information and Orders

→ Information and Interception Orders

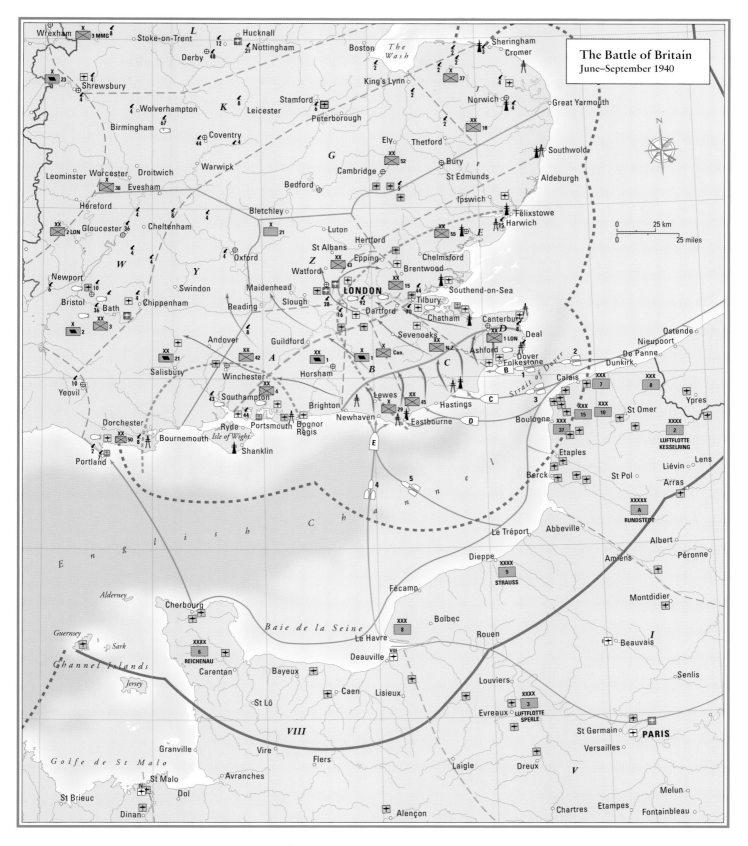

The Battle of Britain
June–September 1940

Holding Out

After the *Luftwaffe*'s failure to destroy the RAF in the Battle of Britain, Hitler decided to destroy Britain's industrial capacity to make war and to break the morale of the civilian population by the night-time bombing of cities. Beginning on the night of 24/25 August 1940, factories, shipyards, oil terminals, ports and urban centres were bombed in what became known as the Blitz. London suffered the worst treatment with half of the 43,000 civilian casualties being suffered there and some one million houses destroyed or damaged. Coventry was badly damaged, its stricken cathedral remaining an icon of the Blitz, while Hull suffered 85 per cent of its buildings destroyed or damaged. Later, large numbers of German bombers were transferred eastwards in May 1941 in preparation for Operation Barbarossa against the Soviet Union.

The notion of breaking morale failed because Britain had prepared itself for an air attack. Gas masks were issued, including those for infants. Trained air raid wardens patrolled the street and blackouts were introduced so that no lights could be seen from the air. Official estimates of possible casualties were wildly inaccurate but fears for the next generation led to 827,000 school-age children being evacuated to the countryside. Pregnant mothers and school teachers eventually followed with some 3.5 million people being displaced, leading to interesting cultural impacts, as portrayed in the film, *Goodnight Mister Tom*. Important targets were defended by barrage balloons, searchlights and scarce anti-aircraft guns.

Early German Blitz daylight raids incurred such losses that night-time bombing became the norm. However, inaccurate bombing meant that collateral damage was enormous in terms of homes, near factories, being damaged. Although civilians' resilience remained strong, the scale of the attacks was daunting provoking thousands to migrate out of the cities over night and returned in the morning, often having travelled for hours. Rural camping was accompanied by the London population being allowed to set up night quarters in the London Underground stations, housing some 177,000 people.

German science had invented radio direction beams known as *X-Gerät* along which allowed pathfinder bombers to be directed towards targets, such as Coventry on 14/15 November 1940. Yet, despite damage, factories would be working again within a few days and the nation's grit, determination and sense of bloody-minded pride ensured an unbroken spirit. Eventually, electronic counter-measures could distort the German radio direction beams to such an extent that bombers were deflected from their targets, dropping their bomb load in the wrong place. Other British innovations were radar-directed guns capable of predicting the height and direction of bombers. Night fighters equipped with radar intercepted the enemy with increasing success. The fire brigade became increasingly skilled, as did rescue teams, which ameliorated damage. Yet an inferno, known as the Second Great Fire of London, witnessed the City of London in flames with St. Paul's Cathedral surrounded by an inferno.

Eventually, the Germans realized that Britain would not capitulate and raids withered as plans against Russia were formulated and German air power moved eastwards. However, bombing continued in a lesser form. After the RAF bombed Lübeck, the *Luftwaffe* retaliated with the Baedeker raids, based on the famous Baedeker historical guidebooks, reprisals against historic cities such as Bath, Norwich and York in Spring 1942. More raids occurred in November 1943, resulting in heavy German losses thereby reducing German capacity to counter D-Day. June 1944 observed the first V-I flying bomb reaching London, followed by V-2

The Blitz

"A string of bombs fell right besides the Thames, their white glare was reflected in the black, lazy water near the banks and faded in midstream where the moon cut a golden swathe broken only by the arches of famous bridges. We could see little men shovelling those fire bombs into the river."

(US reporter, Ed Murrow, 10 September 1940 CBS radio broadcast)

North Sea

*LUFTFLOTTE
from Denmark
and Norway*

Perthshire
Dundee
Argyll
Kinross
Clackmannon   Fife
Dumbarton
Stirling   West
Dumb.   Lothian
Renfew   Glasgow   Eastlothian
Midlothian   Edinburgh
Scotland   Berwick
Lanark   Peebles
Bute
Ayr   Selkirk
Roxburgh
Dumfries
Kirkcudbright
Wigton
Northumberland

Londonderry   Antrim
Tyrone
*Northern
Ireland*
Belfast
Armargh   Down

Newcastle upon Tyne
Sunderland
Cumberland   *North
Eastern*
*North
Western*   Durham
Middlesbrough
Westmorland
North Riding
Y o r k s h i r e
Irish Sea   York
Blackpool   West Riding   East Riding
Preston   Leeds   Hull
Drogheda   Blackburn   Bradford
Lancashire   Huddersfield
ELAND   Liverpool   Manchester
DUBLIN   St. Helens   Sheffield
Caer   Cheshire   Lincoln
*Luftwaffe accidentally bombs
the neutral Republic of Ireland on
raids aimed at Belfast*   Flint   Derby
Denbigh   *North
Midland*
Stoke-on-Trent   Nottingham
Caernarvon   Derby   Nottingham
Wexford   Merioneth
Stafford
Shropshire   Leicester
Montgomery   Wolverhampton   Leicester
Walsall
Wales   Birmingham   Isle
Radnor   Coventry   of
Midland   Warwick   Northampton   Ely
Cardigan   Worcester   Northampton   Cambridge
Hereford   Bedford   Cambridge

LUFTFLOTTE 2

Norfolk
Norwich
Eastern
West Suffolk
East Suffolk
Ipswich

Penbroke   Carmarthen   Brecknock
Gloucester   Oxford   Buckingham
Oxford   Luton
Swansea   Monmouth   Hertford   Essex
Glamorgan   Bristol   Middlesex   Southend-Sea
Cardiff   Bath   *Southern*   LONDON
Bristol Channel   Wiltshire   Reading
Surrey   Kent
Somerset   Hampshire   *South   Tunbridge Wells   Dunkirk
Eastern*   Calais
*South
Western*   West Sussex   East Sussex
Dorset   Southampton   Brighton   Boulogne-sur-Mer
Devon   Bournemouth   Portsmouth
Exeter

Cornwall
Plymouth

E n g l i s h   C h a n n

LUFTFLOTTE 2

N

Cherbourg

*Channel
Islands*

LUFTFLOTTE 3

F
R
A
N
C
E

0   50 km
0   50 miles

Global War

To support scattered battle fronts the USA and Britain made a prodigious industrial effort during the war. American and British merchant fleets traversed the seas and oceans of the world, including the dreaded winter Arctic convoys to Russia.

Rockets in September 1944. Despite the loss of life caused some 4,000 V-I bombs were destroyed and V-2 launch pads were gradually captured ending the risk to British citizens, especially in London.

When the war began in Europe, the German Navy believed that 750,000 tons of Allied shipping sunk per month for one year would cause Britain to both starve and surrender. Commerce

raiders such as the *Admiral Graf Spee* sank nine merchant ships before being cornered in Montevideo, Uraguay, by British naval units. Next, U-boats were deployed into the Atlantic from newly-developed French and Norwegian bases but the convoy and escort system reduced merchant losses, as did the ever expanding British and Canadian Navy escort forces. After December 1941, the USA entered the war with

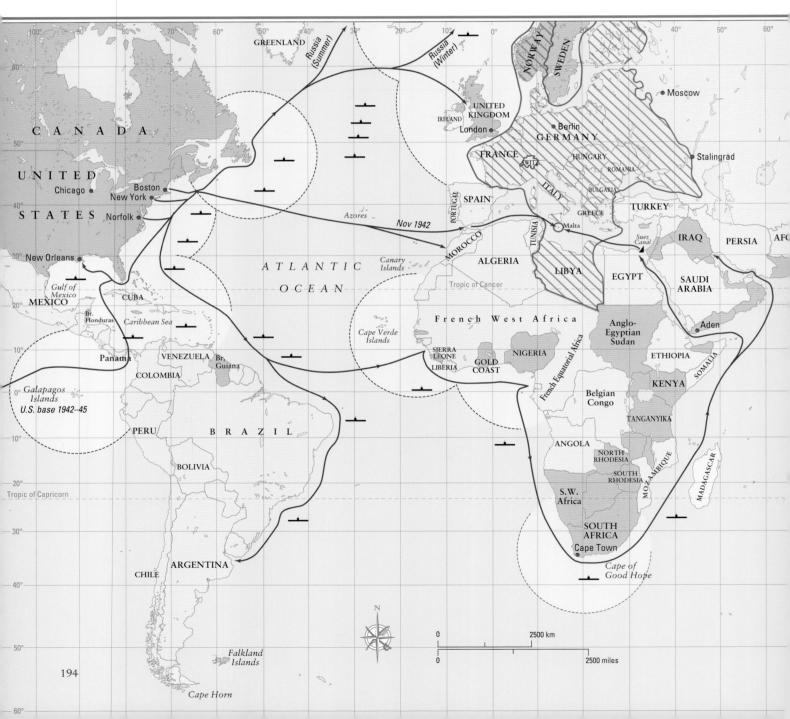

its large and growing merchant fleet, bringing food and fuel to Britain. Improved radar and long-distance patrol aircraft ensured steadily increasing success against the U-boats. The use of Ultra decrypts also allowed interception of submarine signals with 100 U-boats sunk in early 1943. The continuation of British purchases from the USA, after Britain's financial reserves were exhausted, was ensured by the Lend-Lease Act. By the end of 1943, the Battle of the Atlantic was won ensuring supplies of fuel, materials and food to Britain. Additionally, all the resources of men and munitions poured into Britain and trained for the forthcoming invasion of Europe. Although Allied ships continued to be sunk, the German strategic gamble at sea had failed, just as the Battle of Britain and the Blitz had before it.

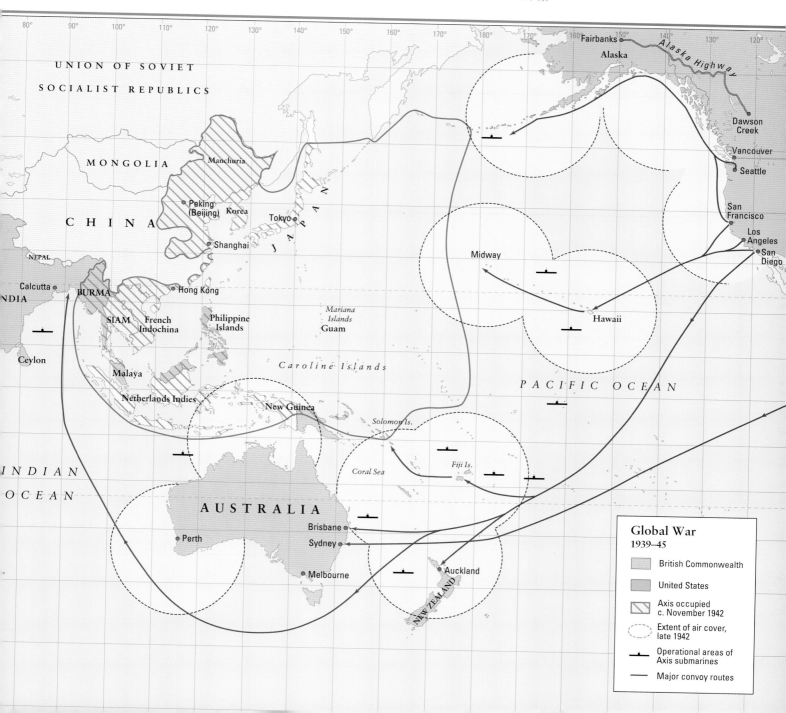

Bomber Command in World War II

When the war broke out, the British abided by an American request to confine bombing to military targets. Bomber command immediately sent some squadrons to France to form part of the Advanced Air Striking Force, which returned to Britain when France was knocked out of the war. During the Phoney War, after the Germans blitzed Rotterdam, Ruhr targets were attacked such as oil plants and industrial targets.

This strategic bombing was not particularly effective but the campaign against German concentrations of invasion barges and materiel in the Channel ports was extremely important and hazardous, with 330 aircraft lost in the last six months of 1940. Over Germany, night attacks were the norm after daylight raids had seen so many planes lost. Berlin and Mannheim were hit and Bomber Command wanted to bomb the heart of Germany as a response to the Blitz. Area or terror bombing was about to commence. However, dead reckoning navigation was not effective enough and raids frequently missed their targets.

Other targets were U-boat pens and construction yards in an attempt to relieve pressure on Trans-Atlantic supply routes. During 1941, Bomber Command realized that so-called precision bombing was inaccurate and aircraft losses were so high that Winter 1941/42 saw a suspension of RAF activity over Germany. Over time, innovations ensured that raids reached their targets. Special Pathfinder squadrons, equipped with de Havilland Mosquitos, would navigate and light up a target with flares and marker bombs for following planes to find. Technical gadgets also helped such as external navigation aids, the Gee and Oboe systems, and the H2S radar installed in the bombers.

The spring of 1942 witnessed Sir Arthur Harris became the new Commander-in-Chief of Bomber Command. New large scale raids were tried, for a time, such as the '1000 bomber raid' on Cologne. The campaign gained a new momentum when the US 8th Airforce built up its strength in England and used precision daylight bombing with US Norden bomb sights. Thus, day and night raids kept German defence forces totally committed. Yet, much of 1942 was used to build up numbers of aircraft and in training crews for later air offensives. In 1943, Bomber Harris began an assault on the Rhine–Ruhr industrial region, iconized by the 'bouncing bomb' attacks on the Mohne and Eider dams. Hamburg was turned into a fire-storm, killing nearly 90,000 people. Yet, high losses were sustained and this affected the US bombing campaign too. Eventually, escorting fighters were fitted with drop tanks enabling them to fly to a target and back. The winter of 1943–44 observed a sustained series of attacks on Berlin, which failed to destroy the city and resulted in the loss of 587 aircraft. Harris became exasperated when his and American efforts were redirected from attacking Germany, instead having to direct resources against the VI flying bomb and in planning for the D-Day invasion.

Bomber Command suffered enormous casualties, running at a 44.4 per cent death rate, with thousands more wounded in action or becoming prisoners of war. The chances of surviving thirty operations were one in six and to live through a second tour, the odds were one in forty. The US 8th Air Force sustained far fewer casualties. The RAF also lost 8,325 aircraft in action. Despite terrible losses, Bomber Command achieved much against oil installations. Most importantly, bombing forced the Germans to divert large-scale resources to defending the Reich itself. By 1943, some 1,000 night-fighters defended Germany. Also, the 88mm tank-busting guns were used in homeland service, with nearly 9,000 being stationed in Germany together with 25,000 other flak guns. Their use in Germany meant that they were not being used on the battle fronts. Additionally, 90,000 personnel were needed in the flak regiments, with hundreds of thousands more required to clear bomb damage and make repairs.

Major Bomber Command Stations of WWII

Besides fighting the Axis along its periphery after 1940 in north Africa and then Italy, the only way Britain, and later its Allies, could bring the war to the German homeland was by a bomber offensive.

To support this war-long campaign Britain's industrial heartlands produced 136,549 aircraft, of which 34,689 were bombers. From factories large and small, these aircraft rolled off their production lines to be delivered to airbases across eastern England. This remorseless campaign lasted until the last day of the war.

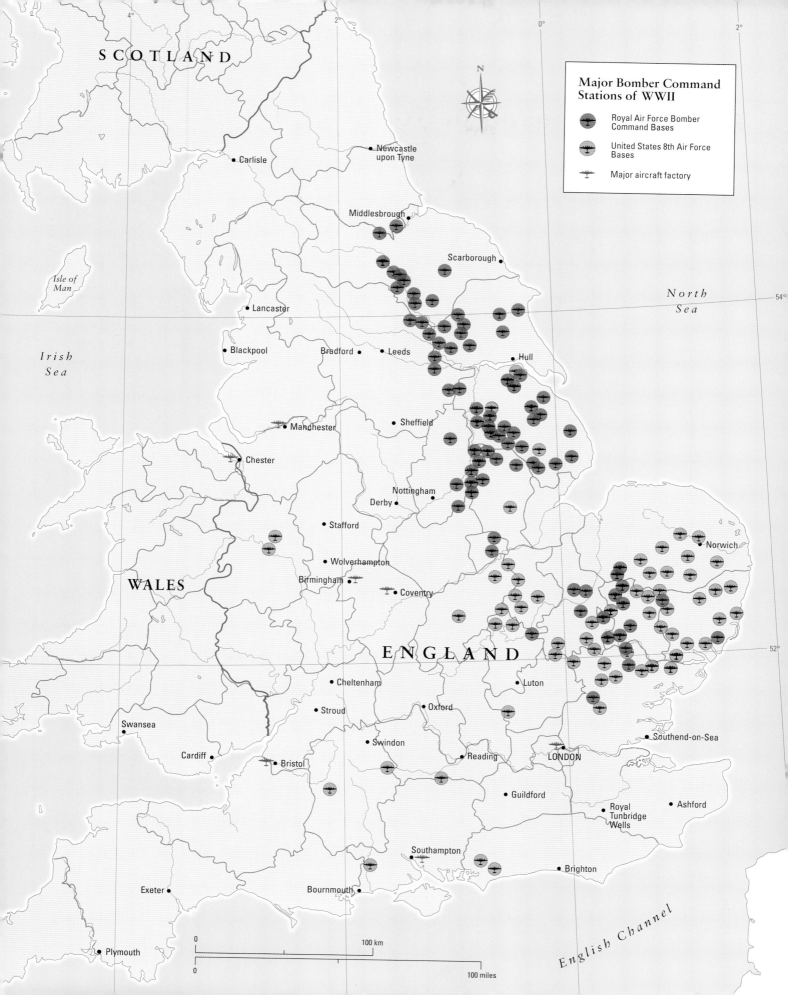

SCOTLAND

Carlisle

Newcastle
upon Tyne

Isle of
Man

Middlesbrough

Scarborough

North
Sea

Lancaster

Irish
Sea

Blackpool   Bradford   Leeds

Hull

Manchester

Sheffield

Chester

Nottingham

Norwich

Derby

WALES   Stafford

Wolverhampton

Birmingham

Coventry

ENGLAND

Cheltenham   Luton

Stroud   Oxford

Southend-on-Sea

Swansea   Swindon   Reading   LONDON

Cardiff   Guildford   Ashford

Bristol   Royal
Tunbridge
Wells

Southampton   Brighton

Exeter   Bournemouth

English Channel

Plymouth

Major Bomber Command Stations of WWII

Royal Air Force Bomber Command Bases

United States 8th Air Force Bases

Major aircraft factory

0   100 km

0   100 miles

The End of the Axis

The Axis Collapse

Five years of war left Europe
shattered with some 43 million
dead, countless wounded and
millions displaced. Much
architectural heritage was
destroyed in all countries and
treasures were looted, some
never to be found. Some villages
and towns were so damaged that
they remained uninhabited,
especially in Yugoslavia, which
lost ten per cent of its
population.

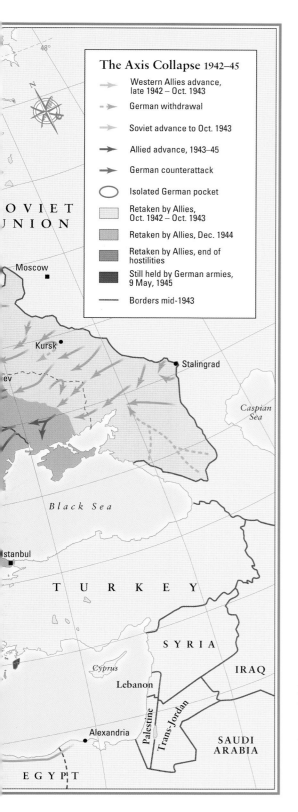

British and Commonwealth forces had engaged in intense combat with Rommel's Afrika Korps in North Africa in a campaign moving backwards and forwards across the desert. November 1942 saw a British victory at El Alamein. That month also saw US and British forces landing in North Africa and the Axis were forced out of the continent into Sicily by May 1943. Allied armies then landed in Sicily, later invading Italy. The Italian fascist government signed an armistice with the Allies and then declared war on Germany. German forces moved into Italy and consolidated a defensive Gothic Line with savage fighting in the autumn and winter, 1944.

Elsewhere, the Soviet Red Army earned a great victory over von Paulus's Sixth Army at Stalingrad in February 1943, followed in July by the vast and bloody tank and air battle at Kursk. Each side sustained huge losses but the Red Army began pushing back the Germans so that, during the winter of 1943–44, the Red Army regained much of Soviet occupied territory and, in April 1944, advanced into Central Europe.

In June 1944, the Allies landed in Normandy, establishing a bridgehead in France and beginning the long-awaited 'Second Front'. By 18 June, the Cotentin Peninsula was secured and British and Commonwealth troops fought their way into Caen. An advance on Falaise was an attempt to surround the German Fifth and Seventh Armies. Fierce fighting supported by continuous air attacks killed some 60,000 German soldiers and destroyed most of their equipment, temporarily shattering German morale. Patton's and Montgomery's forces swept through France into the Low Countries, liberating Paris and Brussels on the way. Despite the setbacks at Arnhem and in the Battle of the Bulge, the Rhine was eventually crossed in February 1945 and the Second Front met the Soviets in Germany. Hitler committed suicide in April in his bunker in Berlin and the German High Command signed an unconditional surrender in May. The bloodiest war in European and world history was over.

Britain and Post-War Europe

The aftermath of World War II saw Britain and Europe struggling to recognize the new dangers posed by the growth of two superpowers and how to prevent a resurgent Germany emerging to destabilize the Continent for a third time. Great Britain and France responded immediately by signing the 1947 Dunkirk Treaty against Germany. This was translated into the 1948 Brussels Treaty with the inclusion of Belgium, the Netherlands and Luxembourg, creating the Western European Union (WEU).

European politicians realized that a new threat was emerging. The Soviet Union had shifted its border westwards by seizing parts of Finland, Estonia, Latvia, Lithuania, eastern Poland, Ruthenia and Bessarabia from Romania. Additionally, a new Poland, Czechoslovakia, Hungary, Romania and Bulgaria became Communist puppet states while Germany was divided between four occupying powers, with neighbouring Austria likewise divided.

The democratic governments of Europe were apprehensive about Soviet plans and needed to face up to other problems incorrectly visualized as monolithic world communism on the march. Communist trade unions in France and Italy, prominent in wartime resistance movements, were so feared by the USA that it began financing the establishment of competing Christian trade unions. 1947 witnessed Britain fighting Communists in Greece, a role passed to the USA, given Britain's weakness after the war. Also, Britain faced a Communist Malayan Insurgency from 1948. Asia posed other problems with the Soviet Union having only just withdrawn its support from Iranian separatists while the Iranian Communist Tudeh Party was backing moves to give the Soviets oil concessions in Iran.

The lesson for Britain and Europe was that each individual state was unable to defend itself and collaboration was essential for security, bearing in mind that Europeans had expended their wealth in a bloody six-year war, and that cities, towns, villages and infrastructure had been devastated. Britain faced an enormous debt owed to the USA, due to massive imports to supply the war effort and huge post-war loans.

The basis for the Cold War was being created by Stalin's paranoid suspicion of the capitalist west while recognizing the USSR's losses of between 15 to 25 million war dead, 1,700 cities destroyed plus 70,000 villages devastated. Matters were enflamed by Winston Churchill's Iron Curtain Speech at Fulton, Missouri, and by American diplomat in Moscow, George Kennan, whose Long Telegram stated that the Soviet Union would only respond to force and containment, not the pre-war concept of appeasement. At this time the USA launched two major policies. Firstly, the 1947 Truman Doctrine aimed to support free peoples resisting violence or outside pressure, with special emphasis on Turkey and Greece. Secondly, America devised the Marshall Plan, which provided finance for a European economic recovery aid package to stimulate development. The plan hoped to stabilize European economic weakness, which national Communist parties might use for their electoral or revolutionary benefit. The Soviets refused the offer of Marshall aid deeming it to be a Trojan horse of world dollar imperialism. Aid certainly helped extend American markets into western Europe.

Another institution established in response to the excesses of World War II was the formation of the 1945 United Nations, which adopted the Universal Declaration of Human Rights in 1948 and remains largely on paper in most countries. The WEU emerged as the military arm of the Council of Europe, which contained most European countries. Finally, the USA joined member nations of the WEU to create the North Atlantic Treaty Organization in 1949, which soon added Italy, Denmark, Norway, Iceland, Portugal, Canada, Greece and Turkey to its membership. NATO became the keystone of the alliance between the USA and Western Europe in the Cold War and after.

Britain and Post-War Europe

Although bankrupted by war and supported by massive American loans, Britain still managed to innovate during peace. A 'Welfare State', the brainchild of Sir William Beveridge, was created in an attempt to end want, disease, ignorance, squalor and poverty. Amongst measures taken was the birth of a National Health Service. However, full-employment was needed to pay for it.

Europe emerged from the war devastated from the Atlantic Ocean to the River Volga. The Continent divided itself along political lines, with Soviet Russia dominated the east and United States influenced and supported the west. The United States poured billions of dollars into its western European Allies under the Marshall Plan.

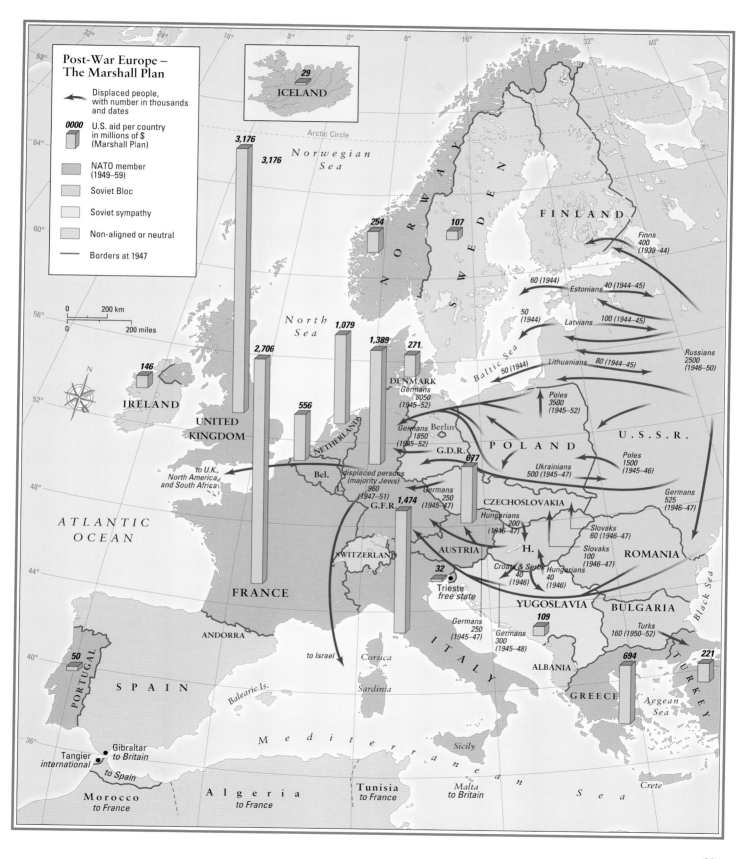

**Post-War Europe –
The Marshall Plan**

← Displaced people,
with number in thousands
and dates

0000 U.S. aid per country
in millions of $
(Marshall Plan)

NATO member
(1949–59)

Soviet Bloc

Soviet sympathy

Non-aligned or neutral

Borders at 1947

ICELAND *29*

*Norwegian
Sea*

Arctic Circle

3,176
3,176

254 *107*

N O R W A Y

S W E D E N

FINLAND

Finns
400
(1939–44)

60 (1944)

*North
Sea*

Estonians 40 (1944–45)

50
(1944)

Latvians 100 (1944–45)

Russians
2500
(1946–50)

1,079

1,389 *271*

Baltic Sea

50 (1944) Lithuanians 80 (1944–45)

2,706

146

0   200 km
0   200 miles

DENMARK
*Germans
8050
(1945–52)*

Germans Berlin
1850
(1945–52)

G.D.R.
677

P O L A N D

Poles
3500
(1945–52)

U. S. S. R.

556

IRELAND

UNITED
KINGDOM

NETHERLANDS

Poles
1500
(1945–46)

Ukrainians
500 (1945–47)

to U.K.,
North America
and South Africa

Bel.

displaced persons
(majority Jews)
960
(1947–51)

1,474

L

G.F.R.

Germans
250
(1945–47)

CZECHOSLOVAKIA

Germans
525
(1946–47)

A T L A N T I C
O C E A N

SWITZERLAND

AUSTRIA

32

Trieste
free state

H.

Hungarians
200
(1946–47)

Croats & Serbs
40
(1946)

Slovaks
60 (1946–47)

Slovaks
100
(1946–47)

Hungarians
40
(1946)

ROMANIA

F R A N C E

ANDORRA

to Israel

Corsica

Sardinia

*Germans
250
(1945–47)*

YUGOSLAVIA
109

Germans
300
(1945–48)

BULGARIA

Black Sea

50

PORTUGAL

S P A I N

Balearic Is.

ALBANIA

Turks
160 (1950–52)

694

221

GREECE

T U R K E Y

Aegean
Sea

I T A L Y

Tangier
international

Gibraltar
to Britain

to Spain

M e d i t e r r a n e a n

Sicily

Crete

Morocco
to France

A l g e r i a
to France

Tunisia
to France

Malta
to Britain

S e a

Baby Boomers and Population Movement

Baby Boomer and Population Movement

The Baby-Boom generation began post-war and it is later associated with the Swinging Sixties. It was a period offering new trends in music, models like Twiggy, the BMC Mini Car and the fashion centre of Carnaby Street. Iconic buildings were designed by Sir Basil Spence: Coventry Cathedral was ground breaking, as were the first buildings for the University of Sussex, symbolized by Falmer House and the Meeting House.

New universities and polytechnics were created with curricula markedly different and cutting-edge compared with traditional red-brick institutions.

The aftermath of World War II witnessed a 'baby boom' as servicemen and women returned home to continue peacetime lives as near normal as possible considering the austere times facing Britain and Europe. Increases in industrial and agricultural incomes also stimulated and encouraged people to have larger families. The definition of these children, members of the baby-boom, are those born between 1946 and 1964. Additionally, medical advances eliminated diseases such as polio and increased numbers of doctors reduced infant mortality. The new term of Golden Boomers has been coined to define this population bulge as it hits retirement age in the twenty-first century and places burdens on the national pension scheme and health services.

The social and political impact of the rise in the birth rate was enormous as the vote was given to 18 year olds in 1969. Governments were also obliged to increase spending on education to prepare pupils for jobs in an increasingly complex economic system. New universities were built to accommodate the population bulge, such as Sussex, Essex, Kent and York. However, education was not democratized with university attendance being confined to the middle and upper classes. Mature students and those from ethnic backgrounds were a rarity.

Baby boomers are often characterized as being critical of their parents' generation, hostile to authority, and demanding of social change. Protest movements and student activism grew up in an era known for the phenomena of Beatlemania. Many people went on the Aldermaston Marches organized by the Campaign for Nuclear Disarmament. Some protesters demonstrated against the Vietnam War outside the US Embassy in Grosvenor Square, London. A particularly significant movement was the Greenham Women's Peace Camp. Here, women, protesting about the stationing of cruise missiles from 1981, kept a presence there until 2000. In 1983, 50,000 women encircled the base, broke down fences and scuffled with the police, leading to hundreds of arrests.

In 2004, the baby boomers owned or controlled eighty per cent of the UK's wealth and have been accused of benefiting from house-price inflation and responsible for the British predilection for house ownership, which is arguably a partial reason for the post-2008 credit crunch. Some have seen this Saga Generation as being fitter and more long-lived than previous generations and are using their wealth for holidays and cars, rather than providing a nest-egg for their children, who will have to work more years to pay the taxes necessary to provide their parents with government-funded pensions.

As well as changes in the demographic pyramid, the British Isles has seen population movements between regions, and between rural and urban areas. The more highly qualified people are, the further they are prepared to move in search for jobs. This particularly applies to students surging into the some 150 universities, with many students seeking to settle near them upon graduation. The South-west, East Anglia and East Midlands have seen population increases from inter-regional movements and from other countries, especially in cities like Leicester. The South-east has seen out-migration over time compensated by the lion's share of international inward movements of people. Northern England tends to lose people through internal migration except for areas where the government has moved its agencies, making areas like Durham dependent on government jobs. With the coalition government's planned spending cuts, areas such as these will suffer and maybe increase out-migration. International financial investment and increased job opportunities has pulled people into the Northeast where companies such as Nissan operate, as does Toyota in Derby. Urban areas tend to have increasing populations; London is peculiar as many former inhabitants are leaving for green counties, while international migrants flood in but not in sufficient numbers to prevent the capital's population decline.

Baby Boomers and Population Movement

● New town

— Motorway opened by 1970

Population increase

Over 40%

5% to 39%

0% to 4%

Population decrease

0% to 4%

5% to 19%

Over 20%

Orkney Islands

Shetland Islands

North Sea

SCOTLAND

Glenrothes

Cumbernauld

Livingstone

East Kilbride

Irvine

IRELAND

Northern Ireland

Irish Sea

Isle of Man

Washington

Peterlee

Aycliffe

ENGLAND

Skelmersdale

Warrington

Runcorn

Telford

Peterborough

Corby

Newtown

WALES

Redditch

Northampton

Milton Keynes

Stevenage

Welwyn

Harlow

Hemel Hempstead

Hatfield

Cwmbran

LONDON

Basildon

Bracknell

Crawley

English Channel

N

0 — 100 km

0 — 100 miles

The European Union

At the end of the Second World War, the founding fathers of the project for European integration, including Robert Schuman, Jean Monnet, Konrad Adenauer, Alcide de Gasperi and Paul-Henri Spaak, sought to co-operate in a spirit of reconciliation to build Europe anew and to strengthen European economic competition in the world market place.

Although the European Economic Treaty was founded by the Treaty of Rome in March 1957, its origins lie in the Schuman Declaration of 9 May 1950, which advocated the pooling together of coal and steel production by establishing a single higher authority that would merge the coal, iron, and steel industries of France, West Germany, Italy, and the Benelux countries. The European Coal and Steel Community (ECSC) was also designed to be an initial step in the federation of Europe, in an attempt to establish peace forever on the European continent by terminating the traditional enmity between France and Germany. The ECSC began to function in July 1952 and would be merged with the EEC and Euratom in 1967, within the European Community.

A second significant development was the unsuccessful attempt to establish a European Defence Community among the six ECSC countries. This plan was launched by French Foreign Minister René Pleven and ratified by five of the member states in 1954 but rejected by the French Assemblée Nationale, due to a growing public opinion concerned with the rearmament of West Germany.

In accordance with the Treaty of Rome, the European Community established common policies among the six member states for: agriculture; transport; the movement of capital and labour; and the erection of common external tariffs. A European Parliament was instituted, meeting alternately in Strasbourg and Luxembourg, alongside the European Commission in Brussels and the European Court. Later, the Lomé Conventions of 1975, 1979, 1984 and 1989 would establish development and technical co-operation aid programmes and would ease the customs duties for over 60 countries.

The United Kingdom, Ireland and Denmark joined the EEC in January 1973, the first of numerous accessions to the EEC and its successor development, the European Union. Numbering 27 states, the European Union has identified candidate and potential members.

More recent developments have been the Maastricht and Lisbon treaties. In 1992, the first established the Single European Act, which is characterized as an amendment of the Treaty of Rome plus citizenship, establishing a single European Act and a peoples' Europe founded upon the three pillars of European security, the European Community and internal affairs. The second, in 2009, made the Charter of Fundamental Rights of the European Union legally binding.

Britain's relationship with the European project has occasionally seemed reluctant, perhaps stemming from French President de Gaulle's veto of the British entry application in 1963. Despite rigorously adhering to European policies, even when against British interests (fishing), Britain refused to join the European currency, the Euro. The strength of antagonism to Europe can be seen in the June 2009 European Elections when Britain returned two members of the extreme right British National Party and the extreme conservative United Kingdom Independence Party with its 13 members. The Conservative-Liberal Democrat coalition government, elected in May 2010, is introducing an EU Bill into Parliament which will require that in any proposed future EU treaty involving the transfer of areas of power or competence from the UK to the EU would be subject to a referendum of the British people. This would bring the UK in line with Ireland, France and Denmark. During 2010, Eire witnessed rejection of the proposed European Constitution. At the same time, Britain stated that it would support measures to strengthen European economic competition.

European Union

The European Union's initial mission was to provide a sense of unity and security for its members in place of the nationalist rivalry, which had devastated the Continent. Its membership has steadily grown over the post-war decades and is due for further enlargement. The candidate countries being Croatia, Iceland, Turkey and the former Yugoslav Republic of Macedonia. Potential candidates are Albania, Bosnia-Herzegovina, Montenegro, Serbia and Kosovo. Outermost regions might join with the dissolution of the Netherlands Antilles; Curaçao, Aruba and St Maarten are now constituent countries within the Kingdom of the Netherlands. Also, Mayotte has become an overseas department of France.

European Union
Development of the European Community

- Signature of the Treaty of Rome, 1957
- EEC member added 1973
- Greece added 1981
- EEC member added 1986
- Became part of the EEC after unification of Germany, 1990
- EEC member added 1995
- EEC member added 2004
- EEC member added 2007
- Membership pending

ICELAND

Norwegian Sea

Faeroe Islands (to Denmark)

FINLAND

Helsinki

Tallinn • St. Petersburg

RUSSIAN FEDERATION

N O R W A Y

S W E D E N

Oslo

Stockholm

ESTONIA

Riga **LATVIA**

Baltic Sea

LITHUANIA

Vilnius

BYELORUSSIA

Kaliningrad • **RUSSIA**

Gdánsk

North Sea

Glasgow • • Edinburgh

UNITED KINGDOM

Dublin

IRELAND

Liverpool •

Birmingham •

Bristol •

London

Calais

DENMARK

Copenhagen •

Hamburg •

Amsterdam •

NETHERLANDS

The Hague •

Brussels •

BELGIUM

L.

GERMANY (GERMAN FEDERAL REPUBLIC)

Berlin

(GERMAN DEMOCRATIC REPUBLIC)

Warsaw •

P O L A N D

UKRAINE

Lvov •

Cracow •

Frankfurt •

Rhine

Prague •

CZECH REP.

SLOVAKIA

Bratislava •

Vienna

AUSTRIA

Budapest •

HUNGARY

ROMANIA

Bucharest •

Paris

F R A N C E

Bern •

SWITZERLAND

Lyon •

Bordeaux •

Milan •

Genoa •

Trieste •

SLOVENIA

Ljubljana •

Zagreb •

CROATIA

Venice •

Belgrade •

BOSNIA HERZEG.

Sarajevo •

SERBIA

Danube

B U L G A R I A

Sofia •

Black Sea

ATLANTIC OCEAN

ANDORRA

Marseille •

Monaco •

I T A L Y

Corsica

Adriatic Sea

MONTE-NEGRO

ALBANIA

Tiranë •

Skopje •

Istanbul •

TURKEY

PORTUGAL

Madrid

S P A I N

Barcelona •

Balearic Is.

Sardinia

Rome

Naples •

Aegean Sea

GREECE

Izmir •

Alicante •

Athens •

Cádiz •

Gibraltar *to United Kingdom*

Almería •

Tangier •

Mediterranean

Sicily

Crete

MOROCCO

ALGERIA

TUNISIA

MALTA

Sea

LIBYA

CYPRUS

Ulster Says No!

The origins of the Irish troubles lie in the past and the partition of Ireland in 1922 failed to solve the problem. Then a sizeable Catholic, basically republican nationalist, minority still lived in the north and felt threatened by the Protestant majority. Simultaneously, these Protestants saw themselves as a minority in Ireland as a whole. The intransigence of each side has been characterized by competing flags, ceremonies, ritual marches, and hostility. The Catholics in Ulster were discriminated against in terms of employment, welfare and housing ,while political rights were infringed by gerrymandering. The bitter rivalry between Catholics and Protestants generated violence and terrorism from either side.

The 1960s saw Unionist leader and prime minister, Terence O'Neill, pursuing moderate unionism, which was detested by militant Ulster loyalists. He wanted to end sectarianism and bring Catholics and Protestants into working political and economic relationships. In January 1965, O'Neill invited the Taoiseach of Eire, Séan Lemass, for talks in Belfast. O'Neill met with strong opposition from his own party, mainly because he informed very few of the visit, and from Ian Paisley who rejected any dealings with Eire. Paisley and his followers threw snowballs at Lemass' car during the visit. In February, O'Neill visited Lemass in Dublin. Opposition to O'Neill's reforms was so strong that in 1967 George Forrest, the MP for Mid-Ulster who supported the Prime Minister, was kicked unconscious by fellow members of the Orange Order.

In 1968, the Northern Ireland Civil Rights Association began campaigning and were banned by the authorities from a peaceful march. Rioting resulted in British troops being sent to keep the peace but their welcome wained and they lost Catholic support, being perceived ultimately as the paramilitary army of a Protestant state. Increasing violence caused many Catholics to look to the IRA as their defence force. The policy of internment and imprisoning suspected terrorists without trial won the IRA further support.

Tension was increased by Ian Paisley attacking any notion of compromise between Catholic and Protestant. His extreme provocation exacerbated civil unrest. That the 1st Battalion of the Parachute Regiment opened fire on a civil rights march in Derry on 30 January 1972, Bloody Sunday, killing thirteen, merely served to dramatically heighten political tension, leading British Prime Minister Edward Heath to suspend Northern Ireland's Parliament at Stormont.

Northern Ireland dissolved into naked aggression with the Provisional IRA attacking British soldiers and the Royal Ulster Constabulary. Social segregation along religious lines and inter-faith murder increased and small parts of Belfast and Derry became temporarily 'no-go' territory, with paramilitaries of both sides policing their areas with corporal punishment, including knee-capping by gun shot. During these troubles, Ian Paisley founded the Democratic Unionist Party in 1971 while Catholics supported the constitutional nationalism of the Social Democratic Labour Party (SDLP) or Sinn Féin (SF), which is republican and was linked to the IRA.

An economic depression in the 1970s multiplied Ulster's problems and violence became extreme, with the IRA detonating a bomb at the Grand Hotel, Brighton where Prime Minister Margaret Thatcher, with her cabinet, were staying during the annual Conservative Party conference. The IRA bought weapons on the world market often with contributions from sympathetic Irish Americans. The IRA campaigned in both Ulster and England leading to armed reaction including a British Army unit killing several IRA members in Gibraltar. Butchery occurred on all sides, especially with 'tit-for-tat' murders. During this violent activity, the British and Irish government were secretly negotiating and reached an agreement in November 1985. This far-reaching accord agreed that: the UK recognized the Irish government's right to design proposals concerning Northern Ireland; the Irish

Ulster's Troubles

The tension between Catholics and Protestants continued after 1985. In May 1987, eight IRA members were shot while on a mission and eleven people died at the Enniskillen War Memorial bombing in November. January 1992 witnessed eight more deaths in another IRA explosion and October 1993 saw a bombing in the Shankhill Road. Eight people were gunned down by Ulster Freedom Fighters at Greysteel in October 1993, revenge for the Shankhill massacre. A loyalist paramilitary group, the Ulster Volunteer Force, killed six and wounded five in a bar in Loughinisland.

Republic recognized that a united Ireland was a long term objective only achievable by majority consent; and, a joint conference was to be established between the two governments to discuss issues of mutual interest and the production of an improved Northern Ireland society.

The Unionist community was totally dismayed at this news and Protestants felt utterly betrayed. Ulster Unionist MPs had been kept in the dark and, as a protest, they all resigned forcing new elections in Northern Ireland. Sinn Féin also opposed the agreement because the Irish government recognized the existence of Northern Ireland. The poll increased the Unionist vote but they lost the constituency of Newry and Armagh to the Social Democratic and Labour Party. The

Unionists campaigned under the slogan 'Ulster Says No' with mass demonstrations led by Ian Paisley of the Democratic Unionist Party and James Molyneaux of the Ulster Unionist Party. The campaign achieved nothing and the Northern Ireland Assembly was abolished on 13 June 1986.

Protestant terrorist groups and the IRA attacked each others communities, resulting in 300 people being murdered between 1984 and 1987. In 1994, the IRA agreed to a cease-fire and hopes emerged that a peaceful solution might be brokered. Protestant terrorist groups became represented by the Progressive Unionist Party and the Ulster Democratic Party just as Sinn Féin gave voice to the IRA. All interests could now be represented in peace negotiations.

Ulster's Troubles

Major terrorist activities

- 1970s
- 1970s–90s
- Real IRA base (late 1990s)
- Major incident with date

Results of General Election 1997

- United Kingdom Unionist
- Ulster Unionist Party
- Social Democratic and Labour Party
- Democratic Unionist Party
- Sinn Féin

Immigration and Diversity

Ethnic Populations

Since 1066, the British Isles experienced limited immigration throughout most of its history. The Norman conquest brought just a 0.5 per cent change to the population. Small communities of foreign merchants lived in London and other major seaports. Few religious refugees, like French Huguenots, established themselves in London and other towns. Africans arrived, mostly via the West Indies, serving in the Royal Navy and as personal servants in Britain. However, none of this made any significant change to the population of the British Isles. It wasn't until the post-WWII period, particularly the late 1950s and 60s, that large numbers of 'immigrants' were seen on the streets and workplaces of the British Isles. By far the largest numbers have settled in London and the industrial areas of England. Fortunately, this massive, and largely unplanned, change has been achieved peacefully. Racism exists in Britain, with violence seemingly being directed against all groups by all groups. The British National Party presents an extreme right-wing image and its leadership claims not to be racist. Far more militant is the English Defence League, which makes anti-Islamic comments. Their marches and demonstrations receive significant police attention.

The British Isles have received migrant populations throughout its history. Celts, Romans, Anglo-Saxons, Vikings and Normans commenced a never ending process. Protestant Huguenots refugees arrived from France in the sixteenth century fleeing from religious persecution led by King Louis XIV and more French arrived in the wake of the French Revolution. Flemings arrived in the Middle Ages and Dutch with William III. The nineteenth century Jews arriving, while Africans and Chinese flourished in sea ports. World War II brought Poles and Czechs to the islands to help fight Hitler and the post-1945 years saw migrants arriving from the British Empire, for many symbolized by the 1948 arrival of the SS *Empire Windrush* with Caribbean families.

The Census of 2001 showed that the population was 85.67 per cent White British and 5.27 per cent White non-British, the remaining population being Indian, Pakistani, Mixed Race, Black Caribbean, Black African, Bangladeshi, Other Asian Non-Chinese, Chinese, Other and Black Other. A major problem with these categories is that people are lumped together who are quite diverse in character. The London Caribbean community contains residents from different islands, each a community in its own right. Arabs have also criticized the Census model for not allowing them a specific category. Another issue can be that some categories contain mutually hostile or racially antagonistic groups. Hence, a high caste Hindu might look down upon a resident of Kashmir owing to their skin shade. This certainly happens in Leicester.

The migrant populations arriving from the Commonwealth and, more recently, Eastern Europe with the widening of EU membership, have arguably created a more multi-cultural society but not necessarily an integrated one. That a Derby Tesco store stocks Polish food products suggests recognition of a minority group but so did the bombing of a local Serbian Orthodox Church during the break-up of Yugoslavia and the desecration of Jewish graves. The multi-cultural state faces racism and racialism in a social and political sense. Hindu might not wish to marry Muslim but the Mixed Race group grew the most between the 1991 and 2001 Censuses.

Migrants have stimulated xenophobia and racism and helped generate extreme right-wing groups and sometimes anti-migrant terror and violence. Racist concepts have been given a new lease of life to racial theories of supremacy based upon physique, ancestry and blood. During times of recession, migrants have been accused of taking white jobs, causing unemployment, damaging the housing market, or if unemployed, a drain on the welfare system and the cause of crime, drugs and prostitution.

In 1972, President Idi Amin of Uganda expelled his country's Asian population giving it 90 days notice to leave. Some 30,000 people with British passports arrived in the UK. This sudden influx gave ammunition to the British National Front in its racist attacks on non-white groups in the country. The successor British National Party has acted in the same fashion but has attempted to distance itself from overtly racist comments in public. However, this party won seats in the 2006 local elections, gained a seat in the 2008 elected London Assembly and has two MEPs. No seats were gained in the 2010 General Election.

Economically, migrants tend to be well educated, taking high-end jobs or have no qualifications, taking more menial positions. In general, migrants have improved the tax base of the UK but Pakistani and Caribbean people are disadvantaged in the labour market, whereas white immigrants' opportunities are no different to native-born white people. The group with the highest incomes are the Japanese. Migrants tend to move to the London region, the south-east Midlands and cities but Yorkshire and Humberside receive considerable numbers. Migrant flow into Britain has increased dramatically in the last ten years.

Ethnic Populations
1991

*Ethnic Minorities as a
Percentage of Population*

Less than 1%
1.1% to 2.5%
2.6% to 5%
5.1% to 10%
10.1% to 20%

Orkney Islands

Shetland
Islands

*North
Sea*

Highland

Grampian

SCOTLAND

Tayside

Fife

Central

Lothian

Strathclyde

Borders

Dumfries and
Galloway

Northumberland

Tyne and
Wear

Cumbria

Durham

Cleveland

North Yorkshire

Humberside

Northern
Ireland

*Isle of
Man*

*Irish
Sea*

Lancashire

West
Yorkshire

Greater
Manchester

South
Yorkshire

Merseyside

Cheshire

Derbyshire

Lincolnshire

IRELAND

Clwyd

Notting-
hamshire

ENGLAND

Gwynedd

Staffordshire

Norfolk

WALES

Shropshire

Leicestershire

West
Midlands

North-
ampton-
shire

Cambridge-
shire

Suffolk

Powys

Hereford and
Worcester

Warwick-
shire

Bedford-
shire

Dyfed

Gloucester-
shire

Oxford-
shire

Hertford-
shire

Essex

West
Glamorgan

Mid
Glam-
organ

Gwent

Buckinghamshire

Greater
London

South
Glamorgan

Avon

Wiltshire

Berkshire

Surrey

Kent

Hampshire

West
Sussex

East
Sussex

Somerset

Devon

Dorset

English Channel

Cornwall

0   100 km
0   100 miles

N

Devolution

After Tony Blair became the British Prime Minister following the 1997 General Election, he was determined to pursue and enact laws, laid out in his Labour Party manifesto, which would democratize politics by giving devolution to Wales, Scotland and Northern Ireland with systems of proportional representation.

Original support for modern Welsh nationalism was more concerned with protecting and preserving Welsh culture and language than with Welsh self-government. The 1969 Royal Commission on the Constitution, the Kilbrandon Committee, recommended devolution for Wales but a proposed assembly was rejected by the Welsh electorate in a referendum in 1979.

A second referendum was held on 18 September 1997 in which the electorate just approved the foundation of a National Assembly for Wales. The executive powers of the Welsh Office were transferred to the Assembly, which was given only secondary legislative powers. It has some extremely limited power over taxes and can largely lay down the amount of grants for local councils while having authority in certain devolved areas of competence, such as ending prescription charges for the National Health Service in Wales.

The Government of Wales Act 2006 altered the electoral system. The first-past-the-post electoral system was changed to a version of proportional representation, the Additional Member System. The Assembly has been criticized by Plaid Cymru for not having full powers and opinion polls in Wales suggest that most Welsh people desire full legislative powers while the AMs would be happy to gain further powers from Westminster. In the meantime, Wales might demand powers similar to the Scottish Parliament, with both countries moving incrementally to gaining more power in different areas with a dream of full autonomy.

A referendum in September 1997 saw the Scots voting for a Scottish Parliament with tax-varying powers and the seat of government being in Edinburgh. Power was transferred from Westminster on 6 May 1999. The electoral system uses a version of proportional representation with seventy-three Members of the Scottish Parliament (MSP) representing individual geographical constituencies elected by first-past-the-post, with another fifty-six MSPs returned from eight additional members' regions. The Scottish Parliament has devolved powers in areas such as education, agriculture, health, and the legal system.

Some critics of devolution feel that full independence might be achieved incrementally, which would leave just the English and Scots crowns unified. Others feel that Scotland has achieved so much power that the SNP will be undermined.

The Labour General Election victory in 1997 began a process leading to the 1998 Good Friday Agreement or Belfast Agreement. Crucial elements included: a devolved assembly for Northern Ireland elected by the single transferable vote system of proportional representation and with legislative and executive powers; an executive comprising ten ministers to be allocated according to the d'Hondt process to ensure proportionate power sharing; and, parallel referenda in both parts of Ireland to ratify the agreement. The electorates endorsed this political programme but Ian Paisley's hostility and the issue of decommissioning IRA weaponry remained on the agenda.

Since the Assembly has been created it has been suspended on four occasions: 11 February – 30 May 2000; 10 August 2001 for 24 hours; 22 September 2001 for 24 hours; and 14 October 2002 – 7 May 2007. On 28 July 2005, the IRA stated that it ordered an end to the armed campaign and instructed its volunteers to assist the development of purely political and democratic programmes through exclusively peaceful means. The future of Northern Ireland is uncertain. Demographic trends suggest that a nationalist Roman Catholic majority will emerge and Irish unification might be demanded although this dream has been deleted from Eire's constitution.

Devolution

Elections to the 2007 Scottish Parliament saw the Scottish National Party winning 47 seats to Labour's 46. Leader Alex Salmond formed a minority government receiving Green Party support in certain circumstances. Despite this success, it seems unlikely that the Party's aims of secession from the United Kingdom and full integration with the European Union will be realized. Its peculiar strand of nationalism, left of centre, is comparable to Celtic Cornish Mebyon Kernow and Welsh Plaid Cymru.

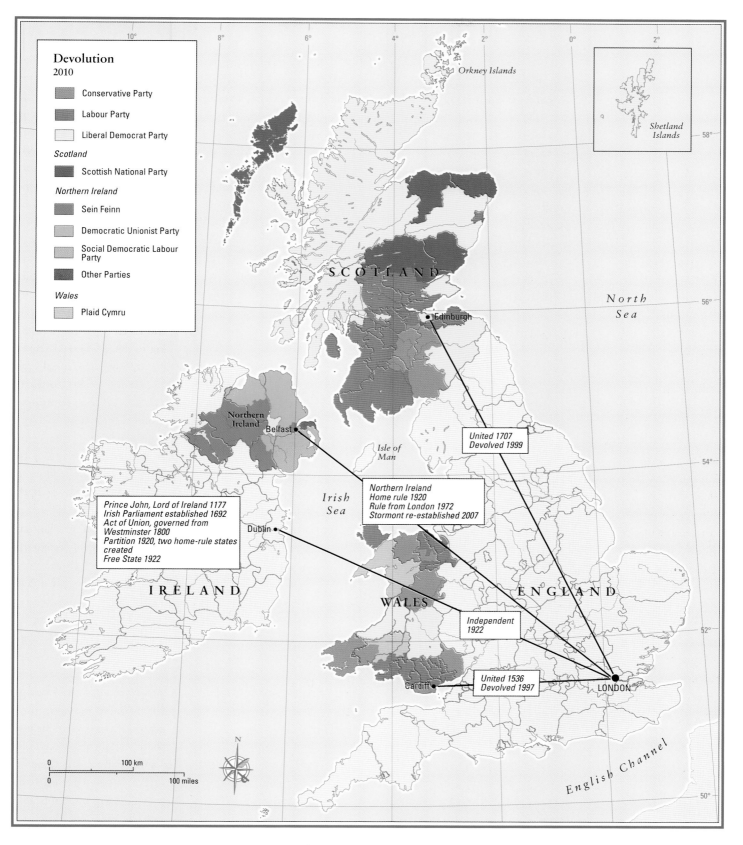

Devolution
2010

Conservative Party

Labour Party

Liberal Democrat Party

Scotland

Scottish National Party

Northern Ireland

Sein Feinn

Democratic Unionist Party

Social Democratic Labour Party

Other Parties

Wales

Plaid Cymru

Orkney Islands

Shetland Islands

North Sea

SCOTLAND

Edinburgh

United 1707
Devolved 1999

Northern Ireland
Belfast

Northern Ireland
Home rule 1920
Rule from London 1972
Stormont re-established 2007

Isle of Man

Irish Sea

Prince John, Lord of Ireland 1177
Irish Parliament established 1692
Act of Union, governed from Westminster 1800
Partition 1920, two home-rule states created
Free State 1922

Dublin

Independent 1922

IRELAND

WALES

ENGLAND

United 1536
Devolved 1997

Cardiff

LONDON

English Channel

0   100 km

0   100 miles

N

Kings and Queens

ENGLAND					
Alfred	871–899	Protectorate	1653–1659	David I	1124–1153
Edward the Elder	899–924	Charles II	1660–1685	Malcolm IV	1153–1165
Athelstan	924–939	James II	1685–1688	William I	1165–1214
Edmund I	939–946	Mary II	1689–1694	Alexander II	1214–1249
Edred	946–955	William III	1689–1702	Alexander III	1249–1286
Edwy	955–959	Anne	1702–1714	Margaret	1286–1290
Edgar	959–975	George I	1714–1727	First Interregnum	1290–1292
Edward the Martyr	975–978	George II	1727–1760	John Balliol	1290–1296
Ethelred the Unready	978–1013,	George III	1760–1820	Second Interregnum	1296–1306
	1014–1016	George IV	1820–1830	Robert I	1306–1329
Sweyn Forkbeard	1013–1014	William IV	1830–1837	David II	1329–1371
Canute	1016–1035	Victoria	1837–1901	Robert II	1371–1390
Harold I	1035–1040	Edward VII	1901–1910	Robert III	1390–1406
Hardicanute	1040–1042	George V	1910–1936	James I	1406–1437
Edward the Confessor	1042–1066	Edward VIII	1936	James II	1437–1460
Harold II	1066	George VI	1936–1952	James III	1460–1488
William I	1066–1087	Elizabeth II	1952–	James IV	1488–1513
William II	1087–1100			James V	1513–1542
Henry I	1100–1135	**SCOTLAND**		Mary	1542–1567
Stephen's Anarchy	1135–1154	Kenneth	842–858	James VI	1567–1625
Henry II	1154–1189	Donald I	858–862	& I of England	1603–1625
Richard I	1189–1199	Constantine I	862–876		
John	1199–1216	Aedh	876–878	**PRINCES OF WALES**	
Henry III	1216–1272	Eocha & Giric	878–889	**(Recognized by King of England or**	
Edward I	1272–1307	Donald II	889–900	**claimants; term is disputed)**	
Edward II	1307–1327	Constantine II	900–943	Owain Gwynedd	1165–1170
Edward III	1327–1377	Malcolm I	943–954	Llywelyn the Great	1230–1240
Richard II	1377–1399	Indulf	954–962	Dafydd ap Llywelyn	1244–1246
Henry IV	1399–1413	Duf	962–966	Llywelyn the Last	1258–1282
Henry V	1413–1422	Culen	966–971	Dafydd ap Gruffydd	1283–1283
Henry VI	1422–1461	Kenneth II	971–995	Madog ap Llywelyn	1294–1295
Edward IV	1461–1483	Constantine III	995–997	Owain Lawgoch	1372–1377
Edward V	1483	Kenneth III	997–1005	Owain Glyndŵr	1400–c.1416
Richard III	1483–1485	Malcolm II	1005–1034		
Henry VII	1485–1509	Duncan I	1034–1040		
Henry VIII	1509–1547	Macbeth	1040–1057		
Edward VI	1547–1553	Lulach	1057–1058		
Mary I	1553–1558	Malcolm III	1058–1093		
Elizabeth I	1558–1603	Duncan II	1094		
James I	1603–1625	Donald III	1093–1097		
Charles I	1625–1649		(Deposed 1094)		
Commonwealth	1649–1653	Edgar	1097–1107		
		Alexander I	1107–1124		

Prime Ministers

Sir Robert Walpole	1715–1742	Whig
Earl of Wilmington	1742–1743	Whig
Henry Pelham	1743–1754	Whig
Duke of Newcastle	1754–1756	Whig
Duke of Devonshire	1756–1757	Whig
Duke of Newcastle	1757–1762	Whig
Earl of Bute	1762–1763	Tory
George Grenville	1763–1765	Whig
Marquess of Rockingham	1765–1766	Whig
Earl of Chatham (Pitt the Elder)	1766–1768	Whig
Duke of Grafton	1768–1770	Whig
Lord North	1770–1782	Tory
Marquess of Rockingham	1782–1782	Whig
Earl of Shelburne	1782–1783	Whig
Duke of Portland	1783–1783	Whig
William Pitt, the Younger	1783–1801	Tory
Henry Addington	1801–1804	Tory
William Pitt	1804–1806	Tory
Lord Grenville	1806–1807	Whig
Duke of Portland	1807–1809	Tory
Spencer Perceval	1809–1812	Tory
Earl of Liverpool	1812–1827	Tory
George Canning	1827–1827	Tory
Viscount Goderich	1827–1828	Tory
Duke of Wellington	1828–1830	Tory
Earl Grey	1830–1834	Whig
Viscount Melbourne	1834–1834	Whig
Duke of Wellington	1834–1834	Tory
Sir Robert Peel	1834–1835	Tory
Viscount Melbourne	1835–1841	Whig
Sir Robert Peel	1841–1846	Conservative
Lord John Russell	1846–1852	Whig
Earl of Derby	1852–1852	Conservative
Earl of Aberdeen	1852–1855	Peelite
Viscount Palmerston	1855–1858	Whig
Earl of Derby	1858–1859	Conservative
Viscount Palmerston	1859–1865	Liberal
Earl Russell	1865–1866	Liberal
Earl of Derby	1866–1868	Conservative

Benjamin Disraeli	1868–1868	Conservative
William Gladstone	1868–1874	Liberal
Benjamin Disraeli	1874–1880	Conservative
William Gladstone	1880–1885	Liberal
Marquess of Salisbury	1885–1886	Conservative
William Gladstone	1886–1886	Liberal
Marquess of Salisbury	1886–1892	Conservative
William Gladstone	1892–1894	Liberal
Earl of Rosebery	1894–1895	Liberal
Marquess of Salisbury	1895–1902	Conservative
Arthur Balfour	1902–1905	Conservative
Henry Campbell-Bannerman	1905–1908	Liberal
Herbert Asquith	1908–1916	Liberal
David Lloyd George	1916–1922	Liberal
Andrew Bonar Law	1922–1923	Conservative
Stanley Baldwin	1922–1924	Conservative
James Ramsay Macdonald	1924–1924	Labour
Stanley Baldwin	1924–1929	Conservative
James Ramsay Macdonald	1929–1935	National Labour
Stanley Baldwin	1935–1937	National Conservative
Neville Chamberlain	1937–1940	National Conservative
Winston Churchill	1940–1945	Conservative
Clement Atlee	1945–1951	Labour
Sir Winston Churchill	1951–1955	Conservative
Sir Anthony Eden	1955–1957	Conservative
Harold Macmillan	1957–1963	Conservative
Sir Alec Douglas-Home	1963–1964	Conservative
Harold Wilson	1964–1970	Labour
Edward Heath	1970–1974	Conservative
Harold Wilson	1974–1976	Labour
James Callaghan	1976–1979	Labour
Margaret Thatcher	1979–1990	Conservative
John Major	1990–1997	Conservative
Tony Blair	1997–2007	Labour
Gordon Brown	2007–2010	Labour
David Cameron	2010–	Conservative (Conservative–Liberal Democrat Coalition)

Battles

ROMANS TO VIKINGS
Dover, 55 BC
Cassivellaunus' Defeat, 54 BC
Caradoc's Defeat, AD 51
Boudicca's Revolt, AD 60
Mons Graupius, AD 83
Mount Badon, c. 495
Nechtanesmere, 685
Ashdown, 871
Ethandun, 878
Brunanburh, 937
Maldon, 991
Lumphanan, 1057
Stamford Bridge, 1066
Hastings, 1066
WALES: CONQUEST AND REBELLION
Rhyd-y-Groes, 1039
Hereford, 1055
Crug Mawr, 1136
Cymerau, 1257
Irfon Bridge 1282
Pilleth, 1402
ANGLO-SCOTTISH WARS
Battle of the Standard, 1138
Dunbar, 1296
Stirling Bridge, 1297
Falkirk, 1298
Bannockburn, 1314
Halidon Hill, 1333
Neville's Cross, 1346
Otterburn, 1388
Sauchieburn, 1488
Flodden, 1513
Solway Moss, 1542
Pinkie, 1547
Inverlochy, 1645
Philiphaugh, 1645
Preston, 1648
Dunbar, 1650
Killiecrankie, 1689
Dunkeld, 1689
Massacre at Glencoe, 1692
Sheriffmuir, 1715
Prestonpans, 1745
Falkirk, 1746
Culloden, 1746
IRELAND'S TORMENT
Clontarf, 1014
Clais an Chro, 1169
Athankip, 1270
Athenry, 1316
Faughart, 1318
Knockdoe, 1504
Affane, 1565
Monasternenagh, 1579
Yellow Ford, 1598
Kinsale, 1601
Dungan's Hill, 1647
Knocknanuss, 1647
Rathmines, 1649
Drogheda, 1649

Scarrishollis, 1650
Bantry Bay, 1689
Londonderry, 1689
The Boyne, 1690
Aughrim, 1691
Antrim, 1798
Vinegar Hill, 1798
Ballinamuck, 1798
Easter Rising, 1916
WARS OF THE ROSES
St. Albans, 1455
Blore Heath, 1459
Northampton, 1460
Wakefield, 1460
St. Albans II, 1461
Mortimer's Cross, 1461
Towton, 1461
Barnet, 1471
Tewkesbury, 1471
Bosworth Field, 1485
ENGLISH CIVIL WAR
Edgehill, 1642
Roundway Down, 1643
Newbury I, 1643
Adwalton Moor, 1643
Cheriton, 1644
Marston Moor, 1644
Cropredy Bridge, 1644
Lostwithiel, 1644
Newbury II, 1644
Newbury III, 1644
Naseby, 1645
Langport, 1645
Rowton Heath, 1645
Worcester, 1651
WARS IN EUROPE
Tinchebrai, 1106
Sluys, 1340
Crécy, 1346
Poitiers, 1356
Agincourt, 1415
Formigny, 1450
Castillon, 1453
Spanish Armada, 1588
Dover, 1652
Kentish Knock, 1652
Dungeness, 1652
Three Days' Battle, 1653
Gabbard Bank, 1653
Lowestoft, 1665
Four Days' Fight, 1666
St. James's Day Fight, 1666
Medaway, 1667
Southwold Bay, 1672
AMERICAN REVOLUTION
Bunker Hill, 1775
Long Island and Harlem Heights, 1776
Valcour Island, 1776
White Plains, 1776
Trenton, 1776
Princeton, 1777

Ticonderoga and Hubbardton, 1777
Oriskany and Fort Stanwix, 1777
Brandywine, 1777
Germantown, 1777
Saratoga, 1777
Monmouth, 1778
Flamborough Head, 1779
Camden, 1780
King's Mountain, 1780
Cowpens, 1781
Guilford Courthouse, 1781
Hobkirk's Hill, 1781
Chesapeake, 1781
Eutaw Springs, 1781
Yorktown, 1781
Saintes, 1782
FRENCH REVOLUTIONARY AND NAPOLEONIC WARS
Glorious First of June, 1794
Cape St. Vincent, 1797
Camperdown, 1797
Nile, 1798
Copenhagen, 1801
Trafalgar, 1805
Maida, 1806
Vimiero, 1808
Corunna, 1809
Busaco, 1810
Barrosa, 1811
Fuentes de Oñoro, 1811
Albuera, 1811
Salamanca 1812
Vitoria, 1813
Bidassoa, 1813
Nivelle 1813
Nive 1813
Orthez, 1814
Toulouse, 1814
Quatre Beas, 1815
Waterloo, 1815
TWO WORLD WARS
Heligoland Bight I, 1914
Dogger Bank, 1915
Ypres I, 1914
Neuve Chapelle, 1915
Ypres II, 1915
Loos, 1915
Jutland, 1916
Somme, 1916
Arras, 1917
Messines, 1917
Ypres III, 1917
Passchendaele, 1917
Heligoland Bight II, 1917
Cambrai, 1917
Kemmel/Somme, 1918
Battle of the Atlantic, 1939–45
Battle of Britain, 1940
The Blitz, 1940–45

Bibliography

The author readily acknowledges the work of the many scholars and published works that have been consulted in preparation of this atlas. Among this selected bibliography are books recommended for further reading and study of the peoples of the British Isles from ancient times to the present.

Allen, Stephen, Lords of Battle. *The World of the Celtic Warrior*, Oxford: Osprey Publishing Ltd., 2007

Aughey, Arthur, *The Politics of Northern Ireland*, London: Routledge, 2005

Barnard, Toby, *The Kingdom of Ireland, 1641–1760*, Basingstoke: Palgrave Macmillan, 2004

Barron, Caroline M., *London in the Later Middle Ages. Government and People, 1200–1500*, Oxford: Oxford University Press, 2005

Bede, *A History of the English Church and People*, Harmondsworth: Penguin, 1962

Bennett, Martyn, *Oliver Cromwell*, London: Routledge, 2006

Bogdanor, Vernon, *Devolution in the United Kingdom*, Oxford: Oxford University Press, 1999

Boyce, D. George, *Decolonisation and the British Empire, 1775–1997*, Basingstoke: Palgrave Macmillan, 1999

Bragg, Melvyn, *The Adventure of English. The Biography of a Language,* New York: Arcade Publishing, 2011

Brendon, Piers, *The Decline and Fall of the British Empire, 1781–1997*, London: Vintage Books, 2008

Brooke, Christopher, *The Saxon and Norman Kings*, Oxford: Blackwell Publishing, 2006

Caesar, Julius, *The Conquest of Gaul*, Harmondsworth: Penguin, 1982

Cassius Dio, *History of Rome*, London: Loeb Classical Library, 1989

Christiansen, Eric, *The Norsemen in the Viking Age*, Oxford: Blackwell Publishing, 2001

Collingridge, Vanessa, *Boudicca*, London: Ebury Press, 2006

Copsey, Nigel and Macklin, Graham, *British National Party:*

Contemporary Perspectives, London: Rouledge, 2011

Cunliffe, Barry, *The Ancient Celts*, Harmondsworth: Penguin, 1999

Daunton, M. J. & Halpern, Rick, *Empire and Others: British Encounters with Indigenous Peoples, 1600–1850*, London: Routledge, 1998

Doran, Susan, *England and Europe in the Sixteenth Century*, Basingstoke: Palgrave Macmillan, 1999

Dorling, Daniel and Thomas, Bethan, *People and Places: A 2001 Census Atlas of the UK*, Bristol: Policy Press, 2004

Duffy, Seán (ed), *The Macmillan Atlas of Irish History*, New York: Macmillan, 1997

Dungan, Myles, *Irish Voices from the Great War*, Dublin: Irish Academic Press, 1998

Elton, Geoffrey, *England under the Tudors*, London: Routledge, 1991

Evans, Eric J., *The Forging of the Modern State. Early Industrial Britain, 1783–1870*, Harlow: Longman, 2001

Ferguson, Niall, *Empire. How Britain Made the Modern World*, Harmondsworth: Penguin, 2004

Ferguson, Robert, *The Hammer and the Cross: A New History of the Vikings*, Harlow: Allen Lane, 2009

Fraser, George MacDonald, *The Steel Bonnets: The Story of the Anglo-Scottish Border Reivers*, London: Harper Collins, 1989

Gillingham, John, *The Angevin Empire*, London: Hodder & Stoughton, 2000

Harriss, Gerald, *Shaping the Nation. England, 1360–1461*, Oxford: Oxford University Press, 2005

Herlihy, David, *Medieval Households*, London: Harvard University Press, 1985

Howard, Michael, *The First World War*, Oxford: Oxford University Press, 2003

Keen, Maurice, *England in the Later Middle Ages*, London: Routledge, 2003

Kenny, Kevin (ed), *Ireland and the British Empire*, Oxford: Oxford University Press, 2004

Kenyon, John, *The Stuarts: a Study in English Kingship*, London: Fontana, 1972

Kinvig, Robert, H., *The Isle of Man. A Social, Cultural and Political History*, Liverpool: Liverpool University Press, 1975

Kirby, D. P., *The Earliest English Kings*, London: Routledge, 1991

Kramer, Jürgen, *Britain and Ireland. A Concise History*, London: Routledge, 2006

Lehmberg, Standford, *A History of the Peoples of the British Isles: from Prehistoric Times to 1688*, (3 vols), London: Routledge, 2002

Leonard, Richard, *A Century of Premiers: Salisbury to Blair*, Basingstoke: Palgrave Macmillian, 2004

MacDonald, C., *Scotland and the Great War*, Edinburgh: Tuckwell, 1998

Manley, John, *Atlas of Prehistoric Britain*, Oxford: Phaidon Press Ltd., 1989

Manning, Roger, *Swordsmen: The Martial Ethos in the Three Kingdoms*, Oxford: Oxford University Press, 2003

Marr, Andrew, *A History of Modern Britain*, London: Pan Books, 2008

Marsden, Peter, *Roman London*, London: Thames and Hudson, 1980

Maund, Kari (ed), *The Welsh Kings: Warriors, Warlords, and Princes*, Stroud: Tempus Publishing Ltd., 2006

Messenger, Charles, *The D-Day Atlas. Anatomy of the Normandy Campaign*, London: Thames and Hudson, 2004

Michison, Rosalind, *A History of Scotland*, London: Routledge, 2002

Morgan, Kenneth, *The Birth of Industrial Britain: Economic Change, 1750–1850*, Harlow: Longman, 1999

Morgan, Kenneth, *The Birth of Industrial Britain: Social Change, 1750–1850*, Harlow: Longman, 2004

Mortimer, Gavin, *The Blitz. An Illustrated History*, Oxford: Osprey, 2010

Moscati, Sabatino et al., *The Celts*, Milan: Bompini, 1991

Neillands, Robin, *The Hundred Years' War*, London: Routledge, 2001

Paxman, Jeremy, *The English: A Portrait of a People*, Harmondsworth: Penguin, 2007

Phillips, G., *The General Strike*, London: Weidenfeld and Nicolson, 1976

Plunkett, John, *Queen Victoria: First Media Monarch*, Oxford: Oxford University Press, 2003

Pollard, A. J., *The Wars of the Roses*, Basingstoke: Palgrave Macmillan, 2000

Power, Daniel, *The Norman Frontier in the Twelfth and Early Thirteenth Centuries*, Cambridge: Cambridge University Press, 2004

Prestwich, Michael, *Plantagenet England, 1225–1360*, Oxford: Oxford University Press, 2005

Raban, Sandra, *England under Edward I and Edward II*, Oxford: Blackwell Publishing, 2000

Robbins, Keith, *Great Britain: Identities, Institutions and the Idea of Britishness*, Harlow: Longman, 1998

Shotter, David, *Roman Britain*, London: Routledge, 2004

Stevenson, John, *The Pelican Social History of Britain: British Society, 1914–1945*, London: Penguin, 1990

Tacitus, *The Annals*, Indiana, Indianopolis: Hacket Publishing Co., Inc., 2004

Thomas, Hugh M., *The English and the Normans. Ethnic Hostility, Assimilation, and Identity, 1066–c. 1220*, Oxford: Oxford University Press, 2005

Williams, Gwyn, *When Was Wales? A History of the Welsh*, Harmondsworth: Penguin, 1991.

Index

Please note that page numbers in *italic* denote maps or plans.

Acknowledgements

Design: Malcolm Swanston

Maps: Jeanne Radford, Alexander Swanston,
         Malcolm Swanston and Jonathan Young

Editors: Matt Jones, Malcolm Swanston

Typesetting: Jeanne Radford

Production: David Hemingway

Frontispiece photograph: Ivan Sendall